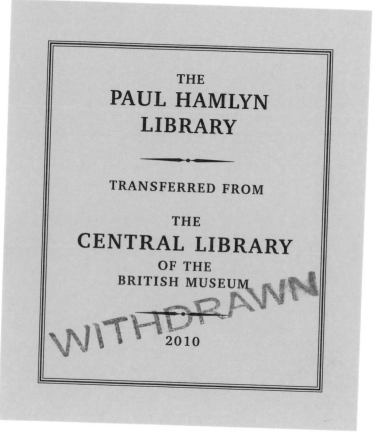

ASLIB READER SERIES

We would point out that the material for this publication has been extracted from numerous sources, consequently the reproduction varies according to the quality of the original copy and is the best the printer can average.

©1979 Aslib
Published by Aslib, 3 Belgrave Square
London SW1X 8PL

ISBN 0 85142 114 8 (hardback)

ISBN 0 85142 116 4 (paperback)

Printed in Great Britain by Henry Ling Ltd., at the Dorset Press, Dorchester, Dorset.

ASLIB READER SERIES

VOLUME 1

NATIONAL LIBRARIES

EDITED BY
MAURICE B. LINE & JOYCE LINE

Aslib

SERIES EDITORS: PETER J. TAYLOR & RUTH FINER

CONTENTS

This book consists of three main sections on specific themes, each section consisting of a group of readings preceded by the editors' commentary. An extensive list of annotated references to further reading following the structure of the main sections is also provided, together with an author index to all literature cited.

Maurice Line is the Director General of the British Library Lending Division, having previously been Librarian of the University of Bath and the National Central Library, and having worked in four other university libraries. Following the report of the National Libraries Committee in 1969, he carried out in 1971-2 for the UK Department of Education and Science a feasibility study into the application of automation to the national library. He has headed several other major research projects, and written four books and over a hundred articles. He is a Professor Associate in the University of Sheffield and also Director of the IFLA Office for International Lending.

Joyce Line, like her husband, is a qualified librarian. She has indexed numerous books and assisted in several research projects. She recently carried out for the British Library a study of archival collections of non-book materials in the UK.

INTRODUCTION

It is easy to think of national libraries as a well established category of library, like public, university or industrial libraries — a readily recognisable genus of libraries, occupying similar positions and fulfilling similar roles in most if not all countries. Yet national libraries are surprisingly difficult to define, and they exhibit great variety, in size, nature and function. Not only that, but in some countries there is no clear dividing line between National Library planning and national library planning — various libraries in these countries may be fulfilling national roles to a greater or lesser degree. Some countries have neither a National Library nor a national library service; in many countries the National Library is by no means the largest or the best library; and in some federal nations each state has its own national library.

The very concept of a national library is remarkably recent. It is true that national libraries, in essence if not in name, have existed since at least the 18th century, and some claim much earlier beginnings, usually as royal libraries (which some are still called). In the 19th century, several countries, mainly in Europe, consciously created national libraries, but more often they developed them from pre-eminent existing collections, or labelled such collections as National Libraries and gave them national status. Nevertheless, it is fair to say that until the present century the typical national library was, or aimed to be, to books what the national museum was to artefacts — the finest collection of books in the country, the national book archive, and a source of national pride *(see Further reading, Ref.1)*. Any discussion of its role and function would have seemed strange and unnecessary.

In the 20th century, the mere collection and preservation of books, and their availability for consultation, did not constitute by any means all the library roles that needed to be carried out at a national level, and additional national functions began to be performed by existing libraries, individually or in co-operation, or by newly created national organisations. National bibliographies became established or were re-organised, by no means all of them produced by national libraries. Interlibrary lending, at first a small activity, became too large for national libraries to handle with their existing organisation. The needs of science, technology and medicine became pressing, and could not be met by the humanistic book museums that many national libraries essentially were. The problem of how to reconcile collection and conservation with service became a major issue — the collection being a natural base for bibliographic, lending and information services, but the services putting the collection in some danger.

One country's solution to these new needs can be seen by looking at the situation in the United Kingdom in 1970. The British Museum Library remained essentially a national collection devoted to the humanities, and to a lesser extent the social sciences. The National Reference Library of Science and Invention had been created a few years earlier as a semi-autonomous department to serve science and technology. Since 1950, the British National Bibliography Limited, a totally independent body, had been producing the national bibliographic record and offering cataloguing services to other libraries. Interlending needs had been catered for first by the creation of the National Central Library, founded as the Central Library for Students in 1916, and then by the National Lending Library for Science and Technology, established in 1961 — the latter created directly by the Government, and the former largely supported by the Government. In effect, there were five national library organisations serving the United Kingdom, and other libraries could claim to be serving more limited national functions.

In the last 25 years, the issues mentioned above have become more pressing, and, together with a number of other factors, have led to extensive discussion on the nature and function of national libraries. The other factors include the increasing size and complexity of national libraries, a great growth in libraries of all kinds and a desire for library planning and co-ordination at a national level, the emergence of new nations and their wish to create their own national libraries, and the development of a more analytical and systematic approach to library planning. From 1955, when an early issue of *Library Trends* was devoted to national library planning, numerous papers and books on national libraries began to appear, whether general, comparative or specific to particular countries.

The discussion was greatly stimulated by a series of seminars and meetings funded by Unesco on or relevant to national libraries, covering various areas of the world. These were:

1955, Delhi	— Unesco seminar on the development of public libraries in Asia
1958, Vienna	— Unesco symposium on national libraries in Europe
1964, Manila	— Unesco regional seminar on the development of national libraries in Asia and the Pacific
1966, Quito	— Unesco meeting of experts on the national planning of library services in Latin America
1967, Colombo	— Unesco meeting of experts on the national planning of library services in Asia.

Another relevant conference was organised in the United Kingdom in 1963 by the University and Research Section of the Library Association. Within individual countries, not only were plans made for new libraries, but major reappraisals took place of some existing national libraries, notably in the UK and USA, and at least one massive reorganisation took place, in the UK.

While it is very difficult to find any writings on national libraries before 1955 beyond out-of-date accounts of particular national libraries, after 1955 the problem is one of selection — in the first place from general papers, e.g. on the functions of national libraries, and in the second from papers on specific libraries. General papers tend to be repetitive not only in subject matter but even in their content, since many of them rely heavily on, or refer constantly to, the two key articles by Humphreys published in 1964 and 1966. These two articles, and a few others, constitute the first group of papers in this selection.

There follows a group of papers dealing with particular aspects of national libraries. Here we have chosen articles covering a fair range of aspects, as well as two 'reviews' — one an analytical review of functions and types of national library, the other a review of national libraries in developing countries.

The third and final group, consisting of papers on individual libraries or countries, proved the hardest to select, since such papers are numerous, they are often little more than barely descriptive, and they are soon out of date. Rather than attempting to choose the 'best' papers, we have tried to achieve as wide a spread of geographical areas and types of country as possible.

In making our selection, we have had to exclude many worthy papers, and some excellent ones that touched on but were not specifically concerned with national libraries. In particular, we have not included any papers on national library planning, in the sense of planning the nation's library resources, and our selection is confined to articles on national libraries as such. A selection of the 'best' articles relevant to national libraries would have been substantailly different from the present collection, which endeavours to present a reasonably representative picture of national libraries now and since the war.

The following are among the main types of national library:

1.   Comprehensive (e.g. National Library of Canada)

2.   Limited by function (e.g. British Library Lending Division)

3.   Limited by subject (e.g. US National Library of Medicine)

4.   'Sub-national', serving a state or country within a federal nation (e.g. Yugoslavia)

5.   Sharing major national with other functions (e.g. State and University Library of Aarhus)

6.   Providing a limited (e.g. by subject) national service as part of a different service (e.g. Library of Parliament in Helsinki).

All of these, not always in a 'pure' form, are represented in the following pages.

1. THE NATURE AND AIMS OF NATIONAL LIBRARIES

This section consists of general articles on national libraries. The first paper is also the earliest of the articles in this volume. Written as an introduction to a 1955 issue of *Library Trends* devoted to 'Current trends in national libraries', this percipient and in places prophetic article makes a fitting introduction to the present volume, as it identifies many of the key problems and aspects of national libraries that occupy the attention of writers of later articles. It is significant that the latest article cited by its author, David Mearns, is dated 1937, while Mearns' own article is the earliest cited by many later writers. The points he covers include the wide diversity of national libraries, their archival functions, the compilation of current national bibliographies, relationships (with other state bodies, with users, and with other libraries), financing, innovation versus traditionalism, the problems of serving science and technology, dispersion versus unification, and national libraries as symbols of or contributors to national prestige.

The symposium on national libraries in Europe held in Vienna in 1958 was the first of several meetings on national libraries organised by Unesco, and the published proceedings mark a further step forward in identifying, and proposing solutions to, the problems faced by national libraries, in particular in identifying their actual and desirable functions. Inevitably in view of the place and time of the symposium, there is a heavy emphasis on acquisitions and bibliographic functions, but problems of staffing and building also receive much attention *(see also Further Reading, Ref. 9)*.

One important paper given at the Vienna seminar was that by Francis. It reappraises Panizzi's ideas in the light of a vastly increased volume of publication, and, especially, of the needs of science and technology, which Francis sees as unsatisfiable by the traditional large comprehensive library and as requiring decentralisation into more specialised sections.

The second Unesco seminar on national libraries was held in 1964 at Manila, and was the first of several devoted to national libraries in developing countries, although the 1955 Delhi seminar on public libraries in Asia had many relevant things to say on this topic (see the article by Anuar later in this volume). Functions mentioned are rather more inclusive than those discussed by the Vienna symposium, and emphases are different; for example, legislative reference services, retrospective bibliographic control, national library planning in the wider sense, and library training receive extensive discussion *(see also Further Reading, Ref. 5)*. The gaps between the ideal and reality are recorded in an Appendix to this paper, briefly summarised in this volume.

The following two articles, by Humphreys, on the role and functions of national libraries *(see also Further Reading, Ref. 48)* must be two of the most quoted of all library articles. The first paper, prepared for the International Federation of Library Associations, quotes the stated functions of several national libraries, and categorises functions as 'fundamental', 'desirable' and 'inessential', the last being national library service functions which do not necessarily have to be carried out by the National Library. This categorisation is expanded in the second paper, and is used as a frame of reference for many later articles on national libraries. The papers, associated as they are with IFLA, represent a fair consensus among senior librarians concerning the functions of national libraries, and their influence has been great, although there have been other categorisations (for example by Gittig, quoted in Thompson's article). To date, Humphreys' categorisation has not been seriously challenged, and challenge in the immediate future seems unlikely, if only because practical measures in several countries have been based upon his categorisation.

To present a non-European slant — in fact, a very Indian one — two very short articles by Ranganathan conclude this first group of papers. Ranganathan sees the solution to the problem of combining deposit, conservation and service in one library in the establishment of the tripartite system — a national copyright library, a national 'dormitory' (i.e. repository) library, and a national service library (or rather, a whole series of national service libraries).

Papers in other parts of this volume are also relevant to the general aims and functions of national libraries notably those by Anuar and Thompson already referred to, and those by Berry and Magnussen.

The aims and functions of national libraries will doubtless continue to be discussed. Changes in emphasis can be expected as national libraries in developing countries become more numerous and significant, since their priorities and emphases are somewhat different from those of the traditional European national library.

Current Trends in
National Libraries

DAVID C. MEARNS

Summary

THE MANAGING EDITOR has decreed that this number must have a "summarizing chapter," containing "observations on this important phenomenon of librarianship: the national library." He insists that the "world needs to know what a national library is, where they come from, what seem to be their basic functions." Perhaps he is right; perhaps the world will one day hit upon a definition; but the foregoing statements (limited, as they are, to institutions in the free world) provide ample evidence of the fact that just now national libraries are in ferment; that they are wondrously complicated organisms; that whereas some among the newer institutions are frankly imitative, most are conspicuously differentiated one from another; that they defy or elude simple categorization; that they have come to possess separable personalities and bear proud markings of dissimilarity.

In consequence, there is danger of blurting out inanities, for national libraries have but few common characteristics and to every one, generally applying, it would be possible to adduce an exception. Perhaps it could be accurately, albeit redundantly, said that most national libraries are maintained primarily at public cost with funds allotted from, and disbursed by, national treasuries. Again, it might be represented that most national libraries are parts of national governments; that some are directly subordinate to ministries of education or parliamentary bodies, whereas others have attained a degree of greater autonomy, but are nonetheless ordinarily subject to the policy controls and decisions of superior and officially-constituted boards or commissions.

Arundell Esdaile, an authority on the subject, writing in 1934, referred to "that comparatively modern product, the national library," adding that "the idea of a national library has for over a century, and for longer still, if we consider it rightly, been expanding." [1] It is expanding now.

National libraries have had various origins. Some, for example, were established for the purpose they presently serve. Others came to being as a result of the dedication to public use of great private collections. Many have developed into their contemporary stature through a gradual extension of their privileges and facilities to an ever-enlarging patronage.

Reprinted from *Library Trends*, vol. 4, no. 1, July 1955, p. 96-104, by permission of the author and the publisher. Copyright by the Board of Trustees of the University of Illinois.

Either from their beginnings or along the way, national libraries were recognized as the natural conservatories of the records of their peoples' genius however expressed, whether in print, or in manuscript, or facsimiled on film, or in musical notation, or in embossed characters, or in glyphs; whether charted on maps and graphs, or depicted, or reproducible from captured sound. As preservators of the national literature, national libraries were designated as legal depositories and offices of record for the product of the national press.

Thus they became the principal sources of information for the compilation of current national bibliographies. Once the work of private and commercial organizations, there would seem now to be a trend on the part of national libraries themselves to assume responsibility for the preparation and publication of national bibliographies, and to the extent that the techniques employed bibliographically are compatible with their somewhat rigid cataloging practices, national libraries are thereby enabled and compelled to achieve currency in processing the issues of their domestic press.

Inherently the collections of national libraries are encyclopedic in their range and coverage, and because the lives and fortunes of the people they exist to serve are conditioned by the civilizations and societies and progress of other peoples, national libraries must acquire substantial portions of foreign literature in every field and discipline. This obligation is an obligation to collect materials abroad in quantities and concentrations beyond the duty and abilities of the other learned libraries of the land to collect for themselves.

To this end, national libraries engage in large-scale undertakings of exchange. Some of these are arranged by agreements diplomatically negotiated through foreign offices and embassies and departments of state; others are fulfilled in response to private contracts. As old as Vattemare, the smaller, post-war world would seem to have given fresh impetus and new urgency to international exchanges.

Implicitly, then, national libraries are universal in scope. But apart from such routinized sources of accession as copyright deposits, exchanges and intra-governmental transfers, the greatest asset to, and assurance of, their development is prestige. For they flourish most in those communities where their strivings and aspirations and capacities are best understood, are generally approved, and are widely honored. Their prestige is measurable primarily in terms of the eminence of their staffs, the amounts of their annual appropriations, the dimensions of their endowments, and the quality of the gifts of material they attract. National libraries, to a far greater extent than is generally realized, are dependent for their steady enrichment on private, public-spirited, patriotic, generosity.

In addition to the functions of internal management, the administration of a national library is the administration of relationships: relationships with other agencies of government, with learned societies and professional associations, with universities and colleges, with collectors and connoisseurs, with statesmen and scholars, with industrialists and philanthropists, with scientists and technicians, with authors and publishers, with outstanding leaders in every noble cause and the semi-anonymous and unexceptional citizenry, with the press and the pulpit, with fellow-craftsmen and the anointed disciples of librarianship at large. For it seems to be a rule of life that where national libraries prosper, their activities are identifiable with, and allied to, the interests of many and diverse groups.

All national libraries do not occupy the same position in the library systems of their country. Some may conceivably be independent or aloof; others are legally charged with fixed responsibilities and firm primacy; others still, exercise authority loosely and only by common consent. No national library is, perhaps, quite exempt from rivalry and competition dissidence and the threat of pretenders, and, on the whole, this is salutary for national libraries. It keeps them alive and alert; it makes them show cause for their persistence; it rouses them to contemporaneity; it adduces them to bestir themselves.

But whatever their status in the library scheme, there is gratifying evidence that in many parts of the world the national library's pursuits are integrated with the pursuits of other types of libraries. Not only for itself but for those others as well, the national library is devising, developing, and refining technical standards and promoting their general adoption. It is compiling, publishing, and distributing codes of sound practice. It is performing functions of centralized catalogation through the printing of cards and making them available to other institutions. Either as the initiating force or as a cordial participant, the national library is involved in great, cooperatively sponsored, bibliographical enterprises in the national interest.

Precisely because they are national, national libraries are constructing union catalogs of printed books and other research materials. Thus it is possible for them readily to locate unique, uncommon, or unusual works and to make them available to scholarship by acting as clearing-houses for interlibrary loans. Thus, too, it is possible for them to appraise the resources of a nation's libraries, to discover their deficiencies, and economically to undertake joint acquisitions programs for their improvement. By reference to union catalogs, excessive or need-less or expensive duplication can be minimized. Not only are union catalogs conducive to the betterment of the nation's collections con-sidered in their totality, but they provide arguments for moderation or abstinence on the part of the national library, and for the fusion of its objectives with the objectives of other institutions however tenuously they may be constitutionally affiliated.

From this it follows that in one important aspect a national library, at its best, is a libraries' library. It provides them with materials super-fluous to its own needs. It undertakes studies and investigations which are beyond their capacities singly to attempt and shares its findings with the rest. It contributes to their wise planning. It is their champion and advocate. It is a reservoir of large experience and intensive spe-cializations, and content at once profound and vast, on which all may draw. It is neither master nor servant but is inseparably part of themselves.

Presently national libraries are manifesting an excited interest in gadgetry. They are experimenting with contrivances of many kinds, designed for the "simplification" of their technical processes and refer-ence procedures. Perhaps the Age of Mechanized Librarianship is at hand. There may be those who feel that the need of personal media-tion between men and materials will one day be removed and libra-rians will be superseded by intuitive engines and the chauffeurs of literacy. This is in no way intended to disparage the prevalent en-thusiasm; it is inescapable and contagious; it may lead to practical adaptations and to benign consequences. The worst that can be said in criticism of the vogue or fashion is that it may be wastefully diver-sionary from other and more pressing concerns. At this juncture it is too early to stand in judgment, but as a "trend" it cannot be ignored.

Many national libraries have installed or propose to install well-equipped photographic laboratories. These provide an alternative to the loan of rariora by supplying applicants with reproductions at mod-erate cost. Where reproduction of many pages is required, the usual medium is microfilm. This has several advantages: it is relatively in-expensive; it is, when carefully exposed, satisfactorily durable; and, for the largest group of purchasers, which is composed of other libraries, it is convenient to shelve. Microfilm reproductions now represent, numerically, a large part of the collections of national libraries, where special reading rooms, with appropriate projectors and ancillary ap-paratus, have been set apart for their examination.

The regard in which microfilm is held cannot be said to be unanimous, but it is generally considered in terms of a *faute de mieux*. For infrequently or briefly or casually consulted series, it provokes no serious qualms. It is a means of transferring and preserving the contents of newspapers originally printed on wood pulp. It can be used economically for making "service" or "insurance" copies. It can, when necessary or expedient, be restored to legibility either by enlarging it upon a screen or by making enlargement prints from it.

But aside from microfilm, there are now on the market reproductions of library materials made commercially by many other processes of microphotography or microprinting. These, collectively, constitute a formidable body of sub-publication. Their eccentricity of format creates no storage problems, but the fact that each type can be satisfactorily enlarged only on its own especially designed projector, which in itself calls for a not inconsiderable investment, deprives them of some of their general applicability. How national libraries will resolve the dilemma remains to be seen, but it is possible that, working in concert with other libraries, something can and will be done to reduce their multiplicity.

No national library can be greater or perform better services than its financial support allows. This is to state the obvious, but it explains why it is so heartening to learn that the budgets of many national libraries have been increased in the decade following the second war. Even so, it is extremely doubtful that anywhere they have attained adequacy. Until they do, national libraries will not realize their potentialities and confer their fullest benefit upon their constituencies. Meanwhile, they must fall short of the expectations of the uninformed, and operate by compromise and makeshift.

For the older and larger national libraries the situation is, perhaps, peculiar. Their glory is the glory of a continuum. They have survived fires and floods, wars and invasions, occasional periods of public apathy and indifferent direction. They have achieved dignity and renown and distinction. The value of their collections is incalculable. The sum of the funds devoted to their operation through the years, if tabulated, might be surprising even to themselves. Their roots run firm and deep. They are, today, administered with competence and imagination. They are neither old nor listless. They are mature. They are the product of their own tradition, their own practices, their own experience, their own past accomplishments, and their own present preoccupations. Their condition is enviable and admirable.

But are there limiting factors? It may be that the answers are esoteric, metaphysical, exquisitely subtle, but the questions persist.

Have they given precious hostages to fortune? Are the older and larger national libraries, for example, resistant to an augmentation of their activities? Quite obviously not, for, as previously stated, many have assumed and are assuming, new functions. But are these new functions merely extensions, or developments, of old, familiar and congenial labors? Could they, in other words be classified as objectives long denied and only recently authorized?

Are the older and larger national libraries opposed to innovation? The evidence would seem to deny it. Perhaps, then, it would be fairer to enquire if they are only hesitant to reverse their fields, change their course, and adopt new emphases. This would seem a reasonable explanation. For that, if imposed upon them, could mean a repudiation of the way they had come to greatness, the scrapping of a national capital investment, and the abandonment of tested and cherished achievements. It may be that the older and larger national libraries have developed a momentum that thrusts them forward, that makes them expand, but is lacking a magic to transform themselves. Perhaps they are confined to the patterns time has made for them.

But there have been instances where older and larger national libraries have, whether by default, or impotence, or enforced surrender, or unwitting consent, allowed national library functions and services to devolve on new and separate institutions. These new institutions are not always completely independent. Not infrequently the national libraries are represented on their governing boards, where they can exert some influence and insure cooperation. But what wise purposes are served by these alienations of responsibility and diffusions of authority?

Again, it is perfectly clear that the older and larger national libraries are pre-eminent centers for research and the patient tedium of scholarly investigation, but is it possible that they are not always so organized as to permit effective and "spot" reference service? If this is not possible, why is it that in so many cases they have forfeited that requirement to special libraries and information bureaus. This would seem to be conspicuously the case in the fields of the natural and applied sciences. Perhaps it is because the size of the collections in the older national libraries and considerations of practicality and economy prohibit the molecular separation and identification and analysis of subject-content which are essential in the day-to-day experiments in the laboratories and in the testing rooms of factories. This suggests that in the future national libraries may organize their collections and services in two parallel but distinguishable lines: the humanities being treated in accordance with established bibliographical principles, and the natural sciences and technology being processed by the newer and more elaborate methods of documentation and automation. Otherwise, national libraries may become the repositories of material only for retrospective or historical study, and thereby influence the present only by precedents and examples.

It would seem to be not unlikely, however, that the trend toward a dispersion of national library functions will soon spend itself, and will be succeeded by re-unification and reintegration. Satisfactory administration would appear to demand it. Moreover, the diffusion will almost certainly be arrested by improvements and renovation in physical plants. For some, new buildings or extensions have been completed; for others, new buildings are in course of construction; for others still, new buildings are on the drawing boards. These will not be the monumental piles erected by a previous generation, with ornate lobbies, and gilded halls, and "grand" stairways. Modern architecture, with insistence on functional adequacy, will not only relieve overcrowding and correct clumsiness, but will permit the execution of functions and services long deferred or relinquished or temporarily abandoned largely because of spatial constrictions and want of applicable funds.

In some regions of the earth, the progress of national libraries has been seriously retarded by the prolongation of the Cold War. Intellectual and cultural advances cannot be constant and consistent in a climate of fear, suspicion, and despair.

And yet, partially offsetting this uneasy and untoward abatement, is the fact that as new states and new sovereignties come to being, the establishment of national libraries is among the early objects of governments. This convincingly attests to the respect held for the achievements of their counterparts throughout the world. Moreover, in those nations where modern librarianship has not been fully developed, schools of library science and service are being conducted, either directly or indirectly, under the sponsorship of national libraries. It is not unusual for national libraries to provide quarters and secretarial assistance for the professional library associations.

The personnel of most national libraries is part of the national civil service. It has been occasionally difficult to persuade the classfying officers of the grades and salary levels required for professional librarianship, but much has been and is being accomplished along that line. The staff of a departmentalized national library must be administered by experts comparable to a university faculty. In addition to

men and women trained in the arts of cataloging, classification, acquisition, reference, and general bibliography; national libraries require
competent musicologists, geographers, scientists, archivists, lawyers,
linguists, and other scholars of highly specialized abilities. These must
be capable not only of understanding the collections for themselves
but of interpreting and propagating them in behalf of the public. That
national libraries have succeeded in securing the services of so many
distinguished representatives of the world of learning is a further
indication of the intangible and imponderable, but sensitive and ex-
hilarating compensations which are their dowries.

It may be that there is an increasing public awareness of the
capacities and resources of national libraries. Certainly the libraries
themselves are more conscious than ever before of their opportunities
affirmatively to contribute to national life. They no longer shun pub-
licity, nor disdain popularity. On the contrary, they cheerfully, openly,
welcome both. It should be understood, however, that this stems from
no selfish conceits, or impulses for arrogant charity, or instincts for
dominion, but from a new and quickened sense of duty to their second
privilege. If it is their first privilege to conserve the records of the
past for a future infinite and eternal, it is their second privilege to
justify conservation in terms of widest usefulness and the promotion
of understanding. This may, as it often does, require delicate balances
and rare detachment, for neither preservation nor utility can be
mutually exclusive. This realization is radical and revolutionary.

For whereas the accent may have been once thrust harder upon
the doctrine of immobility, the penitentiary, the mortuary, or the deep
freeze, national libraries are now become extrovert and gregarious.
They have allied themselves with their own days. They are taking a
chance on the present. They have aligned themselves with immediacy.
They are risking their materials to accidents of transit and are sending
them on loan to remote places where they cannot supervise the treatment accorded them. They are preparing exhibits at once edifying
and enjoyable, and are sending them on tour. They are opening their
halls for lectures and concerts; the subjects of the lectures and the
music selected for the concerts do not have to be recondite, precious
or beyond the appreciation of the average citizen and other mytho-
logical characters in the audience. They are publishing bulletins,
bibliographies, facsimiles, and annotated texts. The libraries of the
free nations of the world are defending the freedom to inquire and
the freedom to inform. They are alert to resist and combat any force

that would restrain mankind from the accumulated knowledge so hardily gained by the human family.

Of course, national libraries are instruments of national policy: of national policy in education; of national policy in research; and, to some indefinite, unspoken, unrealized extent, of national policy in foreign relations. For national libraries are not grim memorials, or beautiful monuments, or hallowed shrines that visitors from abroad view with approval or disapproval. National libraries are the resort of searchers from overseas or across boundaries. Their quest is truth. When a national library contains and discloses truth, it fulfills its purpose and confirms its power.

This is important for the reason that, as an instrument of national policy, a national library might be committed to distort, dissemble, disguise, degrade, even to destroy, the verities. An Orwellian imagination could convert national libraries to infamy and outrage and the ultimate perversion.

Happily among the Western powers, at least, there is a comity of national libraries, an understanding of common problems, constant intercourse, the occasional interchange of personnel. Their directors are on familiar terms with one another. In response to invitation they make official visits. They meet as delegates at sessions called by I.F.L.A. and F.I.D. and Unesco. They undertake joint programs. They collaborate in the cause of universal copyright. They agree upon international standards. Together they make discoveries and find solutions. They debate practices and give counsel. There are now the beginnings of a confraternity, based on confidence, conspicuity and courage; dedicated to the shimmering shadow of an image that may be, must be, coming into sight, whose advent has been too long awaited and too long delayed, bearing a promise and exacting zeal. National librarians are well enough stocked with fervor; the rest will be up to peace.

General References

1. Esdaile, A.: *National Libraries of the World*. London, Grafton and Co., 1934.
2. Vorstius, J.: *Grundzüge der Bibliotheks geschichte*. Leipzig, O. Harrassowitz, 1935.
3. Burton, Margaret: *Famous Libraries of the World*. London, Grafton and Co., 1937.
4. Loffler, Karl, ed.: *Lexikon des gesamten Buchwesens*. 3 v. Leipzig, K. W. Hiersemann, 1935-1937.

SUMMARY OF THE DISCUSSIONS
OF GROUP I

In general, it may be said that the national library of a country is
the one responsible for collecting and conserving the whole of
that country's book production for the benefit of future generations.

However, the very diversity of the libraries represented in
Vienna was an illustration of the wide range of institutions covered
by the term 'national library', and for that reason the symposium
considered it pointless to try to define it. The view was taken that
the real problem was, rather, to identify the functions and responsibilities of a national library, for which the tasks primarily involved were of national and international significance going beyond
the normal scope of learned libraries.

It was deemed essential, however, to make a careful analysis
of the functions currently devolving upon the majority of national
libraries, so as to see whether they were in all cases justified and
properly fulfilled, bearing in mind, first, the types of service at
present expected of libraries, and second, the increase in the
number of libraries and particularly of special libraries.

ACQUISITIONS

On the subject of acquisitions of printed material published in a
given country, it was agreed that the national library had the
ineluctable responsibility of acquiring the whole of the national
production, but that in the case of ephemeral material (job-work,
commercial material) it should be free to make a selection and
eliminate any of it according to its own established principles. If,
for any reason, certain types of printed material (e.g., material
of purely local interest, such as regional editions of newspapers,
publications by local authorities) were acquired and stored elsewhere, the national library should have a record of them. It retained full responsibility, in any event, for ensuring that the whole
of the national production was conserved, whether stored in its
own depots or in other institutions.

Reprinted from NATIONAL LIBRARIES: their problems and prospects. Symposium on National Libraries in Europe, Vienna, 8-27 September 1958. Paris: Unesco, 1960 (Unesco Manuals
for Libraries – 11). Chapter III: Summary of the discussions of Group 1 (Organisation of
National Libraries and General Questions), p. 34-45, by permission of the publisher.

The problem of acquisition was considered to be far more complex in the case of foreign publications.

The national libraries, and especially the oldest of them, still cling, to some extent, to the encyclopaedic approach which governed the development of their old and modern collections at the end of the nineteenth century and made them storehouses not only of the national production but also of the principal foreign publications on all subjects. But that policy was designed for collections far less varied than they usually are today and intended for uses very different from those of the collections of modern libraries. The symposium therefore went into the question afresh in order to determine whether it was legitimate to urge national libraries to pursue that same aim as the guiding line for their policy on foreign acquisitions.

How far, and how successfully, have national libraries held fast to their encyclopaedic principles?

In the case of the science disciplines, marked by such rapid advances, most national libraries do not seem to have been able, for some time past, to maintain their collections at a level adequate to the needs of research scholars, who were the first to acquire the habit of working in special libraries. The same situation is gradually developing in regard to the economic and social sciences. The size of newspapers and the multiplicity of printed material of all kinds are speeding up this trend, which is now affecting even the humanities, although these have long been regarded as the particular province of the national libraries.

The symposium recognized that the national library was under the obligation of collecting foreign printed material concerning the country, no matter where published, but that practices might vary according to the volume and nature of that section of foreign literature (with a moderate output the procedure would be one of systematic research and acquisition, whilst a voluminous output would be subject to selection).

This difference is particularly marked in the case of translations of the works of national authors, and some national libraries of great powers (the British Museum, for instance) make no attempt to acquire the host of editions that appear. However, works concerning the activities of a country should be collected in that country's national library, and it was recommended that a system of co-operation be instituted between the national libraries of different countries, so as to make those collections as complete as possible.

As far as foreign publications not directly relating to a country are concerned, it was felt that the only possible solution was the policy of national co-ordination of acquisitions, which the national libraries tend to favour. Such co-ordination, which is a practical

necessity, is calculated to benefit the user, augment existing national library collections and promote a rational development of
other libraries. It was strongly recommended, however, that the
national library should still have due responsibility for ensuring
that a country had all the foreign literature it required. In that
respect, too, collaboration between national libraries could be of
great value.

The conservation of contemporary manuscript documents of
national importance is one of the functions of the national library,
and the acquisition of that material involves problems of selection
and decentralization. In most countries, responsibility is divided
between the national archives, the national library and local
libraries and archives. While recognizing that national arrangements must take account of this distribution of work, the symposium considered that the national library had the responsibility
of collecting and maintaining a central inventory of contemporary
manuscript collections.

Owing to the greatly diminished supply and the constant rise
in prices, the acquisition of early manuscripts of national interest
tends to raise new problems; competition arising between docu-
ment-collecting institutions as a result of these circumstances
might have an adverse effect on the basic interests of all. The
symposium accordingly advocated that the utmost fairness be
used whenever valuable documents bearing on the cultural
heritage of a country came on the market.

The conservation of national publications for an indefinite
period is the second major function of a national library. Its
collections acquire to some extent the importance of archives and
therefore need to be preserved in their original form. Hence
microcopying, particularly of newspapers, cannot be regarded
as a justification for the destruction of the originals.

NATURE AND ORGANIZATION OF THE SERVICES
OFFERED BY A NATIONAL LIBRARY

A problem on which the group's deliberations largely hinged
was that of the policy to be adopted in order to ensure the full
scientific utilization of collections. The traditional ideal of universality pursued by most national libraries has proved difficult,
if not impossible, to maintain. The very size of their collections
has often become an obstacle to the full utilization of the resources
they contain. In addition, and especially in the fields of the exact,
natural and applied sciences, technology and industry, many
national libraries have failed to keep pace with the requirements
of specialist users.

Habits of work, too, have changed; there is less and less time and taste for painstaking research, and the public demands easy and rapid access to documentation prepared in advance.

The national libraries thus find themselves in a quandary: are they to leave certain fields of study to special libraries— existing or to be created for the purpose—because of the quality of the services that these libraries can provide (such as ease of access, availability of specialized catalogues, analysis of articles in periodicals), or are they to develop an internal system of specialization by subject as well as by type of material?

There could clearly be no question, the symposium considered, of ignoring the existence of special libraries or denying their obvious value, but that very specialization which justified their existence and enabled them to render unrivalled service in their particular sphere was also a limiting factor. National libraries, on the other hand, with the whole range of their collections of early material to rely on, could and should retain a very wide field of action even if only to make marginal studies or works of synthesis generally or to ensure the permanent conservation of extensive stocks.

Partial or provisional solutions of this difficulty have already been found, in some countries, outside the national library. The discussion brought out the following points:

1. The national library, because of the extent and variety of its collections, the quality of its staff and the resources at its disposal, should be in a position to offer the best and most economical solution to the problem.

2. Taking as examples the specialized sections already existing in large libraries (music, maps, manuscripts, prints and engravings, etc.), the symposium noted that it was in those sections that the staff was best equipped to carry on its work, whilst users were afforded a reasonable volume of material in certain well-defined fields as well as receiving authoritative advice. The general feeling, therefore, was that, without belittling the peculiar role of special libraries or deliberately rejecting the possibility of apportioning subjects among a group of libraries given national responsibility in those particular subjects, a certain degree of specialization according to subjects within the vast complex of the printed production departments of national libraries was to be recommended. This policy of decentralization would lead to the creation of special collections, with their own reading rooms and specialized staff.

But this course involves a much more extensive operation than is usually supposed. Reorganization on the suggested lines calls for a bold approach.

3. Where such decentralization within the national library is undertaken, it should be planned so as to give the newly created divisions wide responsibility. It was observed in this connexion that, in very large libraries, the specialized divisions might contain upwards of half a million volumes, which would itself be sufficient justification for a large measure of independence.

It was pointed out, however, that—in view of the variety of types of national libraries and the conditions under which they operated—it was impossible to devise an optimum structure for a decentralized library on the proposed lines, and the manner of undertaking the study of that problem should be particularly objective and flexible.

4. The symposium found in conclusion that, whatever method was adopted for solving this important problem of making the widest use of large collections, the national library should play an essential part in the matter of co-ordination and should itself serve as the centre where full information was available on national collections. But it could fulfil that role only if its services were of the highest calibre and earned the respect and confidence of the users.

On the subject of loans, the symposium made a rapid survey of present practices, the wide variety of which was noted (and considered to be justified). It approved the proposal that a distinction should be made between loans of national and of foreign publications. It was generally agreed that, in view of their function as archives of national publications, national libraries should lend only duplicates of such publications. But, whether at the national or the international level, loans should normally be made to libraries only.

The symposium stressed the importance of making international loans for exhibition purposes, where such loans were compatible with the conservation of documents, and considered this practice as a valuable means of enlarging the national library's field of activity.

PERSONNEL PROBLEMS AND PROFESSIONAL TRAINING

The symposium turned its immediate attention to the difficulties encountered in recruiting and retaining scientific staff. The main difficulties noted in connexion with recruitment were:

1. The lack of candidates in certain specialized fields (science and technology, manuscripts, incunabula, orientalia, etc.).
2. The relatively low salaries offered by libraries.
3. The unpopularity of the profession as compared with university careers, and the absence of certain material advantages.

But the most serious problem is that of retaining staff, which has become more and more difficult on account of the discontent inevitably resulting from the routine aspects of the profession. All the members of the symposium were aware of that feeling, and discussion ensued on some of its many manifestations, such as:

1. The tendency shown by some librarians specializing in particular fields of indubitable scientific importance to fear that their advancement might be jeopardized by colleagues more familiar with general library problems.
2. The antagonism between the staff of special departments or services (maps, prints, manuscripts, music, orientalia and rare books) and that of the printed books and periodicals departments, where the day-to-day workload is particularly heavy and runs the risk of lowering the standards of scientific staff.
3. The danger that librarians engaged in day-to-day work might lose interest in general library problems on account of the departmentalization dictated by the size of the collections.
4. The conflicts between the individual work of the specialized librarian and the general work programme of the library.
5. The attraction exercised by research work and university teaching.

A variety of palliatives were considered, as follows:

1. Attention to be paid to the professional training of librarians recruited on the basis of their previous specialization and, at the same time, specialization facilities to be provided for librarians whose previous training has been on broad general and professional lines.
2. Encouragement to be given to personal work by librarians whose professional duties are of a wholly unspecialized nature.
3. Particular librarians to be made responsible for conducting university courses or lectures for which their work has equipped them.
4. Opportunities to be provided for instruction in librarianship at the university level, thereby facilitating recruitment, as students would learn something about the profession while still at university.
5. The number of librarians dealing with a special field and capable of serving as intermediaries between the library and the research worker to be increased, so as to ensure the fullest use of the library's collections.
6. Personal work and the general interests of the library to be co-ordinated.

The methods adopted to meet the difficulties arising will probably vary considerably, depending on the extent and range of the library's collections, on whether or not it operates as a university library, and on the material and psychological conditions involved in each particular case. The symposium insisted, however, on the point that the library's field of influence and, in short, its proper functioning depend on the standard of its scientific staff, which should include as high a proportion as possible of trained research workers. It is also important not to underestimate the need for encouraging a sense of general responsibility among the scientific staff, so as to provide for recruitment to senior posts.

Following this exchange of views, it was decided to recommend that the professional status of librarians should be considered as equivalent to that accorded to careers at universities, and that their further professional training should be encouraged on the same grounds as research work in all other fields, by such means as appropriate salaries, hours of work, vacations, fellowships and study tours.

The symposium also agreed that development of the qualifications of the library-assistant grade had a beneficial influence on the work of the senior staff. Attention was drawn to the experiment, conducted in some countries, of training up a category of assistants whose professional level tended to approximate to that of the senior staff.

Library assistants had at first been employed in general departments, where the range of tasks entrusted to them had become increasingly wide (from the preparation of author catalogues to the tracing of current references); their value was now coming to be appreciated in the special departments also. The proportion of assistants to senior librarians was given as 2 or 3 to 1.

The possibility of promotion to the senior grade was discussed. It was noted that some countries allowed for this promotion, provided certain conditions were met.

The symposium went on to deal with the question of professional training. Despite the differences that were noted in regard to the conception and organization of the professional training of scientific staff—differences which were gone into thoroughly in the course of a broad exchange of views and information—a strong tendency emerged in favour of professional training superimposed on academic training.

Professional training, it was considered, should include both theoretical instruction and practical work. Discussion ensued on whether it would be better for the theoretical instruction to be given at a university and open to students of all faculties, or for it to be given in a special school, perhaps attached to the national library. It was agreed, finally, that theoretical instruction—wherever imparted—should be given by librarians, whilst practical work should be carried out in the national library or in other large libraries.

Note was taken of the efforts being made in a number of countries, for practical reasons, to combine professional training either with university studies or, more commonly, with work in a library (generally on a part-time basis and at a lower salary).

Stress was also laid on the importance of organizing professional training for the library-assistant grade with due regard to the growing number of tasks now entrusted to it.

BUILDINGS AND PREMISES

The question of premises was approached in the light of the symposium's conclusions concerning the nature and organization of the services offered by a national library. The view was taken that there was urgent need to relate plans for library construction to all the services offered; that aspect of the organization of libraries was of psychological importance both to the staff and to the users. Consideration was given to some questions relating to library construction which the responsible bodies tended to overlook. In this connexion, the symposium concluded that it was a mistake to regard storage space as a more important problem for national libraries than the provision of adequate and well co-ordinated reading rooms and staff premises. It was essential to plan for the decentralized type of service mentioned above, which would imply the provision of special reading rooms adjacent to the collections. In some cases (e.g., maps, prints and engravings, musical scores), it would also be necessary to provide special premises where manuscripts and printed books could be consulted at the same time. Emphasis was also laid on the importance of well co-ordinated work-rooms for the staff and of the provision of common rooms.

The following further points regarding construction also emerged from the discussion.

1. The only acceptable site for the national library is a central one; the division of collections into 'modern books' and 'old books', with the effect of keeping one or other group in decentralized depots, was unanimously rejected; subsidiary depots, away from the main library, usually sprang from necessity, but they offered advantages as well as limitations.

2. The provision of only one reading room is not to be recommended; it is better to provide a set of reading rooms for different purposes, preferably adjacent to the stocks, thereby increasing the number of volumes freely available to readers: reference books, texts, periodicals and monographs most frequently consulted (50,000-60,000 volumes). But this arrangement necessitates additional staff.

3. The provision and equipment of exhibition and lecture rooms
   are of particular importance to national libraries, even where
   these also serve as university libraries.
The symposium was in favour of collaboration at the European
level in the matter of library construction, so that each country
might derive maximum benefit from the experience of the others
and that the all-too-summary information contained in documentation on the subject might be supplemented by real and
prolonged contact. Such collaboration should be brought about
through the National and University Libraries Section of IFLA.[1]

The symposium also referred on several occasions during its
discussions to the desirability of pursuing inquiries on the material
arrangements and technical equipment required for the operation of libraries.

Unesco was urged to promote such inquiries in all suitable ways
(e.g., through meetings of experts and contracts with specialized
institutions). The results of these studies should be incorporated
in articles similar to those which Unesco published in *Museum*;
meanwhile, the articles might appear in the *Unesco Bulletin for
Libraries*.

LEGAL DEPOSIT

The problems involved in legal deposit were touched on rather
briefly: the symposium was concerned with defining the proper
aims and scope of legal deposit rather than studying the laws in
force in the different countries.

While recognizing the advisability in certain cases of adopting
other methods for acquiring national publications, including
arrangements with publishers' associations, the symposium took
the view that, in general, legal deposit was the best means of
ensuring the recording and conservation of national material.
Legal deposit regulations, it was added, should not leave out of
account privately printed publications.

So far as newspapers with multiple editions were concerned,
it was felt that the national library should take the necessary
steps to see that the several editions were conserved, at least
locally.

The legal deposit of photographs, films, gramophone records
and tape recordings entailed complex problems of selection and
conservation; it was for the national library to see that the necessary studies were undertaken, so that practical solutions to those
problems might be found.

---

1. A resolution on these lines was in fact adopted by IFLA at its Madrid session (see Annex II.1).

FINANCE

The symposium next considered methods of financing national libraries and their relation to public expenditure.

It may be said that, in each country, the over-all budget of the national library is financed by a number of different methods and from a number of different sources. Generally speaking, a maximum flexibility should be exercised in the use of funds, with the possibility of transfers from one section to another and a carry-over from one year to another; special subventions may also be necessary.

The discussion clearly indicated how essential it was for a national library, if it was to develop, to be in a position to make its needs known as directly as possible to the competent authorities, so that the appropriations for it could be determined. The financial authorities, for their part, should recognize that the normal growth of a national library automatically entailed the organic development of all its services and hence a periodical increase in its budget.

It is also necessary for a national library to be able to make known its specific needs in all spheres (buildings, materials, etc.) where the conduct of the work comes outside the purview of the central administration.

Receipts (from admission fees, sale of publications and duplicate books, photocopies, etc.) should be regarded as supplementary income to be left at the disposal of the library, possibly in the form of a cash reserve, to enable it to develop its activity in further ways.

Funds should be suitably apportioned between the various types of acquisition: current collections (including a large proportion of periodicals and serials), old or rare books and exceptional items. It is most important, in the last-mentioned case, to have special funds available at very short notice so that the national library (often the only one in a given country to have that responsibility) may be in a position to acquire works of capital importance for the national heritage.

Precise methods of budgetary evaluation have been investigated in a number of countries but the attempt to prepare an ideal budget for a given type of library has proved disappointing; even less, then, is this experiment capable of extension to national libraries. However, there is no reason why they and other libraries should not try to work out average figures for the execution of current work so as to have definite data as a basis for budgetary proposals.

The symposium noted on several occasions the growing importance of exchanges of staff and foreign travel, and the desirability of providing adequate funds for those purposes. (The question of exchanges and travel was discussed in Group III.)

PROTECTION AND CONSERVATION OF DOCUMENTS

Finally, there was a brief discussion on the problems of protecting and conserving documents, including the provision of special storage facilities for rare books, special reading rooms and facilities for consultation, constant inspection of the collections, etc. It is the normal practice in all national libraries to make special arrangements—of a widely different nature, incidentally, including separate store-rooms, horizontal storage for large-size books, air-conditioning, glass cases, and strong room—for the books regarded as the most valuable in their collections. A figure of 4-5 per cent was mentioned as the proportion of such material to total stocks. The criteria for selecting works for storage in the rare books room were also discussed.

The symposium felt that there must be a certain quantitative limitation so as to ensure optimum material conditions for conservation in the rare books room, but that account should also be taken of the fact that even the most recent works would become rare in the course of time (perhaps even in a fairly short time) and that steps must be taken to save them from disappearing. A satisfactory solution might be found on the basis of collaboration with specialized institutions or local libraries, which would be in a position to apply less restrictive criteria in their own spheres of work. The national library should make its experience available to other libraries both in that matter and in regard to technical methods for the physical conservation of books.

On the international level, the International Centre for the Study of the Preservation and Restoration of Cultural Property, in process of being set up in Rome under Unesco's auspices, was expected to play an important part in providing documentation and giving advice.

The symposium considered that the question of the export of books, including rare works, should be studied afresh in the countries where it arose. In this study, due account should be taken of the provisions of the Unesco Agreement on the Importation of Educational, Scientific and Cultural Materials.

The symposium also considered, in connexion with the export of books, that Unesco might usefully undertake: (a) a general survey of existing regulations and practices—its Bureau of Legal Affairs and the national libraries to work in co-operation on the matter; and (b) a study of the conditions under which national libraries could assist in the application of such regulations as might be established.

The symposium took the view that the International Convention on the Protection of Cultural Property in the Event of Armed Conflict did not relieve national libraries of the necessity of going resolutely ahead with the constitution of reserve film libraries.

It also recommended that requests for microfilms of documents of national interest conserved in foreign libraries should be given favourable consideration, within the limits imposed by the amount of work the photographic services were capable of doing, the precautions to be taken for the conservation of the originals and the conditions specified by Group III (see Chapter X).

SUMMARY OF THE DISCUSSIONS
OF GROUP II

THE ROLE OF THE NATIONAL LIBRARY
IN THE BIBLIOGRAPHICAL ACTIVITIES OF A COUNTRY

The symposium was unanimously of the opinion that one of the most important duties of a national library was to ensure the publication of a current national bibliography. An exchange of information on the situation in various countries showed, however, that in many cases (particularly in Western Europe) publication is ensured by other methods. In some countries a parallelism is found between official bibliographies based on legal deposit and bibliographies produced by the book trade; the former often appear with several months' delay while the latter contain serious omissions. Elsewhere, the national bibliography is compiled by bodies specially set up for the purpose. In Eastern Europe, on the other hand, the publication of a national bibliography is the undisputed task of the national library—a task, incidentally, which is understood in a very broad sense, going so far as to cover not only specialized bibliographies, but also bibliographies of articles published in periodicals and newspapers.

In view of this diversity of practice, the symposium considered that the national bibliography might be produced either in the national library by the library's own staff or by a completely independent bibliographical institute—the latter course, however, being justified only where special conditions required it. Production by a semi-independent institute might be desirable to ensure the speed and regularity of issue required by the commercial interests concerned, including the book trade.

In view of this situation, the symposium agreed that all the points made in the present chapter concerning national libraries applied equally to independent or semi-independent bibliographical institutes (the term 'bibliographical institute' being understood to refer to a body entirely devoted to the preparation of bibliographies and not to a documentation and reference centre). However, it was recognized that some countries already have institutes whose normal programme includes other work in addition

Reprinted from NATIONAL LIBRARIES: their problems and prospects. Symposium on National Libraries in Europe, Vienna, 8-27 September 1958. Paris: Unesco (Unesco Manuals for Libraries – 11). Chapter VII: Summary of the discussions of Group II (Bibliographical Activities of National Libraries), p. 71-80, by permission of the publisher.

to the production of current and general national bibliographies. The reason why the national library is primarily made
responsible for the production of a current national bibliography
is that, in most countries, it receives a copy of every book published
there under legal deposit regulations. Moreover, the national
libraries created during past centuries possess most of the earlier
printed material, which means that they are best qualified to
produce a general retrospective national bibliography when the
need for one is felt. That task cannot so easily be transmitted to
an independent or a semi-independent institute which has neither
the basic stock nor the union catalogue which the national library
often possesses and which helps it to trace the books and periodicals missing from its own collections.

The production of specialized national bibliographies does not
devolve upon the national library to the same extent. These bibliographies can, of course, be produced by the national library on the
basis of its own stocks but they can also be produced by specialized bodies such as learned societies, scientific institutions and
documentation centres. In these cases, the main responsibility
of the national library is to give guidance to the bibliographers,
supply them with the necessary documents and see that their
activities are reasonably co-ordinated.

The discussion revealed that in practically every country
scientists and research workers, including teaching staffs at universities, show a regrettable lack of understanding as far as bibliographical work is concerned. Students are no longer made familiar
with the bibliographical tools which they should be using regularly, because introductory courses are no longer given on the
subject. Specialists are too prone to entrust the compilation of
bibliographies to persons without training in bibliography or
librarianship. The only way to redress the situation, the symposium held, was to institute bibliographical courses at the universities and give specialists training in bibliography. It is essential to
promote co-operation between specialists and librarians and to
get the former to realize how useful the librarians' advice can be
to them for the proper compilation of their bibliographies.

A fitting task for the national library would be to compile and
publish at regular intervals a bibliography of the bibliographies
issued in its country. Lists of this kind are already appearing in
some countries but, where they are not, the national library
should fill the gap. The bibliography of bibliographies might serve
as a basic instrument in the fulfilment of an important task devolving upon the national library—the co-ordination of the country's bibliographical activities. The conference on the improvement
of bibliographical services convened by Unesco in 1950 strongly
recommended the establishment of national planning bodies:

(a) to promote the development of bibliographical and information services; (b) to stimulate research in the field of bibliographic methodology and to serve as a clearing house of information about research completed and research in progress in that field; (c) to co-ordinate the various tasks, and assist in the determination of priorities; and (d) to act as a link with international bodies concerned with the planning of bibliographical and information services.

The national library should naturally work in close co-operation with national bibliographical commissions, where they exist. The staff of the national library have the necessary experience to be able to advise on bibliographical methodology, and their experience should be drawn upon in an endeavour to establish sound bibliographical standards for the guidance of the compilers of specialized bibliographies and to standardize cataloguing practice. The symposium recognized that standardization might be difficult to achieve in the matter of classification but felt that the national library should take the lead in formulating standards of bibliographical description in its own country and proposing methods for the professional training of bibliographers.

The co-ordination of bibliographical activities can be furthered by the regular dispatch of questionnaires to bodies engaged, or likely to be engaged, in the production of specialized bibliographies. The questionnaires should cover planned as well as existing bibliographies, thus preventing duplication and revealing gaps. The results of the inquiries should be published by the national library, which might also call conferences of people interested in the production of specialized bibliographies.

Again, the national library can further the production of specialized bibliographies and the inculcation of sound bibliographical methodology by having such bibliographies compiled by specialists coming to work in the library for that particular purpose and for a specific period.

The symposium agreed that the training of bibliographers is an important part of the work of a national library, especially in countries where there is no school of librarianship. Discussion centred on two aspects of that problem: the training of future compilers of (a) general bibliographies and (b) specialized bibliographies.

Theoretical training should be supplemented by practical work; this should be done either in the national library, where special sections might be set up for the purpose, or in a university library or a library of similar type.

Specialized bibliographies should, as far as possible, be compiled by bibliographers qualified in the speciality in question. Co-operation between bibliographers and librarians, on the one hand,

and scientists on the other, is always desirable; it might be promoted in certain fields by the establishment of joint committees or advisory boards. For the human sciences in particular (history, social sciences, psychology, etc.), a bibliography should be selective and critical if it is to be fully efficacious; the bibliographer may be incapable of effecting the necessary selection and evaluation without the help of a specialist on the subject.

Steps should be taken to include courses on bibliographical methodology and the use of bibliographies in the programmes of regular work for university degrees. It is particularly desirable for such courses to form part of the training of post-graduate students intending to take up a scientific career.

In addition, a manual of instruction in bibliographical method, compiled under IFLA's auspices should be published for the guidance of compilers of specialized bibliographies.[1] This manual might be translated into several languages, possibly with the help of Unesco.

Lastly, the national library should inform the compilers of specialized bibliographies that they can always apply to it for advice and guidance.

THE NATIONAL LIBRARY AS A NATIONAL CENTRE OF BIBLIOGRAPHICAL INFORMATION

For a number of reasons the national library is the institution that is best qualified not only to compile current and retrospective bibliographies but also to serve as a bibliographical information centre. In the first place, its collections are generally far larger than those of any other library in the country—a fact that is sometimes apt to be overlooked. Then, even in countries where this is not the case, it is in its collections that the material for a national bibliography is to be found. Its catalogues are, therefore, a major source of bibliographical information.

Again, the national library often possesses the cards on which the current national bibliography is based. It is obviously important that it should keep a series of these cards, either indefinitely or for a reasonably long time, so as to be able to use them as a source of reference. By compiling specialized indexes and enumerative and analytical bibliographies covering its own holdings, or, better still, its own and those of other libraries, it can anticipate requests for information in certain cases.

In each country, it is usually the national library which posesses, in addition to the union catalogue, the best collection of biblio-

1. See Annex II.2.

graphies, works on librarianship and related publications. It should make it its business to acquire as full and up-to-date a collection of these works as possible.

Lastly, it has the trained staff required for it to serve as a centre of bibliographical information; it is often the only institution in the country to combine all three requisites—stocks, staff and catalogues.

Where the national library is responsible for producing the current national bibliography, it should issue it in a form (i.e., on cards or printed on one side of the paper only) which is not only convenient for filing but also allows of selective subscription to one or more subject groups.

Despite its abundant resources, the national library cannot be expected to deal with all requests unaided. It should therefore have full and accurate knowledge of all sources of bibliographical information in its own country so as to be able to refer any inquiries it cannot handle itself to the proper quarter. It is in its own interests to maintain the closest possible relations with specialists and specialized industrial and commercial documentation centres able to provide bibliographical data. It should also publish, or encourage others to publish, a guide to sources of specialized information.

So as to be able to answer inquiries, the national library should keep an up-to-date central register of bibliographies compiled by other libraries in the country and should make arrangements for it to be published from time to time. The staff should therefore have a first-hand knowledge of the bibliographical work done by the other libraries. This could be ensured by providing for exchanges of staff or some other suitable arrangement.

As part of its bibliographical information service, the national library should be prepared to supply basic information such as dates of publication, exact titles of books and the like. However, it remains free to decide whether or not to compile bibliographies on particular subjects or authors, depending on the amount of work involved and the originator of the request. It is under no obligation to supply such bibliographies to those who can compile them themselves, and particularly to students, who ought in their own interests to learn something about bibliographical work for themselves. On the other hand, requests from certain other categories of person, such as persons living abroad, should be given more favourable consideration.

The symposium also considered the question of remuneration for this type of work. It agreed that information should normally be given free of charge but that exceptions might be made in certain cases, for instance where extensive research was involved or where the information was requested for commercial purposes.

The symposium took the view that the provision of information services for private individuals and public bodies was an essential task of a national library, and that any library which had no information department should take steps to establish one.

In a national library with a lending department close co-operation should be established between that department and the information department. Similarly, where a national library has relations with a national lending service outside itself, there should be close co-operation between that service and the library's own information department.

NATIONAL BIBLIOGRAPHIES
AND SPECIALIZED BIBLIOGRAPHIES

Special importance was attached to the question of the contents of general national bibliographies and their relation to specialized bibliographies. It was agreed in principle that every work published in Europe should be recorded at least once in a current national bibliography, and that the national bibliographies should supplement each other. The symposium therefore welcomed, for example, the production of a national bibliography of Monaco to supplement the *Bibliographie de la France*. One difficulty noted was the fact that in some countries it was only the printer, and not the publisher, who was required to make legal deposit, and hence books printed abroad might be omitted from the national bibliography.

Notwithstanding, the symposium laid down the principle that every current general national bibliography should aim at total coverage of the country's book production, irrespective of language.

A certain amount of duplication with other national bibliographies was regarded as justified, and it was recognized that a national bibliography might also include publications which, though issued abroad, were of interest to the country by reason of their author, subject or language. The last-mentioned point, however, was not to be interpreted as justifying the publication of bibliographies based exclusively on language considerations and hence going far beyond the scope of a national bibliography in the true sense.

It was further urged that foreign publications also listed in the bibliographies of their own countries should be cited in such a way as to distinguish them clearly from home publications, for the symposium fully realized that national book production statistics should be based essentially on the national bibliography and that international statistics would become misleading if certain works were counted both in one country and in another.

For the same reason every national bibliography should include a statement of the basis on which it was compiled. Where the bibliography was issued in one of the less widely known languages, the statement should be translated into one of the principal European languages. The symposium also considered it essential, for the purposes of compiling international statistics, that a uniform method should be adopted for national statistics. This question was discussed more fully by Group III.

Another very important point discussed was that of the types of document to be covered by the national bibliography. The symposium decided that it should list not only books and pamphlets, by whatever process they were produced, but also maps, atlases and musical scores. It might also cover other material such as theses, prints and engravings, microfilms, gramophone records, etc. The entries for such material might be included in the regular issues of the current bibliography under special headings, or they might form the subject of special supplements.

The current national bibliography should also include entries for official publications, data on new periodicals and newspapers, and notices of changes of title. Information concerning the discontinuation of periodicals and newspapers might usefully be recorded but such information would be of a strictly unofficial nature.

The symposium fully appreciated the desirability of also publishing a current national bibliography of articles appearing in periodicals and newspapers as is already done in a number of countries (e.g., Czechoslovakia, Poland, USSR), but considered it inadvisable to include them in the current national bibliography unless they were listed in a separate section or in a supplement. Any other course would be misleading to statisticians.

With regard to retrospective general bibliographies, the symposium recommended that such bibliographies should be made as exhaustive as possible. They should include all publications printed within the present boundaries of the country in question and might also mention publications issued abroad which had a bearing on the country's cultural history.

Apart from current and retrospective general bibliographies, the national library should concern itself with the preparation of all bibliographies which, as a general rule, might be based primarily on its own collections, e.g., catalogues of manuscripts, incunabula and early printed books.

Lastly, the symposium viewed with favour the prospect of issuing selective national bibliographies of new publications, with brief notes in one of the principal European languages, and expressed its opinion that the national library was the most suitable institution to carry out that task. It recommended that the International Advisory Committee on Bibliography take up the question.

PROBLEMS OF CATALOGUING AND CLASSIFICATION

The symposium evinced keen interest in the work done by IFLA in connexion with the formulation of principles of cataloguing on which international agreement could be reached. As the question was being considered by the competent committee of IFLA under the chairmanship of Mr. Francis, the symposium did not think it appropriate to discuss its substance. With the aid of a subvention from the Council on Library Resources, IFLA was preparing an international conference on the subject, and a successful outcome could be expected. The national libraries, as producers of national bibliographies would be among the first to benefit from these proceedings. The symposium took note with approval of the paper submitted to it by Mr. Chaplin and asked him to submit it also to the IFLA commission of which he was the executive secretary.

The symposium took the view that it was for the national library, in co-operation with other libraries in its country, to promote the adoption throughout the national territory of common rules for the compilation of catalogues. In doing so it should take account of the recommendations of the IFLA committee.

The discussion on the classification of titles in national bibliographies revealed the multiplicity of methods employed: by main headings, by decimal classification, by subject matter and alphabetically. All those methods were justified provided they were clear to the user. The symposium saw no need to recommend any one of them, its view being that a national bibliography could be classified either by subject or by author. In general, a preference was expressed for subject-arrangement, on the ground that it might be easier to include periodicals in this kind of classification. But whichever system was adopted, an index in the other form was essential. Furthermore, an author index should include entries for anonyma.

Cumulative volumes might be more conveniently arranged by author, but in that case they would have to be supplemented either by a cumulative list of subjects or at least by a subject index giving cross-references to author entries.

NEW METHODS AND TECHNIQUES IN THE STORAGE
AND RETRIEVAL OF INFORMATION

Generally speaking, the national libraries have made practically no attempt to apply new techniques, such as punched cards, Hollerith machines, etc., for their cataloguing work. The symposium was therefore not in a position to reach definite conclusions on this subject. It was informed of some not very encouraging experiments. On the other hand, the members paid an extremely interesting visit to the library of the International Atomic Energy Agency in Vienna, where they heard a talk on those new bibliographical methods and were able to appreciate some of the practical results.

The symposium was, however, mindful of the fact that most national libraries already had vast holdings which were daily becoming more unwieldy. At the same time, the demands on them for new services were constantly growing. It was therefore most desirable that the national libraries should keep themselves constantly informed of all possible means of facilitating the rapid use of their collections. To this end, they would have to maintain close contact with the special libraries which were trying out new methods of storage and retrieval.

The symposium warmly approved the initiative of Unesco in exploring the possible applications of those new methods and techniques and expressed the hope that the Organization would continue to interest itself in the question.

In addition, the symposium recommended the holding of regular conferences of librarians and documentalists (perhaps in connexion with IFLA and FID meetings) to study these problems, discuss their experiences and determine their needs.

FUNCTION OF THE NATIONAL LIBRARY
AS REGARDS INTERNATIONAL CO-OPERATION
IN THE FIELD OF BIBLIOGRAPHY

The national library is usually the most suitable institution to undertake the distribution and exchange of bibliographical information at the international level. While there is no doubt that other institutions of a more specialized nature can often carry out this task more effectively, the national library will always be able to channel requests for information to the right quarter.

It will take a close and active interest in all bibliographical work and it will co-operate, in particular, with organizations and institutions responsible for preparing international specialized bibliographies.

National libraries seeking to collect bibliographical data on foreign documents bearing on their own countries should negotiate bilateral agreements with other countries to that end.

There should be regular exchanges of information between national libraries concerning the unpublished bibliographical tools at their disposal (e.g., card-index catalogues).

It is for the national library to see to it that reports are given from time to time, in the international professional publications, on the progress of bibliographical work (including planned or current work) whether carried out by the national library itself or by other libraries or institutions in the country. It should also ensure that similar information concerning bibliographical work abroad is reported in the professional publications of its own country.

National libraries are asked to send to Unesco each year, for publication, a list of the new periodicals issued in their respective countries.

THE ORGANIZATION
OF NATIONAL LIBRARIES

by
F. C. FRANCIS [1]

Development in the conception of library service during the past
25 years, and particularly since the beginning of World War II,
makes it imperative that national, comprehensive libraries should
examine afresh their position in the community and see how
far they are able to satisfy current requirements.

The concept of a national library is, I think, fairly generally
understood, even though national libraries differ in size and
scope from country to country. Speaking broadly the national
library in any country is the library which has the duty of collecting and preserving for posterity the written production of that
country. To this basic duty other duties are added, depending on a
variety of factors, such as the quality and range of the collections
which form the main stock of the library, the conception of the
library's purpose held by the government, the size of the country
and the existence of other comprehensive collections within easy
reach of each other, and so on.

National libraries like the British Museum, the Bibliothèque
Nationale in Paris and the Library of Congress, to name three of
the largest and best known, offer not only comprehensive collections of the literature of the United Kingdom, France and the
United States respectively, but also very large collections, both
historic and current, of the literature of other countries. The
scope of such libraries was best indicated by Sir Antony Panizzi,
the Italian-born former principal librarian of the British Museum,
when he spoke of the British Museum providing the necessary
means of information on all branches of human learning from all
countries, in all languages, properly arranged, minutely and fully
catalogued and capable of keeping pace with the increase of
human knowledge.

By following a policy based on these ideas a national library
could provide for the use of the citizens of the nation—as well as
for citizens of other countries—all the essential information on
all subjects and could enable basic research in any field of study

---

1. Director and Principal Librarian, The British Museum, London, United Kingdom.

Reprinted from NATIONAL LIBRARIES: their problems and prospects. Symposium on National Libraries in Europe, Vienna, 8-27 September 1958. Paris: Unesco (Unesco Manuals for Libraries – 11), p. 21-6, by permission of the publisher.

to be carried out successfully. There is no doubt that this is the service which the British Museum (to speak of the library with which I am familiar) has endeavoured to offer, and which indeed it has been able to offer in many subjects. It has to be realized, however, that this policy was enunciated well over a hundred years ago and the time is ripe to consider if it is still valid, and—still more important—if it is possible under modern conditions and with the enormous increase in the world's literature which has taken place in the past twenty or thirty years.

The policy for a national library enunciated by Panizzi was based on the traditional idea of the library as a place for study, a place where a scholar would be able to find the materials with which he would carry out his studies and compose his own contributions to learning. The very act of searching among the treasures of a great library was a valuable part of the scholar's work and contributed greatly to his success as a scholar and a polymath. The field of knowledge itself was also limited, in the sense that it was largely conceived of as academic knowledge.

Looking back, it seems clear that, far-reaching though Panizzi's ideas were, they were conceived in terms of a much smaller range of material than we are accustomed to regard as normal for a library and for a very different kind of use than that which a modern library is subjected to. It is right, therefore, that we should look once again at these ideas and see if we can conscientiously adopt them as valid for a national library today.

It is not only on theoretical grounds that a reappraisal is necessary. It would be idle to deny that in the past quarter of a century or so there has been a movement away from the large comprehensive libraries and a tendency to look upon the special, highly concentrated, library as the best and most promising instrument of research. This is truest in the field of science and technology, but it is also true in certain other subjects, such as economics. There are a number of reasons for this development, and as they are highly significant for the future development of library services, it is as well to set them out in detail. First, these subjects have to a greater or less extent been neglected in many of the older libraries, based as they are on the 'humanities'. It is especially true in the case of science and technology where developments have been so rapid in recent times. Second, research in scientific and technical subjects and in economics is based largely on periodicals and comparatively little on books and thus makes demands which the comprehensive libraries have not been equipped to meet, and which indeed they have been slow to understand. Third, the libraries have not had specialist staff able to deal with these subjects. Fourth, perhaps most important of all, the type of service which is required by scholars in these subjects is entirely different from that which libraries have offered in the past and, speaking broadly, it is beyond the capacity of almost every comprehensive library, as at present organized, to give it in the manner in which the scientist and technologist and perhaps also the economist require.

It is not only in the fields of science and technology, however, that the great comprehensive libraries are experiencing difficulties. The fragmentation of knowledge is so great, and the output of printed material so large, that libraries find it next to impossible, owing to lack of funds and lack of staff, to maintain comprehensive collections even in the subjects they have always looked upon as appropriate to them. Moreover, a generation of library users seems to have grown up which has not the will nor the interest to devote time to search among the large collections of a comprehensive library, but demands easier and more direct access to the material required than is usually offered in the unwieldy catalogues of such a library.

I have painted a deliberately gloomy picture, with the object of highlighting the problems which face the large general library. As I made clear at the beginning of this paper, not all national libraries are the same and not all attempt to provide comprehensive collections on all subjects and in all languages, but I believe that these problems face all general libraries in some degree and I do not think that the solution to them has yet been found.

I suppose I have not been alone in wondering from time to time if the day of the comprehensive library as anything but a storehouse of older books and periodicals—a sort of museum— was perhaps over, and if the main burden of bibliographical and information work should not be handed over to small, highly organized libraries. A moment's reflection, however, is sufficient to dispose of any such alarmist views.

The problem of providing information through libraries and similar institutions has not changed in principle throughout the ages. Changes, however, have taken place in the type of service demanded. These affect the large comprehensive libraries in two special ways: first in the matter of the speed with which information is required, and second the range of publications called for. Whereas up to a few years ago a library was looked upon as the natural resort of scholars for the study of books, monographs and periodicals (usually in that order of importance), nowadays, for a variety of reasons, study of the old-fashioned kind appears to be rarer and a considerable proportion of the demands made upon libraries is for quick reference to specific information, largely in periodicals and in what is now called report-literature. There is a perfectly understandable insistence on speed and immediacy which puts out of question the leisurely browsing among catalogues and bibliographies which is typical of many of the older libraries, and which makes it essential in the case of reference, i.e., non-lending, libraries to provide the closest possible approximation to an over-the-counter service if they are to satisfy the research worker and the scholar in the exact sciences and in technology and industry. The special libraries which have sprung up in the last few years endeavour to supply such a service and their success has underlined the need for library service of this kind. The large comprehensive library cannot, even if it wishes, avoid responsibility here, because it often has material which is not available in the special libraries. In any case the popularity of the special libraries has shown that speedy service is highly appreciated by library users, and the big libraries should surely rejoice in the challenge presented by this new requirement.

It is essential for the full use of printed information that the special libraries should continue to exist. They have undoubtedly a most important part to play in technological, industrial and commercial development. The services which these libraries can perform, however, are limited: special libraries connected with societies, commercial firms, research associations and professional bodies have their own local problems to meet and despite the useful and at times very impressive system of mutual aid they have built up, they are limited in the range of their operation—one has only to think of the information already coming or likely to come from far-distant countries using unfamiliar languages, of the cost of purchasing such material and of storing it, to realize that the large comprehensive library cannot avoid responsibility in these areas of study.

The growth of knowledge and the enormous increase in the number of publications, particularly periodicals, in which it is transmitted are responsible for the second of the major problems affecting the national libraries. This results in the intensification of the quality of reference work, which places a considerable additional burden on these libraries. It can be argued that one of the main services which the national library can perform is to supplement the books and periodicals held in other libraries by providing secondary and 'fringe' material. This is true in humanistic as well as in scientific and technological studies—indeed it is truer in respect of the humanities than of the sciences—and it puts a heavy strain on the financial and staff resources of the library, besides making bigger demands on its storage space.

I consider that national and other comprehensive libraries must endeavour to meet these demands on their services. Only by so doing can they, in my view, fulfil their proper role in society and bring their influence to bear on the intellectual and even commercial development of their country.

It is by no means easy, however, to suggest how this can be done. Example is better than precept, and I wish I could point to instances in Europe where a great national library, with the burden of the past lying heavily on its shoulders, had readjusted itself to modern conditions and was fulfilling the purpose I have outlined above. Of all the national libraries the Library of Congress in Washington comes nearest to the ideal, and there is much in that library which most European librarians would like to copy if they could ever get over the feeling that the Library of Congress with its budget of 10 million dollars and its staff of 2,500 seems to belong to an entirely different world. I believe, however, that by its emphasis on decentralization the Library of Congress is on the right road, and I would like to see, myself, a determined effort in one of the larger European libraries to create within its ambit a series of specialized sections. I have written elsewhere—in the paper prepared for the world congress in 1955 at Brussels—of my conviction that there is a great danger in mere size. I believe that size (coupled with complexity) is an unexpected enemy of library service. Up to a certain point, size increases the value of a library and engages the respect of its users; beyond that point it has to be controlled. Otherwise, it bemuses the reader and stifles the proper interest in the staff. I believe that it requires an almost superhuman effort, or a supreme disregard for one's general duties, to be a real bookman in a large undifferentiated collection.

Speaking once more of the library I know, it is a fact that the specialized sections—music, maps, State papers—provide the most satisfactory work for the staff, present the user with a well-defined body of material and provide him with expert assistance. Is it not possible to extend this system to other parts of the collections? I am aware that such a system would create difficulties of its own: with the small staffs common in European libraries, problems of promotion might prove difficult; duplication of reference material might make serious inroads in the diminutive funds available for purchases; planning, especially as it would involve not only the provision of special reading and staff rooms but a redistribution of the book stocks, would be difficult if not impossible in all but a few library buildings—unless one could start with an entirely new building.

Such a change would obviously have to be rather long-term, but I believe that all the difficulties I have outlined are capable of solution: they would be much less formidable if an example could be produced of such a scheme working satisfactorily.

There is a second important development which must be

undertaken by national libraries if it is not to be forced on them by circumstances: a determined effort to organize a system of national co-operation. It has already been admitted that no library can aim at completeness in all subjects: even the Library of Congress concedes the work of collecting books on agriculture to the Library of the Department of Agriculture, of medical books to the Army Medical Library, and so on. In the case of libraries in less wealthy countries, it is essential, if information work is to be properly carried on, that all available resources should be effectively mobilized. This is already being done I believe in a number of countries where the national librarian has a kind of roving commission and a general responsibility for library provision. In the United Kingdom effective steps have yet to be taken to secure fully effective use of library resources, though there is already a large degree of useful voluntary co-operation, and financial considerations are likely to carry the movement still further.

The two major developments outlined here carry with them a host of complementary developments which need consideration. Some of these I have outlined above, such as redeployment and training of existing staff; recruitment of new staff; new library planning, in particular the co-ordination of special reading rooms with the general library and with each other; enhanced funds; cataloguing arrangements so as to provide for a general and a number of special catalogues; the machinery of consultation and co-operation between the major libraries.

REGIONAL SEMINAR
ON THE DEVELOPMENT
OF NATIONAL LIBRARIES IN ASIA
AND THE PACIFIC AREA

Manila, Philippines, 3-15 February 1964

ORGANIZATION OF THE SEMINAR

Encouraged by the success of the Symposium on National Libraries in Europe, held in Vienna in 1958, and in response to requests received from a number of Member States in Asia and the Pacific area, Unesco, in co-operation with the Government of the Philippines, organized a seminar on the development of national libraries in Asia and the Pacific area which was held in Manila from 3 to 15 February 1964. The purpose of the seminar was to bring together directors and other senior officers of national libraries and potential heads of such libraries in countries which have not yet established them with the view to an exchange of ideas and experience and the formulation of recommendations for concrete action leading to development of national libraries throughout the area.

Twenty-four participants from the following countries attended the seminar: Afghanistan, Australia, Ceylon, China, Hong Kong, India, Indonesia, Iran, Israel, Japan, Korea, Laos, Nepal, New Zealand, Pakistan, Philippines, Thailand and Viet-Nam (See Annex A, List of Members of the Seminar).

Various observers also took part in the meeting.

Mr. Liebaers, director of the Royal Library in Brussels, Belgium, and Mr. Rogers, Deputy Librarian of Congress, Washington, U.S.A., attended as consultants. A considerable number of visitors from Philippine libraries was present at many of the sessions.

Mr. Kesavan was director of the seminar, Mr. Quirino, deputy director and Mr. Abella, co-ordinator of the local preparatory committees. Mr. Graneek and Mr. Harley were appointed rapporteurs. The foregoing and Mr. Petersen, chief of the Libraries Division of Unesco, with Mr. Dastagirzada, Mr. White, and the two consultants, constituted the steering committee of the seminar. The meeting was held in the building of the World Health Organization, Manila.

The inaugural session opened with a declaration of background and purpose by Mr. Petersen. He proposed that the seminar should aim at reaching agreement on the functions which a national library should carry out and state as clearly as possible the task which each country should undertake in furtherance of the development of its national library. Mr. Kesavan, director of the seminar, welcomed the guest speakers and invoked an abiding faith in the perfectibility of man as an essential element for the success of the ensuing proceedings. The Honorable Geronima T. Pecson, chairman of the Unesco National

Reprinted from *Unesco Bulletin for Libraries*, vol. 18, no. 4, July–August 1964, p.149-64 ©
Unesco 1964. Reproduced by permission of Unesco.

Commission of the Philippines, welcomed the participants and introduced the Honorable Alejandro R. Roces, Secretary of Education. Mr. Roces referred to the special significance of the seminar not only in respect of library development but also as a contribution towards the deepening of understanding among the people of the countries concerned. He urged the members of the seminar to explore ways in which national libraries could attract public interest and support.

In the succeeding sessions discussion leaders were as follows:
Organization of national libraries—Mr. Kesavan.
Acquisition policies of national libraries—Mr. Suzuki.
International exchange of publications—Mr. Suzuki.
Bibliographical activities of national libraries—Mr. Pearson.
Legislative reference services—Mr. Rogers.
National library buildings—Mr. White.
Protection and conservation of publications—Mr. Liebaers.
Professional training of librarians for work in national libraries—Mr. Mulay.
Co-operation of national libraries with other libraries—Mr. Wormann.
Role of national libraries in relation to scientific and technical information
    service—Mr. Liebaers.
Cataloguing problems of national libraries—Mr. Rogers.
Documentary reproduction and copyright—Mr. Graneek.
A list of working papers distributed to participants in advance of the seminar is given in Annex B. Three of these papers are reproduced in this issue of the *Bulletin*.

Questionnaires were distributed in 1963 with the purpose of collecting data and statistics on national libraries in the region. An analysis of the replies is given in Annex C.

Summaries of the discussions at each session were distributed twice daily.

The proceedings were enlivened by the preparation of a 35mm. documentary film of about 15 minutes' duration designed to demonstrate the contribution that national libraries can make to national development.

FINAL REPORT

INTRODUCTION

There are many countries with an ancient cultural and library tradition. Though the cultural tradition has survived, modern national libraries have not grown directly from it, but perhaps more from an awakening national consciousness. Over twenty of the world's four score national libraries are in Asia.

The nations of Asia and the Pacific region vary tremendously in size, population and wealth. Their national libraries vary similarly, but not in any direct relation to these factors. The variations displayed by these libraries are apparent in their age, size, method of growth, present condition, expenditure, function and organization.

Despite such differences, there are nevertheless many problems shared in common by the national libraries in the region. There are common economic, staff training and bibliographical problems; problems of acquisition, linguistic problems, and those consequent upon the poor physical quality of book production and damaging climate. Sometimes the same situation has been arrived at in different ways. Many national libraries in Asia provide public library service: in India, this is regarded as an onerous extension of the proper work of a national library; in Hong Kong, on the other hand, an institution conceived as a public library is drawing to itself a number of the functions of a national library.

Participants expressed their concern with the structure of library service, in particular the relationship among libraries within each country and of national libraries to those in other countries. Although there are common regional problems, and although there exist in the national libraries of Asia and the Pacific region notable differences from the older national libraries of the world, a national or even a regional organization alone is not sufficient. Perhaps a national librarian is in a better position than most people to maintain both a national and an international outlook.

But the very breadth of such an outlook creates its own problems. The proliferation of printed and other library materials in each country is aggravated by its multiplication upon an international scale. The difficulties in dealing with this experienced by libraries with limited staff and resources are easily apparent, especially when contrasted with the resources—still admittedly insufficient—of those national libraries which have achieved a more advanced state of organization, and which may be regarded as setting standards of operation for the developing libraries of the region.

Possibly the most encouraging fact to emerge from discussion was the understanding and appreciation which participants displayed of one another's problems and their willingness—indeed eagerness—to assist and co-operate with one another. The sharing of common difficulties and the pursuit of common aims in providing facilities for the preservation of mankind's national and international cultural heritages, together with facilities for scholarly research and for the support of educational programmes, are things which can plainly lead to a larger international understanding. If with them are combined youthful zest for development and the wisdom and cross-fertilization of ancient civilizations, the future promises well.

It is noted, however, that for co-operation to be successful there should be some activating and co-ordinating body, and that the techniques of co-operation must be carefully planned and supervised.

FUNCTIONS OF A NATIONAL LIBRARY

Initially, the functions of an individual national library may be largely defined by the social, cultural, economic and geographical conditions. There are nevertheless certain functions which it is the responsibility of the national library to develop. Broadly, these are:
1. To provide leadership among the nation's libraries.
2. To serve as a permanent depository for all publications issued in the country.
3. To acquire other types of material.
4. To provide bibliographical services.
5. To serve as a co-ordinating centre for co-operative activities.
6. To provide services to government.

ACQUISITION

A national library should serve as a permanent depository for all publications issued in a country, and should enjoy the benefit of legal or copyright deposit free of all charges and inclusive of all material both printed and audio-visual.

It should further acquire, preserve, and make available all library material concerning the home country wherever and whenever produced. It should have a comprehensive collection representative of all civilizations and providing a comprehensive subject coverage for purposes of research, study and inquiry.

It is considered desirable that a list should be prepared of collections of

Asian and Pacific manuscripts and printed books of outstanding importance in libraries in Europe and America and such materials should be readily available on microfilm to libraries requesting them.

INTERNATIONAL EXCHANGE OF PUBLICATIONS

Of the States represented at the seminar, only China, Israel and New Zealand have ratified the 1958 Unesco Convention concerning the International Exchange of Publications. The same States with the addition of Ceylon, have ratified the Convention concerning the Exchange of Official Publications and Government Documents between States.

It was agreed that:

1. All possible steps should be taken to persuade governments to ratify both conventions with a minimum of delay.
2. In countries where there is not yet a national exchange centre, the national library should be designated for this purpose.
3. Governments should provide the necessary funds and facilities for the establishment of such centres.
4. Centres should handle, as far as possible, non-official as well as official publications.

BIBLIOGRAPHICAL ACTIVITIES OF NATIONAL LIBRARIES

A national library has the responsibility of providing or co-ordinating the bibliographical services of a country. Typical activities are related to: (a) a current national bibliography, including all published materials both printed and audio-visual, with a roman transliteration; (b) retrospective bibliography; (c) subject and selective bibliographies; (d) union catalogues facilitating inter-library co-operation; (e) contribution to national and international bibliographical projects; (f) periodical indexing.

A national bibliography should include all books published in a country, whether written and printed there or not. The scope of other materials to be included may depend on the national deposit law. If a romanized script is used it is essential that a standard form of transliteration be adopted.

Where the publication of small national bibliographies is a problem it may be possible to print them in a learned periodical. The United Nations Economic Commission for Asia and the Far East (UNECAFE) publishes an Asian bibliography which could include national publications if information about them were made available. Unesco is prepared to consider requests for advice, guidance and assistance in the production of bibliographies. There are also a number of foundations from which funds might be sought, and attention is drawn to the possibilities of publication under the Colombo plan and with United States bilateral aid.

Although the production of a complete national bibliography is of prime importance, libraries of the Asian and Pacific regions may be thought to have a special responsibility for the preparation of select bibliographies of materials relating to the region, and published in their own country. These need not be evaluative, but should give annotations or at least indicate the type of publication.

Difficulties in compiling retrospective bibliographies of national publications were noted, such as that of locating material which is very often no longer in the country of origin. Indeed, national libraries may not be the most competent bodies to undertake the work. Several retrospective bibliographies some of which are based on the catalogues of overseas libraries are, however, in progress. In connexion with bibliographies of works about a country either some form of assistance from libraries in other countries or travel grants may be necessary.

Another difficulty noted in the compilation of a union catalogue of monographs was the immense and unwieldy size to which it may grow. Regional catalogues may offer a partial solution to this. A union catalogue of serials is a less complex matter and is considered essential. Manuscripts and incunabula lend themselves to union cataloguing.

CATALOGUING

The *Statement of Principles* of the International Conference on Cataloguing Principles, 1961, was considered.

The principles relating to corporate entries are controversial, for example the requirement that a body be entered under the name by which it is most frequently known in its publications which, if adopted, would mean changing millions of existing entries under the geographical location of the body, with the accompanying cost or acceptance of super-imposition.

The question arises whether the present situation is so unacceptable that new rules must be adopted. The possibility of publishing existing catalogues in whole or in part in order to permit a new beginning was discussed.

It was thought desirable that a study should be made of ways in which the Paris Principles might be adapted to the needs of the many Asian languages, and that the International Federation of Library Associations (IFLA) committee on this subject would be the appropriate body to undertake such a study.

It was agreed that catalogue cards which are to be sent abroad, and also national bibliographies, should incorporate a transliteration in roman script.

It was further agreed that the national library has a responsibility to promote agreement in catologuing and adoption of the Paris Principles insofar as they are applicable to the needs of a particular language.

LEGISLATIVE REFERENCE SERVICES

The types of legislative reference service which may be called for include the provision of factual data; the formulation of arguments for or against a given proposition or arguments in support of pre-determined actions; and assistance in speech writing both within and outside the legislature.

Information is almost always required to be supplied at very short notice and it is imperative that the research staff should have ready access to a highly organized collection of basic reference tools and a wide variety of vertical file material supplemented by the tools of micro-reproduction and an efficient messenger service.

The legislative reference staff need not consist only of professional librarians, but may include specialists in various fields. The staff must above all else be impartial and discreet and in no way directly involved in public affairs.

In the United States and Japan the legislative reference service is an integral part of the national library but this is by no means a universally desirable pattern. In the interest of democratic government in those countries where the national library is under the executive branch of the government, it is desirable that the legislative reference service should be independent of the library and responsible directly to the legislature.

It was agreed that legislative reference services are an essential adjunct to enlightened government and the requisite finance and facilities must be made available whether the service is offered primarily by the national library or by an independent unit responsible directly to the legislature.

THE ROLE OF THE NATIONAL LIBRARY
IN SCIENCE AND TECHNOLOGY

The experience of such a highly developed service as the United States Library of Congress would seem to show that a national library has duties in this field. This implies adequately trained staff (trained, that is, in science and or librarianship) and comprehensive science collections, especially periodical material and, nowadays, technical reports. Copyright deposit and exchange arrangements are important in building up collections. A referral service is important and may be supplemented by printed guides to sources of information; there is also the need for a strong section dealing with science bibliography. The work of other sections (e.g. the photo-duplication service) may be concerned to a greater or less extent with science. Promptness and the co-operation of scientists and librarians are to be emphasized, and also co-operation with other libraries.

Not all countries locate their chief science services in the national libraries, and no national library can handle all these services. It thus needs to draw upon or refer to other libraries. Traditionally, national libraries have avoided heavy scientific responsibilities, but it is felt that if the national library can take on this work it should do so.

The role of the public library in supplying scientific information should be noted, and the need to make specialized collections and services available to the public.

Some duplication is unavoidable in developing national services in science and technology, and is to be welcomed if it is necessary to the provision of adequate services.

Where circumstances permit, a national library should assume its proper responsibilities in the fields of science and technology, since these differ in degree rather than in kind from its responsibilities in other fields. These responsibilities in no way diminish the importance and duties of specialized libraries.

DOCUMENTARY REPRODUCTION AND COPYRIGHT

Documentary reproduction has two aspects: one in furtherance of acquisition policies, and the other in furtherance of scholarly activities and research. In the latter case, due regard must be paid to copyright legislation; the interests of the author and publisher must be reconciled with those of the scholar and the researcher. The inquiry carried out by the Bibliothèque Nationale (France) in 1962[1] revealed a common trend towards the application of copyright provision with sufficient flexibility to avoid hampering scientific work. For the most part photographic reproduction is permitted provided that the copy is for private study and not for publication. Specific legislation relating to documentary reproduction (as in the United Kingdom and the Federal Republic of Germany) is likely to have a limiting and restrictive effect and libraries are much better placed in those countries where reproduction is sanctioned by a general 'fair dealing' clause. Governments should be urged to adhere to the International Copyright Convention and to frame their regulations relating to documentary reproduction as liberally as possible and with a minimum of prescription.

CO-OPERATION

The national library must assume responsibility for initiating and promoting co-operation betwen itself and other libraries, nationally, regionally and inter-

1. See *Unesco bulletin for libraries*, vol. XVII, no. 4, item 255.

nationally. This is more difficult in Asia than in Europe owing to enormous social and cultural differences, problems of illiteracy and the diversity of vernaculars. A primary task is the planned acquisition of foreign literature based on a policy of national co-ordination on the lines of the Farmington Plan, the Scandia Plan and the programme of the Deutsche Forschungs-gemeinschaft.

Union catalogues are essential for identification of the national literature when it is dispersed in a number of libraries and private collections, and for the facilitation of inter-library loans. The national library should act as an information centre and assist in the formulation of rules and conditions for such loans. It should also serve as a clearing house for the exchange of books and periodicals including duplicates and be responsible for the planned co-ordination of national bibliographic activities.

National libraries can make a considerable contribution to library development by promoting knowledge about library resources through publications, by assisting library associations, providing photographic and other technical services and establishing and administering storage libraries.

It is advocated that in smaller countries the functions of the national library and the central library bureau should be integrated and that the national librarian should be the official adviser to the government for the whole library service.

In the field of regional co-operation, efficiency and economy can be achieved by co-ordinating acquisition of foreign, less used and expensive literature in neighbouring countries with common cultural affiliations. Many of the literary treasures of the Asian and Pacific area are now housed in libraries in other parts of the world and the only way to make them available in the country of origin is by systematic microfilming.

Internationally, national libraries should subscribe to the IFLA Agreement on International Library Loans, should contribute data to the Unesco *Index translationum* and to Unesco's Major Project on Mutual Appreciation of Eastern and Western Cultural Values, and should participate generally in the activities of IFLA and the International Federation for Documentation (FID). They should also initiate the compilation and publication of selective national bibliographies of new publications with brief annotations in one of the principal European languages.

Member States should note the extent to which co-operation exists within their borders, and where it is not yet fully operative should take steps to encourage the creation of appropriate machinery. Governments should be urged to introduce the necessary legislation to give formal sanction to co-operative activities.

National libraries should provide storage libraries and supervise the systematic withdrawal of superseded and obsolete material in local libraries with a view to preserving at least one copy of every publication.

Unesco should be requested to appoint a regional expert to advise and otherwise assist in the development of libraries in the Asian and Pacific regions. It is thought that such an expert would not need to concern himself with all countries.

PROFESSIONAL TRAINING OF STAFF

The need for trained staff is inherent in the very functions of a library, for they cannot be adequately performed without a trained staff with varying degrees of specialization and skill, competent also to carry ont many supplementary tasks and to deal at the appropriate level with persons using the library.

Training in Asia and the Pacific region involves special problems, e.g.

the recruitment of adequately equipped trainees; the use of textbooks and library tools in foreign languages; the fact that experience gained abroad may not be applicable at home; the need for specialists in many languages and in subjects of special interest to a particular country. This is not, however, to stress unduly the differences of the needs of the region's librarians, for these are probably outweighed by their similarity to the needs of librarians elsewhere.

The provision of different levels of service within one library implies differing requirements in training programmes for the various levels of staff. Orientation programmes, in-service training and continuing training and guidance are also necessary and must be related to the requirements of the particular library.

Although it is desirable that each country should be able to provide training in librarianship both the advantages and the disadvantages of overseas training should be recognized.

Training abroad is suggested for persons competent to establish library education within a country and able to acquire knowledge of training systems abroad while also understanding the home country's special needs. Such persons must have adequate knowledge of the language of the country in which they study.

In many countries it would be difficult to provide special training for the staff of a national library, but basic library education should be such that the necessary special knowledge can subsequently be added to general library knowledge. A training institute has, however, to be organized for a continuing programme, and not merely for occasional bursts of activity.

The library science material and textbooks produced should relate to conditions which students will find in the region's libraries. National libraries should also take a lead in organizing exchanges of personnel between different types of librarians and between different countries.

For professional or semi-professional positions all library personnel require basic library training. Each country should provide this training, and the special needs of a national library should be provided for also, where necessary.

Adequate rewards and incentives should be offered in order to attract staff of the standard required to the national library. The professional status of librarians should be considered as at least equivalent to that of careers in equivalent academic institutions, and librarians should receive the same treatment as workers in other academic fields with regard to salaries, vacation, travel, etc.

NATIONAL LIBRARY BUILDINGS

Designing a building is an operation which involves not only the architect and librarian, but the government, the city planning authorities, the Library Board or Council, the staff, and others. However, once the purposes of the building have been formulated, the architect should be allowed freedom to make a complete proposal before details are discussed. It is also essential that those concerned with design should have the opportunity to inspect national libraries elsewhere, and that the main control should be exercised by the librarian and architect. The librarian should, of course, exercise major control of library aspects of the design.

The building must be flexible, though not over-flexible, and large enough with possibilities for expansion. A noble, well-sited building is likely to attract desirable support for the library, but it should not be merely a monument. Monumentality should in any event be limited to the exterior and entrance.

The functions of a national library building must be very carefully defined, and should be a combination of those of libraries in general, those of a national library in particular, and those appropriate to the specific situation. The prime function is to serve the users and adequate exhibition space is considered desirable.

The problems of wooden construction are well known, in particular those of termite-proofing and earthquake-proof construction. All aspects of maintenance are, of course, important and in this, as in all other aspects of the question, the value of outside assistance based on genuine experience in the field was emphasized.

Since the quality of national library building design should set a pattern of excellence for library design in the country, expert advice should be called upon in the formulation of an objective and experienced view concerning the solution of the problems of design. The opportunity for local librarians to study buildings abroad should also be provided. But given the necessity of adapting the library to the local situation and requirements successful design also calls for the development of a body of informed opinion within the country.

The wide range of materials handled and of readers served necessitates a variety of special features in national library design. The need for growth must be borne in mind, and also the possibility of future installation of air-conditioning, fire protection equipment, etc., if not installed in the first instance.

A standardized description and ordered listing of the elements in library buildings should be prepared and it is urged that Unesco should commission this work.

CONSERVATION AND PRESERVATION OF MATERIALS

The question of protection and conservation is basic to the tasks of a national library. There are three kinds of potential destructive factors; temporal, climatic and human. Modern documents constitute a special problem in that the paper used is often of poor quality. There is little that librarians can do to make good this deficiency except to encourage the use of very durable paper for documents of any significance.

In Asia and the Pacific area, climatic conditions are exceptionally inimical to the preservation of library materials. The most serious damage arises as a result of wide variations of temperature and humidity. Full air conditioning for stack areas is a *sine qua non* for libraries in tropical regions. Unfortunately, such installations are expensive and governments are not always able to make available the necessary funds.

Microfilm makes an important contribution to conservation, despite the risk of damage arising from the filming process and the doubt concerning the durability of even properly processed film housed in good conditions. The Unesco mobile units are prepared to undertake projects in Asia at the specific request of governments. Depositories having staff members with the requisite linguistic competence and the technical resources for reproduction of copies from master negatives might be established in India, Japan, Australia and the Philippines.

Little can be done about negligence or incompetence on the part of human agents but steps can be taken to guard against the ravages of war or natural disaster. The question of dispersing original materials to safeguard them from such disasters and deterioration due to climatic conditions should be studied.

To sum up the question of protection and conservation let us say that prevention is better than cure. To this end the means of mechanical and chemical protection of books and manuscripts should be investigated, with special reference to devising equipment for thermostatically controlled air-conditioning that would demand a minimum of foreign currency for installation and maintenance.

Government departments should be required to produce limited editions of significant publications on very durable paper and commercial publishers should be encouraged to do likewise. National libraries should set an example in this matter.

National libraries should undertake the microfilming of newspapers and back sets of periodicals and of all rare, valuable and unique materials in their possession.

LIBRARY ASSOCIATIONS

Steps should be taken to encourage the formation of national library associations. IFLA should be requested to set up a section which would devote itself to the affairs of library associations in Asia and the Pacific region and to the organizing of conferences in that area.

With a view to following up the work of the seminar, Philippine participants agreed that the Philippine Library Association should be asked to collect and disseminate through IFLA information on national libraries in the region, whether or not separate publication is undertaken.

CONCLUSION

At the penultimate session participants paid tribute to the generosity and helpfulness of their colleagues, to the personal friendships established, to the hospitality of their Philippine hosts, and to the work of Unesco in arranging the seminar.

It was made clear that there was among participants a determination to see that the information and ideas gained at the seminar should be put to use in developing individual libraries, and that it should lead to a continuing communication between participants and national libraries throughout the region.

MAIN RECOMMENDATIONS

The seminar recommends
1. That Unesco:
    (a) Appoint a regional expert to advise and otherwise assist in the development of national libraries in Asia and the Pacific area.
    (b) Commission the compilation of a list of collections of Asian and Pacific manuscripts and printed books of outstanding importance in libraries in Europe and America.
    (c) Initiate a study of the inclusion of transcription in roman script in national bibliographies and on catalogue cards produced for distribution abroad.
    (d) Initiate a study to determine how the *Statement of Principles* of the International Conference on Cataloguing Principles may be applied to cataloguing in Asian languages.
    (e) Commission the preparation of a standardized description and ordered listing of the elements in library building.
    (f) Provide increased funds for the development of national libraries in Asia and the Pacific area through provision of experts, fellowships and equipment.
    (g) Make arrangements to hold another seminar on library development in the region in about five years' time.
2. That Member States in the region:
    (a) Establish as soon as possible a national library in each State where one does not at present exist.
    (b) Encourage the formation of a library association in each State where one does not at present exist.

(c) Ratify or accept the 1958 Unesco Convention concerning the International Exchange of Publications and the Convention concerning the Exchange of Official Publications and Government Documents between States.

(d) Ratify or accept the International Copyright Convention and pass legislation or frame regulations relating to documentary reproduction, in as liberal a manner as possible and with a minimum of prescription.

Annex A is a list of members and Annex B a list of documents distributed to seminar members. Annex C, 'Analysis of replies to questionnaire on national libraries in Asia and the Pacific area', may be summarised as follows:

Questionnaires were sent out in 1963 to gather factual data on national libraries in Asia and the Pacific area. Information in this document, which is based upon the 18 completed questionnaires received, covers size of collections (the majority being modest — only 12% having collections over a million volumes); departments and services (public library service being offered by 61% of the libraries); interlibrary loan (55% do not act as interlibrary loan centres); bibliographical activities (61% compile and/or publish the national bibliography); legal deposit (in effect 94% receive the benefits of legal deposit); operating expenditures (average proportions of budget for various items are as follows: 25% for books and other material, 55% for salaries, 20% other expenditures; proportion spent for each of these by individual libraries ranges from 7% to 50% for books etc., from 38% to 77% for salaries, and from 3% to 32% other); national library buildings (only 33% reported that they are housed in a building that is exclusively for the library's use; only 22% indicated that their quarters were adequate); personnel (over half the staff in 50% of the national libraries have neither a university degree nor training in library science).

The Rôle of the National Library:
A preliminary statement

Paper read to the Section of National and University Libraries
at the IFLA Council Meeting, Rome 1964

by K. W. HUMPHREYS

In 1962 at Berne this section of IFLA considered the document on the long term programme of IFLA (*Les bibliothèques dans de monde.* La Haye 1963) with special reference to the work of national libraries:

"In the previous chapters due attention has already been given to all the different aspects referred to here, such as the 'dépôt légal', the national bibliography, the union catalogue, the care and restoration of material and training. So it is not necessary to express any particular wishes in this respect. What does need emphasis, however, is the question, which has a direct bearing on all this and has by no means been answered yet, of how we should imagine the future development of the national library and what should be its place in the whole of the national library system."

It was resolved that a study be made of the bibliographical and professional responsibilities carried out at a national level by national libraries or other appropriate bodies.

The problem of the duties and functions of national libraries had already been discussed in detail at the Symposium on National Libraries in Europe at Vienna in 1958 organised by UNESCO and certain of the conclusions and recommendations which were agreed upon were clear and specific for national library policy, e.g.:

"It is the responsibility of the national library to acquire and conserve the whole of the national production of printed material ..."

"It is recommended that a national plan for the acquisition of foreign materials should be established in countries where no such plan exists."

"The national library is responsible for the bibliographical service of its own country ... It is also the national library's responsibility to undertake the production of current national bibliographies, and also of retrospective national bibliographies where needed."

"It is the responsibility of the national library to assemble material for a central register of manuscript collections and to keep it up to date."

Reprinted from *Libri*, vol.14, no. 4, 1964, p. 356-68, by permission of the author and the publisher.

(*National Libraries: their problems and prospects*. Paris: UNESCO, 1960).

The great variety of national libraries and the divergent views on their place in relation to libraries and librarianship in their own countries impelled IFLA to attempt a further assessment of their responsibilities.

The matter should have been dealt with in Sofia last year but I was unable to be present and Miss Razumowsky had time only to prepare a brief outline of some of the views expressed by the directors of some of the largest national libraries. At the conclusion of its meeting at Sofia this Section included in its resolutions the following:–

The section has decided to put on the agenda once more the comparative study of bibliographical and professional responsibilities to be carried out at a national level by national libraries or other appropriate bodies. The Section has estimated that this study should draw principally, but not exclusively, on the experience of the British Museum in London, the Lenin Library in Moscow, the Bibliothèque Nationale in Paris and the Library of Congress in Washington.

I have now attempted to consider the problem in this paper which, as you will be aware, is little more than a further step on the path towards the fulfilment of one of IFLA's aims. Whilst my brief may seem to be clear, however, the ultimate purpose may not be so evident. I have perhaps exceeded my brief by attempting to look beyond or outside it to consider the ultimate use to which any recommendation of IFLA will be put.

I start by outlining the duties of certain national libraries in extension of the information circulated at Sofia by Miss Razumowsky. Not all the four libraries which are named in our terms of reference have given a full account of their functions but it is possible, nonetheless, to list those they have responsibility for.

The Librarian of the Library of Congress detailed the duties accepted by his library in considering the report on its work prepared by Douglas W. Bryant.

"The Library of Congress today performs more national library functions than any other national library in the world. The functions of such libraries vary, but each of them engages in some, and the Library of Congress in all, of the following:

1. Maintains comprehensive collections, especially evidence of the national heritage, for the use of the Government, the scholarly world, and the public making it a national center for research.

2. Benefits from official, intergovernmental exchange of publications.

3. Receives through copyright or legal deposit materials for the enrichment of its collections.

4. Receives gifts to the Nation in the form of collections of personal papers, rare books, and other valuable materials and in the form of trust funds and bequests, which enable it not only to enrich the collections but to present cultural programs in such fields as literature, art and music.

5. Develops a comprehensive classification system, which is widely used by other research institutions, and cataloging codes, which are nationally accepted standards.

6. Serves as a center for co-operative cataloging of books and other forms of material by the Nation's libraries.

7. Provides a national catalog card distribution service.

8. Maintains national union catalogs on cards, which serve as guides to the Nation's research resources in various forms (such as books and manuscripts) and in various fields (such as Hebraica and Slavica), and furnishes information about the location of needed materials to those who cannot personally consult these tools.

9. Publishes in book form a national bibliography, or a major contribution thereto, such as the Library's *National Union Catalog*.

10. Gives reference service on its premises and provides extensive information from and about its collections by mail.

11. Participates in a nationwide inter-library loan system, which enables it to share collection responsibilities with other libraries and to make research materials generally available, thereby strengthening smaller libraries throughout the country by supplementing their research resources through those of the national library.

12. Has an active bibliographic program and makes the results of it widely available through publication.

13. Administers the national books-for-the-blind program.

14. Presents exhibits selected from the national collections for the education and enjoyment of the general public, and circulates exhibits at home and abroad as evidence of the national history and culture.

15. Experiments and conducts research in the area of library technology.

16. Engages in national and international co-operative bibliographic projects and works with other national libraries and international organisations to achieve standardization of rules in order to increase the accessibility of the materials of knowledge without regard to national boundaries and language barriers.

(Annual Report of the Librarian of Congress for the fiscal year ending June 30th, 1962. Washington, D.C. 1963).

The raison d'être of the Lenin Library is set out in the Statute of the Library from which I abstract the following sections which are relevant to our present purpose:–

1. The Lenin Library is the central library of the Soviet Union; the national repository for publications of the peoples of the USSR, of foreign publications,

manuscripts and manuscript books; a center for the compilation of bibliographies of recommended reading; and an all-union research institution in the fields of library science, bibliography, and the history of books.

The Lenin Library is open to all citizens.

Services are provided without charge.

2. The Lenin Library contributes to the development of communism in the USSR. It publicizes Marxist-Leninist doctrine, decisions of the Communist Party and the Soviet government; participates in the Communist education of workers and in the development of all branches of the national economy, science, technology, literature and art through extensive utilization of its holdings.

3. To achieve these goals the Lenin Library:

a) services readers in its reading rooms with publications, microfilms, and manuscripts. If materials requested by readers are not in its possession, it shall borrow them on a temporary basis from other Soviet or foreign libraries;

b) loans publications and microfilms to readers, central agencies of the party and government, libraries, and other institutions, in conformance with rules governing the interlibrary loan service;

c) aids readers in book selection through the compilation of bibliographies and catalogs, card files, book exhibits, surveys, and information on bibliography, and conferences as well as making available microfilms, photographs, translations, typewritten copies of printed and manuscript material as requested by institutions, organisations, and individual citizens;

d) provides bibliographic service to central agencies of the party and government, educational institutions, and libraries;

e) collects and preserves publications and manuscripts in all branches of knowledge, written in the language of the peoples of the USSR; receives a deposit copy of all publications printed in the USSR regardless of the type of publication and distribution; acquires and retains foreign publications of scientific, historical, artistic and practical value;

f) catalogs and classifies the library's holdings. Organizes readers' and official catalogs and bibliographic card files;

g) carries on book exchanges with Soviet libraries, using its duplicate holdings for this purpose. It exchanges books with foreign libraries and other academic institutions, using for this purpose legal deposit copies and additional purchased publications;

h) performs research and guidance work in the field of library science, bibliography, and the history of books. Compiles and publishes bibliographies, lists of recommended reading, printed catalogs of books and manuscript collections, *Trudy* (Transactions) and *Uchenye zapiski* (Communications) dealing with problems in library science and bibliography;

i) participates in the expansion of the library system in the USSR. Provides guidance in problems of library science to republic and province libraries; gives assistance in library techniques to mass and research libraries by compiling manuals, studying and publicizing modern practices, holding conferences, organizing group and individual consultation services.

(*Osnovnye polozheniia instruktsii Gosudarstvennoi ordena biblioteki SSSR im. V. I. Lenina.* Moscow 1957, quoted by P. L. Horecky, *Libraries and Bibliographic Centers in the Soviet Union.* Washington, D.C. 1959).

The British Museum's functions may be summarized as follows:-

1. The depository for all national literature (printed books, manuscripts, prints, drawings, etc.).
2. The collection of representative literature on all subjects in all languages.
3. Houses the British National Bibliography.
4. Offers photographic services.
5. Preparation of catalogues.
6. A reference service.

The Bibliothèque Nationale, Paris has very similar functions:-

1. The depository for all national literature (printed books, manuscripts excepting material collected by the Archives Nationales etc.).
2. The collection of representative literature on all subjects in all languages.
3. Offers photographic services.
4. Preparation of catalogues.
5. Inter-library loan service, national and international.
6. Foreign exchange service.
7. Preparation of national bibliography.

Statements on the duties which national libraries should perform have been made by several librarians of national libraries:

At the International Congress of Libraries and Documentation Centres at Brussels in 1955 Dr. Stummvoll gave the following list:

a) Coverage of the entire national output of printed matter with the greatest possible completeness through free copies (deposit copy or presentation on a voluntary basis).

b) Inter-library lending within the country and abroad.

c) Training of librarians at a library school, connected with the library or through in-service training with corresponding courses and terminating examination.

d) Publication of a national bibliography covering the national book production as well as all books written about the country concerned or by a citizen of that country which have been published abroad. With this is connected the keeping of statistics of book-production.

e) Publication of catalogues (union, special, newspaper and other catalogues.)

f) Printing of catalogue cards for the other libraries of the country.

g) Centre for a bibliographical information service.

h) Centre for international exchanges.

i) Valuation of duplicates.

k) Technical installations serving as models for other libraries (bindery, printing department, repair departments, photographic installations, microcopying laboratory, etc.).

l) Collection on librarianship.

m) Collections concerned with special fields: manuscripts, incunabula, copper-engravings, medals, coins, stamps, theatre, music (gramophone records), films, photos, tapes, negatives, books for the blind, etc. in as far as these fields are not already covered by other institutions (museums).

In the same year in the number of *Library Trends* devoted to "Current Trends in National Libraries" (*Library Trends*, Vol. 4, no. 1) he gave a similar list:–

1. The maintenance of a comprehensive collection of national writings, acquired as far as possible through copyright deposit either as required by law or by the voluntary gift of their authors.

2. The issuance of a national bibliography which contains all the literature written either about a country or by the nationals of a country.

3. The administration of international interlibrary loans.

4. The training of librarians in an affiliated library school.

5. The publication of catalogs (general, special, serial, etc.)

6. The printing of catalog cards for other libraries of the country.

7. The compilation of bibliographies of reference value, the preparation of indices, and the maintenance of a national union catalog.

8. The organisation of international book exchange channels.

9. The public utilization of duplicates.

10. The development of technical standards for other libraries in the country, including binding, printing, restoration, photoduplication, and microfilm reproduction.

11. The collection of such specialized material as manuscripts, incunables, books for the blind, dramatic compositions, engravings, medals, music scores, cinematic films, photographs, sound recordings, and coins; unless these materials are already collected in other institutions or museums.

At the Conference in Bangor in 1963 of the University and Research Section of the Library Association (*National Libraries*. London, Library Association, 1963) Mr. Ib Magnussen, Librarian of the Statsbiblioteket, Århus, summarized a national library's functions under seven heads:

1. Collecting national literature.
2. Collecting foreign literature.
3. Serving as a book museum.
4. Giving the public access to the collections.

5. Carrying out information service and bibliographical activity.
6. Functioning as a training centre.
7. Participating in national library planning.

This is perhaps sufficient evidence of the variety of the views of national librarians on their duties and at the same time in part an indication of the diversity of functions at present undertaken by certain national libraries. From this evidence it should be possible to deduce various categories of these functions. Firstly, those which are fundamental to the existence of a national library; secondly, those which it is desirable should be accepted by the central or single national library; thirdly, those which can be undertaken by other agencies whether under the control of the central national library or not.

The remainder of this paper (pp. 362-368) is developed in the next paper in this volume.

National library functions

by K. W. Humphreys, Librarian,
University of Birmingham Library

Introduction

The present paper is an extension of that presented to the National and University Library Section of the International Federation of Library Associations (IFLA) at Rome in 1964 ('The role of the national library: a preliminary statement', *Libri*, vol. XIV, 1964, p. 356). The Rome paper was to have been preliminary to a full-scale statement on the functions of a national library to be compiled in the light of the discussions there, but no discussion was, in fact, possible at Rome. However, a very useful meeting was held in Helsinki in August 1965 at which the paper was approved for publication, with certain amendments incorporating the suggestions put forward by members of the section.

I have also taken note of the discussions held at Manila in 1964.[1]

In attempting to classify the functions of a national library system which may be undertaken by the national library, I have assumed that a country has only one such library (see illustrations). Of course this assumption will not be true of many large and highly developed countries, but it may be true of smaller, newly emergent countries—and it is mainly for these that I am writing. At the same time, for reasons of brevity, I have not here discussed the effect on a national library's functions of its accepting additional responsibilities as a university library or even as a city library, although this may be the position of the national library in a small country.[2]

I examined the various activities of several great national libraries (see *Libri*, vol. XIV, 1964, p. 356 ff.) and classified them according to my own view as to their appropriateness to the aims of national libraries generally. Where there is only one national library and bibliographical centre, it must probably accept all the responsibilities mentioned and there are many advantages in centralizing them.

In the following pages, I have divided the national library activities into three categories—essential, desirable and inessential. There will be some shading over between the categories I have designated but the distinctions, however rough, will indicate the general trend of my proposals.

I regret that in order to be able to publish some account of my views on this subject in this journal it has been necessary greatly to compress my original statement. I hope that it will be possible to issue a full statement later.

---

1. *Unesco bulletin for libraries*, vol. XVIII, 1964, p. 149-64.
2. Cf. C. Wormann. National libraries in our time. *Libri*, vol. IX, 1959, p. 273-307.

Reprinted from *Unesco Bulletin for Libraries*, vol.20, no. 4, July–August 1966, p. 158-69. ©
Unesco 1966. Reproduced by permission of Unesco.

Fundamental functions of a national library

The outstanding and central collection of a nation's literature.

Whatever other function of a national library is undertaken elsewhere, the collection of the nation's literature is its basic aim. The types of material which are included in this collection may vary according to the country's particular needs and historical development, and the national collections may, as in many countries, be preserved separately from the other collections. Obviously, however, printed literature must be fully covered, although there will be some division of opinion about the value of retaining centrally such items as local newspapers, book-jackets, jobbing printing of all kinds, diaries and similar ephemera. Arrangements should be made by the national library to ensure that university, public or special libraries maintain files of local newspapers and other material of regional, rather than national, interest.

The national library should receive at least one copy of every book published in the country (see '*Depôt légal*' in the next section), all privately printed items and all books printed abroad which describe any aspect of the life and cultures of that country. In some libraries, like the British Museum, no attempt is made to obtain the vast number of editions of translated works, but a selection, at least, of the first issues of such translations should be acquired. National libraries should not, however, take too narrow a view of this aspect of acquisition—particularly in the newly emergent countries.

The acquisition policies of national libraries will vary from country to country. The collection of printed books and usually of manuscripts will be common to most, but other types of material may not always be included. Maps are commonly deposited under the *dépôt légal*, as also are music scores, but gramophone records, films, engravings, medals, coins and magnetic tapes (recording sound) are not always so treated. In some countries gramophone records are deposited in the national library to accompany, as it were, the musical scores. The Library of Congress not only receives films, but also publishes a catalogue of them as a section of the national union catalogue.

Many European national libraries have included in their functions the preservation of engravings, coins and medals, but in countries where national library services are developing these items would be better dealt with in a national museum or art gallery.

Editions of books, periodicals, theses, etc., which are produced only in microtext form should be considered in the same way as editions of printed books and preserved accordingly. The national library should also attempt to have a complete collection of printed books in microtext or other photocopy form when no copy is available in the country. A number of national librarians have also initiated the copying of manuscripts held in libraries outside their own countries which are known to have been produced originally in their countries. Some libraries also undertake the planning of a national scheme for the microfilming of domestic and foreign newspapers; this operation may facilitate the publication of a union catalogue of newspapers.

It is assumed that all current published material will be obtained by means of *dépôt légal*. All other national publications which are not received by gift will need to be purchased. It is, therefore, vital that adequate funds should be available to the national library for purchases. These will generally be of two types—recurrent and non-recurrent. The recurrent grant will be used for normal day-to-day acquisitions, but will probably not be sufficient for the occasional important—and therefore usually highly expensive—item which is offered through private sale or in the market. The national library must be always in a position to apply for additional money to buy these outstanding books or manuscripts so that they may not be lost to the country. In countries where the financial resources of the national library are not sufficient to ensure the retention in the country of any item of national importance, then the literary (including the scientific and artistic) heritage of the nation must be safeguarded by other means. Many countries have found it necessary to set up some machinery for the control of the export of books and manuscripts. Legislation designed to stop the outflow of the nation's literature must be fully effective and not, as is the case in Britain, only partially satisfactory.

What is the proper use of the national collection? Unique and very rare items in the library should not, of course, be available for loan and, if the national library is to take part in the country's inter-library lending scheme, probably it should restrict this function to duplicated items and to more recent material. General access to the books in the national library for consultation should, in theory, be granted to any member of the public, although in practice this privilege would not be given to anyone irrespective of the level of their requirements.

Dépôt légal

Dépôt légal may have several aims—to protect the rights of authors, to maintain a system of press censorship and to ensure the preservation of a nation's literature in a national library. The earliest attempt at legal deposit was aimed at the enrichment of a library. By the Montpellier Ordinance of 28 December 1537, every printer and publisher in France was required to send a free copy of every new book published to the Royal Library at Blois. The earliest British arrangements were made with a similar object in view, but the later depository scheme has been associated with the law of copyright and therefore with the rights of authors. This, however, is unusual; the majority of European countries operate a system designed to benefit scholarly libraries. This does not, however, exclude another form of obligatory deposit. In Spain and Italy a deposit in connexion with an author's rights is maintained in addition to the legal deposit, and in Germany, France, Luxembourg, Sweden and certain East European countries one copy must be delivered for censorship purposes as well as one by legal deposit. In these cases the one copy is delivered to an administrative department of the State which may pass it on to a library freely or by statute.

Whatever method is used and whatever the purpose of legal deposit, in every country at least one copy of everything printed or published should be legally required to be deposited in the national library. The obligations of printers to the national library should also be complemented by a regulation binding the national library to retain, preserve for posterity and make available to the public, one copy of everything delivered under the law.

There is considerable variation in the number of copies which are deposited, ranging from only one in a few countries like Japan to as many as forty-one copies of certain kinds of material in the U.S.S.R. In some countries the regulations for the number of copies deposited of periodicals, official publications, engravings, films and sound recordings differ from those for books. In the case of official publications it is common practice to receive extra copies for exchange purposes.

In most countries one copy only is considered inadequate. In order that at least one copy of everything published may be preserved the national library should be in a position to obtain, preferably by legal deposit, not less than one additional copy for loan or to replace items in constant demand. It has been represented to me that three copies should, ideally, be supplied—one for normal use, one to be available on inter-library loan and one to be preserved. The practice in a number of countries of providing additional copies for regional libraries is obviously of great benefit to scholars, supplementing the services offered by the national library. It is, however, a great mistake to treat all these copies as reference-only material, as has happened in the United Kingdom.

As for the number and the nature of the copies required to be supplied by legal deposit, it is assumed that all items must be complete and perfect and in the usual state as retailed to the public. Where a work is produced in a normal and a 'de luxe' edition, the national library should receive copies of both editions.

The regulations in most countries which impose the duty of legal deposit normally require the printer or the publisher to present the copies, although one or two put the onus on the author. It would seem sensible to expect the publisher to deposit copies of his productions, except where works are unpublished, and then the printer should be held responsible; it is too heavy an imposition to place on the author. The law should include some administrative and punitive sanctions in the event of non-execution of the act of deposit. In some countries the depositor is required to make restitution to the libraries concerned, which can institute legal proceedings for non-compliance with the law. Other sanctions include requisitioning of copies, demanding a photographic reproduction of a work no longer available in the original, and seizure of the whole edition of the work which, until deposit has been made, is on sale illicitly. In Italy the printer can be prevented from carrying on his trade for a period of three months or more, while in the United States of America, where the author's rights are connected with deposit, the author can lose his copyright.

It has been laid down above that the national library should receive at least one copy of everything that is published or privately printed and that the law of legal deposit should require the depositor to send his copy direct to the national library.

The copy which is delivered should be dispatched to the national library before the date of publication although, of course, it cannot be made available to the public earlier than the publication date. The national library which should be responsible for, or should house, the national bibliography will be in a position to prepare entries for the bibliography which can then be issued simultaneously with the publication of the books it lists. The major criticism of the legal deposit system in which books are sent to government departments in connexion with press control is that the departments cause long delays in dispatching material to the national library. In cases where a book is banned or censored it should be included in the normal deposit but retained separately from the other material and not made available to the public until, if ever, the ban is lifted.

Finally, it should be stressed that no matter for what purpose the legal depository system of a country has been instituted, the important consequence is that the national library should receive all the books, periodicals and whatever other material it has decided to collect which are printed or published in that country. Although the national library will receive the benefit of free copies of the production of its national press it must at the same time accept responsibility for the many tasks which follow from legal deposit.

Coverage of foreign literature

At the Vienna meeting on National Libraries in 1958[1] the role of the national library in the provision of foreign literature within its own library and within the country generally was fully discussed and it was recommended that a national plan for the acquisition of foreign materials should be established in countries where no such plan exists. It was clear from the discussions that members were concerned that a country should have as full a coverage as possible and also that there were doubts in the minds of many about the efficiency of the continuing encyclopaedic nature of a national library. It was felt that the enormous growth of the world's literature and the changing attitude of readers had created problems which a monolithic type of library could not solve without

---

1. *National libraries: their problems and prospects. Symposium on national libraries in Europe.* Paris, Unesco, 1960.

radical reorganization. In order to meet the problem of size many members of the symposium looked, it seems, with some envy at the example of large university libraries which, especially in the United States, tend to decentralize their collections. In view of the methods proposed, however, it is clear that any process of separation of parts of the collection is expected to be based on subject divisions which reflect the interests and the varying methods of working of different types of scholars. It is often suggested that, for example, science, medicine and the social sciences all demand different approaches from those of the humanities and that they should be split off from the old national library, leaving it to devote its attentions only to the humanistic subjects. This is surely, however, a counsel of despair and accepts the view that the new methods of librarianship cannot be adopted by the national library; clearly this is not necessarily true.

The hiving-off of subjects of this type from the national library may be the means of offering scientists and scholars a service which the national library is unable to provide. In countries where it is possible to support only one central library it is important that even though it is under one roof it should be divided according to the many functions it must perform. It is necessary for example to have reading areas for manuscripts, maps, prints and drawings separate from those for printed books. The traditional single, monumental reading-room should be replaced by several reading-rooms devoted, for example, to science, medicine, law, economics and social sciences, languages and literatures, history and geography. Each of these rooms should, as far as possible, be contiguous or one above the other, and connected as closely as may be practicable to the bookstacks. All material should be processed immediately on receipt and made available to readers and, in addition to their library training, the staff should have had professional training in the subjects with which they are concerned.

The question of co-ordination is central to the role of the national library in relation to the coverage of foreign literature throughout the libraries of the country. The immense range and scope of foreign scholarly literature is a formidable barrier to full coverage by one library and it has been usual to share this responsibility among a number of libraries. Thus, the important co-operative schemes of this type—the Farmington Plan in the United States, the Scandia Plan and the West German system organized with the aid of the Deutsche Forschungsgemeinschaft—are relevant to this study. Under the terms of these plans the co-operating libraries ensure varying degrees of coverage of foreign literature. The Americans have been very careful to make critical surveys of the results of their Plan and have shown that it has enabled the United States to collect a large number of important items which would not otherwise have been acquired by any American library.

Nonetheless there have been many criticisms of the scheme and more recently strong doubts have been expressed about the usefulness of dividing up the fields of knowledge among a number of libraries. It has been suggested that it would be preferable for the national library to collect all material from all countries to be made available for loan to any library. The particular advantage of this arrangement, it is advocated by its proposers, is that the national library is in a position to offer catalogue entries not only for the books published in the country, as it is a depository library, but also for books in all other languages. The national library can therefore offer a centralized cataloguing service based on the co-operative acquisitions scheme and reach a high standard of inter-library lending without the necessity of maintaining a fully comprehensive union catalogue.

Whatever method is adopted the national library should encourage the collection of a wide coverage of the scholarly literature of other countries. It should be at the centre of any plans for developing the resources of the libraries in its country. If it can combine a coverage scheme with inter-library lending and shared cataloguing, it will have made a splendid contribution to the national library system.

Publication of the national bibliography

The publication of the national bibliography is related to the practice of dépôt légal. When the current national output is deposited at the national library it is usual for that library either to prepare the national bibliography itself or to house the organization responsible for compiling the bibliography. Where the dépôt légal is centred on a bibliographical institute or other non-library institution the national bibliography may be prepared there. In East European countries the book chambers which collect the national or republic literature produce the national or republic bibliography. Whatever system is used for the collection of the dépôt légal it is vital that the books should be received immediately after publication or, if possible, before the publication date so that the national bibliography may be compiled and issued with no delay. Unfortunately many existing national bibliographies do not appear until several months after the publication date of the books they record.

The form in which the national bibliography is published will depend on the needs of the publishers, booksellers and librarians in each country. Normally, weekly parts are cumulated into quarterly or annual volumes. Each entry may also be available on a card or a slip for sale to libraries.

The content of the national bibliography varies considerably from country to country. 'If we examine the impressive series of current national bibliographies now available we can see clearly that there are certain fundamental differences between them: some cover all printed publications in a single language (for instance, *Bibliographie de la France, Deutsche Bibliographie*), others cover all publications printed in all languages in one country only (for instance, the Yugoslav bibliography), others again contain not only publications printed in the given country or in its languages, but also foreign publications of interest to it on account of their authorship or subject *(Bibliographie de Belgique)*. Bibliographies differ too in the type of material they deal with. Some include maps, atlases, plans, engravings, prints and musical scores, as well as printed and multigraphed publications (the German and Austrian bibliographies); others include these types of material in supplements *(Bibliographie de la France)*; and others again omit these types of material either altogether, or in part (the *British National Bibliography*). It might perhaps be possible to reach agreement on the categories of material to be included in national bibliographies.[1] Certainly any co-operative effort aimed at uniform treatment of material to be listed in national bibliographies would be very welcome.

National bibliographical information centre

A conference on the improvement of bibliographical services was held by Unesco in November 1950, and among its recommendations was the proposal that every country should establish national planning bodies (a) to promote the development of bibliographical and information services; (b) to stimulate research in the field of bibliographic methodology and to serve as a clearing house of information about research completed or in progress in that field; (c) to co-ordinate the various tasks, and assist in the determination of priorities; and (d) to act as a link with international bodies concerned with the planning of bibliographical and information centres.

Such a planning body may be either the national library or a distinctly separate organization or, perhaps preferably, a separately administered body housed in the national library. Of course, if the national library has the privilege of legal deposit and maintains the national union catalogue, no other library or institu-

---

1. Mirko Rupel. The bibliographical activities of national libraries. *National libraries: their problems and prospects.* Unesco, 1960, p. 52.

tion in the country will have comparable sources of information. The specialist knowledge of a large staff backed by the finest library resources in a country will also be a vital element in the servicing of the bibliographical centre. However, in many countries with well-established national libraries there is a serious lack of accommodation and the out-dated methods of processing materials used in some national libraries are not conducive to the acceptance of the new attitudes to bibliographical work requisite for the establishment of a national biblio-graphical centre. For these reasons an autonomous centre, housed in or adjacent to the national library, may be more satisfactory than a centre which is an integral part of the library.

The Unesco conference also made more detailed recommendations concerning the functions of the centre. In all countries the national library would be the co-ordinating centre for all specialized information centres. Where certain libraries are concerned with particular subject fields they will be in a better position to prepare specialist subject indexes than the national library, which should stimulate the compilation and even the publication of such indexes. The national library should, therefore, not only be aware of the existence of all insti-tutions having specialist interests but should also indicate the desirability of their bibliographical services which are not otherwise available. The national library should maintain constant contact with these institutions, providing as well as receiving information and referring to them inquiries relevant to their special subject fields. In this connexion, reports on bibliographical research in progress will be sent to the national centre which can make use of this information in answering inquiries.

Finally, it may be assumed that the national library will be the obvious focus of bibliographical inquiries from abroad. Since it will have so many points of contact with other national libraries it must be responsible initially for dealing with all questions relating to the publications issued in its own country. This is in any case an extension of other aspects of its international work and no other library can be more favourably placed to undertake this responsibility, given the experience of its staff and the strength of its stock.

Publication of catalogues

In a previous section I suggested that, if possible, the national library should be responsible for the compilation of the current national bibliography. Where the national library has this responsibility it is important that it should also prepare a retrospective bibliography of the national literature. The catalogue of the contents of the national library will provide a firm basis for the compilation of the bibliography and, until it is practicable to commence work on the bibliography, the catalogue of the national library should be published. It will be a valuable reference work in other libraries in the country, and, if the library is a large and important one, the catalogue will be useful in other countries as a substitute for a national bibliography.

Whatever the position of the national library in relation to the preparation of the current national bibliography, its responsibilities to the world of scholar-ship generally in bibliographical work and publication are considerable. All items—books, periodicals, maps, etc.—received must be fully and adequately described for ready consultation by readers in the library. Catalogues of the national library should be available in libraries throughout the country as an invaluable aid to scholars. The national library should therefore make every effort to publish catalogues of its holdings in printed books, manuscripts, prints and drawings, maps, etc., and should issue lists of its periodical holdings and bibliographies of the national periodical publications. The national library should likewise sponsor publication of a union list of the nation's holdings of periodicals.

Exhibitions

The most obvious means of making its collections known to the public is through exhibitions and the library should, where possible, provide travelling exhibitions to tour the country. The establishment of a post of permanent public relations officer to foster an interest in the work of the library would also lead to an informed understanding of its functions and its needs.

Desirable functions of a national library

Inter-library lending

It has been suggested in a previous section that the regulations for dépôt légal should include the authorization given to the national library to claim an extra copy of every publication so that it may be available for loan. In many countries the possibility of using material for lending purposes has influenced the choice of the centre for national and international loans. Where the national library is maintained as a reference-only collection, it is usual for the inter-library lending system to be based on another library or on a bibliographical institution.

There is no doubt that if the national library can lend its own material, it is a suitable place from which to organize the inter-library loan system. It has the largest stock of national and foreign literature covering all fields of knowledge; it has the richest collection of reference books and bibliographies; and it has the most experienced staff trained in the widest language and subject fields. For these reasons it has been argued that it is best suited to be the national centre for bibliographical information and the same reasons clearly apply in the choice of the national centre for inter-library lending.

As the country's focal point for bibliographical and library services, it will have the confidence of the centres in other countries which address inquiries to it for loans or for bibliographical information. It would be unfortunate if in fact there were many centres in a country performing a number of slightly different but nevertheless allied tasks. If the national library can accept all these responsibilities, this will be the most economical and satisfactory solution for the development of the country's library services.

If the national library cannot itself undertake the responsibility for inter-library lending it should ensure that this duty is accepted by another library or institution. The inter-library loan centre should be in close proximity either to the national library or to a library with a similarly comprehensive stock. Whatever system is adopted, the relationship between the national library and the inter-library loan centre should be as cordial as possible.

Manuscripts

As the central repository for the nation's published literature, almost inevitably the national library will have a large and comprehensive collection of manuscript material. It may, in fact, be the country's largest manuscript and archive centre and may therefore need to take upon itself the functions of co-ordinator of the country's manuscript and archive activities. On the other hand it may be preferable, as in the United Kingdom and France, to have a national archives repository separate from the national library and collecting all documentary material relating to history, literature, science and other aspects of the cultural life of the country. The tendency in the past has been for certain national archives to be concerned only with historical documents, so that literary manuscripts were dealt with by other libraries; on the whole, also, scientific manuscripts were disregarded. In such cases it is essential that the national library should ensure the preservation of all types of manuscripts in the country.

Research on library techniques

It has already been pointed out that the national library possesses a number of advantages over other libraries as the centre for all kinds of library activity: its staff, stock and additional bibliographical aids make it the obvious choice for any new or supplementary service. At the same time, as I have attempted to indicate, there may be some disadvantages in continuing to aim at encyclopaedic coverage and over-all responsibility. The national library should, however, be the focal point, if not necessarily the initiating centre, for research on library techniques.

If funds for staff and library accommodation are available for this purpose, the national library may be in a position to conduct its own research projects. If such is not the case, it should make every effort to stimulate research within its own country, whether by other libraries, particularly in the fields of science and technology, or by associations of librarians and documentalists. Whatever may be the solution to the problem for any individual country, it is vital that the national library should be concerned with research on library techniques, adopting any new methods which are appropriate to its needs and obtaining full information on all projects in course of development. It should therefore be the central body to which all inquiries may be addressed on this subject and it should be in a position to apply special funds for the purpose of library research.

Functions of the national library service which are not necessary functions of the national library

International exchange service

The position of the national library in relation to a country's book exchange programme has been a subject of debate for many years. There is a strong body of opinion which favours the centralization of all exchange activity but a very forceful case can also be made for complete decentralization. There are two main types of material which need to be dealt with. The arrangements made between governments or between national libraries for the exchange of official publications should be distinguished from those which concern other publications. The national library should always be the first recipient of government publications from other countries and it is a great advantage if these can be sent automatically and free of charge to the national library, in return for similar material sent directly by the government stationery (or publications) officer to the other countries.

The distribution of other types of exchange material may be the responsibility of a national exchange centre which might be housed in, and even under the aegis of, the national library. Most commonly this material is issued or published by universities and research institutions, and therefore exchanges are usually arranged directly between libraries having similar interests, so that there is no need for the service of an intermediary. University libraries often develop extensive exchange programmes on the basis of the publications of their own university presses and are thus in a strong position to make their own arrangements. Research institutes also prefer to send their publications to similar establishments abroad.

Some points in favour of setting up an exchange centre in each country are the possibility of including in its functions the issuing of lists of duplicates not required by libraries in its own country, the receipt and dissemination of lists from other countries and the distribution to other countries of lists of material from institutions which do not have regular contracts. The arguments put forward earlier for the centralization of international relationships are here again relevant to the position of the exchange scheme in relation to the national library.

Distribution of duplicates

This would not normally be a function of the national library, although some librarians consider it an important task to be undertaken on behalf of the country's library system. However, if there is no other centre to organize this kind of work, there may be some virtue in the national library dealing with it. Certainly it is a function which should be related to any centrally organized exchange system.

The arguments for and against centralization in connexion with the exchange scheme are also relevant here. Most libraries having formal exchange relations probably send their lists of duplicates to the libraries with which they have exchanged agreements, both within and outside their own country.

Of course, no national publications should be immediately offered as duplicates by libraries in the country to foreign libraries. There is a chance, particularly with older material, that it may not be in the national library or that it may have been lost. Thus the national library should have the first chance of obtaining it for its own collections. This is obviously the main point in favour of dealing with duplicates centrally, i.e., so that duplicate material may be offered to libraries within a country before being offered abroad; this may apply equally to foreign books and to the publications of the country concerned. Some control of the export of duplicate material may, therefore, be beneficial to the national book resources and the national library could be in the most favourable position to exercise such control.

Books for the blind

Special library services for the blind are not often included as a function of the national library, although the Library of Congress does so. There are a number of advantages in associating this service with a national library, particularly if that library is the country's inter-library lending centre. With its large stock and staff, its bibliographical works and possibly a union catalogue, the national library is the obvious organizer of this service. If it is responsible for inter-library lending the national library will already be in touch with all types of library in the country and will therefore readily fit the special requirements of the blind into the lending pattern.

Professional training

This is clearly not the place for a discussion of the full implications of the training of librarians, but rather of the position of the national library in relation to the system of training as it is organized in any country.

The first distinction which should be drawn is that between theoretical and practical training. We are here concerned mainly with the latter, but some comment is called for on the former. It is normally required that qualifications be given, either by a university or similar body responsible for a school of librarianship or by a library association, on completion of theoretical training in a school of librarianship. In either case, the granting of the final certificate may depend on the student's having gained some experience in practical work through employment in a library.

The nature of theoretical training need not, according to Dr. Liebaers, be different for national library staff, 'especially in its preliminary stages—from that received by their colleagues in other libraries; first, because national libraries have to a very large extent laid down the requirements of the profession in general, and second, because the differences between a national library and other libraries are only to a minor degree the result of differences in training. The profession of librarianship, wherever it may be exercised, is primarily practical. Theory is certainly necessary, but is not sufficient in itself. It matters little whether the theoretical training of the scientific staff is provided by the library staff, by a school un der its auspices, or by a university'. [1]

It may be established, therefore, that theoretical training should be of a high academic standard and may be appropriate to potential staff of almost any type of library. On the other hand practical training must be related to the type of work to which the trainee expects to devote himself. The national library should be in a position to offer opportunities for training to those interested in becoming members of its staff and instruction for all types of academic librarians.

The national library should also be the best training ground for research librarians. Its staff usually includes experts in every aspect of scholarly library work—bibliographers, palaeographers, scientists, binders, cataloguers, etc., any one of whom may be most outstanding in his field, and for that reason the most obvious tutor for trainees. The conditions under which the student works are also excellent since the national library has the finest collection of books, manuscripts and other materials. Finally, the national library usually offers the best and most up-to-date services in the country, whether in connexion with readers, cataloguers, or book description. It is probably the most mechanized, since it has to deal with a vast amount of literature, and it has the largest library staff in the country; it should also be in touch with all the latest developments in library science both within its own country and in countries abroad.

With all these advantages for the instruction of young librarians, the national library must have a very strong sense of responsibility to the profession in its own country. It should shape the present and the future both by its example in developing new ideas and procedures and by making these known and understood by those entering the profession. It is a very necessary part of the duty of the national library therefore to be associated at least with the practical aspects of library training.

Although this section is included under the heading of desirable but not essential functions of a national library, it should be stressed that in newly emergent countries this would be an essential service to be undertaken almost from the library's inception—particularly if, as is likely, it is the only body capable of giving library training.

Assistance in library techniques

The relationship between the national library and other libraries in the country has many different interpretations. In some countries the national librarian may have no specific duties outside his own library, whilst in others he may have wide-ranging responsibilities to other libraries. The Director of the British Museum, for example, has no authority over public libraries, university libraries or even over the other national libraries like the National Central Library or the National Lending Library for Science and Technology. On the other hand, the Director of the Bavarian State Library in Munich would seem to have very clear commitments with regard to every type of library in his area, even including the accommodation for public and monastic libraries.

In the U.S.S.R. and East Europe, too, the library services are organized in various ways by one of the national libraries. These countries have built up a careful system of chains of responsibility for different types of library, from small local areas through districts, provinces and republics to national library centres. The Lenin Library, for example, offers bibliographical and methodological assistance to mass libraries (i.e., to public libraries) throughout the country. It produces bibliographies of all kinds for circulation to libraries, specimen book lists, stock lists, catalogue cards, basic rules for cataloguing and classification and

1. *National libraries: their problems and prospects.* Paris, Unesco, 1960, p. 32.

instructions concerning the special needs of readers. Other national libraries perform similar duties for scholarly libraries.

It may not always be practicable or even appropriate to provide services of this type, but the national library can give the lead in library matters in a number of different ways. Cataloguing and classification are two obvious matters for which the national library may have some responsibility. A national committee may meet to discuss these subjects, but the national library is the most satisfactory and acceptable body to issue proposed new rules.

The best example of the influence of a national library on classification is the Library of Congress, whose scheme has been put into practice not only in United States libraries but in many other parts of the world. The constant attention which is paid by the staff of the Library of Congress to changes in subject fields and the proposals for amendment which are issued at frequent intervals are of benefit to a large number of libraries.

The more technical aspects of librarianship—binding, photography and duplication, and the use of mechanical aids—present a number of special problems. Since these various technical services are usually most highly developed in a national library, it should be able to give advice to librarians on the setting up of technical departments, on preparing standards for binderies, on photocopying and on problems concerned with the preservation or repair of valuable books. Undoubtedly, national libraries as a rule are very generous in assisting other libraries to overcome their difficulties in technical matters but here again there is need for more leadership in this aspect of library service. The establishment of various kinds of standards, for example, could well be undertaken by the national library on the basis of its experience and research carried out in its workshops and laboratories.

Library planning

The foregoing would suggest that in almost every aspect of the library system in any country the national library (or libraries, if the functions are divided among several) should be the central agent, receiving information and inquiries and initiating library services for the common good. This should be the situation everywhere, irrespective of whether a country is organized centrally or is decentralized. The national library should be the prime mover in library matters and should be expected to be the leading library in all fields.

The national librarian, too, should play a central role in all systematic planning of a country's library services. He should be called in for advice and consultation on inter-library lending, on the development of libraries in new universities, on the future of the public library service and so on. He will be able to see the country's library system as a whole and the relationship of the national library to it, thus ensuring that the various strands in the organization continue to form a golden chain of responsibility for service, from the smallest to the largest library and from the richest to the poorest.

SYSTEM OF
NATIONAL CENTRAL LIBRARIES

S R RANGANATHAN

1 Days of Single National Central Library

Two or three centuries ago some of the countries in the West were in the active phase of their life. Each of them naturally wished to have a National Central Library. In those years, the number of printed books accumulated through decades was not very great. Nor was the annual addition very great. Therefore, naturally each country established a single National Central Library to serve all purposes—not only service to readers but also other purposes, such as those enumerated and described in the later sections of this paper.

2 Need for a System of Triple National Central Libraries

Today, the annual output of printed books in India it as high as 12,000. The annual output is the highest in the USSR—about 76,000. It is also very high in UK, USA—about 35,000 and 60,000 respectively—and other countries. Further the cumulated number of volumes of the past has gone beyond a few millions in the National Central Libraries of many a country. For example, in the Library of Congress (USA) it is about 60,000,000; in the Lenin Library (U S S R) it is about 25,000,000; in the British Museum Library it is about 9,000,000; and in the Bibliotheque Nationale (France) it is about 7,000,000. In India too it has already reached about three millions. In a library of such huge size, books without any demand will hide away the few thousand books currently in demand. With the result, the library is unable to discharge its essential func-

Reprinted from *Herald of Library Science,* vol. 11, no. 3, July 1972, p. 247-9, by permission of the publisher.

tion of serving readers. As the first step to get over the difficulty the single National Central Library should be divided into the following three kinds of National Central Libraries:

1 National Copyright Library ;
2 National Dormitory Library ; and
3 National Service Library.

3 National Copyright Library

A National Copyright Library will consist of all the books deposited under the Copyright Act and/or the Delivery of Books Act. Its books will not be lent out to any but a court of law. Usually, no book in its collection is given even for consultation within the library premises till the expiry of 10 years of its publication. The purpose of the National Copyright Library is to serve as a collection of the intellectual remains of the Nation and to show the cultural and authorial progress of the Nation. As this library will be ever-growing at the rate of about 25,000 volumes per year, as it is today, it will require an ever-increasing accommodation. It may therefore be located at some distance from Delhi, the Capital City, where land is cheap and available in plenty and to which access is not difficult. If any reader desires to have any books from it, they can be borrowed by the National Service Library.

31 State Copyright Library

A State Copyright Library also may be maintained and managed on the analogy of the National Copyright Library.

32 Delivery of Books and Newspapers Act (1954)

Under the Delivery of Books and Newspapers Act (1954) four sets of copyright collection are to be formed and one of these sets is to be deposited in Bombay, Calcutta, Delhi, and Madras respectively. The Government of India appointed me as the Chairman of a Committee on the housing of the National Copyright Library in Bombay. I do not know whether any action has been taken on the recommendations of that Committee by the Government of India. However, this gave me an opportunity to study the utility of having four National Copyright Libraries. I found that one was sufficient. The other three appear to have no substantial purpose to serve, more than what a single Copyright Library can. On the contrary, the rate of annual growth demands an annual extension of the stack-room to house about 25,000 additional volumes received each year. This means finding additional building space, fittings, and furniture every year, and what is worse, additional cost every year. The Delivery of Books and Newspapers Act (1954) was a wrongly conceived one. Therefore, the Act may be either repealed or brought into inaction in any other way. Incidently this would mean that the publishers need not give to the Government, three additional copies of every publication now liable to be demanded under the duress of law.

4 National Dormitory Library

A National Dormitory Library will consist of one sound copy of each of the books weeded out from any of the libraries in the country—whether public library or academic library or any other library. These books are mostly out-of-date ones. But there is need to preserve them to serve specialist readers engaged in antiquarian and bibliographical research. It is, however, important that the needs of such workers should be fully met. The annual growth of the National Dormitory Library will be very much larger than that of a National Copyright Library. Therefore, in view of this and of poor demand for the books in it, it may be located at some distance from Delhi, the capital city, where land is cheap and available in plenty and to which access is not difficult. If any reader desires to have any books from it, they may be borrowed by the National Service Library.

41 STATE DORMITORY LIBRARY

A State Dormitory Library also may be maintained and managed on the analogy of the National Dormitory Library.

5 National Service Library

After making the National Copyright collection and the National Dormitory collection independent libraries, the volumes left over will be those of current value and in fairly frequent demand. This residual National Library of live books will truly become a National Service Library. Its collection may normally be below 300,000 and occasionally it may reach 500,000.

Its outmoded books will be weeded out in the same way as in any other service library in the country. The size of its building will not go beyond certain limit. Indeed its size will be small enough to have it housed in the city of Delhi itself. In fact, it will have to be in the City to facilitate easy approach to its potential readers.

51 STATE SERVICE LIBRARY

A State Service Library also will be automatically formed on the analogy of the National Service Library.

6 Break-up of the National Service Library into Several National Service Libraries

The time has already come even for replacing a single National Service Library by a multiple system of National Service Libraries. This subject is discussed in detail in the next article.

SYSTEM OF
NATIONAL SERVICE LIBRARIES

S R RANGANATHAN

1 Need for a System of Multiple National Service Libraries

The time has already come when even a National Service Library becomes too large and too unwieldy for efficient service. Therefore, a single National Service Library should be replaced by two or more National Service Libraries, each devoted to restricted subject areas such as, Natural Sciences, Humanities and Generalia, and Social Science. As time goes on, the number in the system of National Service Libraries may have to be increased gradually.

2 System of Multiple National Service Libraries in Denmark

Even as far back as 1948, I found that Denmark was maintaining two National Service Libraries—one for Natural Sciences and the other for all the other subjects.

3 System of Multiple National Service Libraries in U S A

U S A has begun to develop what are virtually National Agricultural Service Library and National Medical Service Library, quite independent of the Library of Congress—the old single National Central Library.

4 System of Multiple National Service Libraries in U K

Even in the conservative U K, as far back as 1956, Dr Urquhart had been endeavouring to have a National Science Service Library. He has now succeeded in his endeavour. He has further demonstrated that this has resulted in some national economy. For, it functions as a National Central Service Library in Science with the functions such as those described in connection with the State Central Library.

5 Unconscious Attempt in India

India entered into library field with some zest only during the last few decades. She was in a state of cultural exhaustion before that. This does not mean that India should wait for a few centuries to have a multiple system of National Service Libraries, as some of the countries in the West did. On the other hand, pressure of fast developing scholarship has already resulted in consciously or unconsciously thinking of independent National Service Libraries for Pure Natural Sciences and for Medical Sciences. The Indian Council of Social Science Research, formed in 1969, is working actively for a National Service Library for Social Sciences.

6 Need for Conscious Attempt in India

The idea should be consciously and deliberately developed by the library

Reprinted from *Herald of Library Science,* vol. 11, no. 3, July 1972, p. 250-1, by permission of the publisher.

profession, and the authorities should be persuaded to give effect to their finding. As time progresses, similar National Service Libraries for other subject areas may become necessary.

7 Subject Field for the Present National Library

Perhaps the now existing National Library may be made to function as the National Service Library for Humanities and Generalia. In doing this, many of the volumes in its present stock will have to be distributed to the National Dormitory Library and to the National Copyright Library. Of the remaining volumes in current demand, books in subject-fields other than Humanities and Generalia will have to be distributed to the respective National Service Libraries in different fields in Natural and Social Sciences.

2. SPECIAL FUNCTIONS AND ASPECTS OF NATIONAL LIBRARIES

The articles in this group consider in more detail some of the types and functions of national libraries.

Burston's analysis, confined though it is to developed countries, usefully demonstrates the wide variety of national libraries, in particular showing how national library functions in many countries are divided between different libraries (an aspect taken up in Rojnić's article in the next section), how some libraries combine national and other functions, and how in some countries there are subject-specialised national libraries or regional or state 'sub-national' libraries. It is clear that in some countries one cannot talk of a National Library as such, only of a national library service.

Burston's analysis is complemented by Xuereb's article on national libraries in developing countries *(see also Further Reading, Ref. 10)*, though Xuereb's presentation is by country rather than by function. The different emphases in developing countries emerge clearly – conservation and bibliographic control are less important than leadership, co-ordination of the nation's library services, the need to link library with information services (especially to the Government and in science and technology), and service to the public, including in some cases to children. The problems are also apparent: huge areas and widely distributed populations in some countries, small resources in most. Xuereb's paper can also be regarded as updating the information gathered for the Manila seminar held in 1964 (summarised above).

If national libraries in some developing countries, such as Singapore *(see Further Reading, Ref. 35)*, are also public libraries – in fact, the leading public libraries in their countries – then in developed countries, especially in Scandinavia, they may also serve as university libraries; or rather, university libraries may fulfil some national functions, including the fundamental ones of collecting the nation's literary output and producing the national bibliography. As Rojnić's article shows, while most such libraries admitted to no difficulty in fulfilling a double function, some tensions are inevitable, and some national functions, for example interlending, may be hard to fulfil when there is an equal or greater commitment to a local clientele *(see also Further Reading, Ref. 43)*.

One responsibility of national libraries – that of organising national interlending systems and in particular of ensuring the supply of national imprints on loan or by photocopy to libraries at home and abroad – has until recent times been generally seen as a minor one, and was classed by Humphreys as 'desirable' rather than 'essential'. The great growth of publication and literacy in the last twenty years, and the consequent increase in interlibrary borrowings, have changed the situation radically, and it could be argued, as Urquhart does, that the supply of literature to distant users – and in most countries the great majority of users *are* distant from a national library – is at least as important as the accessibility of the national collection to nearby users. The great volume of demand on the British Library Lending Division in a country as small as the UK – about 2,230,000 requests were received from British libraries in 1977/78 – would seem to support this view. Yet, as several writers (e.g. Xuereb) point out, many countries, especially developing countries, cannot afford separate reference and lending collections. Urquhart suggests that national libraries can be designed to fulfil both functions.

The importance of supply is mentioned also by Kalaidzieva, who reviews the solutions adopted by various countries. Her wide-ranging paper also gives special attention to the growing and special needs of science and technology – needs which have in several countries been responded to by the setting up of separate science libraries or documentation centres, largely or wholly independent of existing national libraries (one example is Canada). The problem of combining cultural conservation with a current service in science appears in several other articles, notably those by Francis and Mumford *(see also Further Reading, Refs. 2,3,41)*.

Anderson's comprehensive study of the bibliographic functions of the national library seems likely to become as classic a statement as Humphreys' general statement of functions. As she points out, the national bibliography has in some countries preceded the creation of a national library. She reviews the solutions adopted by different countries, and outlines a model National Bibliographic Centre, placing it in a context of Universal Bibliographic Control *(see also Further Reading, Refs. 6,7)*.

Whatever the demands of modern society and the needs for bibliographic control, the national heritage of books, like the national heritage of paintings and artefacts, has to be conserved. Wilson's paper emphasises this need, and the two main means of meeting it — expertise, and optimum storage conditions. He sees these last as demanding closed stacks, and therefore good communications to bring books to readers.

Chaplin's paper is included as a forward-looking statement of the need for, and nature of, a national information and referral service — something certainly lacking in the British Museum Library in 1963, and lacking in many national libraries now.

Referral and information services are discussed also in Mumford's paper, in the context of science and technology. He considers how the Library of Congress, a fairly comprehensive national library (though the USA has also National Libraries for agriculture and medicine), has endeavoured to serve science and technology.

The last paper in this group is Thompson's on national library buildings, arising from the colloquium on national library buildings in Rome in 1973. It is useful in relating buildings to national library functions.

National Libraries: An Analysis

GODFREY BURSTON

INTRODUCTION

Owing to the importance of the national library or libraries in the overall library pattern of a country, the characteristics and functions of national libraries have been much reported on and discussed in many countries for a number of years and have also been debated at meetings organized by international bodies. Two regional conferences on national libraries have been held by UNESCO, one for Europe and one for Asia and the Pacific area.

In the foreword to the report of the UNESCO Symposium on National Libraries in Europe, held at Vienna in 1958, Pierre Bourgeois, director of the *Bibliothèque Nationale Suisse*, wrote that "we still do not know what a national library really is, nor can we name with certainty the qualities a library must possess or the functions it must fulfil in order to be rightly called 'national' ". The group debating the organization of national libraries did, however, state that "in general, it may be said that the national library of a country is the one responsible for collecting and conserving the whole of that country's book production for the benefit of future generations". Writing in the same report on the needs of national libraries as regards professional training, Herman Liebaers, director of the *Bibliothèque Royale de Belgique*, said that "the main characteristic of a national library is without any doubt the leading place it occupies compared with other libraries in the country". He considered this position "due to the extent and encyclopaedic character of its collections, the variety of material held and the diversity of specialised departments and services".[1]

The International Federation of Library Associations (IFLA) takes a broader view, considering that "the term 'national library' covers a wide range of institutions, all of which, however, have responsibilities and tasks of national and international significance. That is what

[1] UNESCO (1960). *National Libraries: Their Problems and Prospects.* Paris: UNESCO.

Reprinted from *International Library Review*, vol. 5, no. 2, April 1973, p. 183-94. With permission of the author and *International Library Review.* ©Academic Press Inc. (London) Ltd.

makes them different from university and other libraries".[1] This
concept accords closely with that of the National Libraries Committee,
set up in the United Kingdom in October, 1967, by the Secretary of
State for Education and Science "to examine the functions and organization of the British Museum Library, the National Central Library,
the National Lending Library for Science and Technology and the
Science Museum Library in providing library facilities; to consider
whether, in the interests of efficiency and economy, such facilities
should be brought into a unified framework; and to make recommendations". This committee believed that "national library institutions
are intended to complement other types of library by providing services
which for economic or administrative reasons cannot be justified on a
regional or local scale".[2] According to this statement, national libraries
are those libraries whose community is the nation at large, or any
section of the nation widely scattered socially and geographically. An
encyclopaedic stock is not a necessary characteristic.

. So-called national libraries have very distinct personalities and they
may or may not be specifically designated "national". This dissimilarity is immediately apparent from the list of 34 libraries from 25
member states represented at the UNESCO Vienna Symposium. It
includes two libraries in the United Kingdom: the British Museum
library and the National Library of Scotland. Both these libraries have
a legal right to a copy of every work published in the United Kingdom,
but only of the former could it be said that its community is the whole
nation. One of the three libraries of the Federal Republic of Germany
represented at Vienna, the *Bayerische Staatsbibliothek* (Bavarian State
Library) has something in common with the National Library of
Scotland, being the state library of the largest of the 10 Länder (states)
of the Federal Republic, the former Kingdom of Bavaria, which, as
the largest of the original German states after Prussia, still has separatist
tendencies. However, it has a local not a national legal deposit right
and, unlike the National Library of Scotland, which fulfils no central
functions, is the centre of the Bavarian state library system of provincial,
university, municipal and parochial libraries, and has a school of
librarianship. It is the largest library in the Federal Republic, with a
stock of over three million volumes.

CULTURAL NATIONAL LIBRARIES

The definition of a national library appears to need extending to

[1] IFLA (1963). *Libraries in the World: a Long Term Programme for IFLA*. Hague: Nijhoff.
[2] National Libraries Committee (1969). *Report. Cmnd.* 4028. London: H.M.S.O.

include those libraries, such as the *Bayerische Staatsbibliothek*, the National Library of Scotland and the National Library of Wales, which offer services over a major administrative region, formerly independent, and with some political and cultural cohesion—a sub-category of cultural national libraries. Within this fall the state libraries of the autonomous Soviet republics, the Slovak national libraries, and those of the constituent republics of Yugoslavia, some of which were previously part of other countries. According to the director of the Lenin State Library, Moscow, the national sovereignty of the different peoples of the U.S.S.R. "has found its expression in the creation of their own institutes, industrial and agricultural establishments, scientific institutions, theatres, their own literature, and also a national library of the republic, which occupies a place of honour among the cultural organizations".[1]

In Yugoslavia there is no federal national library as such, but the national libraries of Serbia, Croatia, Slovenia, Bosnia, Macedonia and Montenegro are all federal legal deposit libraries. In this respect they closely resemble the National Library of Scotland, but they receive an additional copy of works published in their respective republics.

The interests of cultural national libraries may transcend national borders. The National Library of Wales covers the cultures of the Celtic peoples generally. The founding of the Jewish National Library antedated the founding of the state of Israel by over 50 years.

Dual-purpose Libraries

The *Bayerische Staatsbibliothek* also has something in common with other libraries throughout Germany which, like it, were founded by the rulers of the former independent German states but which, unlike it, mostly now aspire to no grander title than that of *Land- und Stadt-Bibliothek* (state and town library). They fulfil the functions of regional reference libraries and can be considered to form the upper tier of a public library service which provides two levels of library of which the *Stadtbüchereien* (popular public libraries) are the lower one. Some of these libraries have a dual or even treble role to play. The university library in each of the city states of Hamburg and Bremen, for instance, serves also as the state library and, for major enquiries, as a city reference library. *Hamburg Staat- und Universitätsbibliothek*, like the *Bayerische Staatsbibliothek*, has a local legal deposit right and houses the regional union catalogue. The city fathers of the *Freie und Hansestadt*

[1] I. P. Kondakov (1966). La bibliothèque nationale en URSS. *Bull. bibliothèques France* **11** (3), 93–104.

Hamburg are highly independent—the popular public libraries are here called *Öffentliche Bücherhallen*—but it is a proud and prosperous free city, a former Hanseatic city, not a cultural region.

National-academic Libraries

The Vienna Symposium included four libraries with the functions of both national and academic libraries: Helsinki University Library, Oslo University Library, the Croatian National and University Library, Zagreb, and the Jewish National and University Library, Jerusalem. Arundele Esdaile, a former secretary of the British Museum, considered national libraries "a comparatively modern product".[1] The impressive *Festschrift* produced for the fiftieth anniversary of the founding of the *Deutsche Bücherei* (German Library) ascribed a definite country and date, France in 1789, the year of the French Revolution, to the advent of the national library.[2] It is perhaps to be expected that a volume with a foreword by Walter Ulbricht, at that time Chairman of the National Council of the German Democratic Republic, should seek a revolutionary origin for its subject. It is at least certain that the establishment of national libraries has been part of the development of the modern state and whereas the *Bibliothèque Nationale* in Paris is an example of the transformation, whether revolutionary or evolutionary, of the royal library in older countries into a national library, and whereas some national libraries, such as the Canadian National Library and the *Deutsche Bücherei* itself have been founded as completely new institutions, in several relatively recently independent, small countries, such as Norway and Finland, the major university library has assumed the functions of a national library. The opposite occurred with the Jewish National Library, which took on the functions of a university library. Several of the Yugoslavian states have dual-purpose national and university libraries. A Yugoslav librarian, Matko Rojnić, has "no doubt that reasons of economy played a decisive role in prompting a national or regional library to extend its services to the university and a university library to become exceptionally important for a country or a province".[3]

In Sweden, in addition to the national services provided by the *Kungl. Biblioteket* (Royal Library) Stockholm, three university libraries have the right of legal deposit and consequent obligations to the

[1] Arundel Esdaile (1957). *National Libraries of the World: Their History, Administration and Public Services;* 2nd ed., revised by F. J. Hill, London.

[2] Deutsche Bücherei (1962). *Deutsche Bücherei, 1912–1962: Festschrift zum fünfzigjährigen Bestehen der deutschen Nationalbibliothek.* Leipzig: Deutsche Bücherei.

[3] Matko Rojnić (1966). University libraries in a double function. *Libri* 16, 140–47.

nation at large.[1] The legal deposit right, however, does not, of itself, confer the title of national library on a university library. The Bodleian Library of Oxford University and Cambridge University Library both have this right but have no reciprocal duties. In South Africa, in addition to the two national libraries, two public libraries and the Library of Parliament have the right of legal deposit.

The majority of the libraries covered by a survey conducted by the University Libraries sub-section of the International Federation of Library Associations "consider their simultaneous functions equally important although in practice their obligations to universities prevail over their function of national or regional or municipal libraries".[2] This is hardly surprising, for even national libraries which do not specifically function also as university libraries are likely to be heavily used by members of the university which will usually be found in the same city. In the British Museum library, a status-biased, multi-lingual, encyclopaedic library, a survey showed that over two-thirds of the readership consists of academic staff and students, half of these being post-graduate students and the majority of the rest university staff. Thirty-five per cent of the university readership came from the University of London.[3] About half the entire student body of Leipzig University uses the largely mono-lingual *Deutsche Bücherei*, which is more liberal in seating accommodation, opening hours and access than the British Museum library.

National-public libraries

Whereas the considerable overlap in clientele may enable an institution to function efficiently both as a national library and as a university library, the same cannot be said of one which attempts to provide both national library and public library services. The two South African national libraries, the South African Public Library in Cape Town and the State Library in Pretoria, both formerly functioned also as public libraries, the former until 1954 and the later until 1964, but the public library functions proved to be a handicap to their roles as national libraries.[4,5] National-public libraries are a feature of developing countries. India, a federal country with national libraries for some of

[1] Lennart Grönberg (1967). University libraries—national libraries: aspects of the problem in Scandinavia, especially Sweden. *Libri* **17**, 59–62.

[2] Rojnić, *op. cit.*

[3] National Libraries Committee, *op. cit.*

[4] Loree Elizabeth Taylor (1967). *South African Libraries*. London. Clive Bingley.

[5] G. v. N. Viljoen (1965). Die nasionale biblioteke van Suid Afrika. *S. Afr. Libr.* **33** (2). 46–54.

the constituent states, also has a federal national library in Calcutta, which has the additional functions of the city public library. Singapore National Library, the former Raffles Library, is an example of a library in a small, developing country fulfilling the dual roles of a national library and a public library. In Japan, the National Diet Library has a branch which is the public reference library for Tokyo but is eventually intended to be handed over to the local authority.

National-parliamentary libraries

The National Diet Library of Japan is, furthermore, an example of a national library which serves also as the library of the country's legislative body. The prototype of such an organization is the Library of Congress in the United States, one of the world's largest libraries. It was founded in 1800 to provide services to the government and is intended primarily to assist Congressmen in preparing laws, having a large legislative reference service, which answers as many as a thousand quick reference enquiries a day at the height of the Congressional session. Being also designed to undertake analytical research, this service completed 8070 studies for Congressional committees in the financial year 1967.[1] There is also a law library, of which the American–British division has a branch in the Capitol which is solely for the use of Congress. The Library of Congress has, however, evolved as a national library, a status which it can probably be considered to have reached in 1897, when it moved from the Capitol to its own building. All scholars may use its research facilities.

The National Diet Library is modelled on the Library of Congress as a result of the American occupation of Japan and on the recommendations of Verner Clapp of the Library of Congress and Charles Brown of the American Library Association. There are, however, unique features to its organization which are the result of domestic political considerations. It was founded in 1948 as a multi-purpose library. One of its seven departments is a detached library in the Diet and there are 30 branches in government departments. This organization is intended to promote maximum use of materials and aid Diet control of the executive bureaucracy.[2] Some authorities believe that services to the government are an essential function of a national library.[3]

[1] Library of Congress (1968). *Annual Report of the Librarian of Congress for the Fiscal Year Ending June* 30, 1967. Washington: Library of Congress.
[2] Chin Kim (1969). A new national library: the National Diet Library of Japan. *J. Libr. Hist.*, **4** (3), 225–38.
[3] UNESCO (1964). Regional seminar on the development of national libraries in Asia and the Pacific area. *UNESCO Bull. Libr.* **18** (4), 149–64.

NATIONAL SUBJECT LIBRARIES

The enormous world output of literature has made it impossible for any one library to attain complete coverage of all significant information, wherever it originates. This ideal is, however, feasible in a subject field. Thus a further type of national library, which has evolved recently, is the national subject library. The director of the Lenin State Library writes that "The system of national libraries in the U.S.S.R. includes also the great national subject libraries. These are, for example, the Scientific and Technical Library of the U.S.S.R. and the state libraries of agriculture, medicine and the social sciences. Their functions have features in common with those of national libraries and they may be considered as such. It is thus that particular conditions in the U.S.S.R., taking into account certain historic traditions and the existing network of libraries, led us to a wider conception of the national library and these are the factors which have determined our library system".[1]

There are national subject libraries also in the autonomous republics of the U.S.S.R. Thus the Ukrainian S.S.R. has a National Medical Library and a National Scientific and Technical Library at Kiev and a National Agricultural Library at Kharkov.

One national subject library which was represented at the UNESCO Vienna Symposium is the Slovak Central Technical Library, Bratislava. Founded in 1938 to serve this ethnic region of Czechoslovakia, it is one of three national subject libraries serving the region, the others being the Central Economics Library and the Central Library of Agriculture. The State Central Technical Library in Prague, however, serves the whole country.

Ideally this sub-category of national library seeks complete coverage of recorded information in its field from all over the world. Its growth has been most notable in science and technology, where the advance of knowledge has been most rapid, the consequent output of information has been increasing at a logarithmic rate, the library materials are therefore largely recent and the return on the investment is comparatively concrete. It has also been restricted to the developed countries, which need such libraries and have the resources to establish and maintain them.

A national subject library may cover the whole of science and technology, as does the National Lending Library for Science and Technology in the United Kingdom, or a limited part of it, as do the

[1] Kondakov, *op. cit.*

National Library of Medicine and the National Agricultural Library
in the United States. A university library may also function as a
national subject library. Lund University Library in Sweden acts as
the national technological library.[1] In the Federal Republic of Germany
four university libraries function as national subject libraries. The
Technische Informationsbibliothek at Hanover Technical University is the
Central Technical Library and national translations centre. The
Central Agricultural Library is at Bonn University, the Central Medical
Library is at Cologne University and the library of the Institute of
International Economics at Kiel University also acts as the national
subject library in its field.

In the United Kingdom there are libraries of institutions in some
subject fields which have names suggesting that they function as
national subject libraries in addition to meeting the needs of their
institutional communities. One of these is the British Library of Art at
the Victoria and Albert Museum. In his evidence to the National
Libraries Committee, John Pope-Hennessy, director of the Museum,
pointed out that the library "was originally planned as the National
Art Library and has been maintained as the National Art Library for
the past ninety years".[2] It covers a wider field than that covered by the
Museum's collections of art objects, being a reference collection of
some 400,000 volumes covering the fine and applied arts of all periods
and countries. It also collects books as works of art. It is a working
library for the museum staff but is also open to members of the general
public and is much more accessible to undergraduate students than is
the British Museum library. It is thus a dual-purpose library, a national
subject library which is also a special library for the Museum staff.

According to the evidence submitted to the National Libraries
Committee by the London School of Economics, the British Library of
Political and Economic Science, founded in 1896, was from the outset
"intended to serve not only as the working library of the School but
also as a national collection". It is further stated that "reference
facilities are made freely available to researchers and public officials"
and that the library "is in fact, though not in name, the national
library for the social sciences".[3] There is no access for students of other
institutions except during vacations, but the library does supplement
the social science loan facilities of the National Lending Library for
Science and Technology. However, K. A. Mallaber, librarian of the

---

[1] Grönberg, *op. cit.*

[2] National Libraries Committee (1969). *Principal Documentary Evidence Submitted to the National Libraries Committee.* London: H.M.S.O.

[3] *Ibid.*

Department of Trade and Industry, in his evidence to the Committee, states that "the general impression one gets at the moment is of a library almost overwhelmed by the demands of its primary clientele at the School". He considers that there "are now unfillable gaps in its collections from a national library point of view" and that it is not feasible "to attempt now to implement the intentions of its founders".[1]

Reference and Lending Libraries

The stock of a national library may be available for reference only, or part of it may be available for loan, either directly or through other libraries. It may also be specifically a lending library, sending re- quested documents to other libraries and organizations. In this case the lending and reference functions will have been allocated to two separate national institutions and in the United Kingdom this is still the case at present with both the national general libraries and the national subject libraries. The British Museum library is the national general reference library, the National Central Library is the national general lending library, and the National Reference Library for Science and Invention, a detached part of the British Museum Library, is the counterpart of the National Lending Library for Science and Techno- logy. Subsequent to the British Library Act, 1972, the unification of the national lending facilities is, however, imminent, though it is likely to be at least a decade before the national reference library is brought together on one site. Even then, it would be remarkable indeed if it were found to be truly unified.

National Libraries for Handicapped Readers

The Library of Congress is a national general library which has a nation-wide responsibility for providing materials for handicapped readers, all persons who are physically incapable of reading or handling ordinary printed matter. This is an extension, since 1966, of the functions of its former Division for the Blind, now officially renamed the Division for the Blind and Physically Handicapped. In the United Kingdom a separate institution, the National Library for the Blind, was founded in 1882 to provide for the needs of this major category of handicapped readers over the whole country. It has a branch in Manchester to serve the eight nothern English counties. The National Library for the Blind is providing services which could not be justified on a purely regional

[1] *Ibid.*

or local scale to a particular section of the community which is widely scattered both socially and geographically. It is thus a national library.

THE IMPACT OF HISTORY AND CULTURE

Also represented at Vienna were two Italian national libraries: the *Biblioteca Nazionale Centrale* at Florence and a library with the same title at Rome. There are two "national central libraries" in Italy because Florence was the capital of newly united Italy until French troops were withdrawn from Rome in 1870. They centralize nothing. They are called "central" simply to differentiate them from the six *biblioteche nazionali* (national libraries) which, like the *Land und Stadtbibliotheken* in Germany, are, with the exception of that at Bari, the former national libraries of the small states which came together to form the present political entity. They could not, however, be termed cultural national libraries. Of the autonomous regions of Italy only two, Trentino-Upper Adige and Aosta, have a predominantly non-Italian population and none of the so-called "national" libraries is located in either of these regions. Discussing the system of national libraries in Italy, Salvatore Accardo said that "the picture presented is one of historic tradition and above all a reflection of Italian history and culture".[1] The Italian *biblioteche nazionali* are libraries which, for historic reasons, no longer function as national libraries, although they retain the title as a matter of cultural tradition allied to the political reality that Italian unity is a fragile thing.

A part of Europe whose recent history has had a profound effect on its national libraries is Germany, though a comparison of the library systems as a whole of the Federal Republic of Germany and the German Democratic Republic shows that the likenesses imposed by a common history to 1945 and a common tradition of library organization are greater than the differences superimposed upon them by the present opposed politico-socio-economic systems. Pre-war Germany had two national libraries, the *Preussiche Staatsbibliothek* (Prussian State Library) in Berlin and the *Deutsche Bücherei* (German Library) in Leipzig. The *Preussiche Staatsbibliothek* had its origin in the royal library of the electors of Brandenburg, who became the kings of Prussia and eventually the German emperors.[2] The *Deutsche Bücherei* was set up by the German publishers themselves in 1912 in what was then the world's largest

[1] Salvatore Accardo (1969). Accademie e biblioteche per la diffusione della cultura. *Accademie e biblioteche d'Italia* **37** (3), 181–86.
[2] Staatsbibliothek Preussicher Kulturbesitz (1972). *Geschichte der Staatsbibliothek vor dem Krieg*. Berlin: Staatsbibliothek Preussicher Kulturbesitz.

centre of the book trade. It received, by voluntary agreement, a copy of every work published in Germany or German-speaking countries. By 1941 it also sought to obtain a copy of every work in German, translated from the German, or about Germany or the German people, published anywhere in the world. Its intake enabled it to publish the *Deutsche Nationalbibliographie* (German National Bibliography) and various German bibliographies of special materials. It did not collect foreign language material extensively, this being the function of the *Preussiche Staatsbibliothek*, which also housed the German national union catalogue.

The division of Germany left both these libraries in the Russian zone and ultimately in the German Democratic Republic. Political division had a traumatic effect on the *Preussiche Staatsbibliothek*, then renamed the *Deutsche Staatsbibliothek* (German State Library). It was divorced from much of its stock, of which part had been evacuated to territory which had become Polish and of which over one million volumes was at Marburg, in the West. It caused the founding of a new national library for the Federal Republic at Frankfurt-am-Main and a rival current national bibliography, the *Deutsche Bibliographie* (German Bibliography). Moreover, another national library for the Federal Republic, a new *Staatsbibliothek Preussicher Kulturbesitz* is being built on the other side of the wall from the former one and will house that library's former stock. Part of a new cultural complex, it is expected to be completed in 1974. The decision to build it was taken in 1962. It is seen in the Federal Republic as the legal successor to the former *Preussiche Staatsbibliothek*. Thus it has acquired a million books from Marburg, the former stock of the present *Deutsche Staatsbibliothek*, which are housed in a temporary structure, and like that library is a national library for foreign language material. Whilst there are no subject exclusions in its periodicals intake, its book selection policy excludes books in the fields covered by the Federal German national subject libraries. It also has the legal right to receive a deposit copy of every book published in West Berlin.

The *Deutsche Bücherei*, in Leipzig, emerged from the war relatively unaffected. Its stock had been stored safely in the enormous monument to the Battle of the Nations on the outskirts of the city; it still receives voluntary deposit copies of most books published in the Federal Republic and other German-speaking countries; it still scans other national bibliographies and requests items within its scope; and it still publishes the most comprehensive bibliography of German books.

The library services of a state are the product of its geography, history, traditions and political, social and economic conditions. The relative influence of all these factors will vary from country to country.

The recently established national libraries of many newly independent countries have not grown from cultural tradition but rather sprung from an awakening national consciousness,[1] though their organization and functions may have been influenced by foreign advisers. But in any country, despite the wide divergences caused by a variety of factors, the national library is by its very nature at the centre of the problems of contemporary library economy. This has been nowhere better illustrated than in the United Kingdom over the last decade by the impact, both direct and indirect, of the National Lending Library for Science and Technology. It would be surprising if even the British Library Act, 1972 were to cause any significant liberalization at Bloomsbury, but its ultimate impact on the British library scene elsewhere would seem likely to be considerable.

[1] UNESCO (1964), *op. cit.*

NATIONAL LIBRARIES
IN DEVELOPING COUNTRIES

Paul Xuereb

Most of the national libraries represented at the Unesco Vienna symposium in 1958 were old, some of them ancient, institutions which had evolved gradually with the history of their country. Their status as monuments of the nation's culture seemed at the time to impose on them a freeze on their development, which it was partly the aim of the symposium to thaw. The self-questioning by the national libraries of the western world, done in a spirit of open-mindedness, while it led to the isolation of certain essential functions to be performed by national libraries, also made them realise the dangers of erecting a rigid model: 'the real problem, then, is not to determine the status and structure of an ideal national library (which would never become a reality) but to state quite clearly the tasks which every country should undertake both in its own interest and in order to retain its due place in the international network of cultural relations'. (1)

This pragmatic attitude to the rôle of national libraries had been prefigured to a certain extent in the resolutions of the Unesco Seminar on the Development of Public Libraries in Asia (Delhi, 1955), which had stated that in certain circumstances, particularly where local government was weak, it would be advisable to fuse the national library with the public library system, and that 'in some countries, particularly smaller countries, the functions of the national library and the central library board should be integrated for better and more economical development'. (2) In 1955 few libraries in Asia and in other developing countries have been set up or reconstituted in the 'sixties and 'seventies (3) in the spirit of national pride engendered by political independence, and in the knowledge that if a great new enterprise is being undertaken, it is wise to set it up on the firmest foundations and with the most practical considerations in mind.

National cultural prestige and an understandable desire to use the national library as the nerve-centre of an efficient, nation-wide library

Reprinted from LOCK, R. Northwood, *ed*. Manual of library economy: a conspectus of professional librarianship for students and practitioners. London: Bingley; Hamden, Conn: Linnet Books, 1977, p. 47-60, by permission of the publisher.

network are evident in the legislation, statements of policy and observers' comments in developing countries. The Nigerian National Library
Decree of 1970 lays down that the duties of the National Library Board
include that of setting up and maintaining collections considered 'appropriate for a library of the highest standing', and at the inaugural
meeting of that country's National Library Board, a government minister said that the Board would be responsible for building a headquarters
for the Library which 'befits the nation and the enhanced status of this
national institution'. (4) Sometimes, one can detect a mentality nur-
tured on the European idea of a national library as being preeminently
a custodian of higher learning and research and nothing else, 'a Library
of Libraries to be approached with reverence only when other kinds of
libraries fail to satisfy the needs of the readers'. (5)

Political independence brings about almost inevitably a search for
national identity and so a heightened awareness of the national culture.
The national library, like the national museum and the national archives, becomes a mausoleum of the cultural heritage, as well as a
means of propagating it and renewing it. In theory, therefore, it occupies a position of prestige, particularly if, as Trinidad and Tobago's
Draft plan for economic development, 1968-83 states, the nation's very
survival is 'directly related to the survival of its culture'. (6)

The preservation of the national culture, however praiseworthy,
would not have been enough to prompt the search for new functions,
new roles for the national library in the new nations. The important
factor was the realisation that this type of library could be a powerful
means of furthering the nation's material and intellectual progress as
well as its spiritual and artistic one; that it would be a valuable instrument of national progress. The fear of neo-colonialism in the emerging
countries has led more than one librarian to see the national library
as important for the attainment of full independence. Thus one of
the architects of the Nigerian National Library, Carl M White, saw one
of the library's roles as 'planning for a free way of life, to ensure not
only political but also intellectual and economic independence' (7),
whilst a Nigerian, writing on libraries in general in the decolonisation
process, seems them—and, one must assume, the national library at
their head—as 'an aid in social engineering', and then adds that the library does not create a new social order but 'helps to stabilise an agreed
social order' and this 'by identifying itself with the problems and aspirations of its social milieu'. (8) The dangers of this identification, should
it become complete, have been pointed out. The library as a liberator

of the individual mind is greatly endangered if it becomes a tool in the hands of the state to produce uniformity of thinking. (9)

The development of national libraries in Asia and Africa, and the way they are likely to develop in the Caribbean, is due to a considerable extent to the findings and recommendations of the Manila Unesco Regional Seminar on the Development of National Libraries in Asia and the Pacific 1964, the Quito Meeting of Experts on the National Planning of Library Services in Latin America 1966, and the Colombo Unesco Meeting of Experts on the National Planning of Library Services in Asia 1967. All three of these meetings emphasised the national library's fundamental rôle as the leader of the nation's libraries, together with a number of other functions regarded as more or less essential. The Manila seminar said that national libraries must 'provide leadership among a nation's libraries' and 'serve as a coordinating centre for cooperative activities'. (10) The Quito meeting said that a national library must 'co-operate, whenever its own organisation and the development of planning render it advisable, in the extension and improvement of school and public library services', (11) whilst the Colombo meeting said the national library ought to be 'an active organisation with dynamic leadership', one of whose main aims should be to develop 'systems and procedures which will make available the total library resources of the nation for the benefit of the whole national community'. (12)

Though this fundamental role has been widely accepted, not just in the developing countries but in some of the developed ones as well, the way in which it is exercised has understandably varied from one country to another, owing to different degrees of political development, constitutional frameworks, geography and communications. The advice given at the Delhi seminar and the Vienna symposium has not been forgotten. Thus Nigeria, a large federal country, seeing the importance of tailoring Nigerian institutions 'to fit Nigerian needs and to respond to Nigerian aspirations', (13) is setting up branches of the national library in the various states, side by side with the public libraries, which are a state and not a federal responsibility. This will enable the public libraries to spend their scarce resources on materials other than those of the National Library's areas of specialisation, those reflecting the socio-economic aspirations of the country. Moreover, the presence of the National Library's branches in the states 'will bring the specialised services of the Library closer to the state governments and to many more of the people of this country'. (14) A similar policy is being carried out in Pakistan, where the National Library is at Islamabad, with a regional national copyright library at Karachi, the Liaquat Memorial Library.

Indonesia is another large and sprawling state, with provincial governments as well as a central one; communications within this huge archipelago are poor. For these reasons, although Unesco consultant A G W Dunningham advised in 1969 that Indonesia should set up a national library system headed by the proposed National Library—thus placing the public and other libraries under the National Library—he could suggest only a limited measure of control, such as the submission of annual reports and statistics to the National Library. As Paul W T Poon has suggested, 'in the Indonesian situation, co-ordination and co-operation with other types of libraries, rather than direct control, would be more practical'. (15) The provincial libraries thus remain the responsibility and property of the provinces, even though they are normally set up with an initial five-year subvention by the central government.

A small country like Singapore, on the other hand, has been able to set up a strongly centralised system, such as always attracts countries unwilling to waste meagre funds and a small number of trained staff on duplicated or uncoordinated efforts. Singapore's National Library Act (16) includes the following among the National Library's various functions listed in section 5: '(a) to promote and encourage the use of library material and information therefrom by the establishment of lending and reference libraries and mobile library services; . . . (g) to obtain and provide central information on the resources and services of libraries in Singapore; (h) to participate in national planning for all types of library service in Singapore, and to conduct research to determine library needs and possibilities.' The Singapore National Library carries out many of the functions associated with the older national libraries, but, more important yet, it is the motive force behind the national library network, over which it exercises close control. Of it one can quote what is stated of Trinidad and Tobago's proposed national library, that 'it should not be confused with the headquarters of a central library service. It is the focus of all library activities in the country and the custodian of library standards. . . '. (17) A similar system has been adopted in other countries. In Egypt, the National Library is at present responsible for the public library service, but its official guide says that in future it will attempt to be 'the peak of a national library system which brings together in close coordination the service of university, research, special, public and school libraries'. (18)

The Solomon Islands have adopted a curious variant of the centralised system in their recent statement of policy. (19) Since lack of funds does not allow the state to set up and run at its expense a network of libraries, the new National Library, established in 1974, aims at assisting in the foundation of new libraries by training and advising all people engaged in library work, and by making bulk book loans, against a small membership fee, to all libraries wishing to join the National Library Service. The National Library selects the books sent in these bulk loans, and operates a request and information service, which includes free loans of books from its stock, to members of the service. A measure of control is exercised over member libraries by making National Library aid conditional on the libraries being run according to a reasonable standard.

If the relationship between the national library and a country's other libraries may vary according to circumstances, in one fundamental point national libraries must be identical, whichever country they may be in. They should always be organically connected with a lively library network, giving it life and deriving life from it. They must never be, to use Hedwig Anuar's excellent metaphor, an apex without a base. (20) There are few things more futile than a massive national library with a splendid collection of the national literature and perhaps first-rate services to scholars, existing in what is, library-wise, one large desert. This can also happen, as Anuar has pointed out, 'where the infrastructure of library development is wholly or partly absent' (21), where the setting up of the national library comes before plans for a systematic nationwide library service. This exists to a certain extent in Malta where the National Library (formerly the Royal Malta Library) has formal connections solely with the public libraries, all of which fall under its jurisdiction. Libraries in institutions of higher learning and libraries in governmental ministries, or departments, or para-statal bodies, are independent of the Library. Recently, however, the stocking of libraries in state secondary schools has become the responsibility of a unit falling under the National Librarian, though the school libraries themselves and their staff remain the responsibility of the Director of Education.

In some countries, such as Burma, the national library evolves materially out of an existing university library of long standing and rich resources. This arrangement avoids the setting up of what is found to be to some extent a rival body competing for the same human and financial resources, though actual duplication of stock can of course be avoided by a carefully worked out cooperative acquisition agreement.

In Indonesia, where the fundamental functions of a national library are largely being carried out by an existing group of libraries, and other institutions such as the Perpustakaan Museum Pusat (Central Museum Library), or the Kantor Bibliografi Nasional (National Bibliographical Centre), it has been recommended that the institutions carrying out these functions should be the nucleus around which a unified national library could be built. (22)

Each country, in fact, has to seek the least painful and most economical way of creating a national library. In Malta, the National Library is evolving from an ancient public library, set up in 1776, which has the outstanding collection of the national literature and houses an important collection of archives, rather than from the more modern library of the University of Malta, which is a semi-autonomous institution, whereas the National Library is and has always been a state library. In actual fact, however, the University Library carries out some of the functions of a national library, such as lending to other libraries out of its own stock, or putting such libraries in touch with likely sources of material, lending to foreign libraries, and supplying information to government departments. The likelihood is that in future, the National Library and the University Library in this country will draw closer together, and another stage in the evolution of Malta's National Library will have been reached.

In Malawi, a country as yet without a national library, it would be safe to forecast that the headquarters of the present National Library Service, which already has a good collection of Malawi material and is going to house a major reference library service, will grow into the National Library, should that country decide to set one up.

Whichever way it evolves, a national library in a developing country will almost certainly be a leader of the nation's library development. In addition, it will carry out a set of varying functions, some of which are common to practically all of them. Of these, acting as permanent depository for the national literature is paramount, and usually precedes the designation of a particular library as the national library, as has happened to the (Royal) Malta Library. It is essential that legal deposit be regulated by legislation laying down clear procedures for the deposit of materials (which ought not to be restricted to books, but should cover maps and audio-visual materials), and sanctions against contraveners. Some countries, such as Malta, oblige all printers or publishers to make regular returns, say once a quarter, of all the materials they have produced, to make it easier for the national library to check on the national production and claim material that has not been deposited. Unless copyright legislation is well-drafted, the national library's collection of the country's literature, far from being that coutry's or even the world's outstanding collection in the field, may well have serious gaps. Naturally, the comprehensiveness and hence the usefulness of the national bibliography based on this legal deposit will depend on the effectiveness of the relevant legislation.

Young national libraries, particularly those which have not evolved out of older libraries or groups of libraries, are at a disadvantage in discharging another basic function, that of acting as the national bibliographical centre both within the country and in relation with other countries. Such libraries may find that their bibliographical resources are far inferior to those of established libraries in their country. This happened to the National Library of Nigeria during the first period of its existence, when the resources of the University of Ibadan were already very strong, whilst those of the National Library were being built up from scratch. During this period of any national library's existence—and in some countries this may be a very long period—the success of its bibliographical services to other libraries in and outside the country will depend heavily on the experience of the staff recruited, and particularly on their knowledge of other libraries' resources. The service will thus be, to a considerable extent, a referral service, which is likely to be more efficient if the national library has good links by telephone and telex with other libraries.

Unlike some of the older national libraries, few in the emerging countries, because of the emphasis on economic and social development, can afford to keep away from setting up or at least coordinating bibliographical and information services in science and technology, including medicine. The Manila seminar's recommendation was that 'where circumstances permit, the national library should assume its proper responsibilities in the fields of science and technology, since those differ in degree rather than in kind from its responsibilities in other fields'. (23) Again, it is likely that the service provided will take the form of referring inquiries to the best source known to the national library, or of collecting the information from the various academic and special libraries in the national network. A few countries, like Malta, have followed the pattern of some of the older national libraries by passing over responsibility for services relating to science and technology to other libraries. Thus in Malta there is an understanding that the University Library is to cater for science and technology, including

medicine. In some other countries, the national library passes on the
responsibility to the national documentation centres set up with
Unesco help in the 1960s.

Whether it be in the arts and social sciences, or in science and technology, the national library cannot afford to be standoffish and biased
in favour of the advanced research worker. In many developing countries the national library must constantly be seen to be useful to a
broad spectrum of readers. It was no rhetorical flourish for the National Librarian of Singapore to state in her annual report for 1974 that
during the year covered by the report 'the Library assumed a greater
share of the social responsibilities and became more actively involved
with the community. It further strengthened its role as an information,
cultural and resource centre, alive to the needs of the readers it serves.'
During this same year this lively National Library continued to lay special emphasis on 'strengthening the Library's resources in science and
technology', whilst its Reference, Information and Bibliographical
Services Division produced indexes of such periodicals as the *Singapore
government gazette* and *Singapore trade and industry*, 'to meet the demand for current information'. Similarly, the Cuban National Library's
Department for Scientific and Technical Information has compiled a
union catalogue of scientific and technical journals in the country, as
well as compiling and updating 'either on request or in accordance with
its own national-development forecasts, bibliographical information
on specific economic and technical subjects'. (24)

The national library's bibliographical and reference services grow in
importance in proportion to the weakness of the public library's reference services. This can lead, as pointed out earlier, to the National
Library setting up branches in other parts of the country, whilst the
public library system provides mainly lending services. Other countries
think it more advisable to develop local reference services within the
public library system, since they are likelier to be alive to local needs
than services depending on a central policy-making body, which can see
the country's needs as a whole better than it can those of the various
localities.

The superb service given by Washington's Library of Congress to
congressmen and senators has inspired some young national libraries
to provide an information and reference service to their country's par-
liamentarians, in addition to the more widespread service to ministries
and government departments. This type of service was well described
at the Manila seminar as consisting of the provision of factual data, the

formulation of arguments for or against a given proposal or in favour of pre-determined actions, and assistance in speech-writing both within and outside the legislature. The seminar warning about such services not being 'a universally desirable thing' as an integral part of national library functions, should be heeded. The seminar in fact recommended that when the national library as a whole is under the executive branch of the government, the legislative reference service ought to be independent of the library and responsible directly to the legislature. (25) This, of course, would make it easier for the service to be unbiased towards all the political parties in the legislature.

There are no reservations regarding reference services to government bodies and para-statal corporations, since such services can be regarded as one of the national library's main contributions to a developing country's progress towards economic and social prosperity. This service becomes extremely valuable in those countries where no properly organised and developed libraries exist in the various ministries and departments. The constitution of some national libraries emphasises this role. Thus section 5 of the National Library Act of Singapore lists among the national library's functions: '(e) to provide reference, bibliographic and inter-library loan services to government departments and to Parliament; (f) to advise on and co-ordinate the resources and services of government department libraries and other libraries with those of the National Library'. This National Library produces a promotional leaflet describing its services to government departments and statutory bodies. Its help to these bodies does not stop at such services, for staff from the National Library visit them from time to time in order to advise on reorganisation of libraries and other technical matters; thus in 1974 advice was given to the Jurong Town Corporation on the setting up of a photographic library.

These last activities are a good illustration of the national library as a leader in the nation's system, and as the principal advisory body to the state on library matters. Further pertinent instances can be quoted from the activities of the National Library of Nigeria. This library has been providing technical assistance to the state governments which are setting up new library services; this 'may take the form of training for junior staff, experience opportunities for qualified personnel, conferences and seminars for various grades or specialities of practising librarians'. (26) Members of this national library's staff were requested by the federal government to report on war damage to Nigerian libraries, and are designated by the Ministry of Establishment's examiners for the promotion within the Civil Service of staff in the library service. Like the Singapore National Library, the Nigerian gives direct assistance to government departments by assigning qualified personnel to supervise the development of departmental libraries; in addition, the National Library provides a cataloguing service for these libraries. (27)

Other national libraries extend their advisory and training services to libraries other than governmental or para-statal ones. Thus the Cuban National Library has advised and trained the staff of many specialised information centres set up throughout the country. In the early stages of a nation's library development, the national library can perform a very useful role by acting as a national methodological centre for libraries and information centres.

On the face of it, one of the most obvious fields where the national library could give a lead and lighten the burden of the nation's other libraries is that of cataloguing, and in fact all those national libraries issuing or cooperating in the issue of current national bibliographies are already playing a significant part in this field. On the other hand, the national literature often occupies only a minor, and sometimes tiny, proportion of the bookstock in the nation's libraries, so the national bibliography and any printed card service based on it, such as the one issued by the Nigerian National Library, does little towards reducing the workload of understaffed cataloguing departments in other libraries. National libraries can help, however, by keeping other libraries informed of current printed card services available from other countries.

Effective leadership is much more possible in the acquisition of foreign library materials, which constitute most of the various libraries' purchases and are often essential for technological and economic development. An acquisitions policy for the national library is soundest when made in the context of a well-planned library system with efficient cooperative mechanisms. This means that few of the new national libraries will aim at the old ideal of a collection covering all subjects in depth and coming from all countries. The Manila seminar suggested a policy of national coordination on the lines of the Farmington, Scandia and similar plans; this naturally assumes that all the cooperating libraries have enough funds to permit them adequately to carry out their part of the scheme. In addition to purchasing in depth within those areas assigned to it under the cooperative purchasing plan, the national library can follow a suggestion in the report of the Vienna symposium, by acquiring secondary and 'fringe' materials as a supplement to the acquisitions made by the other libraries in the plan.

In developing countries where libraries have restricted budgets, and inadequate acquisitions departments, the national library can perform another useful role by acting as a central agency for the purchase of foreign materials. (28)

Few national libraries lend books out of their stock to individual readers, though of course when the public library system is fully integrated with the national library, as in Singapore or Cairo, lending is normal from certain units within the system. It may happen that when an existing public library starts functioning as the national library, it sheds off its lending department, which can even become semi-autonomous. This happened in Malta in 1974 when the Royal Malta Library, which was renamed the National Library in June 1976, stopped lending books, and transferred the responsibility to a new public lending library which, however, was placed under the jurisdiction of the parent library.

Lending to other libraries and acting as the nerve-centre for the inter-library loan system, both nationally and vis-à-vis foreign libraries, are two functions undertaken by most national libraries in developing countries. Normally, however, books acquired under legal deposit legislation are not lent, so it is a frequent practice to purchase one or more copies in addition to the one deposited, which are made available for lending. The national library's lending function is of considerable importance in countries where it may be one of a very few libraries with a large stock of learned books. On the other hand, few such libraries can hope to satisfy most requests out of their stock, so they must rely on efficient cooperation with other libraries. Despite the criticism levelled, with some justification, at national union catalogues, national libraries must often depend on them to some extent in order to satisfy many requests for inter-library loans. In countries having only a few important libraries, a national union catalogue is not the daunting enterprise it can be in a country like Britain or the Federal German Republic.

One should note Anthony Thompson's remarks on 'a new and very important trend' among national libraries, that of separating the national library's reference functions from the lending ones, and his forecast 'that in future each country may have to plan *two* national libraries, one for conservation and reference, and the other for lending and photocopying'. (29) A separate building for lending and photocopying would, of course, be needed only if national libraries operated their lending on the style of the British Library Lending Division, which requires a large area and a form of management different from that of the traditional library. It is, however, doubtful whether many of the new national libraries would need to run their lending on these lines, since the majority of loans would not be out of their stock. More important still, few if any of them can ever hope to have first-rate stocks in both their reference and their lending divisions, as would be necessary for the system to be worthwhile.

Some national libraries, such as those of Algeria and Nigeria, are given responsibility for the national archives, and all national libraries have substantial collections of manuscripts. The Manila seminar recommended that an independent body should run the national archives, with close cooperation between this body and the national library. Since in most countries where the national library and the national archives are separate, they come under the same ministry, this cooperation is possible and excessive centralisation is thereby avoided.

REFERENCES

1 *National libraries: their problems and prospects; symposium of national libraries in Europe*, Paris, Unesco, 1960, foreword.

2 *Public libraries for Asia: the Delhi seminar*, Paris, Unesco, 1936, as quoted in H Anuar: *The planning of national libraries in Southeast Asia*, (paper read at the IFLA General Council Meeting, Washington, 1974), para 11.

3 Some examples: National Library of Nigeria, 1962; National Library of Malaysia, 1971; National Library of the Solomon Islands, 1974; National Library of Iraq, 1963.

4 A Enahoro: Inaugural address (at the first meeting of the National Library Board), *Nigerian libraries*, 7 (1971), 1 7 2, p 62.

5 T D Waknis: Observation on the National Library Bill, *Indian librarian*, 28 (1973), 3, p 105-106.

6 Trinidad and Tobago—Education Planning Unit, *Draft plan for educational planning in Trinidad and Tobago, 1968-1983*, para 7.20.

7 Carl M White: *The National Library of Nigeria; growth of the idea, development and progress*, quoted in S B Aje: The National Library of Nigeria, *Nigerian libraries*, 4 (1968), 3, p 79-80.

8 S G Ikoku: The Library in the de-colonization process, *Nigerian libraries*, 7 (1971), 1 & 2, p 18.

9 cf G Jefferson: *Libraries and society* (Cambridge, J Clarke, 1969), p xii, and G Chandler: *Libraries in the East* (London, 1971), p 2-3.

10 The Manila conference's final report was published in Unesco *Bulletin for libraries*, 18 (1964), 150-183.

11 Quoted in Anuar, op cit, para 15.

12 The Colombo meeting of experts final report was published by Unesco in 1968.

13 R A Adeleye: Vote of thanks [at the first meeting of the National Library Board], *Nigerian libraries*, 7 (1971), 1 & 2, p 64.

14 op cit, p 65.

15 P W T Poon: A proposed national library system in Indonesia, *Australian academic research libraries*, 1975, I, p 28.

16 Chapter 311, 1970 edition of the statutes of Singapore.

17 op cit, para 7.3.

18 Quoted by G Chandler, op cit, p 31.

19 Ministry of Education and Cultural Affairs of the Solomon Islands, *National library policy, 1975-1979*. Mimeographed.

20 Anuar, op cit, para 20.

21 Anuar, op cit, loc cit.

22 P W T Poon, op cit, p 26.

23 Unesco *Bulletin for libraries*, XVIII (1964), 4, p 154.

24 G Ramos: Twelve years' work at the National Library of Cuba, Unesco *Bulletin for libraries*, XXVI (1972), 4, p 212.

25 Unesco *Bulletin for libraries*, 18 (1964), 4, p 153.

26 S B Aje: The place of the national library in a multi-state federation with special reference to Nigeria, *Nigerian libraries*, 6, (1970), 3, p 176.

27 S B Aje: The National Library of Nigeria, *Nigerian libraries*, 4, (1968), 3, p 81.

28 cf C D Wormann: Cooperation of national libraries with other libraries in the same country and in other countries, Unesco *Bulletin for libraries*, XVIII (1964), 4, p 167.

29 A Thompson: Some recent trends in national library buildings, *Libri*, 24 (1974), 1, p 75.

University Libraries in a Double Function

National and University Libraries, Regional and University Libraries,
City and University Libraries and their Double Function

by MATKO ROJNIĆ

In his study published in Libri 1959, under the title National Libraries in our Time, our distinguished colleague, Dr. Kurt Wormann, Director of the Jewish National and University Library of Jerusalem, gave a careful analysis of the discussions and results of the Symposium on National Libraries held in Vienna in 1958. In this study Dr. Wormann also referred to the problems of those national libraries which are at the same time university libraries. Dr. Wormann said: "It would be a good thing if the competent Section of IFLA were to establish the facts, and to publish a research study on the strength of them, analysing the advantages and disadvantages of this double function of certain libraries."[1]

This problem was also given attention in the Long-Term Programme adopted at the IFLA meeting in Berne in 1962. In the chapter of the Programme relating to university libraries the following recommendation is made: "In view of recent developments a study should be made of the problems of university libraries serving at the same time as national libraries."[2]

It is easy to notice a slight difference between the suggestion made by Dr. Wormann and the recommendation as formulated in the Long-Term Programme. In Dr. Wormann's study the emphasis is on national libraries, whereas in the Long-Term Programme the whole problem is considered from the point of view of university libraries. The essntial point, however, is the same – the problem of the double function libraries which are both national and university libraries.

However, the problem of the double function of a library cannot be restricted to national and university libraries, since there are other types of libraries, such as regional and city libraries, which in addition to their primary tasks serve as university libraries. On the other hand there are also university libraries which in the course of time have assumed the tasks of regional libraries. As far as I know there is no university library which has

Reprinted from *Libri*, vol. 16, no. 2, 1966, p. 140-7, by permission of the author and publisher.

additionally taken upon itself the function of a city library. In any case the whole problem of the function of various libraries which serve as university libraries may be considered in a fairly broad aspect.

A study of this problem would represent a step towards the fulfilment of the Long-Term Programme as far as university libraries are concerned. We must, however, admit that on this occasion we can give only a brief report on this problem, a report compiled on the basis of an enquiry organised for this purpose by our Sub-section. I am very grateful indeed to the libraries which took part in the enquiry and answered the questionnaire sent to them by the Sub-section.

It is only logical to presume that national libraries which serve as university libraries and vice versa will have more or less the features common both to national and university libraries. Analogously the same holds true for regional or city libraries having the function of university libraries.

As is well known there are differences among national libraries in their function, activities and the role they play in the library system of their countries. This was the reason why no attempt was made at the Vienna Symposium on National Libraries to give a valid definition of this most eminent type of library. In the Summary of the discussions at the Symposium the point was made that in general "the national library of a country is the one responsible for collecting and conserving the whole of that country's book production for the benefit of future generations".[3] In fact, this broad characterisation of the national library is only a repetition of what Sir Frank Francis considered in his paper presented to the same Symposium on the basic duty of a national library.[4] Certainly, this will correspond to a general conception of the national library. Nevertheless, we think that Dr. Herman Liebaers was also right in stressing the leading place national libraries occupy compared with other libraries in the country. According to Dr. Liebaers the position of the national library "is due to the extent and encyclopaedic character of its collections, the variety of material held and the diversity of specialized departments and services."[5]

As to university libraries one might simply say that their main tasks consist in helping the educational and research work of their universities. No doubt, this conception of the university library would not be fully adequate, since the university libraries of Europe have long since extended their activities and services beyond their universities and, consequently, have become institutions of public interest. Very often university libraries have been given the privilege of deposit copies. This has increased the significance of university libraries for the national culture and has enabled them in a great measure to assume the function of national libraries in their countries.

The common feature of all these libraries, national, regional, city and university, is the encyclopaedic character of their collections. This was a prerequisite condition which enabled some of these libraries simultaneonsly to take upon themselves tasks in the field of knowledge and education.

Naturally, there were also important historical reasons why university libraries in some countries were given the function of national libraries. In general the establishment of national libraries went along with the development of the modern state. In many European countries the former libraries of the sovereigns have been transformed in the course of time into national libraries. In other countries national libraries were founded as completely new institutions. In some countries, however, the duty of collecting and preserving the books of the country concerned was undertaken by national museums. But there has been another solution to the problem of national libraries. This was particularly the case with those small countries which have achieved their independence relatively late and also with those nationalities which developed in a nationally heterogeneous country. As a rule in these countries the most important university libraries were given the function of national libraries. Thus the University Library of Oslo assumed the function of the National Library of Norway. The University Library of Helsinki is at the same time the National Library of Finland. The national significance of the Helsinki University Library was enhanced long ago by the privilege of deposit copies. Denmark found a satisfactory solution to the problem of the double function of the national and university library in 1943 when the two biggest libraries in the country, the Royal Library of Copenhagen, which is the National Library of Denmark, and the University Library of Copenhagen were put under the same administration. The two libraries are directed by the Office of the National Librarian. The fields of knowledge are divided between the two libraries. The Royal Library covers humanities while the University Library is responsible for natural sciences and medicine. As far as the University is concerned both libraries act as a big university library.

Germany offers several examples of university libraries transformed into state and university libraries. Here we mention only the famous University Library of Göttingen which became the State and University Library of Lower Saxony along with the creation of the State (Land) of Lower Saxony. In France the National and University Library of Strasbourg, founded in 1871 during the German domination as University and State Library, retained its double function after the incorporation of Alsace into France. In fact this library may rather be considered a regional and university library. The Cantonal and University Library of Lausanne had been an academic institution only until 1803, when it was taken over by the cantonal authorities and made a public institution.

In Croatia, which for centuries was in the union with Hungary, the University Library of Zagreb has performed the role of the national library. It was only a consequence of its development that the University Library of Zagreb recently changed its name into National and University Library. The University Library of Ljubljana was also made National and University Library for Slovenia, one of the six Yugoslav republics.

Despite the historical and other possible factors which might have influenced a university library to assume the tasks of a national or regional library, there is no doubt that reasons of economy played a decisive role in prompting a national or regional library to extend its services to the University and a university library to become exceptionally important for a country or a province. Thus the Jewish National and University Library founded as the National Library took upon itself to serve the University of Jerusalem. The National Library of Sarajevo in Yugoslavia, a quite independent institution, is also the main library of the University of Sarajevo. The same may be said of the city library of Cologne transformed into the University and City Library and that of Frankfurt which was made City and University Library.

According to the answers to the questionnaire all the libraries which are both national and university libraries or regional and university libraries receive deposit copies from their territories. This is also the case with the city and university libraries as regards the books published in their cities, the only exception being the City and University Library of Berne, which receives only the theses of its University. Some national and university libraries are given two deposit copies. Two copies are received by the Jewish National and University Library and by the University Library of Oslo, of which one copy is sent by printers and the second one is presented by publishers for the purpose of the Norwegian Bibliography. The National and University libraries of Zagreb, Ljubljana and Skopje also receive two deposit copies, one copy from the territory of their republics and a second one from Yugoslavia as a whole.

The majority of these libraries consider their two functions equally important. The libraries of Cologne, Halle and Lausanne reported, however, that their obligations to the university prevailed over their function as national or regional library. According to the Library of Lausanne this is due to the fact that in this city there are other libraries of a public character. Speaking generally there is no doubt that national, regional or city libraries which serve as university libraries are not less in demand with students and members of the university staff than those libraries which function as university libraries only.

Certainly it is not necessary to argue for the learnéd character of these libraries. It is nevertheless worth mentioning that one of the tasks of the

Cantonal and University Library of Fribourg is help for the general public in acquiring knowledge. This is obviously because this library originally was a city library only.

As is only to be expected, libraries which are both national and university libraries are faced with the same difficulties that other general libraries have in preserving their encyclopaedic character. In selecting books libraries with a double function show a tendency to concentrate on the humanities, no less than other general libraries, as one may conclude from the answers to the questionnaire.

Naturally a large library with different important functions will need greater funds for books than another library which is only a national or a university library. This was confirmed by the answers of some libraries. The greater part of the funds is spent on foreign books and periodicals, the literature of the country being received under deposit copy regulations.

In the field of bibliography libraries with the double function of national and university libraries have particular responsibilities. Work on the national bibliography is their concern. Current national bibliographies are being prepared by the University Library of Oslo, the Jewish National and University Library of Jerusalem, and also by the National and University Library of Ljubljana and that of Zagreb. The University Library of Oslo has published the retrospective national bibliography, while the Library of Jerusalem is working on the retrospective national bibliography. Two Yugoslav libraries, that of Zagreb and that of Ljubljana, are also preparing the retrospective bibliographies of their republics. As to bibliographies for academic purposes, it seems that only the Library of Jerusalem and that of Halle compile lists of the publications of their faculty staff.

A union catalogue of books kept in the libraries of the whole country or of a region would be quite adequate for a national or regional library with the function of the university library. Such catalogues, both of books and periodicals, exist in some libraries, as in Göttingen for Lower Saxony, Halle for Saxony Anhalt and Zagreb for Croatia, while in the Library of Frankfurt there is a regional catalogue of books and periodicals to which, however, the libraries of the University institutes do not deliver their entries. On the other hand the National and University Library of Jerusalem has a catalogue of books and periodicals in the libraries of the University only and a separate union catalogue of scientific periodicals in the libraries of the country.

As to reading rooms, most libraries keep to the traditional scheme of a main reading room, very often intended both for students and other readers, a reading room for periodicals and a reading room for manuscripts and rare books. Instead of the reading room for professors only, there are sometimes one or more reading rooms for research workers. Of course, provision of space for students is a very difficult problem, no less than in libraries which are university libraries only. The Library of Göttingen is planning a separate reading room for students, in Helsinki a students' library was established long ago.

As a rule students and professors are given facilities for the use of these libraries no less than of those which are university libraries only. In general university professors are not charged for the use of the library, and in some libraries: Göttingen, Frankfurt, Halle and Jerusalem students do not pay fees. There are, however, libraries in which students are charged, though in certain libraries they pay lower fees than other readers, as in Berne and Zagreb. Students must also pay fees to be admitted to the Cantonal and University Libraries of Fribourg and Lausanne. Of the libraries which took part in the enquiry, only the University Library of Oslo and of Helsinki do not impose fees on any category of readers.

In principle, libraries of this kind should promote coordination of library activities in two directions. On the one hand they should coordinate the work of the libraries of their University; on the other hand they should be in the centre of the library network of their countries or regions. The coordinating role for the libraries of their universities was reported by the Cantonal and University Libraries of Fribourg and Lausanne and by the Jewish National and University Library of Jerusalem. The University Library of Oslo has established a uniform system of faculty service within the University. The libraries and documentation centres of faculties of the Oslo University work under the guidance of the University Library; they assist the institute libraries in book selection, processing and book loan. But, as is well known, there have always been difficulties in organizing cooperation between libraries within the same university and not only on a national or regional scale. This is particularly the case with some countries of Central Europe where university libraries maintain very loose or no ties with the University administration. In Göttingen the faculty and institute libraries are independent of the State and University Library, while the Library of Halle is aiming to establish cooperation with the libraries of the University. In Yugoslavia the National and University Library of Zagreb is making efforts to coordinate the acquisition of books, and particularly of periodicals from foreign countries. It is also trying to coordinate book exchange between the libraries of Croatia and libraries abroad. However the Library has been more successful as an intermediary in international book loans for Croatia than in coordinating acquisition policy.

To summarize:

In small countries, particularly in those where no Royal or National Libraries had existed, university libraries assumed the function of national libraries. Vice versa some regional and city libraries extended their services to universities. Beside historical reasons there is no doubt that factors of economy also brought about such a development.

The majority of libraries which took part in the enquiry consider their simultaneous functions equally important although in practice their obligations to universities prevail over their function of national, or regional, or municipal libraries.

In building up their collections the libraries of this type show a tendency towards the humanities no less than libraries which are either national, or regional or municipal libraries only.

In view of the significance for their countries, regions or cities, these libraries are given the privilege of deposit copies from their respective areas.

While work on the national bibliography is one of the principal tasks of those libraries which are both national and university libraries, only some of them compile lists of books published by their universities.

Union catalogues covering the whole country or region or city are considered more important for a library with a double function than union catalogues embracing only the libraries within the same university.

Libraries which are both national and university libraries are faced with difficulties in establishing coordination with the libraries of their universities, and of course, still more with the libraries of the whole country.

There are no particular differences between the libraries with a double function and those which serve a university only, as regards the use of the library either by professors, or students or other readers. Deposit copies which are received by these libraries for the purpose of preservation are asked for on loan no less than other books.

Libraries with simultaneous tasks have to some extent greater demands for money, staff and premises than if they were confined only to one of their basic tasks, but, needless to say, two libraries instead of one covering the same tasks would entail much greater expenditures, not to speak of separate premises for the two libraries.

Most libraries stated that there were no difficulties for them deriving from their double function. The National and University Library of Jerusalem did however admit that it had difficulties due to its double function, as regards the acquisition of books, the loan of books, the library organization and the staff, but added that the advantages were substantially greater. In general all the libraries which took part in the enquiry agreed they had very good experience of their double function. No library considered the advantages would be greater if it were a university library only.

NOTES

1. C. Wormann, National Libraries in our Time. The UNESCO Symposium on National Libraries in Europe, Libri 9/1959, p. 293.
2. Libraries in the World. A Long-Term Programme for the International Federation of Library Associations. Hague, 1963, p. 47.
3. National Libraries: Their Problems and Prospects. Symposium on National Libraries in Europe. Vienna, 8–27 September 1958. Paris, UNESCO, 1960, p. 34.
4. F. Francis, The Organization of National Libraries (op. cit., p. 21).
5. H. Liebaers, The Needs of National Libraries as regards Professional Training (op. cit., p. 27).

NATIONAL LENDING/REFERENCE LIBRARIES OR LIBRARIES OF FIRST RESORT

D J Urquhart

The development of the BLLD is briefly described and the desire to set up similar institutions in the USA is discussed. The concept of a single national collection providing both reference and lending services is examined and apparent conflict of interests between visitors and remote borrowers is outlined in the light of the author's visits to Iran and Australia. The questions considered include simplified document retrieval, photocopy facilities and a fast service to remote borrowers on the one hand and the need for some duplication and a browsing capability on the other. It is generally concluded that remote borrowers must be properly serviced since they will form the majority of users.

The idea that there should be a separate national lending library in the UK developed almost by accident. At the time of the Royal Society Scientific Information Conference of 1948 the major lending service for scientific material was provided by the Science Museum Library in South Kensington. This service had been started by S C Bradford and in pre-war days the demand on it had been less than the demand on the Science Museum Library's reference service. But in the early post war years the situation had changed and the lending service had become the major activity of the library. Nevertheless the service did not meet the needs of the growing scientific community because the service was slow at times and the collections of the library were inadequate.

It was found that there was insufficient room for expansion on the South Kensington site, so it was decided to create a separate lending library. Thus the NLLST came into being, dedicated to the idea that it should provide a rapid service to remote users from a more adequate collection than the Science Museum Library had.

The room for expansion which existed at Boston Spa made it possible to collect and to store a larger collection than existed in South Kensington, but the creation of a separate lending library also made it possible to devise new procedures which would facilitate the operation of the lending services.

These procedures resulted in Boston Spa appearing to be so different from other libraries that some said it was not really a library, but a factory. This situation, linked to the rapid growth in demand, produced the idea that other countries needed national lending libraries. As a result

there has been a continuous stream of overseas visitors to Boston Spa to see what the development of separate "lending" libraries in their countries would involve.

In the USA, for instance, the Association of Research Libraries (ARL) started pressing for a central service, at least for periodicals, and plans to develop the Center for Research Libraries (CRL) in Chicago as such a centre have been prepared. Recently the National Commission on Libraries and Information Science (NCLIS) have published a national programme document[1] which states:

> "The Commission believes that the Library of Congress should be designated as the National Library. In its role as a National Library it should accept the following responsibilities ...
> (1)   Expansion of the lending and lending management function of the library to that of a National Lending Library of final resort."

In crossing the Atlantic the national lending library concept has, perhaps unconsciously, been changed by adding the notion of "library of final resort". This notion does not exist at Boston Spa. The library there is to an increasing extent, at least as far as the UK is concerned, the library of first resort when local resources fail. If it were not, the BLLD would not be dealing with about threequarters of all the UK inter-library requests.

The concept of a "library of last resort" involves the idea that users should first shop around to see what they can find before approaching such a library. This might be convenient for the library. It is most inconvenient for the user. If the aim is to provide "realistic and convenient access"[2] to the national resources, what is to be the first resort when local

Reprinted from *BLL Review*, vol. 4, no. 1, January 1976, p. 7-10, by permission of the publisher.

resources fail? Such a resort should be able to supply 80% or 90% of the items which are not available locally. Is the Library of Congress to provide this service? Assuming for the moment this is intended, the question arises whether the same "national library" can provide efficient services both for the visitors to its reading rooms and for its remote users.

This is a question which I have had an opportunity of studying in Iran and in Australia. In Iran the Shah has decided that there should be a Pahlevi National Library and a group of consultants met in Tehran in August 1975 to draft proposals for this library. The state of library development in Iran makes it desirable that the proposed library should serve not merely those who visit its reading rooms but also other potential users throughout Iran. Plans to provide computer retrieval services throughout Iran made it essential to provide a document supply service. But could a satisfactory lending and reference service be provided by the same library from the same collection? In general the experiences of national libraries is against such a development, but it has long been clear that the user of scientific literature was likely to be able to obtain in the reading room at Boston Spa, despite the lending service, more of the items he wanted than in any other reading room in the UK. The essential features of the Boston Spa situation which appear relevant are:

1.   Adequate inward and outward flow arrangements to make it possible to deal quickly with both the inward and outward posts.

2.   A form designed to eliminate clerical activities in the library.

3.   A procedure designed to reduce accounting activities.

4.   A storage system which makes it possible to locate the majority of items required without consulting any records.

5.   A demand which is sufficiently large to justify an adequate organisation to deal with it.

6.   Location of photocopying equipment near the items to be copied.

7.   Mechanical handling arrangements which facilitate the packing and despatch of loans and photocopies.

8.   An adequate collection to satisfy a large percentage of all requests.

9.   Access to the collections of other libraries to supplement the Library's collection.

With the proposed national library in Iran, which will have a building yet to be designed, the major problem relates to proposed storage arrangements. If the major part of the collection was divided up between a number of reading rooms on some subject basis, then the problem of discovering where items have been shelved is made more difficult and the possibility of being able to provide a rapid service to remote users is decreased. On the other hand, if the collections in the reading rooms contain only bibliographies and a limited quantity of publications, then a satisfactory service to remote users should be possible if the bulk of the collection is shelved in some easily findable order in a central store. This store should of course be designed to serve both the visitors to the reading rooms and remote users quickly.

This solution reduces the "browsing" possibilities, but does this really matter? Browsing was no doubt a sensible and necessary activity in the seventeenth century when the total volume of publications was much smaller than it is today and when there were few bibliographies. Browsing is no doubt a useful activity for an undergraduate who does not know what he wants but who must have a book immediately. Because of the existence of bibliographies browsing is now rarely necessary. Is it really a sensible activity in a research library? Does not the research worker really need whatever is published in the world which may be of interest to him, rather than what he accidentally stumbles across in browsing around the shelves? Is the browsing habit but the survival of an ancient custom or does it survive owing to bibliographical laziness or ignorance?

Whatever the real advantages are of a browsing capability are they sufficient to require separate collections for "lending" and for "reference"? As far as runs of periodicals are concerned, the generally accepted answer appears to be "no". This is fortunate, because about threequarters of the remote user demand on a national library is likely to be for items in periodicals. Undoubtedly the advantages of providing browsing facilities for visitors to the library (whatever they are) are of less importance than meeting the needs of remote users, if the demand from the remote users is likely to be greater than that from the visitors. This is likely to be the case in Tehran.

There will of course be other problems facing a library which is trying to provide both an effective reference and lending service. Not least of these will be those concerned with duplication. For periodicals the problem would not appear to be too great, since use studies could easily and quickly reveal those relatively few titles responsible for much of the demand. For monographs the problem would be much greater because of the difficulty of identifying "high use" titles in advance of demand and one is forced to admit that the reference service could be weakened by a parallel lending service. A counter argument of course is that reference demand is likely to be for older material, whereas on the interlending front it is the current literature which will be most in demand. As a start however it would seem sensible to duplicate at least national publications. This would certainly be necessary if the library was to fulfil the role of a legal deposit collection.

The importance of the principles set down for the proposed national library in Iran was confirmed by considering the difficulties facing the National Library of Australia in trying to provide a rapid service to remote users. In particular:

(a)   The inward and outward flow arrangements in Canberra are hampered by the staff organisation and the design of the building.

(b)   The existing forms received by the library are not designed to eliminate clerical activities in the library - requests have to be copied onto other forms and separate address labels made.

(c)   It is impossible to locate items required without consulting any records and the existing location records make the job of finding locations time-consuming.

(d)   The total actual demand is so small that it is not economic to have sufficient photocopying machines to make it possible to provide photocopying facilities adjacent to the item to be copied.

The demand is less than a tenth of what might be expected by analogy with the situation in the UK. This is mainly due to the speed of the service. That a faster service from the National Library is desirable appeared to be the general view of Australian librarians, despite the tendency to be suspicious of "federal" activities. As far as the collection of the National Library is concerned, it should be possible.

Finally, the National Library of Australia has not taken an effective lead in organising interlibrary lending. Indeed, one project in the pipe-line is more likely to disorganise the interlibrary arrangements than help them. This project relates to the publication of the union catalogue of books. This catalogue at present exists only on cards in Canberra. Locations are provided upon request, but this service is not very rapid. To speed it up it is proposed to publish microfilm copies of the union catalogue. Such a move is likely not only to speed up the provision of locations, but also to increase the interlibrary demand. This may be disastrous.

At present the University libraries in Australia are the major element in the interlibrary scene since they provide about half the interlibrary loans in Australia and collectively lend appreciably more than they borrow. No objective data appears to be available about the attitude of the university librarians to interlending, but I have the impression that until recently they were very liberal about meeting the requests they received. More recently, owing to the growing load on university libraries, rising costs, some uncertainty about what copies can be supplied freely under the Copyright Act and above all the limitation of resources due to the current recession, university librarians may have begun to change their policies. This process might be speeded up if the publication of the union catalogue increases the demand on university libraries.

The general situation about interlending in Australia gives added emphasis to the importance of the National Library taking the lead and in particular introducing a prepaid form which would not only cut down clerical and accounting activities in the National Library, but which also could be used between other libraries in Australia — the borrower being credited for the items lent and the photocopies supplied. A faster service from the National Library would of course increase the demand upon that library and ensure that the university libraries remain willing to provide, in particular, items not held in the National Library. This situation would of course tend to make the National Library of Australia a library of first resort when local resources failed.

The interlibrary situation in the USA, whilst it is more complex and has a longer history, appears to be basically the same as in Australia. As Gordon Williams[3] states:

"Nearly every US academic library with a collection of 500,000 or more volumes consistently lends more than it borrows."

"Since most libraries make no charge for loans to another library, those that lend more than they borrow bear a cost that can be met only by reducing services to their own readers."

"...as budgets tighten it puts the library under increasing pressure, both from its users and those who review its budget, to reduce lending to a minimum."

Although there are some differences., the pattern of the interlibrary loan demand in the USA is very similar to that in the UK in at least one important respect. There is a high concentration of use on a small number of journal titles and "the titles found to be most requested on interlibrary loan corresponded so closely to the titles most used in local libraries."

This is one of the reasons why the major requirement is a library of first resort. Whether it would be possible to reorientate the Library of Congress to provide this service is by no means clear. It is, however, clear that if it should be possible, it would be a very difficult task. It might be much simpler in the USA to create one or more separate national lending libraries. Undoubtedly it is more important and in some ways simpler to tackle the periodical problem first. Despite the fear in the USA that the total demand on a central lending library in the USA would be too large for any single library to handle, this is by no means clear. There is so far no obvious upper limit to the total demand which could be handled at Boston Spa. It is however clear that a large part of the collection at Boston Spa is used only infrequently. This situation suggests not only that a national lending library need not necessarily be a duplicate of the complete Boston Spa collection, but also that we should be moving towards a situation in which the responsibility for providing access to rarely used material should be shared between national lending libraries in a number of countries. I cannot however see such a system meeting users' needs unless each national lending library can provide a rapid service.

References

1. National Commission on Libraries and Information Science. *Toward a national program for library and information services: goals for action,* 1975, p 67.

2. NCLIS, loc. cit

3. Williams, Gordon. Interlibrary loan service in the United States. *In* Barr, Keith and Line, Maurice, (eds). *Essays on information and libraries; festschrift for Donald Urquhart,* Clive Bingley, 1975, pp 193-206.

Tasks and duties of the modern national library in building up stocks of foreign literature and documentation for the country's library system

MRS KALAIDZIEVA

Director, Cyril and Methodius National Library, Sofia, Bulgaria

Science in the 20th century is a powerful productive force in the hands of society, a dominant and all embracing field of action, and one of the most important factors in raising the efficiency of labour and promoting the progress of a country and nation.

This accounts for the great interest and active participation of the state in the organization and financial support of research work and introduction of new techniques and methods. More and more resources, both intellectual and material, are being employed to meet the needs of the rapid development of science and technology in every country.

Information in the field of science and technology is now a state problem and part of national science policy. The ever increasing amount of scientific research throughout the world and hence the increasing number of science publications, the risk of overlooking some important novelty, the impossibility of controlling bibliographically and keeping abreast of currently published literature, the increasing cost of library and information systems and other well-known factors have led to the coinage of the phrase 'information crisis' and to a search at a national and international level for ways and means to cope with that crisis.

Every country with developed economics and developed science and technology, which has an ambition to participate in the build up of the world's economics, science and culture, is compelled nowadays to establish a reliable and well-organized information system from which to draw information on the latest and most important developments throughout the world.

In this century of 'information explosion', characterized by an annual production of over half a million book titles (to say nothing of other categories of publications), with a tendency to reach one million book titles per annum at the end of the century, the modern state, as the sponsor of the progress of science, faces the problem of building up a rich collection of science, technology and culture in the world. In point of fact, a number of countries have felt the necessity to check existing library stocks, to provide for a systematic and sensible supplementation with new-published materials, and to ensure that the contents of library documents are fully disclosed to users so that a full and easy usage can be warranted. For it is obvious that if science is the key to universal progress, libraries on the other hand are the key to science.

Libraries should be regarded as a function of the extant tendencies in the development of modern science and publishing and, at the same

Reprinted from BARR, Keith *and* LINE, Maurice, *eds.* Essays on information and libraries: Festschrift for Donald Urquhart. London: Bingley; Hamden, Conn.: Linnet Books, 1975, p. 89-103, by permission of the publisher.

time, as a base that might, if properly organized, influence in a large measure the development of science and technology. In view of this situation, the country's library system should consider the two basic tendencies in contemporary science, *viz* the continuing specialization of human knowledge and, parallel with this process, the increasingly predominant tendency towards interaction of every branch of science with other branches of science *ie* towards an integration of sciences.

Taking into account these tendencies, a number of countries have recently made an important change in the organization of existing library and information systems. Efforts have been made to establish, beside the existing decentralized and specialized research libraries, and information centres, a compact information and documentation system aimed at reflecting the interconnections between sciences.

It would appear that the 'explosion' in information, the integration of sciences, the excessive cost of scientific and technical information, the requirements for speed and reliability, and other factors too, have taken us back to the idea of an encyclopedic library which was rejected a century ago.

Here is, for instance, a passage from an article by the director of the All-Union Institute for Scientific and Technical Information in the USSR (VINITI): 'The creation of VINITI was necessitated not only by the requirements of the planned economy of socialism, but also by an inner logic, by the specific character of the development of contemporary science which is characterized by two opposite tendencies. On the one hand, there is an increasingly deepening differentiation of sciences — as a result of the rapid growth of research work in different areas . . . On the other hand, we are witnessing a process of unification and synthesis of scientific knowledge, an integration of sciences, owing to deeper insights into the essence of the existing reality and owing to a juxtaposition of the results of various researches and to the discovery of organic links, hitherto unknown, between apparently unrelated, disparate and heterogenous phenomena. This leads to the appearance of new border-line disciplines, just on the frontier between two branches of science, where the methods of the one interact with the methods of the other.'[1]

Similar views are expressed in a report of the president of the Science Advisory Committee in the USA: 'Science can flourish only if each scientist interacts with his colleagues and his predecessors, and only if every branch of science interacts with other branches of science; in this sense science must remain unified if it is to remain effective. The ideas and data that are the substance of science and technology are embodied in the literature; only if the literature remains a unity can science itself be unified and viable. Yet, because of the tremendous growth of the literature, there is danger of science fragmenting into a mass of repetitious findings, or worse, into conflicting specialties that are not recognized as being mutually inconsistent. This is the essence of the "crisis" in scientific and technical information.' The report runs further: 'As we have already said, science is really indivisible; if it fragments into a host of wholly unconnected specialties, each specialty narrowing and the number of specialties increasing with time, science as an instrument for probing nature will be greatly weakened. Moreover, in spite of the obstacles to proper communication, modern science tends to become more and more interconnected. Though a scientist chooses to narrow his specialty, science itself creates an ever increasing number of potential points of contact between the scientist's narrow specialty and the surrounding fields. As time goes on, successful pursuit of a narrow specialty requires effective contact with more and more diverse parts of the literature.'[2]

The English, too, have arrived at similar conclusions. Dr D J Urquhart, when director of the National Lending Library for Science and Technology, published the results of a survey of the use of scientific literature by scientists and specialists. He wrote: 'More recently we carried out a survey of the use of scientific literature in all fields. One of the things we found was that half the literature we issued was in a subject which was outside the basic field in which the user has been trained.'[3] And he concluded that the extent to which information in peripheral fields is sought and used is much greater than was previously realised, and that scientists and researchers are, in fact, unaware even of the true number of peripheral sciences that are used today by an individual branch of science. Similar conclusions have been reached by other English authors, too.[4]

Even in the German Federal Republic, the classic example of a decentralized and differentiated library system, there have recently been voices of discontent — in spite of a considerable number of well-organized special libraries. 'Science in the German Federal Republic suffers after the second world war from the absence of a central library — we lack a large scientific central library such as the former Prussian Library in Berlin. If confronted by a serious task, we have to travel today throughout Germany, from one library to another, or visit some major library in a neighbour country.'[5]

In consideration of the latest tendencies in the development of contemporary science, namely the differentiation and integration of sciences, many countries have been trying to create an adequate library and information system in accordance with those tendencies. As is well known, the USSR has founded VINITI, a gigantic institution for centralized abstracting of the world's scientific literature, and the Lenin State Library in Moscow.

It is a remarkable fact that in connection with this problem some countries have either resorted to a reorganization of the national library forming a central science library, or have created a new encyclopedic library for science and technology.

As a practical measure based on the special report on the development of science and information[2], the US Congress enacted the Higher Education Act of 1965 for the development of science and higher education[6] and at the same time increased the budget of the Library of Congress with a view to ensuring for the USA an adequate acquisition and a speedy processing of the world's scientific literature and documentation.

Following the experience of the USA, Japan reorganized[7] the National Diet Library, from which will emerge an encyclopedic library of a new type capable of ensuring that the government and research institutes have access to the basic materials of the world's scientific literature and documentation.

A new national library, the National Science Library, was established in Canada.[8] Its stocks and scientific and technical documentation are used by the country's specialised libraries, industrial companies and research institutes.

Europe, too, despite its old and firmly established traditions, began to adapt itself to the new trends, to gradually change the profile of some national libraries traditionally orientated towards the humanities, and to associate their activities with the development of science and technology. Actually this was the recommendation of the UNESCO Symposium of National Libraries held in 1958 in Vienna.

The first steps were made by Great Britain by the establishment in 1962 of the National Lending Library for Science and Technology. In ten years it has become the richest library of Europe[9] in respect to scientific periodicals (with a collection of 44,000 periodical titles currently obtained in all fields) and in respect to documentation (reports, official publications, publications of international organizations, etc).

The merits of the director of NLL, Dr Donald J Urquhart, who conceived the idea of this remarkable library and created its structure, organization and mechanism of action, cannot be emphasized enough. He was the first to break the old library traditions and to entirely subordinate his library to the requirements of modern science and technology.

I do not think it an exaggeration to say, and this is my personal opinion, that Great Britain has in the person of Dr Urquhart a new Panizzi, a Panizzi of the twentieth century, whose ideas and revolutionary methods in the field of modern library service will receive more and more attention in the future and will be applied not only in Great Britain, but also in library theory and practice all over the world.

A serious attempt at reorganization was also made some years ago by the British Museum Library (hitherto collecting materials chiefly in the field of the humanities and social sciences) when the former Patent Office library became a department of the BM Library, expanding its range into that of an encyclopedic scientific library, known as the National Reference Library of Science and Invention.

The British parliament recently (in 1973) enacted the British Library Act[10] for the establishment of the British Library, to include, as well as the British National Bibliography, two encyclopedic libraries. The first, the former National Lending Library and National Central Library, functions as a lending library; the second, the former British Museum Library, as a reference library. The salient point in the reform, however, is the establishment of an encyclopedic national library of a new type aiming at systematic acquisition of all the world's significant scientific literature, as well as the literature of all other subjects.

Belgium, too, has made radical changes in the organization of the national library.[11] A new Centre for Scientific and Technical Information began functioning at the National Library of Belgium, relying heavily upon its collections of scientific and technical material.

In the German Democratic Republic the functions of the modern national library are performed by two libraries, to wit: the Deutsche Bücherei in Leipzig which collects only literature in German (in all fields and from all German speaking countries) and the Deutsche Staatsbibliothek in Berlin which continues the tradition of collecting foreign material in all fields of knowledge. According to the latest regulations for the development of library services in GDR,[12] the Deutsche Staatsbibliothek will collect a selection of foreign scientific literature from all fields and from all countries focussing on social, technical, and fundamental natural sciences. The two libraries, then, perform together the functions which in other countries are entrusted to one national library only.

Similarly, the German Federal Republic relies upon a few libraries for a combined performance of the tasks and duties of the modern national library, especially in connection with the build-up of the national stocks of literature (including both the country's publications and foreign materials). The Deutsche Bibliothek in Frankfurt/Main, like the Deutsche Bücherei in Leipzig, is a depository library only in respect to German publications (from all fields of knowledge). The new developments in GFR have necessitated the opening of still another national library, an encyclopedic library for foreign literature — like the Deutsche Staatsbibliothek of GDR. Based on the collections of the Deutche Staatsbibliothek, which were evacuated to Marburg during the second world war, a gigantic science library, the Staatsbibliothek der Stiftung Preussischer Kulturbesitz, has been formed in West Berlin. This library collects as completely as possible foreign scientific periodicals and documentation (reports, official publications, dissertations, etc). With respect to periodicals it will probably play the same role as does the British Library Lending Division in Great Britain. Its holdings of monographs, however, are mainly in the field of the humanities. To remedy this and in order to ensure intensive acquisition on a large scale of the world's scientific literature in all fields, a system based on several central federal libraries is being formed in GFR.[13] It will comprise a number of central libraries in the fields of technology, medicine, agriculture and economics. These, together with the Deutsche Bibliothek in Frankfurt/Main and the Staatsbibliothek der Stiftung Preussischer Kulturbesitz in West Berlin, will be engaged in building up, as completely as possible, the national stocks of scientific literature.

As early as 1943 the national library of Denmark,[14] the Royal Library, which collects materials chiefly in the field of the humanities, and the University Library, which concentrates mostly on medicine, biology and natural sciences, merged into a new library with a common budget, pay-roll and manager (National Librarian). In this way it was hoped to avoid unnecessary duplication in the acquisition of library materials and to ensure a wider and better selection. It is incumbent upon the united national library to coordinate the acquisition of foreign literature in a number of major special libraries functioning in a sense as national libraries. These are the Library of Economics, the Library of Technology, the Pedagogic Library, and the Library of

Agriculture. All of them form together with the united national library an 'umbrella', as it were, for the smaller specialized libraries which use their stocks and can avail themselves of their services.

In Czechoslovakia, too, the State Library in Prague[15] is a combination of several libraries: the National Library, the University Library, the Slavonic Library, and the specialized libraries of economics and of French and English literature. All these libraries collect together literature in nearly all fields of knowledge.

Finally, mention should be made of the National Library of Bulgaria, which has been collecting for some decades (since 1944) basic foreign material in all fields (published in those languages that are most spoken and used in Bulgaria). Attention is focussed on the completion of the collections of foreign reference works, scientific periodicals, and basic monographs having the character of reference tools. These collections are placed at the disposal of the specialized libraries which supplement the holdings of the National Library of Bulgaria by the acquisition of highly specialized literature and documentation.

The European national libraries indicated above and the three largest national libraries outside Europe (the Library of Congress in USA, the National Diet Library in Japan, and the National of Library Canada) collect foreign literature on all subjects and in all fields — either alone or in cooperation with some special libraries. Their efforts are directed towards the build up of the country's national stocks of foreign literature and documentation — according to the financial possibilities of the country. They are all depository libraries for the publications of international organizations.

At the same time there is still a considerable number of national libraries in Europe giving priority to the acquisition of materials in the fields of politics and social sciences. The reason lies in the old traditions in acquisition still maintained by these libraries. As examples may be cited the national libraries of Austria, Denmark, Spain, Poland, Norway, Hungary, France and the Netherlands. In collecting foreign literature, however, these national libraries collaborate with a number of special libraries, which are for the most part old libraries with established traditions and well-balanced collections, so the situation is somewhat remedied.

Table 1, in which the national libraries in Europe are arranged in alphabetical order of countries, gives statistics about the acquisition of both foreign literature and the country's own production, and also shows the scope of acquisition.

The organization of the country's national stocks, their contents and structure, present a problem that has been solved in different ways in individual countries, yet despite the variety of solutions there are in my opinion two outstanding instances of organization. In the first case the national stocks simply consist of the holdings of the country's national library or, more often, of the holdings of a limited number of libraries (called in most cases national libraries too) forming a close, organically knit system. In the second case the national stocks are based on the holdings of a number of scientific libraries which coordinate the acquisition of foreign literature, and each is responsible for a specific branch of science.

No matter what solution has been adopted in individual countries, there is a tendency to assign the national library an important role and make it establish and maintain links among libraries, achieve the maximum use of library holdings, and restore the unity of scientific literature through special library coordination forms.

The complete coverage and announcement by the national library of the existing stocks and new foreign accessions of the country's major research libraries is considered today a fundamental duty of the modern national library. This is achieved through the union catalogues and bulletins of new accessions which establish a tie-up among libraries and make their holdings accessible to the whole country.

Table 2 shows the activities in this important field of the national libraries in Europe.

As demonstrated by Dr Urquhart, accessions bulletins and union catalogues for foreign periodicals become unnecessary if the national library can acquire a comprehensive collection of the world's scientific periodical literature. In point of fact, libraries in Great Britain have come to rely almost entirely on the collections and efficient organiz- ation of the British Library Lending Division which provides a dependable, time saving and accurate service.

No less important than the bibliographical announcement of library stocks are the measures aimed at practical utilization of these stocks. The national library has always faced two controversial tasks. On the one hand it has to preserve its holdings for the coming generations; on the other hand it has to provide library service, *ie* to give libraries and users throughout the country an opportunity of using these holdings and relying upon them.

Some of the national libraries collect two (or more) copies of every new-published title of the national book production. One copy is kept as an inviolable archival emergency unit and is not used by readers. The second copy is handled freely and may be lent to users and sent through the interlibrary lending service.

Other national libraries have established a far-reaching interlibrary service covering the whole country, and readers' requests for items of the national book production are handled by some lending libraries which are not depository libraries. In this way the national library is freed from the risk of letting its deposit copies become worn and damaged through continuous use. This is the practice in Bulgaria, Finland, and elsewhere.

Some countries have adopted still another system: they have two national libraries, a reference library (where readers are permitted to use library materials on the premises only, and nothing can be taken out) and a lending library (where library materials are not used in the library building and everything is sent to users through the lending service). This is the system in Great Britain and Canada and will probably be adopted by USA too. However, the strict separation of these two functions and their assignment to two separate libraries is hardly economical and, in any case, financially impossible in small countries.

As is seen from the *Table 3*, nearly all national libraries in Europe (with the exception of the British Library Reference Division and the national libraries of France and Portugal) participate in the country's interlibrary lending by sending library materials of their own.

In most countries the national library combines the functions of a reference library with the functions of a lending library (with an established interlibrary lending service). It should be pointed out, however, that every national library must make a radical reorganization of its interlibrary lending service if it is to maintain its credit and prestige within the country's library system. A good example of how best to organize interlibrary lending is set by the British Library Lending Division[1] where the fulfilment of an order is effected within twenty four hours through a chain-process and with a minimum loss of time. It is true, of course, that interlibrary lending is the basic activity of the Lending Division, yet its methods and organization may be adopted by any national library without affecting the other functions of the library which are indeed numerous. To do so, however, new, modern equipment is needed (reprographic and telex machines of high quality and sufficient in number to meet all needs).

After the second world war the national library has been entrusted with more and more tasks which were not previously part of its traditional duties. In this paper an attempt has been made to examine some new problems the modern national library faces in connection with the acquisition of foreign literature and documentation for the requirements of the progress of science and technology in a country. This is one of the numerous tasks[16] the national library has to perform nowadays as a coordination and organization center for a modern library and bibliographic system which has developed beyond the old traditions — in the interests of the country's scientific, technical and cultural progress.

REFERENCES

1 MIKHAILOV A I: 'Tekhnicheskii progress i zadachi nauchnoi informatsii' *Vestnik AN SSSR* 1962 (2) pp 29-37.

2 *Science, government and information.* A report of the President's Science Advisory Committee, Washington. USGPO 1963.

3 URQUHART D J: 'Rising tide of paper' *Advancement of science 21* (91) 1964 pp 279-285.

4 PAGE B S *and* TUCKER P E: 'The Nuffield pilot survey of library use in the University of Leeds' *Journal of documentation 19* (1) 1959 pp 1-11.

5 TOTOK W: 'Die moderne Wissenschaft. Probleme ihrer organisation' *Borsenblatt der Deutschem Buchhandel 19* (88) 1964 pp 1966-73.

6 Higher Education Act of 1965 *US Statutes at Large 84* 1971 p 190.

7 *National Diet Library law* Tokyo — National Diet Library, 1961.

8 NATIONAL SCIENCE LIBRARY: *NRC Research News 20* (3) 1967 pp 10-11.

9 HOUGHTON B: *Out of the dinosaurs: the evolution of the National Lending Library for Science & Technology* London, Bingley; Hamden (Conn) Archon 1972.

10 *The British Library Act* London, HMSO 1972.

11 LIEBAERS H: 'Problems of library science and information. The Belgian experience' *A report to the International Symposium on European Library Systems* Prague 27 November — 2 December 1972.

12 'Dritte Durch fuhrungsbestimmung zur Verordnung uber die Aufgaben des Bibliothekssystems in der DDR' *Gesetzblatt der DDR* Teil II (81) 1970.

13 ORTEL D: 'Das Bibliothekswesen der Bundersrepublik Deutsch-

land.' *A report to the International Symposium on European Library Systems* Prague 27 November − 2 December 1972.

14 BIRKELUND P: 'The research library system in Denmark: The Royal Library in Copenhagen', *Ibid.*

15 KOZELEK K: 'Funktsiya gosudarstvannoi biblioteki CSR v sistemy chekhskogo bibliotechnogo dela', *Ibid.*

16 KALAIDZIEVA K: 'Rolya i funktsii na natsionalnata biblioteka v bibliotechnata sistema na evropeiskite strani' *Izvestiya na Narodna biblioteka 'Kiril i Metodi' 13* (19) 1974 pp 11-51.

Table I   Statistics of the acquisition of

Country	Annual acquisition of		
	Country's annual book production	foreign literature	
		books (monographs)	periodicals
1	2	3	4
Austria	4781	41237	12679
Belgium	4414	73000	17000
Bulgaria	5000	15000	12000
Czechoslovakia	9041	30285	10500
Denmark	5052	RL 40000	12000
		UL	
Finland	5595	29000	4700
France	22935	22000	6000
German Dem. Rep.	5234	DBu 81723	
		DSB 53167	10043
German Fed. Rep.	45369	DB 105000	30000
		SB 60000	25000
Great Britain	33441	BM 120000	46000
		NLL 92400	40000
Hungary	5238	40638	2665
Netherlands	11159	17000	2500
Norway	4295	25000	6400
Poland	10038	18000	7000
Portugal	5956		
Rumania	7681	17000	7000
Spain	19717	6300	950
Sweden	5543	18000	9067
Switzerland	8321	43415	5700
Turkey	5854	2781	522
USSR	78899	242246	14000
Yugoslavia	8119		

Explanations: RL = Royal Library; UL = University Library; DBu = Deutsche Bucherei;
SSB = Deutsche Staatbibliothek; DB = Deutsche Bibliothek;
DB = Deutsche Bibliothek; SB = Staatsbibliothek der Stiftung
Preuszischer Kulturbesitz;
BM = British Museum; NLL = National Lending Library.

literature by the national libraries of Europe

Scope of acquisition of foreign literature	Acquisition of official publications?	Depository library of international organisation?	Total stocks in millions of volumes
5	6	7	8
humanities	yes	yes	2
encyclopedia	yes	yes	2
encyclopedia	yes	yes	1.5
encyclopedia	yes	yes	4.1
humanities	yes	yes	1.7
science			0.385
humanities		no	1.2
humanities	yes	yes	6
Germanica	yes	yes	3.5
encyclopedia	yes	yes	4.5
Germanica	yes	yes	1.4
encyclopedia	yes	yes	2.5
encyclopedia	yes	yes	7
encyclopedia	yes	yes	1
humanities		no	1.2
humanities			1
humanities	yes	yes	1.9
humanities	yes	yes	2
encyclopedia	yes	no	1
encyclopedia	yes	yes	4
humanities	yes	no	2
encyclopedia	yes	yes	3.5
Helvetica	no		1
humanities	yes	yes	0.5
encylopedia	yes	yes	25
humanities	does not collect foreign literature		

Sources of information: Col 2: UNESCO: *Statistical yearbook* 1971. Paris, UNESCO 1972, 890pp.
Col 4, 6 & 7: Questionnaire sent in February 1973 by the Cyril and Methodius National Library to national libraries of Europe.
Col 5: *International library directory.* 3rd ed London, Wales 1969/70, 1222pp.
Col 8: Inquiry into the state of national libraries conducted by the IFLA Section of National and University Libraries in 1971.

Table II Participation of the National Library in the preparation of
Accession Bulletins and Union Catalogues

Country	Current accessions bulletins	Union Catalogues			
		printed catalogues		card catalogues	
		books	periodicals	books	periodicals
Austria	no	no	yes	yes	no
Belgium	yes	no	yes (c)	no	no
Bulgaria	yes	no	yes (c)	yes	no
Czechoslovakia	no	yes (c)	yes (c)	yes	no
Denmark	yes		yes		
Finland	no	yes	yes	no	no
France	yes, but not by NL	no	yes	yes	yes
German Dem. Rep.	yes	no	yes (c)	yes	yes
German Fed. Rep.	no	no	no	yes	yes
Great Britain	no	no	yes (c)	no	yes
Hungary	yes	yes	yes	yes	no
The Netherlands	yes	yes	yes		
Norway	yes	no	yes	yes	yes
Poland	yes	yes	yes (c) in preparation	yes	yes
Portugal	no	no	no	no	yes
Rumania	yes	yes	yes annual	yes	yes
Spain	yes	yes	yes	yes	yes
Sweden	yes	yes	no	yes	no
Switzerland	no	no	yes	yes	no
Turkey	no	no	no	no	yes
USSR	yes	yes	yes		no
Yugoslavia	no	yes	yes	no	no (in the charge of The Bibliographical Institute)

c = computerized

Table III Participation of the National Library in the country's interlibrary lending

Country	Does the national library lend originals contained in its collections	If not, does it supply microfilms, photo and xerox copies	Does it lend or supply both types of materials	Number of copy machines	Is there a photocopying service at the nat library	Is there a telex at the nat library	Is interlibrary lending organized by the nat library
Austria	yes	yes	yes	4	yes	yes	yes
Belgium	yes	yes	yes	6	yes	yes	yes
Bulgaria	yes	yes	yes	3	yes	yes	yes
Czechoslovakia	yes	yes	yes	4	yes	yes	yes
Denmark						yes	
Finland	yes, only foreign materials	yes	yes	5	yes	yes	no
France	no	yes	no	3	yes	no	yes
German Dem. Rep.	DSB: yes DBu: yes	yes	yes	4	yes	yes	yes
German Fed. Rep.	DB: yes StB: yes	yes	yes	6 2	no	no	yes
Great Britain	BM: No NLL: yes	yes	no	42	yes	yes	yes
Hungary	yes	yes	no	3	yes	yes	yes
The Netherlands					yes	yes	
Norway	yes	yes	yes	5	yes	yes	yes
Poland	yes	yes	yes	5	yes	yes	yes
Portugal	no	yes	no	1	no	no	no
Rumania	yes	yes	yes	1	yes	yes	no
Spain	yes	yes	yes	3	yes	no	yes
Sweden	yes	yes	yes	7	yes	yes	yes
Switzerland	yes	yes	yes	2	yes	yes	yes
Turkey	yes	yes	yes	2	yes	yes	yes
USSR	yes	yes	yes	4	yes	yes	yes
Yugoslavia	Each of the six federated republics of Yugoslavia has a national library and each library participates in the country's interlibrary lending.						

The Role of the National Bibliographic Centre

DOROTHY ANDERSON

THE NATIONAL LIBRARY AND ITS BIBLIOGRAPHIC FUNCTIONS: AN ORGANIZATIONAL PROBLEM

AT THE APEX of the library structure in many countries of the world stands a national library, distinguished by the dignity of its building, the richness of its collections, the wealth of its resources, and the quality of its scholarship. There are national libraries with historical foundations dating back centuries, even to the fifteenth (France) and the sixteenth (Austria) centuries, and whose origins reflect the early enthusiasm for learning of a prince, emperor, or president. Other national libraries, including those in Mexico, Venezuela and Belgium, were established in that enlightened period of national liberation, the nineteenth century. In the past thirty years new national libraries have been created, like those of the nineteenth century, as "an expression of emergent nationalism . . . in the wake of a series of 'national' type institutions like a national archives, a national theatre, or a national museum."[1]

Indeed, the national library has been regarded as an institution familiar but possibly aloof; as a symbol of old-style scholarship and of a more leisurely way of life; and as the pinnacle of, yet somewhat unrelated to, the national library scene below. This was the old-fashioned portrait which is now outdated. In the past twenty years, the image has changed as dramatically as have the role and activities of the national library. Yet, it is still surprising that the role and functions of the national library have only recently come under scrutiny and analysis; only in the past ten years have the national libraries in a number of countries emerged from traditional dignity and obscure scholarship to become leaders in national library development. If this is an accurate reflection of changes in librarians' attitudes and in

Dorothy Anderson is Director, IFLA International Office for UBC.

Reprinted from *Library Trends*, vol. 25, no. 3, January 1977, p. 645-63, by permission of the author and the publisher. Copyright by the Board of Trustees of the University of Illinois.

library technology, it is also revealing to note the chronology of analysis and its documentation. Investigation of national libraries originated with *Library Trends* in 1955, but the emphasis then was on resources rather than on activities: ". . . maintained primarily at public cost with funds allotted from, and disbursed by, national treasuries."[2]

The Symposium on National Libraries in Europe, held in Vienna in 1958, inaugurated the study of the role of the national library and expounded on its functions and its duties. In his working paper for the symposium, Frank Francis of the British Museum expressed its basic purpose and in so doing defined "the national library in any country as the library which has the duty of collecting and preserving for posterity the written production of that country."[3] All other duties stem from that basis.

Nearly twenty years later that duty remains fundamental. Indeed, recent emphasis has been to strengthen that basis, for the national library is now seen as the key to the management of "national bibliographic control"—a rephrasing of Francis's definition. The national library is expected to watch over, collect, preserve, record, and advertise book and nonbook materials which make up the national imprint.

From the examinations of the national library in the issue of *Library Trends* and at the symposium in Vienna emerged an analysis both of the functions already being performed by some national libraries and of the other activities which clearly should come within their scope. The following conclusions of the symposium are relevant in consideration of the present concept of national bibliographic control:

> It is the responsibility of the national library to acquire and conserve the whole of the national production of printed material . . . and it should be responsible for co-ordinating efforts to obtain the foreign literature the country requires. The national library should promote the adoption in its own country of common rules for the compilation of catalogues. The national library is responsible for the bibliographical services of its own country . . . to undertake the production of current national bibliographies.[4]

More probing and analysis from dedicated national and university librarians followed. Significant was the paper by Kenneth W. Humphries prepared for the 1964 International Federation of Library Associations (IFLA) General Council, in which he identified fifteen functions which the national library should perform.[5] Three years later in a report on university libraries in the United Kingdom, a chapter devoted to the national library began:

> It has been extremely difficult for us to relate the position of the university library to the national library scene for a variety of reasons of which the fundamental one is that there is no true apex to the library system of the country. In comparison with the organisation of libraries in other countries which have a national library, Britain is especially wanting in this respect.

The functions were then set out, the first six being the "fundamental duties":

(a) The outstanding and central collection of a nation's literature.
(b) The most important collection of books received under legal deposit or under the terms of the Copyright Act.
(c) The fullest coverage of foreign literature.
(d) The publication of the national bibliography.
(e) The national bibliographical information centre.
(f) The publication of catalogues of material in the National Library and in the country's libraries.[6]

Another seven functions, it was agreed, could be carried out by the national library or, if necessary, could be undertaken by other bibliographic agencies. These functions have been accepted and repeated in countries all over the world as national libraries have been created or restructured to meet new demands of information and service. These fundamental functions are cited in numerous reports of national library commissions or international experts. For example, the *Resumé and Recommendations* of the National Seminar on Library Development in Pakistan notes them as "the modern standard of a national library," but concludes that by these criteria, the national library of Pakistan "seems to be non-existent at the moment."[7]

Acceptance of these functions bestows on the national library the additional role of leader of the national library community: it should give guidance and assistance, experiment, undertake research, and be actively committed to supporting the national library community by interpreting its needs and relating them to the rest of the world. The national library is therefore visualised as having a double role: (1) as the apex of the national library structure, and (2) as the head of the national library system. In one sense, this dual role is exemplified in the six fundamental functions. The first three duties are concerned with the national library per se, the physical objects or "information carriers" that make up its collections, and users of those collections; the other three functions are devoted to the recording and describing of information carriers. Together, these aspects make up the whole of national bibliographic control. Lawrence G. Livingston, Program Officer of the Council on Library Resources, expressd the concept geometrically in a paper prepared for the 1974 U.S. Conference on National Bibliographic Control:

> National Bibliographic Control can be considered as a continuum of parallel lines, one line being drawn by the item of literature itself as it progresses from the mind of the author. . . . The other line is followed by the surrogate for the item, its bibliographic record. The first line is straightforward. . . . It is the line of path followed by the surrogate and the surrogate itself which is of vital concern.[8]

The national library is concerned with both the "item of literature" in its physical form and its "surrogate" or bibliographic record. The functions are different for each, and it is an organisational matter to realize how best they can be performed with a minimum of duplicated effort within one institution.

As the key to the improvement and development of national bibliographic control, the national library can also be considered as the national component in the international communications system which we define as Universal Bibliographic Control (UBC). Again, the national library is concerned internationally with both the item and its surrogate, the bibliographic record. The third function of the national library, noted earlier, is to maintain the country's "fullest coverage of foreign literature." In order to do this successfully, access to the bibliographic records of publications of other countries is required. Advances in library technology in the past ten years offer new possibilities: first, in rapid access to those records, and second, in simplified integration of the records themselves into national catalogues. The development of library mechanisation has widened the library's horizons: it is now possible to imagine a network of mechanised national library systems using the same standards of bibliographic recording and rapid exchange of records. This is the basis of UBC: to avoid duplication of effort internationally by recording information in accordance with international standards for easy acceptance in other library systems.

The administrative and organisational problem is how to create a unit within a national library that can handle bibliographic records in both a national and international context. The solution offered is the national bibliographic centre:

> It is therefore suggested that the national component of the UBC system should normally be the national library receiving all types of published documentary material by legal deposit and hence maintaining the national collection; and that within the national library the functions relating.to national bibliographic control should be performed by an organizational unit, the national bibliographic agency, which will make the authoritative bibliographic record for each item added to that collection, and will carry out all the functions associated with the production of the record: that is, produce the national bibliography and maintain authority files of national authors' names.[9]

(For "national bibliographic agency," read "national bibliographic centre." For some purely terminological reason, *agency* has slipped in popularity; perhaps because it has noninstitutional connotations, *centre* has prevailed.) At the Liber Meeting on Co-operative Cataloguing, Strasbourg, 1972, participants were concerned with the demands of European research libraries in acquiring material from other countries. The same solution was presented:

> Each country should have an official Bibliographic Centre which would be responsible for compiling and making available a complete machine readable record of the country's own output of publications, and for obtaining and distributing within its own country information from the corresponding records of other countries.[10]

If the national library is at the apex of a country's library system, then in terms of its national bibliographic control, the national bibliographic centre is its nexus.[11] It looks inward to provide a service to the country's libraries; it looks outward to interpret for and serve as provider from the outside world.

AN OUTLINE OF SOME EXISTING NATIONAL SOLUTIONS

The national library has been defined and its importance stated as the key to national bibliographic control, and as the national component of the international communications system concept of UBC. There is no insistence, however, that there be one model of a national library, or that its bibliographic services be performed only by a national bibliographic centre. The objectives of national bibliographic control are the same in any country, but differing national literary and publishing histories have resulted in different bibliographic traditions—and consequently, in the creation of varying types of institutions to carry out bibliographic tasks. It is of primary importance that the functions be carried out, whatever the institutional pattern of a national library system. In presenting a structure of national library and subordinate national bibliographic centre, however, we are suggesting an organisational arrangement which appears to offer maximum efficiency and minimum duplication.

In considering the relationship of national to universal bibliographic control, it is revealing to note the changes in organisational structure that are now taking place in a number of countries with firmly established bibliographic traditions and long-established institutions. One of the most recent is the creation within the Bibliothèque nationale (Paris) of a new organisational unit, the Centre bibliographique national, which will take on functions hitherto performed by departments of the Bibliothèque nationale, including production of the national bibliography.[12] In the United Kingdom, following the analysis of the Parry report,[13] came the Dainton report recommending the establishment of a national library.[14] The creation of the British Library from six existing institutions followed; within the British Library is the Bibliographic Services Division, which includes among its functions those of a national bibliographic centre.[15]

Awareness of a vacuum in the existing pattern has led to examination and rethinking in the United States:

> Except for the Library of Congress, the United States does not possess an official national bibliographic center to coordinate the processing and distribution of standard bibliographic records for the use of all libraries and information centers. The current complex pattern of bibliographic services consists of a multiplicity of organizations, in the public and private sectors, providing a variety of products and services. National bibliographic control is needed to identify items of recorded information in all media, to provide intellectual access to each such item of information, and to standardize the processing and communication of relevant data.[16]

The proposition has been put to the American library community: Can the library which was specifically established to serve Congress take on officially the role which it has already been performing? The

Library of Congress has, both de facto and in its relationships to the international library community, been acting as the national library, and its Processing Department has been carrying out the functions of a national bibliographic centre.[17] Following the discussions at the conference in April 1974[18] has been the establishment of the Advisory Group on National Bibliographic Control with the formation of working groups to locate and solve particular bibliographic problems (e.g., journal articles, technical reports, and name authority files). Each project is conceived as "efforts leading towards the development of some of the building blocks from which ultimately will evolve a national system."[19] The advisory group further stated that: "The Library of Congress is the logical agency to become the national bibliographic node in the evolving national network for libraries and information science."[20]

Bibliographic traditions and established institutions can sometimes prevail over the simple and straightforward solution, however. In the Netherlands, the search to establish a new national bibliography—the current bibliography has been produced commercially under the title of its publisher *Brinkman's Cumulative Catalogus*—has indicated its establishment within the framework of a national bibliographic centre, and the concurrent introduction of deposit laws. Administrative problems have unfortunately impeded the proposals, but in 1974 the Ministry of Science and Education provided financial support to conduct preliminary studies to determine both the role of a Dutch bibliographic centre and to which existing institution it should be attached. It has proven to be difficult to convince the publishing and library community of the value of a system of legal deposit when it has managed for so long without one.[21] Meanwhile, discussions are underway to improve the quality of the entries in *Brinkman's*.

In newer countries a conflict can arise because of demands on the national library to extend its functions to include those usually undertaken by public libraries. The national library may be as new as the national library system; the emphasis on it may thus be not as a library of "last resort," but how its creation can assist local libraries: "The greater association of the national library with the development of public library services, hitherto poorly developed, would be a logical development in Southeast Asian countries and should be actively pursued."[22] Under community pressure, the national library's commitment to national and international bibliographic control may be whittled away and the production of the national bibliography given low priority in staffing and services. A volume recording 1972 imprints, if it appears in 1976, may be a fine retrospective reference tool, but it is of little value as an acquisition and cataloguing tool. The solution is simple: "The charge that national libraries of this nature do not function effectively, either as national or as public libraries, could be overcome simply through improved staffing and finance, without which both aspects of service would function below par even if kept separate."[23]

By contrast, the establishment of a professional unit undertaking the functions of a national bibliographic centre may precede the establishment of a national library; it may even be considered as one means of forcing a government's dilatory hand. For example, librarians of the four English-speaking countries in the Caribbean reached agreement in 1974 to establish national bibliographies and to carry out other bibliographic services. In Guyana, the National Library (previously the Public Library) was already fulfilling this task; in the others, the new functions were accepted by libraries which, although designated as national libraries, had not officially been given the necessary resources.[24] New and enterprising is the proposal made by a group of Kenyan librarians to establish a national bibliographic centre before and in lieu of the formation of a national library. It would perforce have to be an independent unit under the auspices of the Kenyan Library Association. From its inception, however, it should seek government endorsement, if not government finance, in order to fit easily into a national library plan at some later stage.[25]

Just as national libraries differ in history and administrative structure, so do the units that undertake bibliographic functions. In Copenhagen, for example, the Kongelige Bibliotek (Royal Library) has been receiving Danish books by deposit law since 1697; Denmark's Royal Library and the Universitetbiblioteket (University Library) are organized as one administrative unit under the Office of the National Librarian. The Danish national bibliography, however, is prepared and published by the Bibliotekscentralen (Danish Library Bureau) in cooperation with the Royal Library and a private publisher. Other functions of the Bibliotekscentralen focus on public libraries and include supplying furniture and equipment. The Bibliotekscentralen has been producing the national bibliography in mechanised form since January 1976, but it is not yet certain if the other functions of the national bibliographic centre will be carried out by the automation department of the Royal Library, or by some new unit which will combine with the Bibliotekscentralen.[26]

In other countries tradition has divided collections according to type; the functions of the national library consequently may be split among different libraries. This situation immediately presents problems in the national and international functioning of the bibliographic centre. In the German Democratic Republic, for example, the Deutsche Bücherei in Leipzig collects German-language materials from all sources and in all subjects, and the Deutsche Staatsbibliothek in Berlin performs its function of collecting foreign literature in all subjects. Various series of the national bibliography are produced by the Deutsche Bücherei; thus the link between national and international exchange is not immediately apparent. In the Federal Republic of Germany there are three major libraries: the Deutsche Bibliothek at Frankfurt-am-Main, the Staatsbibliothek Preussischer Kulturbesitz in Berlin, and the Bayerische Staatsbibliothek in Munich. The Deutsche Bibliothek concentrates on German-language material and publishes the national bibliography, thus serving as the national bibliographic agency for German-language bibliographic records and as a receiving centre for records produced in other countries.[27]

The acquisition of foreign literature in Europe is extensive, particularly for the smaller countries which depend on English-language publications from the United States or the United Kingdom for literature in some subject fields. In Denmark, for example, a country with a long tradition of using literature from other countries, the annual book production is about 5,000 titles, and the number of overseas monographic publications received yearly in the Royal Library is about 40,000. Annual book production in Switzerland is about 8,000 titles, and the National Library aims to acquire annually from other countries more than 43,000 monographs and nearly 6,000 periodicals.[28] Sweden expects in the near future to make use of the tapes recording American, British, French and German publications and thus to have available the records of some 75 percent of the overseas acquisitions.[29] If there are a number of libraries within a country that are building special collections of foreign literature, it would be even more essential that some national bibliographic centre act for all the libraries in obtaining records.

A MODEL SOLUTION: THE NATIONAL BIBLIOGRAPHIC CENTRE AND ITS FUNCTIONS

If the primary purpose of the national library is to build and conserve the national collection, the primary objective of the national bibliographic centre is to produce the comprehensive bibliographic records of the national imprint. All of its other activities evolve from that basis. To perform this primary task, the first requirements of the centre are:

1. To obtain access to the physical items themselves (books, serials, etc.). It is legitimate to assume that the entries in the national bibliography are created from the items themselves, not from information found on book jackets, publishers' lists or advance notices. (Hence, the advantage of the national bibliographic centre's attachment to the national library is that the items deposited by law can be shelved for readers after they have been described.)
2. To establish accepted standards for making the comprehensive bibliographic record, standards both for the content of the record and for the physical forms in which it appears.

These requirements have two implications: (1) the development and acceptance of national cataloguing rules which will prevail throughout the country, and (2) if the record is to have exchange value, some international basis for national cataloguing codes. At the moment the situation is complex and far from perfect, but not unworkable. Although no international code exists, most of the national and multinational codes in use are based on the Paris Principles[30] and many have incorporated accepted international practices such as the International Standard Bibliographic Description for Monographic Publications (ISBD(M)).[31]

Bibliographic records more often appear in the form of entries in issues of a printed national bibliography, proof slips or catalogue cards, or in machine-readable forms such as computer tapes. Printed national bibliographies vary in style, size and layout as much as do national imprints and national resources. Nevertheless, if the style and content of the entries satisfy international and national requirements, then those printed issues are acceptable whatever their form.

For catalogue cards there is already an internationally accepted standard for size. More important is the possibility in the future of making bibliographic records in machine-readable form in accordance with accepted international standards; the developing network of mechanised national library systems is working on some of the problems that must be solved for its effective operation. The draft of the international communications format (UNIMARC) through which exchange can be made is in its final stages,[32] while national processing formats are operational in a number of countries.

From the primary function of the national bibliographic centre, it is apparent that other tasks should be undertaken as natural corollaries. First (because it follows so closely from the preparation of the bibliographic record) is the maintenance of the authority list of national authors' names. In the United States, one working group has been specifically assigned the task of working out the format for an authority list file.[33] In the Netherlands, consideration is being given to a numeric coding device which will be allocated to each author; maintenance of this device will be one of the functions of the new bibliographic centre when it is established.[34]

The national bibliographic centre is best equipped when making the record to ascertain the author's requirements with regard to name usage: this emphasises the basic contention that each country has the knowledge to deal best with its authors' names, whether corporate or personal, and that such an operation in a country where name patterns are fluid can in itself have a standardising influence. Experience has shown the problems at the international level of trying to establish and maintain large-scale authority lists (for example, the International Nuclear Information Systems' preparation and use of its lists of corporate bodies[35]), and it is recognised that each country can best decide the definitive form for its own organisations. In some countries—Singapore is one example—national libraries have already produced authoritative lists of such bodies. At present, however, there is much national variation in determining forms of corporate body names as presented in bibliographic records; acceptance of the simple recommendations made by Verona[36] could help to form an international basis for future national decisions.

One unit of the national bibliographic centre can be the centre for the registration of serials as the national contributing organ of the International Serials Data System (ISDS). The majority of the national serial centres already established are within national libraries and specifically are within their bibliographic divisions. Responsibilities of this unit are both national and international in nature: (1) to record new serials for the national bibliography, and (2) to report new titles to the ISDS centre in Paris. Similarly, the national bibliographic centre can house the national International Standard Book Number (ISBN) agency. The use of ISBN is not yet worldwide, depending as it does on the existence of an organized book trade, but its value to library operations is revealed by the fact that eleven national libraries house national ISBN agencies.[37] Inclusion of the ISBN as an essential element in bibliographic records is likely to enhance its use, and may also encourage the spread of national agencies in national libraries.

Cataloguing-In-Publication (CIP) schemes are underway in a number of countries and in experimental form in others. The basis for these schemes is the demand for speed in producing bibliographic records. It is natural that CIP operations should take place within the national bibliographic centre as part of the cataloguing process.

The function of maintaining national union catalogues has long been carried out conscientiously by national libraries in a number of countries. Essentially, this is a national service relating to national bibliographic control, not so much in the location of holdings but rather in its identification of items which, for a variety of reasons, have not been recorded in the national bibliography. As a retrospective record of national publications and national holdings, its value is immense, but maintenance has been a physical labour that has been proving impossible to perform satisfactorily. There are two possibilities for future improvement. The first possibility is that increased use of national records (i.e., the national bibliographic centre's provision of a centralized cataloguing service) may bring about less variation in incorporating entries. The second possibility is more encouraging from the housekeeping point of view: if union catalogue records can be presented in machine-readable form, the burden of maintenance will be alleviated. The national authority list can also contribute significantly in standardising entries.[38]

Another activity within the province of the national bibliographic centre is the maintenance of the office of deposited publications (the "Copyright Office"). If it is economical to make the description of a publication immediately after its deposit and registration, the national bibliographic centre could supervise the deposit office and, given the necessary instruments, undertake enforcement operations. In many countries, revision of legal deposit is being considered; new laws may strengthen enforcement provisions, as well as extend the range of material to be deposited.[39]

It is apparent from this outline that the national bibliographic centre, if it is to undertake its primary functions and to perform its corollary roles, has another basic requirement: professional expertise and adequate staff and technological resources. The staff of the national bibliographic centre plays an important role nationally in activities relating to cataloguing and classifying. This role consists of: (1) providing leadership in experiment and research in mechanisation, (2) promoting cooperation with publishers, and (3) ensuring awareness of what is happening internationally in order to be able to interpret locally decisions that are made internationally, and to report on trends in other countries. Research, experimentation, and public relations are all facets of the work of the centre, and accompanying these duties are the responsibility to the national library community and a need for sensitivity in relating to its demands.

References

1.   Wijasuriya, D.E.K., *et al. The Barefoot Librarian; Library Development in Southeast Asia with Special Reference to Malaysia.* London, Clive Bingley, 1975, p. 99.

2.   Mearns, David C. "Summary," *Library Trends* 4:96, July 1955.

3.   Francis, Frank C. "The Organization of National Libraries." *In* Symposium on National Libraries in Europe, Vienna, 1958. *National Libraries: Their Problems and Prospects.* Paris, Unesco, 1960, p. 21.

4.   "Main Conclusions and Recommendations." *In* Symposium on National Libraries . . ., *op. cit.,* pp. 112-13.

5.   Humphreys, Kenneth W. "The Role of the National Library: A Preliminary Statement," *Libri* 14:356-68, 1964.

6.   Great Britain. University Grants Committee. *Report of the Committee on Libraries.* London, HMSO, 1967, p. 81. (Known as Parry report.)

7.   [Pakistan] Society for the Promotion and Improvement of Libraries. *National Seminar on Library Development in Pakistan: Resumé and Recommendations.* Karachi, Pakistan, Society for the Promotion and Improvement of Libraries, 1975, p. 38.

8.   Livingston, Lawrence G. "National Bibliographic Control; A Challenge," *Library of Congress Information Bulletin* 33:A109, June 21, 1974.

9.   Anderson, Dorothy. *Universal Bibliographic Control.* Pullach bei München, Verlag Dokumentation, 1974, p. 31.

10.   "Cataloguing News," *International Cataloguing* 1:3, July/Sept. 1972.

11.   *See* "Nexus." In *Oxford English Dictionary.* Vol. VII. Oxford, Clarendon Press, 1961, p. 123.

12.   Pelletier, Monique. Personal communication, April 1976.

13.   Great Britain, University Grants Committee, *op. cit.*

14.   Great Britain. National Libraries Committee. *Report of the National Libraries Committee.* London, HMSO, 1969, p. 158. (Known as Dainton report.)

15.   British Library. *Second Annual Report 1974-75.* London, British Library Board, 1975, pp. 14-16.

16.   National Commission on Libraries and Information Science. *Toward a National Program for Library and Information Services: Goals for Action.* Washington, D.C., NCLIS, 1975, p. 38.

17.   U.S. Library of Congress. "The Library of Congress as the National Bibliographic Center," *Library of Congress Information Bulletin* 34:265, 267+, June 27, 1975.

18.   Anderson, *op. cit.*

19.   U.S. Advisory Group on National Bibliographic Control. "Working Parties of the Advisory Group on National Bibliographic Control," *Library of Congress Information Bulletin* 34:A219, Sept. 12, 1975.

20.   *Ibid.,* p. A221.

21. Heijligers, A. and Owen, J. Mackenzie. "Bibliographic Control in the Netherlands." *In* R. E. Coward and M. Yelland, eds. *The Interchange of Bibliographic Information in Machine Readable Form* (Western European Seminar on the Interchange of Bibliographic Information in Machine Readable Form, 1974). London, Library Association, 1975, pp. 41-43.

22. Wijasuriya, *et al., op. cit.*, p. 100.

23. *Ibid.*

24. Regional Workshop on National Bibliographies of the English-speaking Caribbean—November 25-29, 1974. "Resolutions." "Be it resolved that: 1. The four territories represented at this Workshop implement immediately the decisions taken and recorded in the documents approved at the Workshop with regard to the production of their national bibliographies. 2. In view of the decision taken by the Inaugural Meeting of the Conference of Heads of Government of the Caribbean Community to establish and/or designate national libraries, the representatives of each territory should bring to the attention of their respective governments that the decisions taken in Resolution 1 are based on the realization of the establishment of four national bibliographic centres. In the light of this it is recommended that some action be taken to seek acknowledgment of status, legal and otherwise, of the four national bibliographic centres and in particular of the Editorial Boards in carrying out their functions."

25. "Bibliographical Services Throughout the World: Kenya," *Bibliography, Documentation, Terminology* 15:333, Nov. 1975.

26. Hedberg, Sten. "Current Developments in Scandinavia," *In* Coward and Yelland, *op. cit.*, pp. 11-16.

27. Kohl, Ernst. "Current Developments in Germany and Austria." *In* Coward and Yelland, *op. cit.*, pp. 24-31.

28. Kalaidzieva, N. "Tasks and Duties of the Modern National Library in Building up Stocks of Foreign Literature and Documentation for the Country's Library System." *In* Keith Barr and Maurice Line, eds. *Essays on Information and Libraries.* London, Clive Blingley, and Hamden, Conn., Linnet Books, 1975, pp. 89-103.

29. Hedberg, *op. cit.*, p. 19.

30. International Conference on Cataloguing Principles. Paris, 9th-18th, October 1961. *Statement of Principles.* Annotated ed., with commentary and examples by Eva Verona. London, IFLA Committee on Cataloguing, 1971.

31. Anderson, Dorothy. "The Future of the *Anglo-American Cataloging Rules (AACR)* in the Light of Universal Bibliographic Control (UBC)," *Library Resources & Technical Services* 20:1-15, Winter 1976.

32. The revised UNIMARC format prepared by the IFLA Working Group on Content Designators will be available in March 1977.

33. Advisory Group on National Bibliographic Control, *op. cit.*, pp. A220-21.

34. Van Wesemael, A. L. "Some Remarks on Netherland's PICA Project; State of Art and the Problem of the Authority File." In *Neure Formate für Verarbeitung und Austausch bibliographischer Daten* (Bericht eines Symposiums, veranstaltet von der Arbeitsstelle für Bibliothekstechnik 30 April 1974). Pullach bei München, Verlag Dokumentation, 1975, pp. 50-55.

35. DEVSIS Study Team. DEVSIS: The Preliminary Design of an Inter-

national Information System for the Development Sciences. Provisional Text. [Geneva,] DEVSIS Study Team, 1975, p. 126.

36.   Verona, Eva. *Corporate Headings; Their Use in Library Catalogues and National Bibliographies; A Comparative and Critical Study.* London, IFLA Committee on Cataloguing, 1975.

37.   A survey of ISBN usage in these national libraries has been undertaken by the IFLA UBC Office. *See* R. Kerr's interim report in *Bulletin of the International ISBN Agency, Berlin.* (In press.)

38.   Canadian Task Group on Cataloguing Standards. *Cataloguing Standards.* Ottawa, National Library of Canada, 1972, p. 16.

39.   A survey of existing deposit laws is being undertaken. by Dr. G. Pomassl, Deutsche Bücherei, Leipzig, as background paper for the Unesco/IFLA International Congress on National Bibliographies in 1977.

Pp. 657-661, containing a section on 'Problems within the solution: the interrelationship of international and national demands', deal with such matters as the content of the bibliographic record, Cataloguing in Publication, and the international exchange of computer tapes.

NATIONAL LIBRARIES

Extracts from the proceedings of the
University and Research Section Conference
held at Bangor, April 1963

This is the bulk of R.A. Wilson's prepared contribution to a discussion on Ib Magnussen's paper (see pp. 205-222 of this volume).

I want to talk chiefly about something basic and comparatively limited—the duty of a national library to collect and conserve the whole of the nation's book production for the benefit of future generations: the task that, as Dr. Magnussen has already mentioned, was accepted at Vienna as one of the primary functions of a national library; the function that is so often taken for granted.

This archival function is necessarily in conflict with the duty of the library to give the best possible service to the contemporary user. This is, of course, a commonplace: all librarians, not merely national librarians, are well aware of it. But the conflict is more acute in the national library. Just how acute must vary from country to country, according to the general pattern of library provision. Is there a sufficiency of good public reference libraries? Are there good specialized libraries? Is the lending system separate, as in Britain, or is lending a function of the national library, as in Scandinavia?

However much the position may vary, the duty is at its most onerous in the national library, and it becomes more so as other libraries grow fuller. For as libraries grow fuller, the pressure on space grows more acute and the impulse to relieve space problems by discarding grows stronger. I know that university libraries have not, generally, reached this point, at least in this country, and that intermediate measures are possible for relieving the pressure, such as the establishment of joint depositories; but ultimately it will be the national library that is expected to hold on to a copy of a book, even if it has to outhouse a

Reprinted from NATIONAL LIBRARIES: extracts from the proceedings of the University and Research Section Conference held at Bangor, April 1963. London: Library Association, 1963, p. 35-40, by permission of the publisher.

part of its collections. There is already a widespread assumption in quite a number of British libraries that it is not necessary to keep something that is no longer likely to be called for, because, after all, there will be a copy in the British Museum.

I am not for one moment saying that this should not be so, but if it is true, then the duty of conservation becomes for the national library more important in relation to a given book as time goes on. The likelihood of destruction or disappearance of other copies increases constantly. Anyone who has had anything to do with the task of trying to replace wartime losses will have learned how difficult this task may prove, even in the case of comparatively modern and intrinsically not very valuable books.

If this duty of conservation rightly rests upon the national library, two things follow.

First, its staff must include experts in the means of conservation. It should be the centre of research into the technical side of the task; it should be able to advise others not only on how to preserve books, but on how to preserve maps and films, on how to carry out repairs and minimize the damage that constant use of the material is bound, in the long run, to cause, and slow down the gradual deterioration that, even in the best designed and managed libraries, is one of the worst enemies of the book.

Secondly, the national library must be so planned that the optimum conditions prevail in its own premises. This is not so easy as it seems because the conflict between the two purposes, conservation and reference, makes itself felt in the sphere of physical planning. No one, I think, would nowadays deny the desirability of a certain amount of open access, and a very considerable increase in the open access facilities has been allowed for in the schedule of requirements drawn up for the new Library to be built opposite the present British Museum. It is not possible, however, nor is it desirable, to place the whole of a vast library of this size on open access. There must be very extensive closed stacks. In fact it must be recognized that every book in a national library may eventually become a rare book, that the election pamphlets of 1910 are already, so to speak, well on their way to becoming Thomason tracts, and that all must be given the full 'archive' treatment.

Much has been said in the last 15 years or so about the need for flexibility in the internal design of libraries. The various floors, it is said, should be planned in such a way that they can be used for staff or for stacks or for small reading rooms, and there are various examples, quite effective examples, where this aim has been achieved. But if the aim is to conserve the books, it is not quite so easy. Books should, we believe, be kept at a temperature between 55° and 60° Fahrenheit (say, between 13° and 15° Centigrade). Neither your readers nor your staff are going to be pleased if they are forced to work in that temperature. I have recently been discussing with an American librarian this very problem, the problem of keeping both readers and books comfortable, if I may put it that way. As you know, investigations have been going on and are still going on into the causes of the deterioration of paper, especially that of books published between, say, about 1870 and 1920. This deterioration has been in some cases extremely rapid in American libraries. I do not want to anticipate the results of these investigations, but I shall be surprised if they do not lead to the conclusion that the practice of housing readers and books together in one area, kept at a temperature dictated by the comfort of the reader, has something to do with it. It is interesting to learn that in one great American university where a new library is now being planned, the first consideration is apparently to be the provision of a stack designed strictly as a stack with conditions as suitable as possible for the conservation of the contents.

If the main collections of a national library are to be housed in a closed stack, this immediately brings to the forefront of planning considerations the question of communications. Of course, every librarian knows how important this question is, but the point—the rather obvious point—I want to make is that the larger the library and the greater the area of closed stack, the more good service depends on good communications. If you have your books in one place and your readers in another, and you cannot allow the readers to go to the books, you must be able to bring the books to the readers quickly, safely, and as economically as possible in terms of staff. The delivery point from the main stacks in the British Museum is, I suppose, not more than twenty yards from the centre of the Reading Room. It takes a team of eight men to cope with the trans-shipping and moving that this makes necessary and I remember being told of similar difficulties at the Bavarian State Library at Munich. A horizontal carry plus a vertical carry (in either order) between stacks and reading area may be unavoidable: what must be avoided is a third stage—horizontal plus vertical plus horizontal.

It has also to be borne in mind that the more books there are in the reserved stacks, the more will be sent for at any one time and the heavier the traffic will be; the books will, in fact, not be travelling to and from the reading rooms by ones or twos but by trolley loads. Your communications must therefore be planned as trolley routes: motorways, not packhorse tracks, are required. These routes must not intersect or coincide with the normal lines of movement of readers or staff; the various types of highway user must be segregated so far as this is practicable; and the routes must be free from obstruction by unnecessary doors or differences of level or sharp corners, and provided with lay-bys for parking trolleys not in use. Planning the lay-out of a big library is, in fact, not so very different from planning a modern highway system.

A NATIONAL REFERENCE
AND INFORMATION SERVICE

Introductory paper by
A. H. Chaplin, Department of Printed Books, British Museum

Library services may broadly be divided into lending and reference. By reference I mean the use of books in the library, including their exploitation by the library's staff for the benefit of an absent reader. So defined, the term reference covers a good deal of what is commonly known as information service. It may perhaps also be extended to cover the supply of photocopies, though this is a borderline case: it shares with reference the feature of keeping the book in the library to which it belongs, and with lending that of enabling the user to read it somewhere else; it also has the advantage over both that it allows the reader to keep his copy permanently. To many people, the loan of books may seem to be the principal function of a library, and, generally speaking, borrowing probably most often suits the reader's convenience; but reference becomes necessary—or at least convenient and economical—when the material concerned cannot be lent, or the use to be made of it is 'consultation' rather than 'reading', or large numbers of books are to be used in a short time.

In the United Kingdom, a highly organized system of library co-operation, with special organs of its own at the regional and national levels, has been developed to deal with loans. Lending is the *raison-d'etre* of the regional bureaux and the National Central Library, and discussions in SCONUL (Standing Conference of National and University Libraries), as well as in the Library Association, on coverage and on co-ordinated acquisition policies are directed mainly at ensuring the availability for loan of copies of all books likely to be in demand. Quite recently, the Minister of Education's Working Party on Inter-Library Co-operation in England and Wales confined its attention almost exclusively to arrangements for inter-library loans. But the efficiency of reference services as I have defined them is no less important. Should they not be supported by a national system parallel with

Reprinted from NATIONAL LIBRARIES: extracts from the proceedings of the University and Research Section Conference held at Bangor, April 1963. London: Library Association, 1963, p. 41-5, by permission of the publisher.

that which exists for loan services? If so, what should it be like? And what should be done to bring it into existence?

The fact that reference by definition implies the use of the book in the library to which it belongs may appear to make reference a local matter, inappropriate for national co-ordination. But the user of a reference library may be an enquirer by telephone or by post, and one library may be itself a distant user of another library's reference services, or may provide a reference service on its own premises by borrowing a book from elsewhere. Any library, large or small, may be faced with a request for information which cannot be met from its own resources, and needs to know where to turn for help. The solution may be to refer the enquirer to another library, or it may be for the librarian himself to obtain information from another library and pass it on to the enquirer. In either case what is needed is usually an answer to one of the following questions: who is the person, or which is the organization, most likely to be able and willing to produce the wanted information? What publications are most likely to contain the information, and where are copies of them to be found? What is required is a system on which the librarian can rely to answer these questions.

Many of the elements of such a system already exist. We should not overlook the fact that the best way of distributing information is very often by means of publications, which the librarian can have ready at hand. The *Aslib Directory*; the *British National Bibliography*; the Library Association's *British Humanities Index* and *British Technology Index*; the *General Catalogue of Printed Books* of the British Museum; the *Short Title Catalogues* of English books to 1640 and from 1640 to 1700—all these are examples. They are supplemented by Aslib's information service, by the work of D.S.I.R., and by the bibliographical information services given as a sideline by the National Central Library and the British Museum, as well as the larger university and public libraries, on the basis of their own catalogues and stocks. The regional and national Union Catalogues and the National Lending Library for Science and Technology, though designed as instruments of a national lending service, are also valuable auxiliaries.

In many ways, however, these aids are incomplete, only partially developed, or out of date; some of them are too little used, they are not co-ordinated, and they certainly do not add up to a coherent system. Published directories, bibliographies, abstracting journals and union catalogues can never be complete and up to date. Union catalogues created as auxiliaries to loan services are liable to be deficient in relation to early, non-loanable material. Even an appeal for a rare item to a great national collection like that of the British Museum will fail if the item is not actually held there, through lack of information about the holdings of other large libraries. Another difficulty is the widespread ignorance which exists, among librarians as well as the general public, about the services which are actually available and the best way to use them. It is noticeable, for example, that only a small amount of the information work of the British Museum is done at the direct request of libraries in this country. Foreign libraries, on the other hand, particularly libraries in the United States and Commonwealth countries, account for a large proportion of enquiries and photographic orders, and a good many requests for photocopies from individual students reach the Museum through the National Central Library. Many letters asking for information come from individual members of the public, including not a few schoolchildren and students in training colleges and technical institutes in search of material for projects and essays. A large proportion of these inquiries could have been satisfactorily dealt with by local public libraries.

Deficient as they are, however, the present activities of existing organizations provide the foundations on which a system can be built. The first step would be to initiate discussions between the bodies I have mentioned—the Library Association, Aslib, SCONUL, D.S.I.R., the N.C.L. and the British Museum. They should be asked to survey existing aids to reference services, consider how their own contributions could be extended and co-ordinated, and decide what central services or controlling organization should be set up. Without attempting to forecast in detail what their findings might be, one may be permitted to suggest a few possibilities.

As I have suggested, the need is for a system which would locate and make available documents relevant to enquiries which could not be answered at the place where they first arose. It would not itself attempt to be a universal question-answering organization. Rather, in the first place, it would encourage and assist the referring of enquiries directly to the agency most likely to be able to provide an answer. Where this approach failed, regional centres or centres linking libraries in professional, industrial or subject groups, would normally be appealed to before the central national organization was brought into action. This central organization should be able, in case of need, to scan the whole field of sources of information and of available documents, should actively promote the availability somewhere of all documents likely to be useful, and should be able itself, in the last resort, to procure (often in the form of photographic copies) documents not available through other channels. It would also co-ordinate activities at the lower levels.

The equipment needed at the national level would include:

(1) A register of special sources of information and of the conditions for their use.
(2) An organized collection of bibliographies, including collections of abstracts and indexes to periodicals, with staff trained to use them.
(3) Union catalogues, including catalogues of material *not* available for loan.
(4) Access to a stock of books as nearly comprehensive as possible.
(5) An efficient document reproduction service.
(6) A good communications system, e.g. telex.

It would probably be wise to follow an already established trend, and organize the work at the centre in two branches—one for general information and for the humanities, the other for science and technology. The obvious location for the latter branch would be the new National Reference Library of Science and Invention, which would work in close co-operation with D.S.I.R. Since it has now been decided that the Reference Library is to be a branch of the British Museum, it would be logical to give explicit recognition to the British Museum Library at Bloomsbury as the national reference library for the humanities, and to place the other centre there. It would have to draw heavily, however, on the resources represented by the union catalogues at the National Central Library, and it would be designed in consultation with the members of SCONUL. Both centres would need the goodwill and assistance of Aslib. Both would be in communication—presumably by telex—with other national libraries and with the major public, university, research and industrial libraries through which (acting as regional or subject centres) most enquiries would reach the centre. Each centre would compile the completest possible register of libraries and sources of information and make the completest possible collection of bibliographies in the fields for which it was responsible, and would create a unit of staff trained to use these efficiently. It has been suggested that the scientific and technical centre might also collect abstracts of current literature from the many organizations which produce them for their own purposes, classify them and then retrieve them on demand—probably mechanically, and perhaps on payment of a fee. The humanities centre should also promote the completion and extension of such works as the *Short Title Catalogues*, and should store and make available accumulated information supplementary to them. In general, the enquiries received by the centres would have been filtered through local and regional centres (which would be similarly equipped on an appropriately smaller scale), and much of the central activity would consist of referring enquiries down again to the specialized or local units best able to deal with them. Both centres would, however, use the resources of the libraries in which they were situated to answer queries which could not be dealt with at the local or regional level.

The establishment of such a system would demand financial resources, which would probably have to come ultimately from the Treasury. Its efficient functioning would require an educational campaign to explain it to the public. In both respects, action and propaganda by the Library Association can be powerful instruments. The suggestions I have made have been considered by the Reference, Special and Information Section of the Library Association at its 1962 Conference. As a result, the Library Association Council was asked to set up a working party to draw up a report. The question is raised again in the University and Research Section in the hope that this section will add its weight to the demand that the question of a co-ordinated national reference and information service should be given urgent attention by the people who can join forces to provide it.

THE ROLE
OF THE NATIONAL LIBRARY
IN SCIENCE AND TECHNOLOGY

with special reference to the United States Library of Congress

by L. QUINCY MUMFORD,
Librarian of Congress, Library of Congress,
Washington, D.C.

In very general terms, one might perhaps describe the role of the national library in science and technology as follows: A principal—perhaps the most important—product of scientific and technological research is knowledge. Never before has so much scientific knowledge existed that might be applied to solving human problems. Between this store of information and the problems to which it might be applied are various communication barriers. Libraries acquire, store, make available, and provide bibliographic services on knowledge recorded in a variety of forms. Their role in the scientific and technological complex obviously lies, therefore, in improving the effectiveness of communication among the scientists and engineers who can apply technical information—either directly to the solution of immediate problems or as raw material for further research.

Such is the basic nature of a national library's role in science and technology. Significant aspects of the performance of this role include library organization, the collections, and the bibliographic services.

ORGANIZATION

Whether a national library should consist of one building, a group of buildings in a single location, or a system of separate, co-ordinated but independently administered libraries will vary with a number of national factors—size of the nation, scope of technical and economic interests, particular pattern of government, and so forth. Both extremes and all intermediate possibilities are included in the use of the term 'national library' in this paper. In Washington, for example, there are, in addition to several divisions of the Library of Congress that are concerned with science and technology, a National Library of Medicine, a National Agricultural Library, and more than forty other technical libraries operated by the various research-oriented agencies of the Federal Government. All of these libraries co-operate in the exchange of information and carry on extensive inter-library loan programmes, in which many university and industrial libraries also participate.

In planning its national library system, every nation must decide for itself the extent to which centralization is desirable—balancing the frequently cited advantages of tight administrative control, minimum waste and lost motion, reduced overheads and the like, against such alleged disadvantages as unduly complex internal organization, lack of flexibility, inherent cumbersomeness, and so forth. Probably the most important point to make in this connexion is that there should be careful planning. Regardless of what particular form it takes, the national library pattern that is evolved should be the result of thoughtful, deliberate design—not a consequence simply of chance and the cumulated effect of numerous opportunistic, spur-of-the-moment decisions made to solve immediate problems without regard for long-range implications.

Reprinted from *Unesco Bulletin for Libraries*, vol. 18, no. 4, July–August 1964, p. 172-7, 192.
©Unesco 1964. Reproduced by permission of Unesco.

An obviously important aspect of any library's organizational make-up is its professional staffing. When one considers the role of a national library in science and technology, one must be concerned with both librarianship and scientific competence. The ideal individual whose talents include a high degree of proficiency in both these fields and is, in addition, available, like most ideals, is rarely found. Therefore, one must try to provide for this dual competence in the staff as a whole. In the Library of Congress' Science and Technology Division, for example, the staff of 40-45 professionals includes ten Ph.D.'s, most of whose doctorates are in scientific disciplines, and a number of people with masters' degrees. Also, however, library science degrees and extensive bibliographic experience are well represented there being substantial overlap between the 'science' and 'library' segments. Thus, the Library of Congress is trying to achieve within the group as a whole the most effective combination of training and skill in these two 'worlds'.

For a national library truly to keep its finger on the pulse of the information needs of the scientific community it serves, library planning and practice must represent the best thinking of experts in both areas. Once the establishment is created and staffed, there is the additional responsibility of developing criteria by which the national library's performance can be judged.

COLLECTIONS

The optimum nature and extent of the scientific and technical collections in a national library, or national library system, obviously must depend to a major extent upon the needs and interests of the particular nation. Certainly such a library should house a complete collection of the country's own output of significant scientific documents. Also, the collections presumably should include an authoritative basic representation of fundamental monographs and serials in all fields of science and technology, the exact selection and scope varying somewhat with the nation's size and state of scientific and technological development. Beyond acquisition of these materials, emphasis should be on the development and maintenance of comprehensive collections of the most up-to-date textbooks, monographs and journals in those areas of science and technology most closely related to the nation's welfare and economy. Here it is most important that the library's own staff work closely with the country's practising scientists and engineers to make these collections as useful as possible. Every library is plagued to a greater or less degree (mostly greater) by financial problems; consequently, every national library should take maximum advantage of exchanges and other non-purchase mechanisms for acquiring desired documents.

A few data on the science collections of the Library of Congress may be of interest in this connexion. Its holdings in all areas of science and technology include more than two million books, approximately 20,000 journal and other serial titles, and a collection of several hundred thousand technical reports. (The technical report is a semi-formal kind of publication falling between the personal letter or memorandum and the conventional journal article; these documents gained great importance in the United States during World War II and have been increasing in number ever since.) The library now receives some 50,000 such reports annually. Today, much that is significant in the results of United States scientific research appears first in technical report form. The principal producers of these reports are the United States Atomic Energy Commission, the National Aeronautics and Space Administration, the Department of Defense, and their respective research and development contractors.

In addition to acquisitions by copyright, the Library of Congress receives large quantities of scientific materials through its more than 23,000 exchange agreements with domestic and foreign, government and private laboratories, universities, observatories, and other scientific and technical institutions. Library of Congress periodical publications of importance in science and technology, although they are not limited to these fields, include: *New serial titles; Monthly index of Russian accessions;* and the *World list of future international meetings*.

SERVICES

It is clear that no national library can fulfil its obligations in science and technology (or in any field, for that matter) if it offers its bibliographic services solely on a come-and-get-it basis. Its approach to providing service must be active and dynamic—not merely passive; it must 'do'—not just 'have'. To be fully effective, a library must take vigorous action to bring its services to the attention of potential users—in this case, the nation's scientific and technological communities. Despite the fact that reasonably well stocked and staffed libraries exist in all major communities, universities, and industrial plants in the United States, our experience in the Library of Congress shows that an appallingly large number of people—including scientists and engineers—are very poorly informed regarding these institutions and their capacities for service.

Discussed next are four areas of service in which a national library has particularly important responsibilities in science and technology—referral, reference and bibliography, service to the government, and relations with other libraries.

Referral services

The referral function, as it is understood here, means referring inquiries to sources of information outside the national library itself. Traditionally, of course, such referral is an accepted part of the responsibility of any reference or research library. It is discussed separately here because referral work plays a particularly significant part in an effective national library programme. Far more than conventional reference activities *per se*, they provide a broad overview of all of the information resources that may be available through the complex of international contacts which such a library must maintain.

It should be emphasized that the breadth and depth of referral functions cannot be satisfactorily defined in universal terms. Instead, they must be derived from the requirements and capabilities of the nation that wishes to establish them. They may be restricted entirely or primarily to the usual bibliographic sources of information; that is, they may provide merely the equivalent of a national union catalogue of existing and identified publications. They may go farther afield and identify academic or research institutions concerned with particular segments of scientific knowledge. They may even identify individuals who, in some specialized field of scholarship or research, represent the best sources of authoritative advice and counsel.

In the broad and rapidly developing fields of science and technology, it is probably well to go beyond the conventional bibliographic reference sources, if only because the very growth of science and technology has brought into being such a diversity of actual and potential information resources. There is, for example, the centre that compiles observed data on magnetic tapes or in photographic records; the observatory that may be able to supplement existing astronomical tables or calculations; or the biological institute that may be able to provide vital research findings long before their codification and publication.

If referral functions are formally recognized and allowed for in the formulation of a library programme, they can interlock quite effectively with traditional acquisition, reference, and retrieval functions. In the process of acquiring the publications which it needs to build an appropriate collection, a library can develop—as a relatively inexpensive by-product—a listing or catalogue of the organizations responsible for producing the information contained in the volumes it acquires. Even without such a discretely developed catalogue or register, a reference search can provide not only bibliographic citations, but also the identification of contributing information resources to which a questioner might profitably turn for further information. This is perhaps particularly true on an international basis, where the publications which a library acquires are frequently the best if not the only means of identifying the original sources of published information.

It is a truism that the effectiveness of any library depends upon the strength and excellence of its communication with those who use it, or should use it. This, again, is probably particularly true in science and technology where for many reasons—pressure of time, difficulty in maintaining availability of truly up-to-date research data or the tendency of many scientists and engineers to rely upon their own information-gathering practices it is frequently difficult to establish and maintain adequate communication with the proper community of users. To the extent that referral functions permit the library to act as a necessary intermediary between producers and consumers of information (rather than between users and catalogues, the nature of which the users may not understand or appreciate) they offer an effective means of strengthening the ties that must exist between a library and those who rely upon it. For a national library, which should have within its broad purview an exhaustive understanding of the interplay between producers and consumers of information, the provision of referral services thus offers great benefits.

A National Referral Center for Science and Technology, established in the Library of Congress in 1962, functions upon these principles. It is developing a comprehensive register of information resources of all kinds and, since March 1963, has been providing a centralized technical referral service to the nation's scientists and engineers. As the inventory, or register, becomes more complete, it will provide material for published guides to the information resources in the many fields of science and engineering. It should also prove invaluable to future planners of national programmes in all phases of the accumulation and dissemination of scientific knowledge.

The National Referral Center functions as a division of the Reference Department of the Library of Congress, and works closely with its companion divisions—notably the Science and Technology Division—to ensure that its referral service complements, rather than competes with, the reference services that rely upon the collections of the library itself.

Procedurally, the Referral Center is not essentially different from more traditional library activities. Its central register is nothing more than extremely detailed descriptive and subject catalogue of the varied information resources with which it is concerned. Its indexes are of the co-ordinate type, governed by a carefully controlled authority list derived from the collection and relying, for the present, upon an optical-coincidence (peekaboo-card) retrieval mechanism for experimental purposes. Except that its replies to inquiries cite information activities, rather than bibliographic references, they are quite similar to normal reference correspondence; they present brief descriptive summaries of the suggested resources and leave further action to the discretion of the inquirer.

With all of these basic similarities, there are significant differences in detail, and some of the techniques employed may prove to be of adaptive value to other library endeavours. Even more certainly of value to the Library of Congress is the audience served by the Referral Center; while it is still too early to judge conclusively, this audience already appears to include individuals and organizations not normally included in the Library of Congress clientele. Contact with this broader audience will obviously extend the opportunity for service and, to this extent at least, the formal provision of referral functions offers demonstrable benefits to any national library programme.

Reference and bibliography services

The general nature of conventional library services of these kinds is well understood. Certainly they must be provided efficiently and must be widely available if a national library is to play a dynamic part in the country's scientific and technical development. Essential to any effective reference service activity, of course, are the attributes of accuracy and reliability. In addition, in science and technology, it is of paramount importance that that reference inquiries be answered promptly, that the information supplied be up to date, and that the nature and variety of the services be sufficiently varied and flexible to meet the many and changing needs of scientists and engineers.

The optimum combination of different aspects of the reference and bibliography services should be equally available, although at lower priority, to the scientific community, to other government agencies, and to the general public.

What is done for these users? Answers are given to reference inquiries of all degrees of complexity that are received by letter, by telephone, and by personal visit. Routine, relatively simple requests in science and technology are handled by the General Reference and Bibliography Division. Those of a more complex nature are referred to the Science and Technology Division with its combination of skills in science and librarianship referred to earlier. Three science specialists in this division—one each in the biological, physical, and engineering sciences—devote almost all of their time to answering inquiries from members of Congress when substantial technical background is required. In this activity, they work closely with another technical specialist on the staff of the Legislative Reference Service—a major department of the library that is described briefly below. The Science and Technology Division as a whole handled some 26,000 reference requests during the fiscal year 1963.

The Science and Technology Division also prepares bibliographies and other publications of several kinds for a variety of users. Some of these are initiated by the division and are directed toward bringing some particular segment of the technical collections under better bibliographic control; some fourteen such publications were issued last year. Various other government agencies, taking advantage of the presence in the Library of Congress of both the extensive technical collections and scientific and bibliographic skills, contract for the preparation of special bibliographies to their specifications. Between fifteen and twenty such bibliographies are under way at present in the Science and Technology Division. For these projects, literature coverage may be of any combination of domestic or foreign, published or report material; the bibliographies vary from relatively short, single compilations requiring but a few weeks' preparation to comprehensive, continuing efforts that go on more or less indefinitely (one is now in its fifteenth year); the products take the form of some combination of typed lists, catalogue cards, or published periodic cumulations; the citations are usually augmented with informative abstracts and indexes; and subject matter varies widely as indicated by typical sponsors which at present include the United States Atomic Energy Commission, the National Aeronautics and Space Agency, the Public Health Service, and a number of branches of the military services.

Through a special bibliographic programme initiated several years ago, this division assists industry in a manner not previously possible. Under this 'fee bibliography service', a private organization can request a literature search of whatever degree of comprehensiveness it desires, on any scientific or technical subject it wishes, and be charged at an hourly rate for the service. This is a co-operative programme with the Office of Technical Services (Department of Commerce), and the customer deals with that agency; OTS conducts a search of the technical report literature under its control and the Library of Congress covers the published literature and certain groups of technical reports.

Special services to the Congress

The Library of Congress was originally established in 1800 for the sole purpose of serving the Congress. The Library's role has long since been broadened until it is now essentially that of a national library, but service to the members and committees of Congress is still one of its primary objectives. One department of the library, the Legislative Reference Service, is devoted exclusively to furnishing research and reference assistance to the Congress. Other departments of the library, including the Reference Department and the Law Library co-operate as needed.

In recent years, science and technology have had an increasingly sharp impact on nearly every field of public policy. Consequently, staff members of the Legislative Reference Service concerned with national defence, space, foreign affairs, international relations, natural resources, economics, law, and public administration have come more and more to deal with scientific and technological developments. Generally speaking, the congressional need has been less for detailed scientific data than for information and counsel on science in relation to one or another of the broad fields of governmental action.

At least until quite recently, the Legislative Reference Service has been able to serve the Congress satisfactorily in this area without building up a staff of scientists and engineers. It has had one top-ranking specialist in science and one in engineering, and its staff is supplemented especially by that of the Science and Technology Division, as mentioned previously, on inquiries of a strictly scientific or technological nature. Most of the public policy issues, however, have been dealt with by staff members trained in the social sciences, government, and public law. The rapidly increasing tempo of congressional interest in governmental research and development programmes strongly suggests that in the near future the Legislative Reference Service will need to equip itself with more staff assistants having a combination of training and experience both in science (or engineering) and in government and the social sciences.

Relations with other libraries

To be fully effective in its role in science and technology, a national library must assume responsibilities beyond its own organization, collections, and services. It must provide leadership to the smaller libraries across the country to aid them in planning and developing their programmes. It should maintain close ties with such libraries, support their activities through interlibrary loan and other co-operative ventures, and be a major source of counsel and advice. Only in this way can the nation's total library system—government and private—develop in a manner that will provide maximum over-all service for the manpower and money expended.

Outlined in this paper, in general terms, are what seem to the author to be the principal aspects of the role national libraries can play in science and technology. In closing, three specific points should be emphasized, as follows.

1. National libraries can make an extremely significant contribution to the progress of science and technology in their respective countries.
2. While this role is not greatly different *in kind* from that which libraries can play in other fields, it does require particular emphasis on promptness and up-to-date services.
3. For maximum effectiveness, both the planning and the execution of national libraries' science-related programmes must be based on the best available combined thinking of the library and scientific communities.

Some Recent Trends in National Library Buildings

by ANTHONY THOMPSON

A Colloquium on National Library Buildings was held in Rome in September 1973 by the IFLA Committee on Library Buildings in collaboration with UNESCO and the Associazione Italiana Biblioteche, and I had the privilege of providing for it an exhibition of recent buildings.

This exhibition, shown in the Palazzo Braschi on 37 screens, contained plans and illustrations of 23 complete national libraries, as well as seven recent extensions to existing buildings. During the process of gathering and collating this material, and drawing up comparative tables, some facts have emerged which, at least in their comparative aspect, were probably not known before. I shall attempt here to discuss these facts, some of which can be explained easily, but some of which seem to be inexplicable.

Light was thrown especially on three aspects of national libraries:
1) their functions, which determine, or should determine their design; 2) their size, measured in various ways, by floor area, size of stock, number of staff, and number of seats for readers; and 3) their site and layout, determined by the concentration of population, by economic considerations, by the whims of planners, and even by fashions.

When generalizing about national libraries it must, however, be remembered that 1) most of the older national libraries have grown out of former royal collections, e.g. the Bibliothèque nationale, Paris, still in the original building, now cleverly internally re-modelled; the British Museum, London, and the national libraries still bearing the title "Royal Library" (in Belgium, Denmark, Holland and Sweden), with all the attending weight of tradition in the collections and the buildings.

2) Not every country has one national library fulfilling all the necessary functions. For instance, the Federal Republic of Germany has the "Deutsche Bibliothek" in Frankfurt, and the "Staatsbibliothek Preussischer Kulturbesitz", now moving from its temporary seat at Marburg into the vast new building in West Berlin, while the "Bayerische Staatsbibliothek" in Munich is in fact rather more than a Bavarian State Library, with *inter alia*

Reprinted from *Libri*, vol. 24, no. 1, 1974, p. 69-77, by permission of the author and publisher.

the richest collection of incunnabula on the European continent. The German Democratic Republic has the Deutsche Staatsbibliothek in East Berlin, originally the Prussian State Library, and the Deutsche Bücherei in Leipzig. And Italy has a whole series of "biblioteche nazionali", in Florence, Rome, Naples, Milan, Turin and Palermo, a pattern of decentralization dating back over 100 years before the unification of Italy.

3) Some national libraries also serve universities, a service which modifies their functions, notably those of Denmark, Finland, Norway, Croatia, Israel and Iceland, the last of which is shortly to acquire the new building illustrated in the exhibition.

4) Some serve also their national parliaments, as in U.S.A. and Japan.

5) Here we are concerned mainly with general ("encyclopaedic«) national libraries rather than with national libraries for special subjects, such as Medicine, or those for special groups of readers, such as the blind.

1. The Functions

Since the Unesco Symposium on national libraries of 1958[2] various attempts have been made to synthesize the declared functions of national libraries,[3] and to arrange them in an order of priority.[7][8][9] The results attained by Humphreys[7][8] and by Gittig[9] may be tabulated as shown in table 1.

On examination of these two lists, considerable differences will be observed, and omissions in both. Some functions are increasing in importance to-day, such as the international exchange of publications, an activity for which there are special departments in the national libraries of Austria, France, the G.D.R., Iceland, Rumania, the U.S.S.R. and others. There is also a growing interest in the concept of a national "methodological centre", which has been developed in Eastern Europe; and the importance of book exhibitions must not be forgotten, since it demands special rooms in the building, for the display of national treasures and the storage of equipment. It is almost impossible, however, to arrive at an international standard, since the functions depend to some extent on the cultural and political background of the nation served. (See e.g. the declared functions of the Library of Congress, the Lenin Library of the U.S.S.R., the British Museum, and the Bibliothèque nationale, Paris, quoted by Humphreys.[7]

Table 1.

Humphreys	*Gittig*
Fundamental functions	
1. Collection of the nation's literature	1. Collection of the nation's literary production
2. Legal deposit of national publications	
3. Coverage of foreign literature	2. Compilation of the national primary bibliography currently and with cumulations
4. Publication of the national bibliography	
5. National bibliographical information centre	3. To act as a centre for information on the national literature
6. To publish its catalogues, for use in other libraries	
Desirable functions	
7. Inter-library lending	4. Compilation of indexes to articles in periodicals and newspapers
8. Collection of manuscripts	
9. Research on library techniques	5. International loans centre
	6. International centre for exchange of publications
Other functions, not necessarily of the national library	7. Maintenance of union catalogues
10. International exchange of publications	8. Collection of foreign literature
11. Distribution of duplicates	9. Centralized cataloguing.
12. Books for the blind	
13. Professional training.	

For the purpose of the Colloquium on National Library Buildings in Rome I chose for the questionnaire for the exhibition eleven functions which seemed to be important in influencing the design of buildings, to which I have now added the International exchange of publications. These are listed at the head of table 2, which indicates the functions undertaken by each national library shown in the exhibition: −

Table 2. The Functions of National Libraries

	1 Collect all national publications	2 Collect foreign publications	3 National archives	4 Preserve rare books and documents	5 Serve research workers
ALGERIA Bibliothèque nationale.	x	x	x	x	x
AUSTRALIA National Library	x	x	–	x	x
BELGIUM Bibliothèque royale ..	x	x	–	x	x
CANADA National Library	x	x	–	x	x
DENMARK Kongelige Bibliotek ..	x	x	–	x	x
FRANCE Bibliothèque nationale	x	x	x	–	x
GERMANY Federal Republic Deutsche Bibliothek, Frankfurt	x	x	–	x esp. "Exil-lit"	x
Staatsbibliothek, West Berlin	–	x	–	x	x
GERMAN DEMOCRATIC REP. Deutsche Bücherei, Leipzig* ...	–	x	–	x	x
GREAT BRITAIN Nat. Lib. Wales, Aberystwyth**	x	x	x for Wales in part	x	x
HUNGARY National Library (12)	x	x	x	x	x
ICELAND	x	x		x	x
JAPAN National Diet Library	x	x	–	x	x
NIGERIA National Library	x	x	x	x	x
POLAND Biblioteka Narodowa .	x	x	x	x	x
SINGAPORE National Library	x	x	–	x	x
SLOVAKIA Matica Slovenská	x	x	x	x	x
SWITZERLAND Schweiz. Landesbibliothek	x	x	x	x	x
U.S.S.R. Lenin Library	x	x	–	x	x
U.S.A. Library of Congress..	x	x	–	x	x
YUGOSLAVIA. Serbia Narodna Bibl. Srbije..	x	x	x	x	x

* Functions nos. 1 and 12 are performed by the Deutsche Staatsbibliothek, East Berlin.
** One of the "copyright libraries" of Great Britain, receiving British publications by legal deposit, but specializing in publications from and about Wales.

6 National bibliographical centre	7 National bibliography	8 Printed catalogue cards	9 National union catalogue	10 Interlibrary loans	11 Lending to other libraries	12 International exchanges of publications
x	x	—	—	x	x	?
x	x	x	x	x	x	x
x	x	—	x (foreign periodicals)	x	x	x
x	x	x	x	x	x	x
x	—	—	x	x	x	—
x	x	—	x	x	x	x
x	x	x	—	—	x last resort	—
x	—	—	x	x	x	—
x	x	—	x	x	x	—
x						
x	x	—	—	x	x	—
x	x	—	x	x	—	x
x	x	—	x	x	x	x
x	x	x	x	—	x	x
x	x	x	x	x	x ·	x
x	x	x	x	x	x	x
x						
x	x	—	x	x	x	?
x	x	x	x	x	x	x
x	x	—	x	x	x	x
x	—	—	x	x	x	x
x	x	x	x	x	x	x
x	x only retrospective	x	x	x	x	?

2. *The Size of national library buildings*

This may be indicated in various ways: –

1) for general comparison: by the floor area, and the cubic capacity;
2) for comparison of services rendered: by the number of seats for readers, number of staff, storage capacity (no. of volumes).

The following table is an extract from the analysis of the buildings shown in the Rome exhibition:

Country & completion date	Floor area	Cubic capacity	No. of volumes	Staff. no.	Readers
Algeria, 1958............	4,786 m²	72,520 m³	750,000	70	450
Australia, 1968	28,060 m²	109,600 m³	1,400,000	625	911
Belgium, 1969*..........	73,343 m²	2C8,000 m³	?	?	1,114
Canada, 1967	44,900 m²	?	500,000	413	162
Germany, (Fed. Repub.)					
Staatsbibl., Berlin, 1976?	78,000 m²	400,000 m³	8,000,000	562	1,200
Deutsche Bibl., Fr. ft. 1959	20,761 m²	61,922 m³	1,644,000	320	200
Hungary, 1976?	28,700 m²	250,000 m³	5,000,000	600	500
Iceland, 1978	10,530 m²	41,600 m³	866,000	73	830
Japan, 1968	73,764 m²	206,400 m³	4,500,000	845	1,304
Nigeria, 1975?	22,500 m²	95,930 m³	1,000,000	500	1,764
Poland, 1978?	44,800 m²	174,950 m³	5,000,000	820	800
Singapore, 1960	7,750 m²	?	600,000	203	360
Slovakia, 1975	26,000 m²	95,982 m³	2,700,000	300	200
Switzerland, 1931	**7,675 m²	59,000 m³	1,500,000	85	66
U.S.A.					
LC Annex, 1938	65,000 m²	926,000 m³	4,500,000	?	682
Yugoslavia					
Serbia, 1973	24,900 m²	80,000 m³	1,200,000	300	500

* Date of official inauguration: was already many years in use.
** Parts of the building have been used for non-library purposes for many years, a measure to allow for future expansion of the library.

Note. In Prague the plans are prepared for the new Czech State Library building, providing a floor area of 120,000 m², storage for 7½ million volumes, and seats for 2,000 readers.

Some comparisons of these rough figures will produce thought, and some questions:

A comparison of the floor areas with the cubic capacities reveals some big differences in proportion between them, and therefore some big differences in the economic use of space. The National Diet Library of Japan and the Royal Library of Belgium appear to use their space the most economically. (These figures are of course subject to a certain imprecision, such as floor area being interpreted as "usable space" or total space.)

Similarly one may compare the floor areas and cubic capacities with the number of volumes (storage capacity), and notice, e.g. the comparative extravagance of the Australian Library compared with the Swiss Library, both containing circa 1½ million volumes.

Again, one may examine the number of readers' seats in relation to the number of volumes. This gives some indication of the relative importance attributed to preservation and use, both essential functions of a national library. A trend will be observed for the number of readers' seats to be increased sharply in the more recent buildings. This is a strange phenomenon, appearing at a time when national library networks are being developed in most countries, and one might expect a *de*-centralization of use, rather than a concentration at the national library. One may ask, for instance, whether, in Nigeria, as a national network of libraries develops, the 1764 seats will really be used by readers. Again, one may ask whether in West Berlin, a city with other good library resources, the 1,200 seats in the huge new building will be used; or is this figure caused by the dream of a future unification of the city? A study of the later actual use made of these libraries would elucidate the problem.

3. *Site and layout*

There is still a strong trend, as there always has been, for national libraries to be sited in or near the centre of the capital city, where the population is concentrated and can easily use the Library for reference. Some of the new buildings have, however, owing to the city centres being already crowded, been sited towards the edge of the city, such as the Matica Slovenská (at Martín, Slovakia), and the Biblioteca Nazionale Centrale in Rome. The Lenin Library in Moscow, itself sited in the centre of the city, is now building an annexe for less-used material at Khimki on the outskirts of the city, thus following the policy already long adopted by the British Museum in London and by the Bibliothèque nationale in Paris.

Many of the new buildings are planned to be compact, especially those in Budapest, Belgrade, Martín and Prague. But there are two great exceptions to this, the Biblioteca Nazionale Centrale in Rome, just completed, a spread-out building covering a large site, and the plans for the new Biblioteka Narodowa in Warsaw, which shows the same characteristic.

And finally, a new and very important trend must be mentioned. This is the separation of the two types of use, reference and lending. An eternal problem of libraries has been that of ensuring that the complete collection is always available for reference, and simultaneously to operate a liberal policy of lending. This problem came to a crisis in the Science Museum Library, London, in the 1950s, which at that time was not only serving the Museum staff, but was also lending scientific publications on a national scale.

This problem was solved by the founding of the National Lending Library for Science and Technology in Boston Spa, which undertook the national lending and photocopying service, and has recently become part of the newly-organized British Library.[10] More recently (in 1970) the objectives of the British Library were officially defined,[11] and the most important point here is that *two separate objectives* were set:

"a) preserving and making available for reference at least one copy of every book and periodical of domestic origin and of as many overseas publications as possible.

b) providing an effecient central lending and photocopying service in support of other libraries . . ."

This idea of two separate national libraries, one for reference and one for lending, was supported at the IFLA General Council 1973 at Grenoble, at which the theme was "Universal Bibliographical Control", when Mme. S. Honoré (of the Bibliothèque nationale, Paris) read her excellent paper to the plenary opening session. After emphasizing the importance of a national bibliography based on the legal deposit of publications in a national library, she added: "Il faut songer à compléter le Contrôle bibliographique universel par un réseau de bibliothèques de prêt, chaque pays s'engageant à rendre l'ensemble de sa production nationale accessible au prêt interbibliothèques dans une grande bibliothèque nationale de prêt alimentée par le dépôt légal. Ainsi les deux rôles de conservation et de prêt seraient parfaitement assurés . . ."

It seems that in future each country may have to plan *two* national libraries, one for conservation and reference, and the other for lending and photocopying. The building planners will then need to study the new buildings and equipment of the National Lending Library (now part of the British Library) which was also shown in the exhibition at the Colloquium in Rome.

REFERENCES

1. Esdaile, A. *National libraries of the world.* . . . 2nd ed. rev. by F. J. Hill. (London, Library Association, 1957). First edition was published in 1934.
2. UNESCO, *Paris. National libraries:* their problems and prospects. Symposium on national libraries in Europe, Vienna, 8–27 September, 1958. (Paris, UNESCO, 1960).
3. Mearns, David C., *ed.* "Current trends in national libraries". *Library Trends,* 4 (1) 1955, July, 1–116.
4. Wormann, C. "National libraries in our time". *Libri,* 9, 1959, 273–307.

5. The Library Association, *London*. University and Research Section. *National libraries;* extracts from the proceedings of the.... Conference held at Bangor, April, 1963. London, Library Association, 1963.
6. Quincy Mumford, L. "The role of the National Library in science and technology". *Unesco Bull. for Libraries*, 18, 1964, 172–177.
7. Humphreys, K. W. "The role of the national library: a preliminary statement. *Libri*, 14, 1964–65, 356–368.
8. Humphreys, K. W. "National library functions" *Unesco Bull. for Libraries*, 20 (4) 1966, 158–169.
9. Gittig, Heinz. "Nationalbibliothek". In: *Lexikon des Bibliothekswesens*, p. 464–5. Leipzig, Bibliographisches Institut, 1969.
10. Great Britain (United Kingdom). National Libraries Committee. Report. (Chairman:: F. Dainton). London, H.M.S.O., 1969.
11. *The British Library*. London, H.M.S.O., 1971 (Cmnd 4572).
12. Joboru, Magda. "The function of the national library in the Hungarian library system", *Libri*, 23 (2) 1973, 155–165.

3. NATIONAL LIBRARIES IN INDIVIDUAL COUNTRIES AND AREAS OF THE WORLD

3 NATIONAL LIBRARIES IN INDIVIDUAL COUNTRIES AND AREAS OF THE WORLD

There are many papers concerned with individual national libraries. Most of them describe a particular national library at a particular time, and as a result are quickly out of date. Some are exclusively historical, but this is not a reader on the history of national libraries. The most permanently valuable papers are those that concern a national library at a critical period – on its creation or re-organisation – or that relate its nature and operation to a set of functions such as those listed by Humphreys. In the present selection, some papers are of this nature, while others are chosen as representative of libraries of different types and in different parts of the world.

Berry's paper (which must have been written about two years earlier than the date of its publication) considers the functions of the Library of Congress, and to a lesser extent of the British Library, in relation to the analysis provided by Humphreys' distinction between functions to be performed by a national library and those that are necessary to a national library service but that may or may not be carried out by a national library; and he states his own belief that in large countries the latter area should be a very wide one, and that centralisation may be giving way to co-operative network planning. His view of the British Library's functions is, as noted at the end of this paper, considerably narrower than the reality. In the USA, the relationship of the Library of Congress to national library planning has been thoroughly studied by the National Advisory Commission on Libraries, which reported in 1968 *(see Further Reading, Refs. 23,24)* and by the permanent National Commission on Libraries and Information Science which was set up as a result of this report. Berry concludes that the Library of Congress has a particularly wide range of functions, although he fails to distinguish clearly between activities in which it participates in a limited way (e.g. interlending) and national functions which it carries out to the full. The relationship of the Library of Congress – the de facto national library – to the two libraries that are designated national libraries – the National Library of Medicine and National Agricultural Library – is briefly considered *(see also Further Reading, Refs. 19,21,22).*

Parts of papers by Green and Hookway have been included to give a general picture of the British Library. The creation from several separate organisations of a national library with a very wide range of functions, with the opportunities it provided for co-ordination, rationalisation and change on a scale normally very difficult to achieve in a developed country, could be considered (as it is by Berry) the most significant recent development in national libraries. (It is interesting to compare it with the creation in 1952, virtually from scratch although after many years of planning, of another library with a very wide range of functions – the National Library of Canada – *Further Reading, Ref.16).* Hookway's paper was given just over a year after the British Library came into being, and in the following three years many changes have taken place, as is inevitable in such a new organisation. Numerous papers have been published on the British Library, both general and on particular aspects, and these should be consulted for comprehensive and up to date accounts of the British Library (see especially the remainder of Green's paper and the various essays in *British Librarianship Today – Further Reading, Ref. 45).*

Magnussen's paper, which could perhaps equally well have been included in the first group, considers various national library problems with special reference to Denmark. Denmark, like the other Scandinavian countries and several other smaller developed countries in Europe, has a relatively small population, a high level of education and demand, a large number of well developed research libraries, and a very heavy dependence on foreign publications. In such circumstances it may be difficult to justify comprehensive national libraries, and dispersion of functions and collections has been a common solution. There are however problems with dispersion, which are discussed in Magnussen's wide ranging paper, together with various other aspects of national libraries, especially the relationship of the national library to national library planning *(see also Further Reading, Refs. 43,44)*.

Eastern Europe is represented by papers on the USSR, by Kondakov, and on Hungary, by Jóboru. Both papers contain brief historical summaries. The Soviet Union contains not only the Lenin Library but national libraries of the various Soviet Republics and also national subject libraries — all of these carrying out significant national library functions. Bibliographic functions are more extended than in many capitalist countries, including as they do the production of many specialised bibliographies; and the Lenin Library has an important national role as a centre for library methodology, in effect determining standards and policies for many other libraries in the USSR. The international role of the Lenin Library is also explained. Another useful paper (not included here), explaining the background to the national library network in the Soviet Union and incidentally briefly describing the Uzbek SSR National Library, is by Kaldor *(Further Reading, Ref. 53)*. The National Szechényi Library of Hungary has several similarities to the Lenin Library, apart from being designed to serve the aims of the state. It too has a methodological centre, and serves as a centre of a national network of library services; in Hungary too there are separate national subject libraries (e.g. Medicine and Agriculture). The Szechényi Library is in fact quite limited in subject scope and in its collecting of foreign literature. As for native literature, Jóboru argues that only 'the best products of the age's and nation's mind should be preserved. . . and the second and third-rate material can be neglected'. Bibliographic activities are retrospective as well as current, and national depository problems have received much attention (as indeed they have in the USSR). As in so many other articles, the problem of reconciling collecting with service is dwelt on.

Of all countries in Africa, Nigeria has probably devoted most attention to national library planning; indeed, accounts of national library planning in both Africa and Latin America are very few. Adeyemi outlines the very substantial progress that has been made, in particular by the National Library Act of 1964 and the National Library Decree 1970, but in spite of the provision that the national library should 'establish and maintain a branch of the national library in each state' of the Federation, he argues that much has still to be done in the way of national library planning *(see also Further Reading, Ref. 14)*.

Japan's national library, established in 1948, has its origins in post-war educational and political development, and was planned as one agent in the democratisation of the country. It exhibits a number of unusual features. It is a true, and indeed highly centralised, national library, but is nevertheless basically a library serving the Diet. It consists not only of the central library but also three branch libraries and thirty libraries of government agencies in and around Tokyo.

Sudden and massive wealth from oil revenues has given Iran the chance, grasped with both hands, to create from scratch a national library serving a multiplicity of functions (including that of being very much a public library), containing all forms of recorded knowledge from conventional books to films, globes and computer data bases, and using the most modern techniques. The plan, as described in the paper by the person who master-minded the planning, was developed with the aid of over 100 recognised experts from many countries — surely the most comprehensive and ambitious piece of library planning ever. At the moment it is only a plan, but as such it is of great interest, perhaps as an ideal rather than a model for other developing countries.

South East Asia consists of several countries, in different stages of development, but all with huge problems in common, including the provision of education and of the resources for education, administration, science, technology and medicine. At the same time these countries have little tradition of written knowledge. Library planning is therefore seen primarily not as conservation of the cultural heritage — although this is not ignored — but as a very practical provision of information resources to serve practical needs. Anuar's paper, after reviewing the relevant Unesco seminars on national libraries and national library planning, examines the divergent legal provisions and practical progress that have been made within the different countries. Dates of foundation of national libraries range from 1905 (Thailand) to the 1970s (Malaysia). Numerous plans have been commissioned and reports produced, but few of these have been acted upon to any great extent. Library associations have also had some influence (see Xuereb's paper). Parts of Anuar's article, like several others in this volume, have been overtaken by political events, which can only add to the problems — where the problems have not been dealt with by a Final Solution, as in the Khmer Republic.

Many Latin American countries founded national libraries shortly after they became independent, and indeed partly as a symbol of independence. Despite their relatively long history, their story, as Gropp shows, is largely one of heavy dependence on gifts and of severe regular under-financing, punctuated in some cases by natural and unnatural disasters. Of the nineteen countries whose national library provision is summarized by Gropp, the first three have been included in this volume as not untypical examples of different levels of development, and incidentally of both Spanish and Portuguese America.

The importance of the oral tradition in developing countries is a main theme of Lashley's paper on the West Indies, where he identifies only one 'nearly national library', the West India Reference Library in Jamaica. West Indian society is radically different from that of developed countries, and he sees libraries in the West Indies as essentially 'political' instruments dedicated to the benefit of a society and culture with highly distinctive features and needs, including the identification, collection, preservation and transmission of 'the total racial memory' of the West Indies.

The dedication of the national library to society appears, though in a rather different form, in Ramos' article on Cuba, where the national library has been remodelled and apparently revitalised along socialist lines. It is seen as very much a *public* library, with provision for the visual arts and music, and a Juvenile Department which lends books, prints and pictures to children and also offers exhibitions, competitions, film shows and concerts. More conventional are a Department of Scientific and Technical Information and an extensive programme of bibliographic activity.

The papers included in this group may be supplemented by various sources. A summary account of national libraries in twenty-six developing countries, arranged alphabetically by country, can be found in Aje's admirable survey *(Further Reading, Ref.10).* Panofsky's paper on national libraries in Africa *(Further Reading, Ref.13),* though concerned mainly with bibliographical activities, contains useful information on an area not otherwise well covered; in fact, there are as yet few national libraries as such in Africa, though in several countries various national functions are specifically allocated to other libraries. A select list of references on individual countries may be found under *Further Reading.*

Paul L. Berry National Libraries
in General and in the United States

The Introduction (pp. 34-37) discusses the functions of national libraries as dealt with in the Vienna Symposium on National Libraries in Europe, and by Humphreys.

... the significant aspect of Mr. Humphreys' work is the organization of the functions into categories of importance, as well as the distinction he makes between those to be performed by the national library and those necessary to a national library service. This distinction is worth examining in some further detail.

NATIONAL LIBRARIES AND NATIONAL LIBRARY SERVICE
In describing the functions not necessarily those of the national library, Mr. Humphreys defines them further as '. . . those which can be undertaken by other agencies whether under the control of the central national library or not'.[9] The distinction, of course, was not entirely new, since it was noted in the 1955 *Library Trends* issue: 'All national libraries do not occupy the same position in the library systems of their country. Some may conceivably be independent or aloof; others are legally charged with fixed responsibilities and firm primacy; others still, exercise authority loosely and only by common consent'.[10] The editors at that time, however, saw the trend as being away from separation: 'It would seem to be not unlikely, however, that the trend toward a dispersion of national library functions will soon spend itself, and will be succeeded by re-unification, and re-integration. Satisfactory administration would appear to demand it'.[11] Only by a very extensive study would it be possible to determine the current state of unification or dispersion of functions, but the logic of a single agency is not so persuasive today as it might have seemed in 1955, at least not in the larger countries. It seems almost axiomatic that in the larger countries there must be a sharing of responsibility for library services, since no single library or agency can carry the whole load. In the smaller countries, on the other hand, a centralized agency might well be the most effective and efficient means of carrying out the national responsibility.

The current situations in two countries--the United Kingdom and the United States--may provide some indication of the direction in which the trend is going. In the United Kingdom, of course, the new development is the British Library--that new organization set forth in a Command Paper in January 1971 following an extensive study and report by the National Libraries Committee under the chairmanship of Dr. F.S. Dainton. Action by the Parliament is expected to bring the British Library into existence as a national institution.[12] It is not possible yet to stress the importance of this development, and certainly presumptuous of a distant observer to attempt an evaluation. To judge from the published statements, however, the objectives in establishing the British Library are integrative in only a limited way. The 1971 White Paper opens with the statement that 'For many years librarians and users of libraries have recognized that we have in this country the resources to create a *national library service* without rival in the world' (italics added).[13] It is clear in the remainder of the White Paper, however, that the new British Library is not to be responsible for a complete national library service. This is also confirmed in a recent article by the Director of the National Central Library, Maurice B. Line, in which he states that the units of the British Library '. . . constitute only part of the national library system, in the sense of the library system of the country'.[14] On the other hand, it will certainly be a national library organization of great scope so far as collections, bibliography, and reference

Reprinted from INGRAM, K.E. *and* JEFFERSON, Albertina A., *eds.* Libraries and the challenge of change: papers of the International Library Conference held in Kingston, Jamaica, 24-29 April 1972. London: Mansell, for the Jamaica Library Association and the Jamaica Library Service, 1975, p. 34-46, by permission of the author and the publisher.

services are concerned. Only four former institutions were specifically included in the action recommended by the White Paper: the British Museum Library (including the National Reference Library of Science and Invention), the National Central Library, the National Lending Library for Science and Technology, and the British National Bibliography. 'The National Libraries of Scotland and Wales, the Science Museum Library and other libraries of national importance will remain independent of the British Library.'[15] Certain relationships with other libraries were mentioned, but no total library system or national service was proposed. What is proposed for the British Library is undoubtedly a monumental step forward--and may well be the most significant current development on the national scene in any country--but it does not point toward a unified national library service.

It is interesting to compare the objectives of the British Library with the list of national library functions developed by Mr. Humphreys mentioned previously. Of the six fundamental functions of a national library stated by Mr. Humphreys, the first five are specifically covered in the statement of objectives as set forth in the White Paper. [16] Only the sixth function--publication of catalogues of its holdings of all types of materials--is not explicitly stated, but we can assume from the past examples of the British Museum catalogues that this type of publication can be expected to continue. Of the three desirable functions, only the first--interlibrary lending--is specifically covered. The second--index to locations of manuscripts-- is not a responsibility of the British Library. The third function-- research on library techniques--may receive some attention. The White Paper carries this statement:

> In the past national libraries have not been able to undertake
> sufficient research into the needs of their users and into the
> most efficient ways of meeting these needs. Since the planning of
> the British Library and the design of new buildings should
> anticipate these needs and techniques, research is urgently re-
> quired. The Organising Committee will be in a position to com-
> mission studies to provide both the basis for its own planning
> and the background for future policy decisions by the Board.
> These studies will be directly related to the functions of the
> British Library. Library and information science research in its
> wider aspects will remain a responsibility of the Department of
> Education and Science, and will be closely co-ordinated with the
> research undertaken by the Board. [17]

None of those functions that Mr. Humphreys describes as not necessary for the national library is proposed for the British Library, with the possible exception of assistance to other libraries in library techniques. One of the objectives stated in the White Paper is that of 'providing central cataloguing and other bibliographic services related not only to the needs of the central libraries but to those of libraries and information centres throughout the country . . .' [18] One function not listed by Humphreys is assigned specifically to the British Library: that of providing photocopying service.

In summary, then, the British Library is expected to perform the essential functions of a national library, but there are significant areas of library service that are still not integrated into a single national system in the United Kingdom. That the National Libraries Committee recognized relationships among libraries is evident from this statement in its *Report*:

We early took the view that the National Libraries must be seen
in relation to these other parts of the national information
system. Many of the services of the National Libraries complement
those of other libraries and, in this respect, they form an
essential part of the complete spectrum of library and information
services. We also identified various aspects of library and information activity where there was a need to co-ordinate the efforts
of many different libraries and institutions, in order that the
substantial total resources involved would be used in the best
possible ways. Here an organization administering the National
Libraries has a different, but no less important function to perform. Thirdly, the National Libraries should be the apex of the
library system, representing the best in current practice and
pioneering new developments, as well as covering all subjects and
giving the best possible service to users of all types.[19]

In the United States the most recent national development has been
the establishment of the National Commission on Libraries and Information Science, through an enactment of law in 1970 (Public Law 91-
345). This law was the culmination of efforts over a considerable
number of years to examine needs and to develop plans for a national
programme for library service in the United States. Although much of
the early effort at considering and planning for national library
service was informal and not particularly well-supported, a more
systematic effort was made in the late 1960s when a National Advisory
Commission on Libraries was appointed by President Lyndon B. Johnson.
This Advisory Commission performed a noteworthy service in examining
thoroughly the state of library affairs in the United States and in
identifying those areas where national attention was needed. There is
not space, nor would it be useful to recount the work of the National
Advisory Commission on Libraries in this paper. (Its report and
several studies made for it are contained in *Libraries at Large*.)
Several aspects of its deliberations and recommendations are related
to the topic of national libraries. The Commission was concerned
about the diversity of library service:

> The historical growth of libraries is a vivid commentary on our
> problems today, in fact, for we see at major periods in the past
> the development of one or two particular kinds of library. Today
> we have the whole array of libraries alive at once; our world
> demands this variety, while our achievements and our great need
> grow from it.[20]

An overriding conclusion, however, evident from all the studies
and hearings, is that there is an extremely wide range in both
the character and the adequacy of libary services and library
resources.[21]

Inasmuch as the National Advisory Commission on Libraries was a group
established for a specified period with but the single purpose of
reporting to the President on its findings, it could do little else
but identify problems and recommended some means to pursue their
solution on a more permanent basis. Commission members recommended,
however, that this pursuit be the responsibility of a planning or
co-ordinating agency rather than an administrative agency.

> The Commission believes that the nation's library and other
> information systems will continue to be a shared responsibility
> of Federal agencies, the states, municipalities, educational
> institutions, and many other public and private organizations.

> No monolithic Federal or other centralized administrative control
> seems either feasible or desirable. There will have to be many
> different kinds of information systems and working relationships
> among a variety of institutions if we are to provide effective
> access to relevant information for our society. New systems, roles,
> and relationships are likely to emerge at very different rates of
> speed in response to widely varying user needs.[22]

It specifically recommended, therefore, the establishment of a permanent National Commission on Libraries and Information Science in these
terms:

> In order to implement and further develop the national policy of
> library services for the nation's needs, the most important single
> measure that can be undertaken is the establishment of a continuing
> Federal planning agency. It is noteworthy that almost all represen-
> tatives of library, scholarly, scientific, and other professional
> associations who testified before the National Advisory Commission
> on Libraries gave high priority in their recommendations to the
> creation of such a Federal planning agency.[23]

This recommendation, of the five submitted by the Commission, is the
only one to have been adopted to date. The Congress established the
National Commission on Libraries and Information Science in July 1970,
and the President named its members in June 1971. Since that time the
new Commission has held five meetings but has issued little in the
way of information about its deliberations or plans.[24] As a trend
for the future, however, it is evident from the events of recent
years that national library service in the United States has become
a matter for public attention, but that the rather unco-ordinated
situation will continue for the present. Co-operative efforts of a
voluntary character have occurred and will continue to occur in the
next few years, but more permanent changes will depend upon the
success of the National Commission and the library community in
convincing the President, the Congress, and the American people of
the need for a national library policy and programme.

THE LIBRARY OF CONGRESS AS A NATIONAL LIBRARY
    Although the Library of Congress does not have in its name the
words 'national library' it is, in fact, just that. It is the largest
library in the United States, and is among the largest in the world;
it performs to some degree nearly all of the functions that have
been identified with national libraries. Regardless of the matter of
name, the Library of Congress is recognized at home and abroad as
the *de facto* national library of the United States.
    The Library of Congress was not established with this purpose in
mind, but was at its outset in 1800 intended simply to provide a
necessary service for the legislative branch of the new Nation. Within
a very few years, however, the desirability of having collections of
broad scope was recognized: the Congress appropriated funds in 1815
to purchase the personal library of former President Thomas Jefferson,
a library of remarkable universality. During the succeeding years
more and more materials were added by purchases, by gifts, and by the
enactments of law. The year 1870 was particularly significant, for in
that year the copyright law was amended to locate this function in
the Library of Congress and to place in its collections the two
copies of each book or other work registered for copyright under that
law. This change was not merely a happy accident; it was brought
about as part of the vision of the then Librarian of Congress,

Ainsworth Rand Spofford, who saw the future role of the Library as one of a central library for the country--a 'national library' such as those developing abroad. During the next twenty-seven years as Librarian Mr. Spofford pursued this vision with such energy and success that the Congress provided a monumental building adjacent to the Capitol Building to house the fast-growing collections and to provide suitable space for their use and for the services that properly accompany such collections. The history of the Library of Congress in the twentieth century, furthermore, is one of continued growth and ever-expanding services under several Librarians who have carried forward the vision of a great national library.

A comparison of the functions currently performed by the Library of Congress with the Humphreys list of national library functions is quite revealing. Of the six fundamental functions the Library of Congress performs three completely: (1) an outstanding (but not totally inclusive) collection of the Nation's literature; (2) an extensive coverage of foreign literature; and (3) serving as a national bibliographic information centre. The collections of the Library now exceed 64 million pieces and include almost every form of material appropriate for library collections. Its collections of the Nation's literature extend beyond the printed page to include manuscripts and personal papers of many of the Nation's outstanding statesmen, jurists, scientists, military men, authors, and composers. The collections also include the Nation's heritage in graphic form and in recorded sound. The efforts of the Library of Congress as the national centre for cataloguing are unprecedented, and the technical systems (cataloguing codes, classification schemes, and subject headings) that have accompanied these cataloguing efforts are known and used throughout the world.

Three of the fundamental functions, however, are not as fully developed: (1) legal deposit; (2) publication of the national bibliography; and (3) publication of catalogues of holdings. With regard to legal deposit, there is no legal deposit requirement in the United States and little likelihood of any such enactment. The Library benefits from the nearest thing to this--the deposit of copies of materials registered for copyright protection--and also benefits from provisions of law that bring to it the voluminous publications of the Federal Government. Absence of a legal deposit law, however, has merely stimulated the development of means to acquire the appropriate publications by purchase, gift, or exchange, with a degree of success that is evident from the statistics on the size of the collections. With regard to national bibliography, the Library's lack of a publication limited only to works published in the United States is more than offset by its printed card services, its almost universal bibliography in the form of the *National Union Catalog*, and its more limited accessions lists of special types of materials, such as publications of the States (in the *Monthly Checklist of State Publications*) and the recently inaugurated checklist entitled *Non-GPO Imprints*. Similarly, with regard to catalogues of its own collections, the lack of such catalogues for certain of the special collections is more than offset by the extent to which the most important of the Library's collections have been described. New catalogues are prepared from time to time and older ones are revised periodically.

Of the three desirable functions listed by Mr. Humphreys, all are performed by the Library of Congress. It participates actively in the national and international system of interlibrary lending. Much has been done in the Library of Congress to develop information on the

location of manuscript collections in the various repositories of the
country, as attested to by the nine volumes of the *National Union
Catalog of Manuscript Collections* published to date. Research on
library techniques has been actively pursued by the Library, particularly the cataloguing and classification of library materials. In
recent years research efforts have extended to computer-assisted
techniques used in the Library of Congress and also serving as models
for other libraries. Attention is also being given to basic research
and development relating to the conservation of library materials, a
matter of great concern to many research libraries.

The Library of Congress is involved, in whole or in part, in all
six of the functions that Mr. Humphreys cites as those not necessary
for a national library. It is extensively involved in exchanges, both
domestic and foreign; it distributes duplicates, including many that
are received from libraries of other Federal agencies (but it does
not serve as the central distribution agency for all other libraries);
it has a central role in a national system to provide reading materials
for the Nation's blind and physically handicapped; it provides some
professional training, but does not intrude into the type of training
that is traditionally provided by the many library schools; and it
provides considerable assistance to other libraries in library techniques. From one point of view, the Library of Congress plays only a
small part in the library planning of the Nation, inasmuch as this
policy and funding responsibility is placed by law in another agency
of the Federal Government, the U.S. Office of Education. From the
descriptions of the national library scene quoted above, however, it
should be clear that even the role of the Office of Education is a
limited one. National library planning, therefore, requires consideration of the place of the Library of Congress in the system and of
necessity involves the Library's administrative and technical
specialists.

There are other functions of a national character that are now
performed by the Library of Congress. The more important of these are
listed below:

Administers, under its world-wide acquisitions programmes, the
Public Law 480 Program to acquire foreign materials for other
U.S. libraries, as well as for itself.

Has a national cataloguing data distribution service, distributing
catalogue information on cards and magnetic tape (MARC) on a
weekly basis. Most recently, cataloguing data for individual books
is being supplied to publishers for printing in American trade
publications, through a cataloguing-in-publication programme.

Maintains union catalogues on cards; and is now editing the
National Union Catalog on cards describing pre-1956 imprints for
publication in 600 volumes.

Operates such information 'switchboards' as the National Referral
Center for Science and Technology.

Extends services of its collections through a national and international photoduplication service.

Presents exhibits, concerts, and literary programmes, including
the extension of these programmes to enrich the cultural life of
the nation through travelling exhibits and the broadcasting of the
music and literary programmes.

Conducts a programme for the preservation of library materials,

planned as the nucleus of a national programme to attack the
problem of deteriorating materials faced by all libraries. This
programme has both policy and technical aspects.

Despite the record of the many accomplishments of the Library of
Congress in those activities that are considered appropriate to a
national library, there are always additional needs to be met. An
excellent opportunity to review its status and to consider the future
was presented to the Library during the late 1960s when the National
Advisory Commission on Libraries was studying the matter of national
library service. The results of the Library's review were set forth
in a paper on 'The Library of Congress as the National Library:
Potentialities for Service' which was included in the publication of
the Commission's resource materials entitled *Libraries at Large.*[25]
Further accomplishment of these potentialities, of course, must
depend upon support and appropriations, but the following ten areas
are still considered to merit serious development in the next few
years.

1. Expand its acquisitions actively to all geographic areas and
   types of materials mainly through the National Program for
   Acquisitions and Cataloging, acquiring multiple copies of foreign
   publications for major research libraries from areas where
   acquisition presents difficult problems, as well as providing
   detailed guides to materials available at the Library of Congress.

2. Serve as a national centre for library resources, including but
   not limited to extending its union catalogue activities, preparing
   guides to the total library resources of the United States, serving
   as a national centre for research, guidance, and information on
   preservation problems.

3. Broaden and expand its cataloguing activities, including Federal,
   State, and local publications.

4. Substantially expand its bibliographic services.

5. Serve as a national centre for research and training in library
   and information science.

6. Serve as a national centre for data on serials.

7. Serve as a national technical reports centre.

8. Serve to a greater degree as a national referral service in all
   fields as it does now in science and technology.

9. Serve as the focus of a national interlibrary loan system.

10. Expand the Library's publication programmes.

The completion of the James Madison Memorial Library of Congress
scheduled for 1975 would for the first time in many years provide the
Library with the essential space to carry out many of these added
programmes.

OTHER U.S. NATIONAL LIBRARIES
It is not possible in this brief paper to consider in detail the
many facets of the relationships of the Library of Congress with the
many other libraries of the United States, but a brief consideration
of the relationship with two other U.S. national libraries is essential.
At the beginning of the section on the Library of Congress it is stated
that it is not named as a national library but serves this purpose as

the *de facto* national library. Two libraries in the executive branch
of the Federal Government, however, do have legal designations as
national libraries in their respective fields: the National Agricultural Library (under the Department of Agriculture) and the National
Library of Medicine (under the Department of Health, Education and
Welfare). Within their subject areas these two libraries perform
many of the functions of national libraries and, within their
specialties, perform them exceedingly well. But the laws establishing
the two national libraries do not require any co-ordination between
them or with the Library of Congress. This situation was characterized in the following terms by Professor Richard H. Leach in a
special study commissioned by the National Advisory Commission on
Libraries.

> For the most part the three libraries--the Library of Congress,
> the National Library of Medicine, and the National Agricultural
> Library--function as separate institutions. Certainly NAL and
> NLM have no desire to do otherwise. The fact that they do operate
> independently not only militates against the Library of Congress'
> taking full possession of the national library functions, but
> also produces a situation involving a good deal of overlap and
> duplication in scope and coverage, as well as in processes and
> procedures, on the one hand, and some competition between the
> three on the other. Some duplication is probably inevitable,
> inasmuch as the two specialized libraries have a more limited
> clientele than the Library of Congress, and a certain degree of
> competition is generally regarded to be healthy.[26]

In actual fact, however, there has always been a considerable amount
of co-operation--informal and formal--among the three libraries, and
there have been active efforts in the past five years to increase
this co-operation further. Among several projects the most visible
has been the National Serials Data Program, a co-operative effort
intended to create a national data bank of machine-readable information relating to the location of serial titles held by American
research libraries. Much study has gone into this project during the
past five years, with the result that a start will be made during
1972 on the recording of data. Other areas of common interest that
have been studied have been co-ordination of acquisitions activities,
co-ordination of cataloguing activities (including machine-readable
cataloguing data), reference and bibliographic services, and statistics. All of these efforts are carried out by working groups within
a formal organization given the name U.S. National Libraries Task
Force on Automation and Other Cooperative Services. There is every
reason to expect that this co-operative programme can overcome some
of the problems that concerned Professor Leach in 1967.

NATIONAL LIBRARIES IN THE FUTURE
   A suitable conclusion for a paper on national libraries seems to
require some prediction of their future. This is particularly hazard-
ous, however, when the subject is so imprecise and when the milieu in
which it exists is so susceptible to change. There are just too many
types, sizes, and patterns of national library organization to attempt
current generalization, much less to predict the future. Furthermore,
libraries are more the products than the producers of social and
technological changes. National libraries will certainly continue to
play a significant cultural and educational role in the societies in
which they exist. The question for the future is whether the role will
be central or subsidiary; whether active or passive; whether

progressive or vestigial. Can national libraries really meet the
information needs of their constituents? Can they adapt to changes
in needs and to changes in technologies? In some instances the
changes may be forced upon them from the outside if they do not
change themselves; in some instances they will be by-passed as other
institutions are established to satisfy current needs; in many instances, hopefully, the national libraries will be the initiators of
changes and will anticipate both needs and solutions.

In the 1955 issue of *Library Trends* the editors saw reintegration
as the trend for national libraries, but in recent years the popular
words have been 'networks' and 'information systems'. If there is any
discernible characteristic of the present and immediate future it is
in these areas. A unitary approach to library problems has given way
to the co-operative approach through libraries working together in
larger and larger groupings. One specific application of this approach
was described earlier in the section on the new British Library. This
cannot be demonstrated quite so clearly for the United States, but
there is networking in action for libraries at local and regional
levels if not nationally. There is evidence that other countries are
also experiencing this type of change. A recent statement by the
National Librarian of Canada, Guy Sylvestre, puts this quite well,
and may serve as a summary of where national libraries find themselves in 1972.

> There are from country to country such differences--geographical,
> historical, social, economic, cultural--that each nation must
> find for herself those solutions best suited to her particular
> needs which the human, financial, and other resources available
> to her at a given time make possible. There is simply no single
> ready-made recipe capable of curing all evils everywhere once
> and for all. For systems are not only books, catalogs, and
> hardware, they are also people. People are in turn members of
> individual evolving societies so that information systems and net-
> works must be dynamic, they must respond to changing needs, they
> must be capable of handling dynamic information and knowledge.[27]

Notes

1 Symposium on National Libraries in Europe, Vienna, 1958, *National
   Libraries: Their Problems and Prospects* (Paris, 1960).
2 Arundell J.K. Esdaile, *National Libraries of the World: Their
   History, Administration and Public Services* (London, 1934, and
   2nd ed., London, 1957).
3 David C. Mearns, 'Current Trends in National Libraries,' *Library
   Trends*, 4:96 (July 1955).
4 Frank C. Francis, 'The Organization of National Libraries,' in
   Symposium on National Libraries in Europe, *National Libraries*,
   p.21.
5 Mearns, 'Current Trends in National Libraries,' p.99.
6 United States Library of Congress, General Reference and Bibliography Division, *Functions of Selected National Libraries*
   (Washington, 1958).
7 Symposium on National Libraries in Europe, *National Libraries*,
   pp.111-116.
8 K.W. Humphreys, 'The Role of the National Library: A Preliminary
   Statement,' *Libri*, 14:4 (1964) pp.356-368.
9 *Ibid.*, p.362.
10 Mearns, 'Current Trends in National Libraries,' p.98.

11 *Ibid.*, p.102.
12 This was accomplished on 27 July 1972.
13 Great Britain, Office of the Paymaster General, *The British Library* (London, 1971) Cmnd. 4572, p.2.
14 Maurice B. Line, 'The Developing National Library Network in Great Britain,' *Library Resources and Technical Services*, 16:63 (Winter 1972). For another general description of the current situation in the United Kingdom see Edward Stanford, 'Looking to the Future in Great Britain,' *American Libraries*, 3:157-162 (February 1972).
15 Great Britain, Office of the Paymaster General, *The British Library*, p.3.
16 *Ibid.*, p.2.
17 *Ibid.*, p.5. See also reference to an automation study in Maurice B. Line, 'The Developing National Library Network in Great Britain.'
18 *Ibid.*, p.2.
19 Great Britain, National Libraries Committee, *Report* (London, 1969) p.iv.
20 Douglas M. Knight, compiler, *Libraries at Large* (New York, 1969), p.[495].
21 *Ibid.*, p.500.
22 *Ibid.*
23 *Ibid.*, pp.515-516.
24 The first *Annual Report* of the Commission, covering fiscal year 1971-1972, appeared late in January 1973.
25 *Ibid.*, pp.[435]-465.
26 Richard H. Leach, 'A Broad Look at the Federal Government and Libraries,' in Knight, *Libraries at Large*, p.358.
27 Guy Sylvestre, 'The Developing National Library Network of Canada,' *Library Resources and Technical Services*, 16:48-49 (Winter 1972).

Berry's comments on the British Library on pp. 181-2 understate its range of functions. There is nothing in the British Library Act to require the British Library to provide an "index to locations of manuscripts", but equally there is nothing to prevent it. Much "research on library techniques" is funded by the British Library Research and Development Department. The British Library is very heavily involved in international exchange, and is the main national centre for the distribution of duplicates.

NATIONAL LIBRARIES: THE BRITISH LIBRARY

Stephen Green

The British Library is the national library of the United Kingdom. The particular needs of Scotland and Wales are satisfied additionally by the National Libraries of Scotland and Wales, which predate the foundation of the British Library. Taken together, these three institutions help to provide at the national level a balanced pattern of comprehensive service to institutions and individuals, irrespective of their geographical location in the United Kingdom. The British Library takes account of the views of its Scottish and Welsh colleagues wherever appropriate, a feature which is reflected in the membership of its Board, its Advisory Council and Committees, and in the less formal channels for liaison.

Just as this working relationship turns to constructive advantage an historically-determined situation, so also in a similar spirit was the British Library itself conceived. The British Library, which began operation on 1 July 1973, could not be planned in the abstract on a *tabula rasa* in Whitehall. The main objective of its creators was to weld into a coherent and flexible entity a variety of national or para-national institutions which had previously functioned independently, in a way which would yield the maximum benefit to the communities they served. It was recognised that central planning and management could eliminate unnecessary duplication, allow new techniques and systems to be developed and used more effectively, provide for a more equitable distribution of the resources available, and could permit the fullest opportunity to be taken of the possibilities for working on a national and international scale. To achieve this, the library departments of the British Museum (including the National Reference Library of Science and Invention), the National Lending Library for Science and Technology, the National Central Library and the British National Bibliography Ltd were brought together to form the British Library. In April 1974 nearly all the functions of the Office for Scientific and

Reprinted from LOCK, R. Northwood, *ed.* Manual of library economy: a conspectus of professional librarianship for students and practitioners. London: Bingley; Hamden, Conn.: Linnet Books, 1977, p. 18-46, by permission of the publisher.

Technical Information, a part of the Department of Education and Science, were transferred to the British Library, thus providing a central library-based focus for a national programme of research and development.

The character and role of any national library is determined to a large part by the continuum within which it operates, and it can assume a large number of organisational forms. Indeed, it may not even be officially declared the national library, as in the case of the Library of Congress. As a logical corollary to this statement, to draw up a model constitution for a national library is an exercise of limited practical value. It is analogous with the exposition of universal theories of democracy: many countries espouse democratic ideals, yet in no two countries will the practice of democracy be identical. The strength of Unesco's programme for National Information Systems (NATIS) (1), in which the national library has a significant part to play, is that it recognises the diversity of character and of interaction with other library institutions that a national library may possess. Thus the French Bibliothèque Nationale is predictably different in scope and emphasis from the National Library being created in Iran, a country which has a heritage of unparalleled richness but until recently had a standard of library provision which was unremarkable for a developing country. Australia's national library utilises in an advanced way the modern concept of networks (2), which fits well with its place in a federal environment. The Lenin State Library of the USSR performs in a highly centralised state economy, yet its role is modified by the existence of numerous, comparatively autonomous, local state libraries. In Zambia, where great priority is given to education, the functions of the national and the university library are combined. Each is a unique solution to a common challenge in pursuit of broadly similar objectives, such as acting as the national repository for legal deposit, or providing national bibliographic services.

In the United Kingdom, it may seem surprising, at first sight, that an explicitly national library was not established earlier, for it is a library concept with a most venerable provenance. However, the creation of the British Library may be represented as the culmination of a long process of evolution. One of the earliest expressions of the idea may be glimpsed in an address from John Leland, Britain's first great antiquary and topographer, to Henry VIII, where he identifies the personal library of the kings of England as the most fitting repository for the libraries of the monasteries which were being dissolved in the 1530s as part of the English Reformation settlement, 'to the intente that the monumentes of auncient writers as welle of other nations, as of this your owne province mighte be brought owte of deadely darkenes to lyvely lighte, and to receyve like thankes of the posterite, as they hoped for at suche tyme as they emploied their longe and greate studies to the publique wealthe'. (3) In essence, it is a plea that the nation's recorded sense of heritage and learning should receive national public support in its preservation and dissemination. 150 years later, in 1697, Richard Bentley (the Royal Librarian of the day) made his famous melancholy plaint in his *Proposal for building a Royal library, and establishing it by Act of Parliament* (4); yet it was not until 1753 that the British Museum was founded, and even then its desirability had to be pressed on a doubting Parliament by the offer of various collections. As it was, the *de facto* national library, in contrast with many other national libraries in Europe, was set up as an integral part of a universal collection of natural and artificial 'curiosities', a decision which has had a significant effect on the structure and operations of the British Library today.

The marriage of museum and library functions under the guardianship of the amateurs of the old antiquarian tradition was increasingly subject in the nineteenth century to stress and challenge from professional and systematic research, a challenge personified within its walls by that great Italian emigré and most distinguished Principal Keeper of Printed Books, Sir Antonio Panizzi, the 'prince of librarians'. (5) It is fair to say that his vision of the national printed archive, systematically acquired, managed and catalogued, with the support of an exhaustive array of specialist subject bibliographies, accords much more closely with the objectives of the British Library in 1976 than those of the British Museum as he found it in the 1830s and 1840s.

Yet Panizzi's vision hardly compassed the growing world of libraries beyond the walls of the British Museum. There was little contact, and less cooperation, with the network of libraries—public, academic and specialist—that was evolving in a haphazard fashion. In this vacuum, the institutions which are now joined with the former British Museum Library in the British Library were created. In 1916, the Central Library for Students, which was to become the National Central Library providing lending services through its own collections and its union catalogues for the humanities and the social sciences, was established. In 1949, the British National Bibliography Ltd came into being with the avowed intention of providing central bibliographic services to the nation's libraries, principally through the medium of the *British national bibliography*. In 1962 the unorthodox National Lending Library for Science and Technology started operations at Boston Spa in Yorkshire to satisfy the growing need, especially of industrial libraries, for a central lending mechanism which could cope with the tremendous rise in the output of scientific and technical literature at a speed consonant with the timescales and demands of modern industry.

It was this uneven mosaic, heterogeneous both in its practices and attitudes, which confronted those whose task it was in the later 1960s to examine the feasibility of a new comprehensive, national library organisation which could group together these activities and services under one umbrella. The first governmental initiative was to set up the National Libraries Committee under the chairmanship of Sir Frederick Dainton. Its report endorsed the practicability, indeed the necessity, of a single authority, centrally financed and managed. (6) The government's legislative intentions to set up the British Library as an independent corporate body were laid out in its White Paper of January 1971 (7). After approval by Parliament, the detailed planning of the new library was entrusted to the British Library Organising Committee, which started work in the same year. Under the chairmanship of the Paymaster-General with special responsibility for the Arts, Lord Eccles, it had a membership which included representatives of the organisations to be combined, and others who could articulate the needs of the major library, academic, industrial and regional interests. It dealt with buildings, staff, finance, management structure and modern library techniques such as automatic data processing. It was assisted by a full-time planning secretariat, and it sought specialist advice where necessary, both within and without the embryonic organisation. It was a highly-controlled operation which permitted the rapid pace of development to be maintained, so that in July 1972 the British Library Act (8) which was based on its work became law; in April 1973 the British Library Board was set up, and from July 1973 onwards the collections, staff and functions of the constituent elements were transferred.

The terms of the Act are significant for their intrinsic flexibility. They attempt to allow future and as yet unforeseen developments, which may bring about radical changes in the functions of a national library, to be accommodated. One will search in vain for prescribed constitutional practices in the Act; it provides basically broad terms of reference that have received Parliamentary endorsement.

This feature is nowhere more evident than in the composition of the Board itself. The Act states that the Library is to be under the control and management of an independent public authority, known as the British Library Board, whose members are appointed by the Secretary of State for Education and Science. It consists of a chairman and not less than eight, nor more than thirteen other members, and at least one of the members must serve full-time. Hence the Act gives a considerable latitude both in the number of members appointed, and in the balance between full and part-time membership.

The Act also specifies that the British Library shall consist of a comprehensive collection of books, manuscripts, periodicals, films and other recorded matter, whether printed or otherwise. The Library shall be managed as a national centre for reference, study and bibliographical and other information services, in relation both to scientific and technological matters, and to the humanities. The Act requires the Board to make available the services of the British Library in particular to institutions of education and learning, and to other libraries and industry. It empowers the Board to carry out and sponsor research and to contribute to the expenses of those providing library facilities, whether for members of the public or otherwise.

So far, the origins of the British Library and the framework within which it was intended to operate have been sketched out. It is now time to examine in more detail what is happening in practice.

THE BRITISH LIBRARY:
ITS STRUCTURE AND MANAGEMENT

The organisational structure of the British Library is represented in diagram 1. The British Library Board is responsible for the determination and control of policy within the remit of the Act, and for the appropriate allocation of resources to carry out its intentions. These resources may be classified into the categories of finance, accommodation and staff.

The Library's annual income is currently over £21 million. It is provided partly by its grant-in-aid (about 89%) and partly by the revenue earned by its bibliographic, lending and reprographic services (about 11%). The grant-in-aid is the technical term for the money voted annually to the Library through the Department of Education and Science by Parliament, after it has considered the detailed estimates submitted by the Board for its necessary expenditure in the forthcoming year, and less detailed projections for the two years after that. Unlike a government department, the Library is allowed to retain any unspent balance

Diagram 1

Structure of the British Library

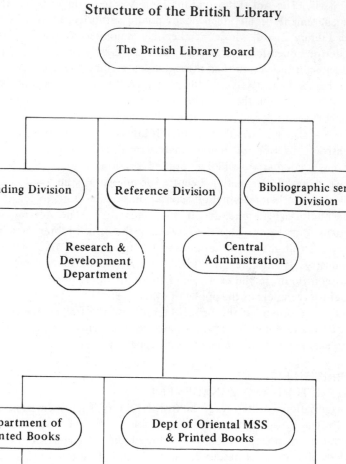

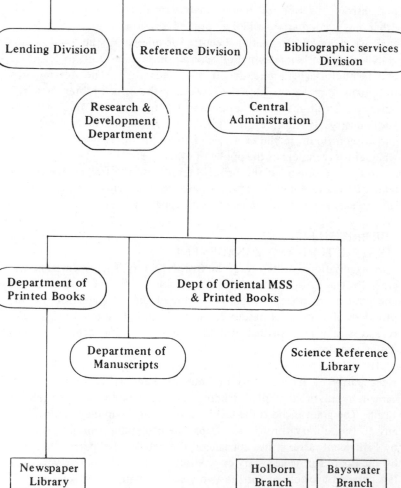

of the grant, and may diverge from the intended allocation shown in the published estimates, subject to certain safeguards. If the Library's costs rise unexpectedly during a year, for instance through a nationally-agreed pay award to its staff, a supplementary grant may be made. The size of the grant takes account both of the national responsibilities of the British Library laid down in the Act (for instance, the Board's contributions to the expenses of other libraries, of which a list appears in its annual report (9)), and the revenue it can derive from recovering some or all of the costs of the services it offers, a matter which is regularly reviewed by the Board. Between 1974 and 1976 the revenue of the British Library increased by nearly 70%, and to a large extent it has been used to improve and expand existing services or to introduce new ones, a pattern which is likely to continue, thus lessening the Library's dependence on its Parliamentary grant. Its annual accounts must be published, and are open to scrutiny by the government's auditors and the Public Accounts Committee of the House of Commons.

In its financial planning the Board utilises the techniques of Programme Analysis and Review—known by its acronym PAR, and a development of the Planning, Programming and Budgeting System (PPBS) —to monitor the effectiveness in terms of both benefit and cost of the divisional objectives it has previously approved. This allows the Board to make realistic forecasts of its needs for Exchequer assistance over the five-year planning periods used by government in framing national expenditure programmes. It is the use of such techniques which has helped the Library to earn already a creditable reputation for financial management in the eyes of the government.

The accommodation needs of the Library have and will preoccupy the Board for some years to come. The Library's London-based activities are carried out in no less than 17 different buildings, some of them relatively unsuitable for the purposes for which they are now used, others geographically inconvenient and disruptive of the speed of service the public rightly expects from its national library, and all of them subject to overcrowding with a deleterious effect on the morale and efficiency of staff and users alike. There will be no substantial amelioration until a new building is constructed which can house under one roof the present fragmented operations and can allow for some physical expansion. Fortunately, after many delays, the Government has given permission for detailed design work to start on the Somers Town site in North London, which it has bought for that purpose. It is hoped that the first phase of the building will be opened by the mid-1980s.

In the meantime, the Board constantly examines ways in which the existing accommodation can be used to the best advantage.

The staff of the Library is regarded by the Board as its most valuable asset. They number about 2,000, of which 680 are professional staff and many previously worked in the organisations which were absorbed in the British Library. Many have library qualifications or equivalent experience, but given the diversity of tasks which the Library undertakes, from the production of catalogues of incunabula to the design of computer systems, professional library qualifications are not invariably demanded. Nevertheless through the introduction of an intensive training programme, the Board hopes to encourage its staff to become qualified wherever appropriate. The major problem facing the Board is that the staff are still on a wide range of incompatible pay scales and conditions of service, largely inherited from their former organisations, pending the agreement of government on a unified pay and grading structure for the British Library. (Most of the staff are on grades which relate to those in the Civil Service and are represented by various Civil Service unions). The Board is convinced that the introduction of an integrated grading structure will enhance career prospects and improve both individual job satisfaction and the Library's management.

These three major areas of concern of finance, accommodation and staff require a Board which is both capable of exercising powerful and knowledgeable control and diverse in its composition. Accordingly, it has been decided that the Board for the time being should have a Chairman serving part-time and a full-time Chief Executive who is also Deputy Chairman. Together they share overall responsibility for all the Board has to do in the initial stages of the library's development. Three other full-time members are the Directors-General of the three Divisions representing the main operational areas of the Library, of reference, lending and bibliographic services, who are responsible to the Chief Executive. In addition there are nine part-time members chosen for their breadth of relevant experience. One is appointed by Her Majesty the Queen; three are appointed after consultation respectively with the Secretaries of State for Industry, for Scotland and for Wales; and one is nominated by the Trustees of the British Museum.

The Board fully apprehends that it operates in a country with an astounding richness of library service, and that its true strength will be realised by acting as the cornerstone in this pluralistic library edifice. The success of many of its policies will depend on their acceptability to the library and information community. For this reason it has been anxious to see an extensive advisory and consultative machinery created. Accordingly, an Advisory Council has been set up to advise on the British Library's relations with other libraries and information services, both national and international, as well as on the nature of the central services to be offered to users. The council's membership is drawn from the nominees of bodies representing both library and user interests. In addition, advisory committees have been set up to provide the expert advice needed for the successful operation of the Library, with their members serving in a personal capacity. So far five committees have been established to advise the management of the Reference Division (Bloomsbury), the Reference Division (the Science Reference Library), the Lending Division, the Bibliographic Services Division and the Research and Development Department.

The remainder of this excellent paper (pp. 26-46) contains sections on National archival and reference services, National lending services, National bibliographic services, and Research and development.

REFERENCES

1 *Final report,* Intergovernmental Conference on the Planning of National Documentation, Library and Archives Infrastructures, (Paris 23-27 September 1974), Paris-Unesco, 1975.

The diversity of national approaches is also manifest in the brief accounts of progress in *NATIS news,* published periodically by Unesco.

2 *National Library of Australia: 15th annual report 1974-75,* Canberra, National Library of Australia, 1975, pp 10ff.

3 *Leland's itinerary,* ed L T Smith, vol 1, pp xxxvii-viii, 1907.

4 [Bentley, Richard, D D] *Proposal for building a Royal Library, and establishing it by Act of Parliament,* [London: 1697].

5 Miller, E J: *Prince of librarians: the life and times of Antonio Panizzi of the British Museum*, Deutsch, 1967.

6 *Report of the National Libraries Committee,* (Cmnd 4028), Her Majesty's Stationery Office, 1969.

7 *The British Library*, (Cmnd 4572), Her Majesty's Stationery Office, 1971.

8 *British Library Act 1972.*

9 See the *Annual reports* published by the British Library, available free on request to library institutions, and to individuals.

10 Houghton, Bernard: *Out of the dinosaurs. The evolution of the National Lending Library for Science and Technology.* London, Bingley; Hamden, Conn, Linnet Books 1972.

A list of publications by and about the British Library was given as Appendix C to the British Library's *Second annual report 1974-75.* It is expected that this will become a regular feature.

The resources of the British Library

H. T. Hookway

Chief Executive, British Library Board

The preceding matter covers very briefly the concept and structure of the British Library, which is dealt with more fully in the paper by Green.

The British Library is the principal national depository for British copyright publications, the producer of the national bibliography, the central library institution for loans, a major developer and operator of computer-based bibliographic and other information services, and the main source of support for research in library and information science. I shall invite you first to look briefly at the Reference Division of the Library;

This Division comprises the former library departments of the British Museum. The nation possesses in the collections of these departments one of the most comprehensive collections of books, manuscripts, maps and music scores in the world. It is no easy task to exploit these outstanding national assets to the full, while bearing in mind the Board's responsibility to conserve the collections for future generations. Until a new building is provided the books—in ever increasing quantity—the staff and the readers must remain where they are, scattered in a multiplicity of inconvenient and outmoded buildings in central London. Much depends therefore on the provision within the next decade of modern premises worthy of the nation and capable of housing the great reference collections of the Library. Nevertheless, much can be done and is being done to ameliorate the situation by better organization and utilization of the limited space available and by rationalization and reorganization of services. Future activities are being planned so as to provide all the essential central reference services on the basis of which other libraries can build up their own collections and services. The reference facilities of a national library are

Reprinted from *Aslib Proceedings*, vol. 27, no. 1, January 1975, p. 2-7, by permission of the publisher.

often regarded as providing Library Services of a 'last resort', or back-up nature and to an extent this is true of the Reference Division of the British Library. However, over 15 million people live within a fifty mile radius of the Division's libraries in central London and in a very real sense it is a library of first resort for them, especially for workers in commerce, planning, science and technology. If the resources of the Division are to be exploited to the full, those who visit the Library and those who study elsewhere must have quickly and in the appropriate form as much information as possible about the nature, scope, and depth of the Library's holdings.

To provide this information requires the development of a wide range of new bibliographic services and the improvement of existing ones. The Bibliographic Services Division will play a major role in providing these services, and others designed to ensure the country as a whole has ready access not only to the collections of the British Library, but in addition, through international co-operative arrangements, with those of other countries.

It is self evident that an effective and economical bibliographic network is essential if libraries are to function at optimum efficiency. The high cost of providing bibliographic access to materials requires the development of co-operative and centralized arrangements for the services required. Computer-based services are obviously attractive in this context because they enable one to process much larger quantities of information than can be done by manual means; the costs of handling these even larger workloads are stabilized—for, unlike manual system costs, machine costs do not rise linearly with the work-load; and new products and services can readily be generated. It is noteworthy, therefore, that the Bibliographic Services Division comprises the former functions of the British National Bibliography together with those of the Copy-right Receipt Office and certain other functions of the former library depart-ments of the British Museum. The operations are already computer based, and the Copyright Receipt Office will soon be providing the listing of all legal deposit material at the library.

The general approach of the British Library towards providing bibliographic services for the Library and information community is that it should provide the route for data communication and transfer between the national biblio-graphic data banks, including of course the British data banks, and the British library community.

In following this policy, the central services provided now by the British Library, and those to be provided in 1975 and later years, have been planned to lead to the rapid growth of computer-based networks in Britain. At present, the Library's MARC tapes service can provide, for current cataloguing, a bibliographic listing, catalogue cards and machine readable cataloguing input. The machine readable input can be processed directly by an individual library, a library authority (where the central library would presumably do the job), by a region, or by the British Library, which is prepared to offer a selective service of catalogue records covering the additions to stock of individual libraries and merging its MARC records with records produced by libraries of books added to stock which are not covered by MARC tapes. The balance of advan-tage as between these various approaches depends on the resources of the library or library system involved. The terms on which the tapes or individual records are made available have been designed to ensure the maximum local utilization of the centrally generated system, while maintaining enough control to avoid the creation of many competing quasi or para-national files.

A further step has been to convert the British National Bibliography, back to its beginning in 1950, to machine readable form in MARC compatible format. This new data bank will be of particular value to the new library authorities described earlier in this paper who face the task of building catalogues of the combined holdings of the former authorities, and whose stocks of material consist largely of items listed in the National Bibliography.

By the end of the year all the regions will be operating a system first set up, with Government development support, by the London and South East Region (LASER) for recording accessions in numerical form by International Standard Book Number (ISBN), with coded library locations, and sorting by computer. The ISBN–location lists are produced as computer output on microfilm and can be used for interlending in two ways: either libraries apply to regional headquarters, which supplies them with a location, or they can buy the microfilm catalogues and borrow direct from one another. The system is both cheap and efficient, and the British Library does the processing centrally at no charge to the regions. It is possible therefore to integrate all the records to make a comprehensive ISBN catalogue for the intake of public libraries in the country. This will be important both at the national and the local level for determining acquisitions policy, as well as increasing the efficiency of interlending.

From 1975, the machine-based current cataloguing activities will be extended to all British Library intake. It will then be possible to provide a range of new services covering the areas of British Library intake that are not part of the MARC service provided at present. On line access within the Library is being provided for, on an experimental basis, and may be available to other users, but in the immediate future the relatively high telecommunications costs in Britain may inhibit rapid growth of use outside the Library. A decision will have to be taken soon on whether to convert the existing manually-produced catalogues. The cost will be high, but the benefits are likely to be great for libraries throughout the world. We should be able to decide what to do later this year, when our analyses of the problems and costs are complete. These developments are likely to be of particular value to university and other research libraries since they will be able to redeploy their own resources more effectively if they accept the new central services and adopt the same standards.

Another effective way of providing access to the collections is of course through inter-library lending which is now a very large operation in Britain. The Library's Lending Division was formed from the former National Lending Library for Science and Technology and the National Central Library, which has been planned to extend and further improve these activities. About two million requests a year are sent to the British Library, and demand is increasing steadily. I should like to make one or two observations of a general nature. First, the main factors accounting for the growth of demand on the central facilities are the acquisition programme of the Lending Division—which now aims to acquire all significant serials and reports in all languages, together with English language monographs—and the speed with which loan requests are met. The Library's Lending Division meets about 84 per cent of the demands made on it by direct loan from the central stock. The main burden of interlibrary lending has therefore been lifted from individual libraries, who are free to adapt their acquisitions and stock-holding procedures accordingly. From the national viewpoint, the interlending process is not only quicker and more efficient; it is also cheaper. But although the central lending collection is large it has to be supplemented by the resources of other libraries, and therefore it has been important to ensure that an appropriate network of cooperating libraries is set up to meet the deficiencies in the central stock. Union catalogues provide access to the holdings of many libraries. In addition, in the interests of efficiency of the overall operations, we have made special arrangements with a limited number of libraries with very large or special resources to provide a back-up service. The number of requests made is fairly substantial, the cost of dealing with the requests is not negligible, and there is need for rapid response. We therefore pay these large co-operating libraries for their services so as to ensure they can deploy adequate resources to meet our requirements.

Finally, a word about research. The research and development department of the library comprises the functions of OSTI, extended to include work in the humanities, together with a systems team concerned with studies and development of the Library's future computing and allied requirements. The pioneering work of OSTI will be continued and extended in the Research and Development Department, and the tradition of consultations and arrangements for independent refereeing of projects will also continue.

THE FUNCTIONS AND PLANNING OF A NATIONAL LIBRARY

Introductory paper by
Dr. Ib Magnussen, Statsbiblioteket, Århus

Before discussing the functions and planning of national libraries, the question naturally arises what is meant by a national library. In 1958 Unesco held at Vienna a so-called symposium on national

Reprinted from NATIONAL LIBRARIES: extracts from the proceedings of the University and Research Section Conference held at Bangor, April 1963. London: Library Association, 1963, p. 7-25, by permission of the publisher.

libraries (Unesco: *National Libraries: their problems and prospects.* Symposium on national libraries in Europe, Vienna, 8-27 September, 1958. Paris, Unesco, 1960.) Here the idea of achieving a clear definition was actually abandoned, but I took part in the symposium myself and can confirm that nevertheless we succeeded in having three weeks of rather profitable discussion. Although it is simplest to define a national library by its functions, it seems reasonable to maintain that one can talk of national libraries in a limited and in a wider sense.

In a limited sense, a national library is the central book museum of a country or, as the Unesco symposium puts it, "the [library] responsible for collecting and conserving the whole of that country's book production for the benefit of future generations." In the light of this, there will normally be only one single national library in every country.

The concept of a national library, however, is generally used also in the wider sense: there may be more than one library in a country which is, in the full sense, a depository library of all printed publications of the nation; there may be national libraries limited by their subject matter—the American National Library of Medicine is an instance—and there are lending libraries aiming at covering the whole country. It may be difficult to draw a line between these last and such university libraries as are open to the population of the whole country. This as a rule applies to the Scandinavian university libraries.

When I use the term national library, I shall mean by this big libraries that are normally depository libraries, but possibly limited by their subject. They are as a rule government-subsidized, or at any rate under public control, and in one way or another they place their collections at the disposal of the whole country. In consequence of this wider application of the concept of national library, part of what I intend to advance will apply not only to national libraries in this wider sense, but also to other major research libraries, including university libraries.

By way of background to what follows, it seems natural briefly to characterize the type of library I personally represent, and the position of my library within the Danish library system. What I aim at is not to give a general description of libraries in Scandinavia; instead, I can refer to a book by K. C. Harrison: *Libraries in Scandinavia* (London, Deutsch, 1961). Even though the library system of the Scandinavian countries may offer dissimilarities from one country to another, one can—by way of summing up—venture to say that Scandinavia is characterized by a rather highly developed public library system on the Anglo-American model, and by research libraries organized along other lines, but in close co-operation with the public libraries. The national libraries of Scandinavia also exercise the function of university libraries, but admission to them is open to the whole population of each country. A resident no matter of how small and remote a town will, normally through a local library, be able to borrow any book from the central libraries of his country.

With one exception research libraries in Denmark are concentrated in Copenhagen, the capital. The Royal Library (in Danish: Det kongelige Bibliotek), the national library proper, contains a very complete collection of printed and manuscript Danica, and at the same time serves as university library and main library of this country for the humanities. The Royal Library does not acquire foreign literature outside the field of humanities, and even inside the humanities certain subjects are left to other libraries, e.g., art. The University Library of Copenhagen is the main library for natural science and medicine, and a number of other subjects are allotted to various special libraries. One may thus say that the libraries of Copenhagen, all of them more or less specialized, together constitute one great universal library.

At Århus, the other university town of Denmark, is found the State and University Library (in Danish: Statsbiblioteket), a minor counterpart to this system and the only universal library of the country. This library receives legal depository copies to the same extent as the Royal Library, but its collections of Danish literature are complete only from about 1800. Although the library still endeavours to add to its earlier collections, it goes without saying that a collection of the oldest literature in the slightest degree admitting of comparison with that of the Royal Library will never be attained. As for foreign literature, the State and University Library as a matter of principle tries to cover all subjects. This, however, only to a certain extent applies to such provinces as technology and agriculture. Within most branches of knowledge, and at any rate within all such as are university subjects proper, one can say that the second largest collection in this country is found at the State and University Library. One may thus perceive that whereas at Copenhagen a decentralized system obtains, we find in the smaller town of Århus a centralized system. This is also indicated by the fact that all the remaining research libraries of Århus—departmental libraries, hospital libraries, etc.—are administered by the State and University Library.

This library, which represents a type of library not found elsewhere in Scandinavia, has two objects: that of functioning as university library and main library to various institutes of higher education at Århus, and that of functioning as general reference library and lending library to the whole country outside Copenhagen. Readers are encouraged to try local resources first and are preferably channelled through public libraries, especially the 33 central libraries functioning as regional centres for local public libraries. The number of books issued by the State and University Library is greater than that of any other Scandinavian research library. About 60 per cent of these books are sent out of Århus. It is calculated that the library is able to execute 75-80 per cent of the requisitions received. The remaining requisitions are distributed, via a central agency at Copenhagen, to the various special libraries of Copenhagen, which also have obligations towards the rest of the country. Should a reader outside Copenhagen feel so inclined, there is nothing to prevent his borrowing direct from a Copenhagen library, just as readers at Copenhagen, should they need to, may borrow from the library at Århus.

Speaking, then, of national libraries in Denmark, we must say that the national book museum and the most complete collection of Danica from the earliest times to the present day are found in the Royal Library, the national library proper of this country, and also the central manuscript library. The State and University Library, Århus, the second in size in this country, is also a kind of national library in so far as it receives our national literature to the same extent as the Royal Library and has a function as national lending library. It should, however, be stressed that this does not mean that the Royal Library is not also a lending library.

The Danish system, relatively simple in comparison with British conditions, is only in a slight degree centrally directed and mainly relies on extensive voluntary co-operation, supported by a fairly elaborate net of union catalogues, especially printed ones, but also card catalogues, comprising both foreign books and periodicals found in about 125 of the most important research libraries in Denmark.

In order to prevent this brief glimpse of the Danish library system from appearing in too rosy a light, I ought perhaps to add that neither the readers nor the librarians themselves are satisfied with conditions. Fundamentally sound though this system may be, we still struggle with the same problems as are frequently encountered elsewhere: restricted grants for acquiring books, in many places a hopeless lack of accommodation and the small number of personnel, especially for the more qualified posts.

What I intend to do in the next part of this paper—namely to separate the mention of the functions of a national library and the planning of a national library—is probably wrong in theory. The two things are closely interrelated. No planning is possible without a thorough acquaintance with and a certain agreement as to the functions and conversely, when analysing the functions, it is necessary to see them as links in the planning both of each individual library and of the national library system. If I nevertheless choose to speak first of the functions and afterwards of planning, this is because it is to some extent possible to treat the functions as isolated phenomena. The planning initially calls for a consideration of the interplay of functions.

In general it may be said that a national library has a series of functions which may somewhat schematically be summarized under seven heads; these, however, often interlock and in several cases are not confined to national libraries only:

1. Collecting national literature.
2. Collecting foreign literature.
3. Serving as a book museum.
4. Giving the public access to the collections.
5. Carrying out information service and bibliographical activity.
6. Functioning as a training centre.
7. Participating in national library planning.

Whereas not all items are of equal importance, none are unimportant. I shall try briefly to describe the single functions. My starting-point will naturally derive from Danish and Scandinavian experiences, and the general statements I propose to advance will probably stand in need of correction if they are to apply to British conditions.

1. *Collecting national literature.*

It would seem that this is everywhere the oldest concern of a national library. This is normally aimed at by means of the copyright law, no matter whether this is imposed on the publisher or the printer. There is no need for me to dwell on the importance of this, but its extent is open to doubt.

In Scandinavia the national libraries in general aim at collecting, apart from printed books and periodicals, manuscripts, music, maps, and prints, whereas it is still an open question whether gramophone records are to be made subject to the law of legal deposit. Posters and graphic work do not ordinarily come within the scope of the collections whereas newspapers do. In certain places these are organized in special collections. There is a definite trend towards the microfilming of all volumes of newspapers, which are not very hard-wearing and require much room, so that they may gradually be relegated to remoter spots in order not to take up precious space in the actual libraries. So far, however, Finland is the only country yet to have accomplished microfilming.

The efficiency and universality of legal deposit is naturally more easily safeguarded in a small country. On the other hand, the national book production in most subject areas is necessarily less important to research, and foreign literature will naturally form a greater percentage of acquisitions than, for instance, in Britain. In Denmark the Royal Library and the State and University Library receive a wealth of material in the shape of leaflets and ephemeral publications which one would hardly expect to find in a copyright library in England; these two libraries have found it necessary to establish special departments for handling this material in accordance with archival principles. Problems in providing the necessary staff and space are created by this material but it is amazing to what an extent it is being used by the public.

Collecting national literature calls for a certain centralization. It would hardly be expedient to spread the legal deposit over a series of libraries according to subject. On the other hand, it seems necessary to ensure the existence of comprehensive national collections in more than one place within a country. In Denmark, as mentioned before, both the Royal Library and the State and University Library receive all printed material from the printers of the country, but in addition the University Library of Copenhagen has the right to request from the publishers one copy of any item it requires. These collections, all of them available for loan, are much drawn on. The State and University Library can allow itself great freedom in lending—with few limitations—even fairly rare material not to be obtained from the booksellers. It is encouraging to note that, in spite of this, the library seldom loses anything from its collections. The real problem is the wear and tear on the books, and efforts are being made to obtain further grants for a more extensive duplication of such parts of the national book production as are much in demand.

Not all aspects of the national collections permit of development in more than one place in every country. I understand that, on account of the wealth of material it is impossible for the British Museum to acquire all translations of the works of British authors. In Denmark, however, this is still within reach, and the Royal Library seeks to acquire all translations into all languages of Danish books and foreign books on Denmark. As this material is for the most part in the nature of museum objects, the State and University Library confines itself to buying a limited selection.

In this connection I should like to stress the importance of a clear agreement as to acquisition policy in countries with more than one national library. This mutual agreement will ensure maximum coverage. A certain differentiation of the aims of national libraries within the same country may have practical advantages, and for the information of the public it is of great importance that each library makes public its policy in this respect.

2. *Collecting foreign literature*

There are national libraries that exclusively collect the national literature and the literature pertaining to the country—Switzerland may serve as an instance. However, the normal thing would be for national libraries to a smaller or greater extent also to occupy themselves with foreign literature.

Whatever divergences may obtain from one country to another, there is still a certain general agreement on the function of a national library towards the national literature. Foreign literature, however, offers greater problems. Wherever a national library serves also as university library, the normal thing is to relate foreign acquisitions to the research and teaching of the university.

Apart from such cases—and this is the normal state of affairs in Scandinavia—there seems to be a general tendency all over the world to develop national libraries from all-embracing universal libraries to special libraries outside the scope of national literature. Natural science, medicine and technology have been abandoned by many national libraries, the social sciences are often surrendered to special libraries, and certain humanistic subjects are only given a restricted amount of attention.

I believe that the problem of centralization versus decentralization is of the greatest importance for national libraries, and one deserving of reflection.

It is evident that the all-embracing universal library of former days, divided by functions and not also by subjects, is impossible at any rate in large countries. Libraries must be selective towards certain subjects; the Library of Congress, for instance, does not collect medicine and agriculture.

Necessary decentralization can be carried out inside each library, which will thus become a framework for subject-divided units of a certain independence. Decentralization may also be attained by surrendering to other libraries.

In a certain sense this last solution is apparently the easiest and at any rate one frequently applied. No doubt it offers a number of advantages. Very big libraries are hard to handle, both for the reader and for the administrator. As the staff grows, so does the number of problems, not least those of internal communication. My daily work is in a library where the staff during the last five or six years has grown from 70 to 140 persons, and although we have taken great pains to solve structural problems as this increase took place, it seems to me that problems grow in number more rapidly than does the staff. Nor can it be denied that special libraries are frequently able to give better and speedier service than the large general library. Presumably it may often be easier to obtain grants for a special library than for bringing up to date a big library, and one notes with regret that in many cases it is easier for a special library—with a not too narrowly defined subject range—to attract specialists to the staff than it is for the larger library of more general scope.

A pronounced development in this direction is not without its dangers both for national libraries and readers. If national libraries renounce too many subjects, there is a risk that they will gradually become isolated within the library system and dwindle into mere museums of national literature, supplemented by somewhat haphazard collections relating to scattered subjects without organic connection. A national library in this plight, and deprived of lively contact with the public, will quickly degenerate and find, amongst other things, that it is even harder to attract qualified personnel. Readers operating in a borderland field, or concerned with subjects cutting across the usual subject division, will also get into difficulties, and entire subjects may be jammed between the various special libraries.

In this connection I should like to give an account of some experiences we have had in Denmark. A report made by a government commission in 1927 effected a very extensive subject division between the research libraries of Copenhagen. In many particulars this still remains a rational arrangement, which has clarified a number of problems and ensured that money is spent on duplicates only in a very restricted number of cases. But the system involves spreading of subjects over a great number of special libraries, whereas, on the other hand, the two main libraries—the Royal Library and the University Library—have given up subjects to smaller libraries. These again have not in all instances been able to live up to the demands made on them, and the main libraries have, to a certain extent, lost their comprehensive survey of the larger subjects.

Last autumn the Ministry for Cultural Affairs held a round-table conference on library problems, and in the interval from then until next autumn when a new round-table conference is to take place, material is being drawn up corresponding pretty well to the report of 1927. An important point will be our proposal to concentrate the responsibility for providing the country with research literature within fewer main libraries. As there is no question of closing down special libraries, this will entail more extensive duplication than formerly, thus radically curtailing the time-honoured 'one book principle', which with increasing use has turned into a menace to Danish libraries and to research. This will naturally involve consider-able expenditure—and we are not yet in possession of the necessary means—but here librarians might well emphasize that when all is said and done, books are about the most inexpensive research material to be found.

It goes without saying that our experiences in Denmark cannot, as a matter of course, be transferred to Britain, where naturally there is a far greater need for duplicating collections than in the smaller country. Still I do think that the bigger libraries, and not least the national libraries, would indeed be well-advised to consider whether or not by effecting decentralization within the individual library they can achieve the most essential advantages otherwise bound up with leaving entire subjects to other libraries. Such a decentralization will largely call for a further increase in staff but it may well be worth the price. Besides this, the demand for highly developed special libraries naturally still exists, presumably in particular within natural science, medicine and technology.

Outside the very biggest towns it is probably very often the case that combining the duties of a national library and a university library will ensure the intensity of use which can justify national libraries receiving sufficient means for improving their collections over a wide front, including foreign literature.

3. *Serving as a book museum*

It is of vital importance not only to much humanistic research, but also to the history of natural science, that there are libraries that, with no eye to demands prompted by current interest, collect printed and unprinted sources on the history of human civilization. The duty of national libraries towards national culture is in this field taken for granted, but it is of almost equal importance that the foreign collections are copious enough to form the basis of thorough studies of the history of the various departments of knowledge, including the history of the book from a historical, sociological or typographical viewpoint.

In certain places there was formerly a tendency to regard national libraries first and foremost as book museums. One may presuppose a general understanding that this, in itself a very important purpose, ought not to stand alone. A national library with no aspirations beyond those of serving as a book museum will easily become isolated inside the library system and lose its central place. Today's acquisitions of literature of immediate importance will also form the basis of the museum treasures of the future.

We librarians ought also to encourage the attitude that the history of knowledge and history of the book is not a somewhat quaint pastime of the librarian, but an important part of humanistic research. This will come all the more easily if we regard the function of book museum not as an aim in itself but as a special province of the duties of libraries towards the public.

4. *Giving the public access to the collections*

Those times when public interest in the collections of the libraries was considered an untimely disturbance of the librarian's quiet work with the collections may well be regarded as a thing of the past. We endeavour to serve the public by giving access to the books on the spot, in the reading rooms of other libraries, by lending for domestic or foreign use, and by collective arrangements such as exhibitions, lectures, etc.

But national libraries have different traditions, to a certain degree different aims, and often different policies in this respect. The most difficult problem for national libraries is probably whether to attach importance to their being reference libraries or lending libraries. National traditions make themselves strongly felt here, and probably there is no universal solution.

In Scandinavia we may be considered as offering a rather extreme instance of lending libraries. Practically all libraries are lending libraries, and even departmental libraries are generally willing to lend—with due regard, however, to the needs of daily research work. This tradition goes far back and may well have contributed towards the fact that the public in our countries has a fairly general suspicion of big, public reading rooms. It goes without saying that old and rare books are to be confined to use in reading rooms, but apart from this there are few restrictions on lending. It has no doubt contributed towards promoting this development that the Scandinavian national libraries usually also serve as university libraries.

Although a national library may also serve as a university library, one must bear in mind that the circle of readers is very wide. In 1960 and 1961 the Royal Library of Copenhagen, which also serves as the University Library for humanistic subjects, carried out a large-scale inquiry with the purpose of collecting information from the public for practical improvements of various sides of library work. The inquiry brought in a profusion of interesting results. Among other things, it proved that far more than half—namely 63 per cent—of the regular readers of the library are not attached to the university, institutes of higher education or other scientific institutions as teachers, students or the like, but belong to the group of 'other readers'. Eighty-two per cent regularly frequent libraries other than the Royal Library, and these are first and foremost public libraries. In Scandinavia, at any rate, it has been noted increasingly that the difference between public libraries and research libraries is to be found not so much in the circle of readers as in the stock of books.

If this development has also been noted in other countries, it will give rise to certain consequences for the policy of national libraries. They must consider carefully the differences in functions of a reference library serving a restricted circle of readers and a library with a wider circle of readers often, as a result of the increasing tendency towards decentralization of cultural life, living in towns other than the home town of the national library. An effective photocopying service may be of great help, and in many cases it will prove necessary to duplicate parts of the stock of books to ensure the presence of important works in the library itself for purposes of consultation.

In many cases the establishment of special lending libraries will be a natural development. This is the case not least when natural science and technology are concerned. Still, it is expensive building up a great network of such lending libraries in all subjects, and in the long run it will, at any rate in a smaller country, affect the size of grants available to the national library.

Proof of the responsibility that national libraries increasingly feel towards inter-library loan is offered by the frequent placing of union catalogues in national libraries or the operation of these catalogues in close co-operation with the national library. This arrangement will also make it possible to serve the sensible purpose of spreading the use so that requisitions may be diverted to less frequented collections, or to libraries with less responsibility as book museums than the national libraries.

5. *Carrying out information service and bibliographical activity*

A national library which is also a depository library forms a necessary basis for compiling a national bibliography. In a country with several libraries receiving depository copies, there is a further possibility of dividing the task by means of a certain decentralization, but such a division naturally involves the danger of lack of co-ordination if there is not a common planning agency for the various parts of the national bibliography.

Besides this obvious task a comprehensive national library offers an exceptional basis for an effective information—or documentation, to use a catch word—service to the public. The considerable growth of research material imposes steadily increasing obligations on the librarians to take over part of the work research workers formerly did as a matter of course. We are here faced by one of the most difficult problems of modern libraries. On the one hand we must admit that many investigations are best and most easily carried out by librarians; on the other hand there may be a valuable educational element in only offering help to a certain degree—helping those who help themselves—whereas at the same time the shortage of qualified personnel sets very narrow limits on what the librarians can cope with practically.

Much of this activity must be left to special libraries, but I believe it would be injudicious and dangerous if national libraries refused to consider such tasks. Indeed, I would say that they must make demands on grant-making authorities for grants for personnel in order to enable them to make their proper contribution to the requests and needs of the public. To prevent abuse, it may in many cases be necessary to let readers pay for investigations carried out. This must be reckoned on the time employed, beyond a certain free minimum. Such payments ought in general to go to libraries, and not to the individual librarian.

6. *Functioning as a training centre*

By tradition research libraries have stressed far more the training the personnel receives in the library than the theoretical training at a library school. The importance of such schools to research libraries is now increasing and that is a tendency I personally find satisfactory, provided that it does not, where librarians are concerned, imply any restrictions on the demand for a previous full university education. In these partially changing circumstances it is important for national libraries to offer themselves as training centres for some of the personnel of other libraries too. It is extremely beneficial, for at any rate part of the staff of the national library, to serve for a period in a special library and here to learn from the often effective service and better contact with the public in a smaller library, and it is of equal importance for the staff of special libraries to be introduced to the special problems of the bigger and more comprehensive library. A good national library system pre-supposes a certain degree of contact between the various types of library during the period of training.

7. *Participating in national library planning*

In most countries there is little centralization in the leadership of the research libraries of the nation. The general trend of development may be towards a certain further centralization, but in many cases there will be sharply defined limits as to how far one can go.

No matter what the degree of centralization aimed at in the individual country, national libraries have a natural duty to take part in the national library planning. If a national library is to live up to its task it must be in lively contact with the other links of the national library system.

After this hasty exposition of some of the most important functions of the national library, many of them limited to general observations that may well seem trivial, I shall try to say a few words on planning: partly on the national level, partly within the individual library, including the planning of a library building.

Planning has always been the necessary background to rational administration, but the present day makes greater demands in this direction than ever before. The rapidly growing demands that research makes on the collections and service of libraries, the intensive growth of research publications, the fact that new countries enter into international scholarly and scientific co-operation, and the great upheavals in the daily life of libraries as a result of new technical devices make planning increasingly necessary, while, at the same time, planning far ahead becomes more and more difficult.

Planning is not a thing to be done once and for all, as, for instance, in connection with the erection of a new building, but a current function to be discharged from day to day, and continually reviewed. Libraries must plan, not only in regard to their own work, but also because of the natural demand from the grant-making authorities for comprehensive plans which may permit the individual grants to be seen as parts of a wider context. Only in this way can the financial consequences of launching a new project be appreciated from the outset.

The planning of the individual library and national library planning are mutually dependent on one another. As the possible grants are in any case insufficient for attaining the ideal solution of all problems, national planning must be able to ensure that the resources of the country are utilized in the best possible fashion. Light must be thrown on the natural distribution of the tasks between the various libraries, and the problems must be solved in accordance with an agreed order of priority. The subject division between libraries must still be brought up to date and the relationship between national and local lending obligations must always be borne in mind. Such provinces as national bibliography and the development of other bibliographical aids, printed and unprinted, are national duties, just as, in another important field, the training of personnel must aim at a certain nationally uniform standard.

We must face the fact that the evolution of modern society will, among other things, result in the central government authorities leaving more and more to lower levels of administrative agencies. Thus a loosely co-operating library system will have a greater chance of shaping the details of its evolution within the financial framework defined on the highest level.

All this is very simple in theory, but exceedingly difficult and complicated in practice. I fear it is inevitable that extensive national planning must involve a certain restriction of the freedom of the individual library to make its own plans. How is the central agency to be established? In certain countries it may be natural to construct a kind of directorate for the entire library system. Such a solution, however, must assume that the management of the directorate has actual knowledge of library problems and not only of administration generally.

In many countries such a structure will seem less natural and at variance with precious traditions. The basis must be co-operation more or less—preferably more—between libraries, co-operation which has been worked out voluntarily, for instance, in the form of a kind of council on which is conferred certain official powers.

In this connection it might seem natural to give a brief account of a discussion which is at the moment taking place in Denmark. Danish research libraries come under many different ministries; certain of them—not, however, the university libraries—are subordinate to various institutes of higher education, and we increasingly feel the need of more national planning of the library system.

A certain centralization has been instituted, and the director of the Royal Library, who is at the same time head of the University Library of Copenhagen, has had imposed on him a number of duties of national character without, however, any direct authority over other libraries. A certain agreement seems to have sprung up inside the library system to go on building on this basis. The gist of these plans is to establish in connection with the central office, which may possibly receive some slight relief in the daily leadership of the Royal Library, certain posts as advisory officers to be at the disposal of the research libraries. This is expected to prove of great importance, not least to the smaller libraries. According to the plans, a council of library leaders is to be attached to this office to keep up current discussion of national planning. This council is not intended to deal with the budget of individual libraries, but only the more fundamental questions of co-operation and of new perspectives and projects. By laying down certain minimum demands, the council might constitute a support for smaller libraries in their relations with the relevant ministries, which may not be sufficiently familiar with library problems. It would be expedient for the council to obtain official status requiring that the individual ministries outside the library ministry proper—the Ministry of Cultural Affairs—had the duty of putting fundamental library questions to the council before the ministry in question makes a decision.

All these are so far only roughly drafted plans, and it is too early yet to say anything about the possibilities of carrying them out. But they may be seen as an example of a possible solution of the problem of national co-ordination for libraries.

No matter what solution the individual country will aim at, it is my opinion that it is very important for national libraries to find a central place in these endeavours and actively advocate a policy of wide co-operation. As conditions are, at any rate in Scandinavia, it would not only be harmful to the library system but in the long run also for the library involved if a national library sought to isolate itself in order to rely instead upon its traditionally close relations with the central government and grant-making authorities.

Planning the individual library is just as important as national planning. The subject is so vast that I can only find time to touch lightly on certain main features. I should like to stress that most of what is to be said in this connection applies not only to national libraries but also to other research libraries. Because of the size and influence of national libraries it is, however, of special importance that one achieves good planning within these libraries.

The background to the planning of every library must be a clear conception of the object of the library, its duty to the public, and to literature. The tasks of the library must be defined again and again, concurrently with evolution. It is thus characteristic that the objects clause of many Danish research libraries is not in keeping with the times, by its narrow concentration on university teachers and under-graduates and disregard for wider groups of other readers.

Whereas the current routine library statistics often have restricted importance—surely many figures are produced in libraries that are not put to any use afterwards—more thorough periodical examinations of limited subjects may be of consequence. I can offer as an instance an investigation into the lending activity of my own library. This examin-ation embraced all requisitions and lending transactions through one month, namely October 1960. For every single subject we tried to cast light on coverage in relation to the requisitions, the percentage of unfulfilled requisitions among titles the library possessed, distribution between periodicals and books, local and out-of-town readers, year of printing and language, and many other things. Allow me to call atten-tion to one single item, which has been of practical importance to us. In our plan of the new building we have just moved into, we had counted on the possibility of placing the most recent books centrally. For practical reasons in Scandinavia the public has not normally open access to the stacks, nor had we, what I personally regret, any possi-bility of introducing this reform in connection with the new building. Our chief stacks are in a 17-storey book tower, and a possible solution would be to place the most recent books in the storey just behind the lending department. The examination showed that the frequency of utilization of the newest books was even higher than we had calculated, namely almost 30 per cent for the last five-year period. Consequently we have decided to place the books published in the last five years or so centrally—simply arranged alphabetically within each year of printing. After about five years they will be distributed according to subjects over the other storeys.

The policy of acquisition is also of importance to the planning of a library, and it must continually be brought up to date, defined clearly and preferably also be published both internally and publicly.

In a big library many details in the process of work may be unpre-dictable, and it easily happens that the historical reason for some detail or other has lapsed without the corresponding process having been changed. Although there may often be a conflict between con-sideration for doing a day's work and planning, we must take time for a continual analysis of even the most trivial mechanical processes. We can often to our advantage call in organization consultants and rationalization experts from outside, but we must understand their limitations. The investigation into work in a library must be carried out with co-operation between librarians and experts from the outside, and in the long run it will, of course, be best for libraries themselves to train rationalization experts.

In this particular we are, at any rate in Scandinavia, far behind the public libraries which both in Sweden and Denmark have instituted extensive rationalization examinations with significant results. Naturally it is more difficult to rationalize research libraries than public libraries which are already more standardized, but if we are to solve our problems in a situation characterized by shortage of qualified personnel, we cannot avoid setting foot on this road.

However unaccustomed it may seem in a library I think we shall have to reach a clear description of the individual processes in special staff manuals, and it is of great importance, not least to new employees, that there is for every post in a library a description which in its details lays down the field of work and competence of every job.

It is important for any planning in a library that it is linked with an adequate staff policy. Planning exclusively from the top will never be fully effective. The whole staff must be informed not only of everything of importance to their daily work, but also of the general policy of the library. Not all decisions can be reached by voting, but there must be channels to ensure that all points of view, including those of the most inferior members, are put forward and taken into consideration. Staff meetings, a joint committee of the librarian and personnel, staff periodicals and many other things are possibilities to be taken into consideration.

It must depend on the size and administrative structure of the individual library whether one actually finds it right to establish special planning departments, but it is at any rate necessary that among the librarians within a library there are persons with ability and interest in planning and who are sufficiently relieved of other duties for them to devote themselves to a suitable extent to such objects.

The planning of a new building is a task that particularly places the librarian in an emergency. The proper solution of the plan presupposes a certain clarification of the national library policy, and of the placing of the individual library within it. Very often this clarificat on is not present during the planning of the building, and important alterations in the wording of the task not infrequently present themselves during the process of construction, just as new technical possibilities continually have to be incorporated into the project on its way. The answer of the technicians to this is the catch-word "flexibility", which may be an excellent thing, but a library has not quite the same ability to use the technically possible flexibility as has a factory, for instance.

Time does not allow of a thorough treatment of the planning for buildings, and I do not intend to spend time on describing more closely the library we have just moved into. Allow me just to put forward a few desultory reflections, also connected with my own experience.

I believe that in our time it is difficult to plan a building in its details for more than 15 or 20 years. The possibilities for extension must naturally be taken into consideration, but it may be unfair to our successors to have laid down in advance future extensions in accordance with too inflexible a plan. For ourselves we count on having to carry out in about 15 years a certain decentralization in the shape of the construction of a special branch library, with open access to the stacks, for natural science and medicine. We have secured a site for it, but have been careful not to stress details.

When planning libraries there is often a tendency to devote plentiful room to book stacks and to rooms for the public, but too little room for the staff who work in it. It may be difficult to bring the grant-making authorities to realize the necessity of sufficient room for working for the staff, particularly in the more distant future, but I believe that it is important to devote much effort on this point. Books can be placed in deposit libraries, but not the staff, and if libraries are to take part in the competition for personnel, one must ensure that the environment for their work is as it should be.

I believe it is decisive for the successful planning of a new building that the librarian does not leave too much to the architect. The project must take shape in close co-operation, and the librarian must share the responsibility for the working out of all details, even though this means that he cannot afterwards blame the architect for the oversights which will always occur in any planning.

When occupied with planning a new building, one must to a great extent depend on the experiences of other libraries. Study tours are useful, but I cannot suppress a sigh that after the process of building so much is written casually and heterogeneously about the new buildings in library periodicals. It may be comprehensible that fatigue sets in after the exertions of moving, but it is unfortunate that many technical details of potential interest to others about to build are not brought out. Far too many descriptions of buildings concentrate in too high a degree on aesthetic details and the artistic presentation of reading rooms. An adequate description with the necessary technical specifications is found for few new buildings.

By way of concluding my contribution I will touch on a subject closely bound up with planning, namely research in the field of library problems. We have, I believe, in Europe, first of all for financial reasons, to a somewhat too high extent been inclined to content ourselves with relying on American investigations, not least the magnificent projects launched by the Council on Library Resources. In all circumstances we shall in a very high degree have to build upon American experience, but in many particulars conditions in European libraries differ from American, and it is desirable that individual investigations be started in a number of countries in Europe—preferably in close co-operation with American librarians—dealing with all aspects of the problems of library work including the purely technical routine aspects. Such an activity within the individual country might advantageously be decentralized, and the tasks delegated to individual libraries or institutions such as library schools, but to ensure national co-ordination there ought to be something in the nature of a research council for this field.

In such a programme of library investigation, national libraries have a natural central position by virtue of their size, versatile staff, and copious experience. National libraries have an obligation not only towards the treasures of the past, but also a responsibility towards the shaping of the library system of the future.

LA BIBLIOTHÈQUE NATIONALE EN URSS.

I. P. Kondakov,
directeur
de la Bibliothèque Lénine.

La bibliothèque nationale, avec ses particularités, ses fonctions, son évolution est au centre des problèmes de la bibliothéconomie 'contemporaine. Plusieurs pays, depuis un certain nombre d'années déjà, cherchent à résoudre ce problème d'une façon rationnelle, en fonction des besoins naissants de la société actuelle.

Ce regain d'intérêt est tout à fait naturel. Les bibliothèques nationales, qui ont un long passé, ont pu accumuler d'inestimables richesses qui reflètent tout le processus de l'évolution culturelle de l'humanité. Elles se sont formées en type particulier de bibliothèques qui jouent un rôle important dans l'exploitation des valeurs culturelles. Certaines — la Bibliothèque nationale de Paris, le « British Museum », par exemple — sont d'une notoriété universelle et très estimées du monde savant pour l'exhaustivité, la variété et la richesse de leurs fonds. Ces bibliothèques sont géantes, de structure interne très complexe et d'un vaste réseau de relations avec l'extérieur.

Mais les conditions nouvelles ont créé un tout nouveau problème des bibliothèques nationales. Certains émettent un doute sur l'opportunité de conserver dans l'avenir aux bibliothèques nationales le même caractère que par le passé. Leurs fonds reflètent un flot sans cesse croissant de production typographique mondiale. Ils grandissent dans des proportions énormes et le problème qui se pose est d'apporter des restrictions à cette croissance. On se demande si les fonctions actuelles des bibliothèques nationales, comprises en tant que conservatoires nationaux des livres, correspondent aux systèmes différenciés des bibliothèques d'aujourd'hui. Le problème est donc posé : universalisme ou spécialisation dans la perspective d'évolution des grandes bibliothèques du monde, bibliothèques nationales y comprises. Ces problèmes demandent à être examinés; de leur solution dépendent le sort et l'avenir des bibliothèques nationales.

Il est évident que malgré les particularités nationales de ces catégories de bibliothèques, les livres constituent un élément commun, qui permet de poser le problème des bibliothèques nationales sur le plan international, et de mettre à profit l'expérience des différents pays pour tracer la voie de leur évolution. Dans le cadre qui nous est imparti il nous est impossible de donner une analyse du développement des bibliothèques nationales à l'échelle mondiale. Nous voudrions tout simplement faire partager notre propre expérience sur la formation d'une bibliothèque nationale dans un pays socialiste, montrer les particularités de son développement, ses devoirs et ses fonctions actuelles et apporter ainsi notre contribution à la discussion générale du problème.

Reprinted from *Bulletin des Bibliotheques de France*, vol. 11, no. 3, March 1966, p. 93-104, by permission of the publisher.

L'ÉVOLUTION DE LA BIBLIOTHÈQUE NATIONALE EN URSS.

Nous pouvons sans hésitation parler de l'originalité de l'évolution de la bibliothèque nationale en URSS. Son histoire reflète les transformations sociales et culturelles du dernier demi-siècle.

La fondation de la bibliothèque nationale date en Russie de la fin du XVIIIe siècle, lorsque fut fondée à Pétersbourg la Bibliothèque publique. En 1810 elle reçoit le dépôt légal et, de ce fait, le statut d'un conservatoire russe national officiel du livre. Sous cette forme elle représente parfaitement les deux notions de bibliothèque nationale d'une part, de conservatoire national du livre de l'autre et reste pendant plus de cent ans la plus grande bibliothèque de Russie.

En 1862, fut fondée à Moscou, à la faveur d'un mouvement social, la Bibliothèque publique Roumiantzev qui bénéficiait également du dépôt légal, élément qui peut être considéré comme une tentative de création en Russie d'une deuxième bibliothèque nationale, prise dans le sens de conservatoire national du livre. Mais elle n'avait pas de caractère officiel et jusqu'à la Révolution de 1917 ne jouissait pas des privilèges accordés à la Bibliothèque de Pétersbourg.

La Russie prérévolutionnaire n'a rien apporté de particulier au concept existant de bibliothèque nationale. Le rôle caractéristique de la bibliothèque nationale, outre son caractère officiel, résidait dans ses fonctions de collecte et de conservation du livre russe. L'accès à la bibliothèque, bien qu'elle portât le nom de publique, n'avait aucune signification réelle, car sa fréquentation était très réduite et la bibliothèque ne faisait aucun effort pour le développer. La bibliothèque nationale russe prérévolutionnaire était isolée des autres bibliothèques du pays et n'exerçait aucune influence sur le développement de la science des bibliothèques sur le plan national.

Les véritables changements de la bibliothèque nationale, si l'on considère sa place dans la société, ses fonctions et ses tâches, appartiennent à la période post-révolutionnaire de la deuxième moitié du siècle. Les nouvelles conditions culturelles et sociales, un changement radical dans la position des bibliothèques devenues institutions de portée capitale sur le plan national et élément de haute importance de tout le système d'éducation nationale, tous ces facteurs ont déterminé la nouvelle conception de la bibliothèque nationale. Il ne faudrait pas par ailleurs perdre de vue qu'il s'agit des problèmes de la bibliothèque nationale d'un pays multinational de plus de deux cent vingt millions d'habitants.

Un des principaux objectifs atteints dans l'organisation du réseau des bibliothèques en URSS réside dans le système de coopération entre bibliothèques nationales qui recherchent en commun des solutions à l'exploitation des richesses culturelles des peuples de l'URSS. Cette coopération s'effectue entre les bibliothèques nationales à l'échelon fédéral, les bibliothèques républicaines et les grandes bibliothèques fédérales spécialisées.

Le rôle prépondérant appartient dans ce système à la Bibliothèque nationale de l'URSS, la Bibliothèque Lénine. Elle a pris son importance sur le plan national après la Révolution. C'est son exemple et son fonctionnement qui ont déterminé les principales caractéristiques et les principales réalisations de la bibliothèque nationale en tant que type particulier d'institution soviétique. L'importance de ses fonds, qui renferment la production typographique de tous les peuples de l'URSS, fait de cette bibliothèque une source importante de diffusion et d'enrichissement pour les cultures nationales soviétiques. La deuxième bibliothèque de l'URSS par son importance est la Bibliothèque publique Saltykov-Ščedrin de Leningrad qui reçoit jusqu'à ce jour un exemplaire du dépôt légal de toute la production nationale. Malgré ses traditions historiques de seule Bibliothèque nationale de la Russie prérévolutionnaire, elle a su rapidement s'adapter aux conditions nouvelles et elle demeure actuellement la deuxième bibliothèque nationale après la Bibliothèque Lénine.

La bibliothèque nationale est devenue une des plus éclatantes expressions de la souveraineté nationale des républiques fédérées et autonomes, membres à part entière de l'Union soviétique. La révolution a justement permis à de nombreux peuples de l'ancienne Russie d'acquérir leur souveraineté nationale qui a trouvé son expression dans la création de leurs propres instituts, établissements industriels et agricoles, institutions scientifiques, théâtres, de leur propre littérature et aussi d'une bibliothèque nationale républicaine qui occupe parmi les organismes culturels une place d'honneur. La création par les républiques fédérées de bibliothèques nationales à caractère encyclopédique, devenues rapidement de grands centres culturels d'importance nationale, est à notre avis un acquis capital pour les nationalités qui peuplent l'Union soviétique.

Le système des bibliothèques nationales de l'URSS comprend également les grandes bibliothèques spécialisées nationales. Ce sont, par exemple, la Bibliothèque publique scientifique et technique de l'URSS, les bibliothèques d'État d'agriculture, de médecine, des sciences sociales. Leurs fonctions ont des traits communs avec celles des bibliothèques nationales et elles peuvent être considérées comme telles. C'est ainsi que dans les conditions spécifiques de l'URSS, compte tenu de certaines traditions historiques et de l'actuel réseau des bibliothèques, nous étions amenés à des conceptions plus larges de la bibliothèque nationale et ce sont ces facteurs qui ont déterminé notre système de bibliothèques.

L'évolution de la bibliothèque nationale en Union soviétique a donné un nouveau sens et une nouvelle valeur à cette catégorie de bibliothèques. A la place de la dominante et presque exclusive caractéristique de conservatoire national (c'est-à-dire de collecte et de conservation de la production typographique nationale du pays — formule révolue), le concept de la bibliothèque nationale est devenu l'expression de tout un faisceau de faits réunissant à la fois l'ampleur et l'orientation de l'exploitation de ses fonds, son rôle dans le développement des travaux bibliographiques et son rôle directeur à l'égard du réseau national des bibliothèques.

LES PRINCIPALES CARACTÉRISTIQUES
D'UNE BIBLIOTHÈQUE NATIONALE EN URSS.

Le caractère d'une bibliothèque nationale en URSS ne peut plus être défini par un seul critère. Elle constitue actuellement un organisme complexe dont les particularités typologiques ne peuvent être définies autrement que par un ensemble de caractéristiques.

a) *La Bibliothèque nationale, conservatoire national du livre.*

La collecte et la conservation de la production typographique nationale est le principal objectif d'une bibliothèque nationale. On connaît, et ceci est vrai pour de nombreux pays, le rôle décisif joué par le dépôt légal dans la formation des conservatoires nationaux de livres. En Russie, le dépôt légal est à l'origine des deux bibliothèques nationales : la Bibliothèque publique à Pétersbourg depuis 1810 et la Bibliothèque Roumiantzev à Moscou depuis 1862, qui réunissent la presque totalité de la production typographique russe.

Après la Révolution de 1917, la loi sur le dépôt légal a été radicalement modifiée. Par une série d'arrêtés, le dépôt légal est devenu la base essentielle de l'organisation d'une bibliothèque nationale. Compte tenu de l'étendue du réseau des bibliothèques, de ses besoins et de la conception nouvelle de la Bibliothèque nationale, le nombre d'exemplaires obligatoires déposés était sensiblement augmenté et un contrôle rigoureux garantissait le bon fonctionnement du dépôt légal.

Parmi les bibliothèques nationales soviétiques la Bibliothèque Lénine occupe par la composition de ses fonds une place particulière. Elle reçoit par la voie du dépôt légal trois exemplaires obligatoires de toute la production typographique de l'Union soviétique, dont l'un est destiné à la conservation et les deux autres sont largement exploités dans l'intérêt de la science, de l'économie et de la culture.

Comme nous l'avons déjà indiqué, la Bibliothèque publique Saltykov-Ščedrin reçoit également un exemplaire du dépôt légal. La croissance rapide des bibliothèques républicaines est très caractéristique, leur particularité nationale se traduit par le souci de rassembler la production typographique de leur pays à l'échelle des grands dépôts nationaux de livres. Ainsi la Bibliothèque républicaine soviétique du Tadzikistan où, à l'époque prérévolutionnaire, les bibliothèques étaient quasi inexistantes, a collecté toutes les publications éditées sur son territoire depuis 1930 (année de fondation de la bibliothèque et où elle a commencé à bénéficier du dépôt légal). La Bibliothèque républicaine soviétique de l'Arménie possède toute sa production nationale depuis la Révolution et aussi de précieux livres anciens, tel le premier livre imprimé en arménien, à Venise en 1512. Ce sont là des exemples typiques pour toutes les autres républiques, sans exception.

Les bibliothèques nationales encyclopédiques ont comme règle la collecte des ouvrages consacrés à la géographie du pays et au régionalisme. A la production nationale assurée par le dépôt légal, s'ajoute celle de l'étranger, concernant soit toute l'Union soviétique, soit une république. Il convient de citer à cet égard le fonds des « Rossica » de la Bibliothèque publique Saltykov-Ščedrin, qui date presque de sa fondation. Des fonds semblables se trouvent à la Bibliothèque Lénine et dans les bibliothèques républicaines.

Certaines bibliothèques spécialisées importantes ont également en URSS des attributions de bibliothèque nationale. Leurs statuts prévoient la collecte, fondée sur un exemplaire du dépôt légal, de la production typographique correspondant à leur spécialisation — technique, industrie, agriculture, médecine, sciences sociales — certes moins complète que dans une nationale encyclopédique mais suffisante pour satisfaire en livres les différents besoins des spécialistes.

Les spécialistes soviétiques de bibliothéconomie n'ont jamais posé le problème des bibliothèques nationales dans la perspective de l'ampleur des fonds. Par leur nature même, ce type de bibliothèques dispose de fonds considérables. C'est surtout vrai pour les bibliothèques nationales soviétiques si l'on considère que la production typographique de l'URSS constitue le quart de toute la production mondiale. Le fonds de la Bibliothèque Lénine compte 22,5 millions de volumes (en 173 langues, plus de 8 millions de volumes seulement en langues étrangères) et la Bibliothèque publique Saltykov-Ščedrin plus de 14 millions de volumes.

Ces fonds proviennent non seulement du dépôt légal, qui leur confère le caractère de conservatoire national, mais aussi d'acquisitions, afin de pouvoir satisfaire tous les besoins de la très grande masse de lecteurs. Ainsi en 1963 le dépôt légal représentait seulement 51 % de l'accroissement total en livres et 20 % pour les périodiques. C'est la raison pour laquelle le problème de l'accroissement d'une bibliothèque nationale doit être réglé en fonction des sources de ses acquisitions.

Il nous semble qu'il ne peut y avoir limitation en ce qui concerne le fonds national de conservation, c'est-à-dire de l'exemplaire d'archives (à la Bibliothèque Lénine et dans les bibliothèques républicaines). Ce fonds doit refléter toute la production nationale, c'est là sa portée historique et culturelle. Des restrictions peuvent être apportées (partiellement en URSS) seulement à l'égard du second et du troisième exemplaire du dépôt légal de la principale bibliothèque nationale et à l'égard des bibliothèques qui n'ont pas le caractère de conservatoire national.

La réglementation de l'accroissement des fonds des bibliothèques nationales ne peut concerner que les fonds complémentaires qui n'ajoutent rien au caractère national de ces bibliothèques. Dans ce domaine, les problèmes sont réglés par la coordination des acquisitions avec d'autres grandes bibliothèques spécialisées d'intérêt national.

b) *La Bibliothèque nationale, première bibliothèque publique.*

L'accumulation d'une masse énorme de livres n'a jamais été considérée en URSS comme une fin en soi, le but étant leur diffusion. Ceci concerne également la bibliothèque nationale qui ne peut aucunement être réduite à un fonds d'archives « mort ».

Au cours de l'évolution historique, les bibliothèques nationales de l'URSS, qui recèlent de grands trésors culturels, sont devenues les plus importantes bibliothèques publiques du pays, largement ouvertes à toutes les couches de la population. C'est l'une des caractéristiques essentielles d'une bibliothèque nationale soviétique.

L'exploitation des énormes fonds de ces bibliothèques nationales soviétiques se fait de deux manières : 1° approvisionnement en livres et en bibliographies des administrations, des dirigeants, des organismes économiques et culturels, des établissements industriels, des organismes scientifiques; 2° service direct d'approvisionnement en livres et en bibliographies du grand public. C'est la fonction même de la bibliothèque nationale qui oriente son exploitation, centrée sur l'aide apportée à la science, à l'industrie, à l'économie nationale et à la culture.

Prenons l'exemple de la Bibliothèque Lénine. Elle compte 215 000 lecteurs dont des scientifiques (22 %), des spécialistes des diverses branches de l'économie nationale et de la culture (41 %), des étudiants (22 %) et même des lycéens (11 %) et autres. La Bibliothèque dispose de 22 salles de lecture et de 2 400 places. Elle reçoit dans une journée 8 à 10 000 lecteurs et elle communique dans une année 14 millions de volumes.

Outre les services directs, le prêt interbibliothèques et la reproduction des documents permettent d'atteindre un grand nombre de lecteurs qui ne fréquentent pas la bibliothèque.

Les bibliothèques nationales sont devenues les plus importants centres du prêt interbibliothèques pour tout le réseau des bibliothèques de l'URSS. Ainsi plus de 5 000 bibliothèques différentes du pays bénéficient des fonds de la Bibliothèque Lénine. Les fonds des bibliothèques républicaines sont exploités par les bibliothèques d'étude et les bibliothèques de lecture publique de la république donnée. Les bibliothèques spécialisées d'État jouent le même rôle à l'égard des bibliothèques spécialisées d'entreprise, d'économie rurale, ou d'organismes scientifiques.

De la longue expérience des bibliothèques nationales soviétiques sont nées différentes formes et méthodes d'exploitation des fonds, du travail avec le lecteur et du choix de la lecture. La première place revient aux catalogues des bibliothèques nationales qui par leur diversité (alphabétiques et systématiques pour les livres, spéciaux pour d'autres documents : les périodiques, la musique, les cartes et plans, les thèses, etc.) et par leur exhaustivité ont la valeur des bibliographies nationales. Les expositions des bibliothèques nationales soviétiques ont pour but de familiariser le lecteur avec les imprimés du dépôt légal (expositions de caractère encyclopédique et spécialisé) et de présenter l'ensemble des documents sur un sujet important (présentation souvent de 8 à 10 000 titres). Une forme particulièrement intéressante du travail des bibliothèques nationales est l'information bibliographique établie à l'attention des administrations et organismes scientifiques, à partir des sources nationales et étrangères.

Le caractère universel d'une bibliothèque nationale en URSS, s'il s'agit de l'exploitation de ses fonds, trouve son expression dans le fait que le travail avec le lecteur est orienté à la fois vers l'assistance culturelle et scientifique, vers la promotion sociale des travailleurs et vers le progrès scientifique et industriel. Cette particularité de la Bibliothèque nationale lui permet d'apporter une aide concrète à la solution des problèmes culturels et économiques du pays.

Ainsi les formes souples et diverses du travail avec le lecteur ont rendu la bibliothèque nationale accessible à toutes les couches de la population de l'Union soviétique ou d'une république fédérée. Les quelques restrictions d'admission à la salle de lecture, souvent fortuites (manque momentané de place) ou de prêt, n'entravent en rien le principe général d'un large accès aux fonds des bibliothèques nationales, fonds exploités également par le prêt interbibliothèques, l'information bibliographique, la reprographie, etc.

c) *La Bibliothèque nationale, centre bibliographique.*

Les fonctions bibliographiques des bibliothèques nationales ont pris en URSS une grande ampleur et des formes multiples. C'est un fait d'autant plus important que le travail bibliographique repose sur la quasi-totalité de la production typographique nationale. Ce travail bibliographique, lié de façon organique au travail de la bibliothèque, devient un moyen important de diffusion du livre et offre la possibilité de déterminer l'orientation bibliographique des lecteurs.

Contrairement à ce qui se pratique dans de nombreux pays, les bibliothèques nationales en URSS n'assument pas l'enregistrement bibliographique courant des imprimés qui est confié à des organismes spéciaux : la Chambre du livre de l'URSS et les Chambres du livre des diverses républiques. L'analyse et le traitement de l'exemplaire du dépôt légal à la bibliothèque nationale a essentiellement pour but la création des répertoires rétrospectifs et des bibliographies recommandées.

De nombreux guides bibliographiques d'importance capitale seraient impensables s'ils n'avaient pour source les fonds des bibliothèques nationales. Prenons quelques exemples. La Bibliothèque Lénine et la Bibliothèque Saltykov-Ščedrin en collaboration avec d'autres bibliothèques publient un travail bibliographique fondamental : « Le Catalogue collectif du livre russe du XVIIIᵉ siècle ». La Bibliothèque Lénine a publié deux volumes de ses archives privées, elle publie un catalogue trimestriel des thèses, etc.

Les bibliothèques spécialisées d'État publient respectivement des répertoires, comme « La bibliographie d'économie rurale de l'URSS », « La bibliographie médicale de l'URSS. ».

Les bibliothèques nationales jouent un rôle important dans le développement des bibliographies recommandées. La bibliothéconomie soviétique considère cette tâche d'une bibliothèque nationale comme essentielle et de haute importance. Nous n'avons jamais considéré la bibliographie recommandée comme une « bibliographie de second ordre » et sommes persuadés qu'elle exige, en tant que genre complexe et important d'activité bibliographique, une analyse profonde et sérieuse des documents, un choix judicieux et une structure spéciale. La solution de ces problèmes est à la mesure d'une bibliothèque nationale qui offre ses bibliographies aux bibliothécaires et aux lecteurs pour le choix de leurs livres. Dans ce domaine, ce travail des bibliothèques nationales joue un rôle directeur à l'égard des autres bibliothèques, en particulier des régionales.

Le principal centre de bibliographies recommandées en URSS est la Bibliothèque Lénine. Ainsi en 1963, elle a publié plus de 70 titres de bibliographies recommandées qui comptaient 3 200 pages imprimées d'un tirage de plus de 1 million d'exemplaires couvrant tous les domaines. De cette masse de publications quelques titres se détachent : « La bibliothèque de l'autodidacte », « Les classiques de la littérature russe », « Nouveautés en sciences et techniques », etc. Ces bibliographies recommandent les meilleurs livres de toutes les disciplines afin d'élargir les connaissances et d'élever le niveau culturel des masses.

La Bibliothèque publique Saltykov-Ščedrin publie également d'une façon régulière des bibliographies recommandées. Ces bibliographies recommandées ne visent pas en URSS seulement un but culturel, mais sont aussi destinées au secteur économique et industriel. La publication de ce dernier genre de bibliographies incombe aux bibliothèques spécialisées d'État. Ainsi, par exemple, la Bibliothèque publique scientifique et technique de l'URSS publie une série de guides « recommandés », tels que le « Guide pour ouvriers polyvalents », « Les nouvelles techniques à l'intention des ouvriers » ou encore « Nouveaux livres techniques pour ouvriers ». L'important travail bibliographique des bibliothèques républicaines connaît également une très large audience. Ce sont elles qui établissent les bibliographies nationales, ce qui se traduit d'une part, par le recensement de toute leur production typographique nationale et de l'autre, par la publication de bibliographies recommandées, ayant pour but d'orienter le lecteur vers les documents nationaux essentiels.

d) *La Bibliothèque nationale, centre méthodologique.*

Les bibliothèques nationales sont devenues de grands centres méthodologiques qui jouent un rôle important dans le développement de la recherche bibliothéconomique et dans l'amélioration de la qualité du travail des bibliothèques soviétiques. L'organisation à l'échelle nationale d'un système harmonieux d'assistance méthodologique à toutes les bibliothèques était à nos yeux une des importantes réalisations et une des caractéristiques de la structure des bibliothèques en URSS. Dans ces conditions il s'agissait de créer des centres (précisément des centres, tenant compte de l'éventail du réseau des bibliothèques de l'URSS) susceptibles d'offrir une aide de tous les jours à toutes les bibliothèques du pays. Ce sont justement les bibliothèques nationales qui sont devenues ces centres méthodologiques, aussi bien à l'échelle nationale que sur le plan républicain.

La longue expérience soviétique a montré combien il était nécessaire d'attribuer aux bibliothèques centrales (dont les nationales) des fonctions de direction méthodologique, puisque seules ces bibliothèques, grâce à leur personnel qualifié, peuvent par des exemples précis d'organisation scientifique du travail, diffuser leurs méthodes dans d'autres bibliothèques.

Les bibliothèques nationales exercent leurs compétences méthodologiques :

1º dans l'étude des principaux problèmes de bibliothéconomie et des problèmes théoriques de bibliographie à la lumière des acquisitions les plus récentes dans ce domaine;

2º dans la recherche des méthodes les plus productives en bibliothéconomie et bibliographie, de rédaction des instructions pratiques pour tous les processus de diffusion nationale du livre;

3º dans la mise en pratique, avec le concours du réseau des bibliothèques centrales (régionales, municipales, centrales scientifiques et techniques des diverses régions, économiques, etc.), de méthodes de travail perfectionnées. On peut encore citer à l'acquis des bibliothèques nationales, l'élaboration, après de nombreuses recherches, de règles souples et efficaces de bibliothéconomie. Diverses formes du travail méthodologique ont résisté à l'épreuve du temps et sont entrées définitivement dans la pratique des bibliothèques nationales : analyse et diffusion des méthodes éprouvées, expérimentation, préparation des publications et des mises au point, édition de recueils et de manuels à l'usage des différents types de bibliothèques, organisation de conférences scientifiques et d'information, consultations méthodologiques, séminaires d'étude et de débats, etc.

A l'échelle fédérale fonctionnent deux grands centres méthodologiques : la Bibliothèque Lénine pour l'ensemble des bibliothèques du pays et la Bibliothèque publique scientifique et technique de l'URSS à l'intention du réseau des bibliothèques techniques; les bibliothèques républicaines exercent ces fonctions sur le territoire de leur république.

LA LIAISON ENTRE BIBLIOTHÈQUES NATIONALES

Il n'a jamais existé et il n'existe pas !en URSS d'alternative « universalité ».ou « spécialisation » des bibliothèques nationales. L'énorme besoin en livres et aussi la ramification du réseau des bibliothèques (on en compte en URSS plus de 380 000) justifient la nécessité des deux types de bibliothèques nationales. Il s'agit seulement de déterminer les justes rapports entre ces bibliothèques, la répartition rationnelle des sphères d'influence et de coopération précise.

L'existence de quelques grandes bibliothèques spécialisées de caractère national amène aux conclusions suivantes : tout d'abord la nécessité d'orienter les fonds des bibliothèques nationales encyclopédiques et de développer la coopération des acquisitions (cela ne concerne en rien, comme nous l'avons indiqué, le fonds de conservation des bibliothèques nationales) et ensuite de préciser les activités des bibliothèques nationales encyclopédiques et spécialisées dans le domaine du renseignement des lecteurs sur des sujets étroitement spécialisés ou sur le plan concret des travaux bibliographiques.

Dans la pratique des bibliothèques soviétiques on retrouve les deux aspects de ce problème. Le premier concerne la coordination du travail, c'est-à-dire une répartition précise des fonctions et des sphères d'influence, la planification (annuelle et pluri-annuelle) pour toutes les activités des bibliothèques nationales.

Le deuxième aspect du problème c'est le travail de coopération, c'est-à-dire l'effort collectif des diverses bibliothèques nationales en vue d'une solution unique des problèmes concrets (catalogues collectifs, par exemple, élaboration de la classification bibliothéconomique et bibliographique, étude des problèmes particuliers de bibliothéconomie et de bibliographie, etc.).

Ainsi les bibliothèques nationales, surtout les encyclopédiques, ont été investies d'une nouvelle fonction, celle de centres de coordination et de coopération du travail bibliographique. La Bibliothèque Lénine par exemple réalise pratiquement la coordination et la coopération des travaux d'information bibliographique des bibliothèques spécialisées, des travaux méthodologiques, de la rédaction de travaux bibliographiques importants effectués au sein des bibliothèques nationales, etc. Les bibliothèques républicaines assument les mêmes fonctions sur le territoire de leur république.

Nous avons esquissé ici à grandes lignes les liaisons existantes entre bibliothèques nationales, leurs principes fondamentaux qui se sont affirmés dans la pratique en URSS. Ce sont en même temps, il faut l'admettre, des aspects complexes de l'évolution des bibliothèques nationales, aspects qui ne sont pas complètement résolus en URSS. Il s'agit de la coordination et de la coopération dans le domaine des acquisitions, solution que nous cherchons actuellement et dont nous partagerons les résultats avec nos collègues aussitôt que nos recherches seront mises en pratique.

RELATIONS INTERNATIONALES DES BIBLIOTHÈQUES NATIONALES

Actuellement, le problème d'acquisition de documents nécessaires au travail scientifique ne peut être résolu que par la plus étroite collaboration entre bibliothèques d'étude de différents pays. Il est évident que dans ce domaine le rôle des bibliothèques nationales, qui disposent de toute la production nationale, est décisif.

La collaboration internationale des bibliothèques revêt divers aspects et couvre des domaines multiples du travail bibliothéconomique et bibliographique : participation à des organisations internationales, à des réunions, à des publications, échanges de livres, prêt, travail d'information bibliographique commun, dont rédaction de bibliographies scientifiques internationales, coopération dans le domaine des acquisitions étrangères, contacts personnels. Ce sont les bibliothèques nationales qui ont le plus grand potentiel humain et matériel leur permettant d'assumer ces tâches et deviennent de ce fait d'importants, sinon les plus importants, centres de coopération internationale pour leur pays. Toutefois, elles ne se réservent pas l'exclusivité, car tout en y prenant une part active, elles coordonnent le travail des autres bibliothèques du pays dans leurs différents rapports avec les bibliothèques étrangères.

Tout cela concerne aussi les activités des bibliothèques nationales soviétiques et au premier plan celles de la Bibliothèque Lénine.

La Bibliothèque Lénine a des relations internationales très étendues. Elle échange des publications avec 3 000 bibliothèques et organismes scientifiques de 84 pays, consent le prêt international à 275 organismes étrangers de 36 pays. Non seulement la Bibliothèque Lénine déploie toutes ces activités mais elle sert aussi de centre de coordination du prêt et des échanges internationaux pour toutes les autres bibliothèques du pays. Elle délivre aux bibliothèques étrangères annuellement près de 1 000 informations bibliographiques complexes. En 1963, 3 500 lecteurs étrangers venant de 74 pays ont fréquenté la Bibliothèque. Une section spéciale étudie la bibliothéconomie étrangère et public le recueil « Bibliothéconomie et bibliographie à l'étranger ».

Les bibliothèques nationales des républiques fédérées prennent aussi une part active à la coopération internationale. Leur participation a une ampleur et des formes diverses, mais accuse toujours une tendance très nette vers une large ouverture internationale. Cela se traduit surtout par l'intensification des échanges internationaux de publications entre les bibliothèques républicaines et des organismes scientifiques étrangers.

Aucune autre fonction des bibliothèques ne dépend autant de la conjoncture internationale que les échanges internationaux. La détente internationale des dernières années a beaucoup favorisé la coopération internationale des bibliothèques. Il est hors de doute que dans la mesure où l'idée de coexistence pacifique des états à structures sociales différentes présidera aux destinées des rapports internationaux, les rapports scientifiques et culturels, et tout naturellement ceux des bibliothèques et avant tout des nationales, ne pourront que s'intensifier.

PROBLÈMES DES BIBLIOTHÈQUES NATIONALES EN VOIE DE SOLUTION

Bien que nous soyions partisans de l'exhaustivité du fonds d'une bibliothèque nationale en ce qui concerne la production nationale du pays ou d'une république, le problème de l'accroissement général des fonds de ces bibliothèques attend sa solution. Elle nous apparaît tout d'abord sous la forme d'une limitation des acquisitions complémentaires nées de la demande sans cesse croissante des lecteurs et ensuite dans la généralisation de la reprographie (microfilms, microfiches, etc.) des fonds à plus faible consultation, sans toutefois étendre cette pratique à l'exemplaire du dépôt légal de la Bibliothèque Lénine ni des bibliothèques républicaines, élément qui confère à ces bibliothèques leur caractère national.

Le moment est venu d'une étude sérieuse de ces problèmes en accord et en étroite collaboration avec les bibliothèques nationales des autres pays et de la confrontation de leurs expériences acquises dans l'accroissement de leurs fonds.

The Function of the National Library in the Hungarian Library System

by MAGDA JÓBORU

This text is preceded by some introductory matter (pp. 155-156).

The history of the national library

The history of Hungary did not make possible the organic development of the great book collections over centuries. In the Middle Ages important ecclesiastical libraries were established and in the fifteenth century the *Bibliotheca Corviniana,* this famous collection of the great Hungarian renaissance king, Matthias, with a great number of codices and with the first products of book printing came into being. It was during the reign of King Matthias that the first book printed in Hungary was published (1473). (The 500th anniversary will be celebrated next year).

However, it was not from this royal library that the Hungarian national library developed, as its holdings were unfortunately dispersed during the one and a half century Turkish occupation of the country. From the Corvina codices only a few dozen could be later on recovered in the nineteenth and twentieth centuries: these are our most precious and carefully kept treasures. (If, after the elapse of 500 years the National Library moves again to the Buda Castle, we can consider ourselves, rightful – to a certain extent – as the descendants of this famous collection).

After the Turkish occupation our kings came from the Habsburg dynasty who established the cultural and political centre for the whole empire in Vienna. The idea of the foundation of a national library was born during the so called "Reform period" in the late eighteenth century, which had under the influence of the French revolution, political objectives and aimed also at the development of the Hungarian language and culture. It was an enlightened aristrocrat, Count Ferenc Széchényi, who donated to the nation his own collection of books, maps, coins and engravings expressively with the intention of laying the foundation of a national library and national

Reprinted from *Libri,* vol. 23, no. 2, 1973, p. 155-65, by permission of the author and the publisher.

museum. This was how our library, bearing the name of its founder even today, and consisting of 13.000 volumes at that time, came into existence in 1802.

The library has borne the features of a national library ever since its foundation: it aimed first of all at collecting the book production of Hungary and that of the *Hungarica* literature published abroad, it enjoyed early the favour of receiving copyright copies. In the period between 1809 and 1948 it made up a single organization with the National Museum, similarly to the Library of the British Museum. Although the number of our documents has increased to approximately five million units during the 170 years since the foundation, and 400 collaborators are working in an ever growing number of fields offering several services in more than twenty special collections or sections, our library is still accomodated together with the National Museum in the building constructed in the middle of the last century, in spite of the fact that the two institutions have organizationally been independent from each other for a long time. The new home of our library will be situated in a part of the Buda Castle under reconstruction which will appropriately and deservedly house the precious collections for a long time to come.

The library system of Hungary

The social, economical and cultural development of our country after the World War II entailed also the development of library life. The Library Act passed in 1956 is one of the most important milestones of the development differentiating four types of libraries: a) national library; b) scientific libraries (both of general and special character); c) public libraries; d) school libraries. The Act gathered the libraries (except the national library) in networks (e. g., the network of the medical, technical and agricultural libraries, network of the libraries of the Academy of Sciences and of its institutions, network of the university libraries etc., in the case of the public libraries regional networks). The centre of each network is a great library having the task »to ensure the planned acquisition of the holdings, its balanced and widespread use, to care for the circulation of the experiences and to efficiently represent the interest of the library branch" (third paragraph of the Act) Such network centres are the National Medical Library and Documentation Centre, the National Technical Library and Documentation Centre, the National Agricultural Library and Documentation Centre, etc.

The Ministry of Education is in charge of the establishment and direction of library policy. In this respect the Ministry is assisted by the *National Library and Documentation Council* as a consultative organ, with the essential activity of outstanding experts of library life. *Professional supervision* belongs similarly to the competence of the Ministry. *The education of librarians* at a high level is carried on in the Budapest University, at a medium level in two pedagogical high schools in the country and in special courses. *The Hungarian Association of Librarians* is a social organization: its task is to provide a possibility for the librarians to discuss the questions of interest to them.

I. The Collections of the National Library

The National Library of Hungary has a double function. On the one hand, in its capacity as a traditional national library it acquires, processes, preserves and makes accessible for the readers the ever increasing number of documents, on the other it functions as a centre of nation-wide library services. As far as the collection and the traditional library is concerned, the first question to ask is what are the documents a national library is charged with collecting? The answer to this question should be, naturally, outlined with a view on the whole library system of the country.

1. *National literature.* It is generally accepted that the first task of a national library is the collection of the nation's literature. Also in the study of Mr. K. W. Humphreys *National Library Functions* the chapter "Fundamental functions" opens as follows: "Whatever other function of a national library is undertaken elsewhere, the collection of the nation's literature is its basic aim".

This goal was envisaged by our library already in the first years of its existence. The founder, Count Ferenc Széchényi, as a bibliophile was led by the passion to collect all books from or on Hungary. Though the example of the great universal libraries in the West (Paris, London, etc.) sometimes raised the suggestion of transforming the national library into a monolithic scientific collection, the original concept remained essentially unchanged.

According to the acquisition principles the term Hungarica-literature comprises all documents issued in the country and from abroad (a) that was written in Hungarian on any subject; (b) that was written by a Hungarian author on any subject and in any language; (c) that refers to Hungary or the Hungarian people by subject written by any author in any language. In this respect the library strives at completeness. The system of the copyright copies is charged with fulfilling this demand. (Our library has enjoyed the supply of copyright copies since 1804, although this service has become regular only since the end of the last century.)

The demand for completeness raises a problem which becomes more and more serious. The rapidly increasing number of publications places the libraries in a difficult situation, among them first of all the national librares functioning on the basis of copyright copies. (The situation is turning out to be even more serious by the development of the techniques of multiplication.) Formerly the case had been quite simple: printing had meant at the libraries in a difficult situation, among them first of all the national libraries same time evaluation, the collecting activity of the libraries could almost be identified with the material being printed. Nowadays, the borderline between the necessary and the negligible is often at an other place, it often happens that the value of documents produced in a small number exceeds several times that of the books printed in a large number of copies. It is quite evident that we cannot be satisfied with the old formal objectives to preserve all printed documents. The best products of the age's and nation's mind should be preserved, i. e. the kind of material which has a documentary value and, after a thorough consideration, the second and third rate material (e. g. reprints, low-level popularizing works) can be neglected. This is a fundemental problem of the national libraries, otherwise they will get drowned in a quantity of waste paper. Our library is trying to determine the lower threshold differentiating the material to be preserved from the ephemeral. (The starting point to be observed is the value of contents, the source value.)

The settlement of this question refers, however, only to the details. The fundamental aim of the national library has remained unchanged: its task is to act as the memory of the nation.

2. *Foreign literature.* Foreign literature is indispensable in a national library. It is, however, not a simple task to decide which type of foreign literature belongs to the duties of the national library as the nation's entire library system must be taken into consideration.

Our opinion and practice is as follows: we have to acquire such foreign works which are, as an international background, inevitably necessary to the study of the national literature. Consequently, emphasis is laid on the different encyclopaedic works, bibliographies, handbooks, etc. In addition we acquire the most outstanding works having connections with the main line of our acquisition policy, i. e., mostly in the following subject fields: linguistics, literature and historical sciences.

The division of labour referred to when speaking about the library system, can be, actually, outlined here. The collection of the literature of the individual branches of sciences on an international scale belongs to the tasks of the great special libraries in Hungary, i. e. to the central technical, agricultural, medical libraries already mentioned, the Central Pedagogical Library, the Library of the Parliament in the field of the political sciences and legal sciences, the Library of the Hungarian Academy of Sciences in the field of linguistics and literature, etc. It means that the National Széchény i Library's activity is restricted to the collection of Hungarica material not only because of its traditions but also in the interest of rationalization. In our opinion we can best keep abreast with the development of sciences if a reasonable division of labour and cooperation can be realized among the special libraries in our library system.

Yet, two additional remarks are here to be mentioned. The first is that the literature of the neighbouring countries takes a special place between the Hungarica and the foreign literature in general. A largescale acquisition is carried on from this type of literature. The other remark is that, in a certain sense, the literature of the earlier centuries is considered as an exception. The specialization of the sciences and the establishment of the special libraries are phenomena of later times, up to late eighteenth century the universal acquisition field was quite natural. Consequently, we do not intend to carry out retrospectively a differentiation according to the present principles of library policy. Thus, our special collection named Collection of Old Prints is built up on other principles than the modern collections. (The collection of incunabula and of the sixteenth century antiqua material are based on similar principles as the national libraries of universal character.)

At the end of 1971 our library's holdings counted two million volumes of books and 200 000 volumes of periodicals. Taking into consideration the other types of publications and the manuscripts too, the number of the holdings exceeded five million units. (5 173 300)

As for the organizational structure of the library, beside the main collection of books and periodicals the following special collections are to be found: Manuscript Collection, Map Collection, Collection of Musical Prints, Theatre History Collection, Collection of Small Prints, the already mentioned Collection of Old Prints and Microfilm Collection. Service to readers and the information service is carried out also according to this organizational system.

3. *Hungarian National Bibliography. Documentation*

In Hungary the national library became connected only in the thirties with the edition of the national bibliography published previously as a private initiative, this many sided activity unfolded, however, only after 1945. In Hungary there is neither a Chamber of Books nor Bibliographical Institution, thus the publication of the national bibliography belongs, according to the disposition of the Library Act, to the tasks of our library. Similarly as in other countries, the copyright copies serve as a basis for the bibliography.

Our current bibliographical activity consists of the following: the bibliography of a) books (and maps) and b) the repertory of periodical articles are published fortnightly, the bibliography of c) music prints and records is published quarterly. The bibliography of books is published in yearly (and several years') cumulations. The bibliography of bibliographies, the bibliography of graphic posters, the bibliography of the text books used in different types of schools appear in cumulative volumes.

The works of the retrospective bibliography are carried on separately but in parallel. During the past twenty-five years considerable results have been achieved also in this field. A retrospective bibliography covering the sixteen years 1945–1960 was published a few years ago and preparations are under way to cover the inter-war period. Beginning with 1960, on the basis of the yearly volumes, an edition of cumulations covering ten year periods is planned, the first cycle (1960–1970) is already published.

Simultaneously with the registration of recent literary production we have begun the new compilation of the bibliography of the earliest prints according to the latest scientific demands. The first volume of the series was published in 1971 covering the Hungarian prints in the period between 1473 and 1600. The eighteenth and nineteenth century bibliographical cumulations have been published in form of reprints partly in enlarged editions.

Great efforts are required also to the processing of the foreign Hungarica material, i. e. of the literature appearing in Hungarian or relating to Hungary published abroad. Recently, the edition of two current quarterly bibliographies have been started and the compilation of retrospective cumulations are also planned in this field.

The Vienna symposium and also the study of Dr. Humphreys range the edition and publication of the national bibliography among the basic functions of the national library. We completely agree with this point of view. This activity ensures that the library – beyond the use of the material on the spot – should act as a general information centre. The situation is more difficult in respect of documentation. It is not a clear question yet what is our task concerning the registration of data and information, beyond the bibliographical survey of the publications. In Hungary the other libraries of a national character have included in their name also "Documentation Centre" (e.g. the former National Technical Library is today: National Technical Library and Documentation Centre) proving also in this way that, in the age of information, it intends to offer more than the traditional library services. It is a statement valid also to us that a modern library cannot be satisfied with the acquisition, preservation, moreover, with the complete registration, the cataloguing of the works and not even with the publication of bibliographies, but it has to offer up-to-date documentation services too. This question is now hotly debated. As for us we are in the following opinion: our library is obliged to offer also documentation services in the field of knowledge of national character: such subject fields are the Hungarian history, literature, linguistics, further the history of the Hungarian science and national institutions. The history of Hungarian book publishing and printing belongs, quite naturally, to this field.

II. National Library Service

In our library system networks were established in accordance with the recognition that there is a constantly growing number of tasks which cannot be performed by the libraries themselves. Co-operation is a modern requirement characteristic to the library life of the whole world. It can be observed all over the world that the libraries are no more isolated, they undertake joint works and even a single library considers itself responsible to carry out certain central services (union catalogue, etc.) In Hungary the organization of the service on a national level falls to the competence of the National Library. These are tasks which are no more (or not only) connected with the holdings of our library. This type of task can be found in the whole field of library activity, in the acquisition, processing, use etc.

1. *Acquisition.* Within the frame of IFLA the Section of the National and University Libraries treated the problem of co-ordinated national acquisition policy within the individual countries. Considering the logical order, this is, without any doubt, the first national task. Co-ordination of acquisition policy is a problem of such a great importance that it was carried out by the Ministry of Education itself. The national system of fields of interest was set up in this way; it refers to hundreds of libraries and is laid down in the Code of Co-ordinated Acquisition. Observing this regulation, the National Library distributes the copyright copies, carries on an international exchange of publications, and the exchange of duplicate copies.

The service of copyright copies means that in Hungary the printing houses supply all (at present 16) copyright copies to the national library which undertakes their further distribution. Centralization has a great advantage. Considering that the libraries with a right to copyright copies are entitled to select the material with a view to their field of interest, each of them claims only a part of the material. Thus quite a considerable number of publications remain in the national library and can be used first of all in the international exchange of publication.

The international Exchange Service deals with a task of greater importance and responsibility, having relations with libraries from all over the world. The actual international exchange of publications is not centralized in our library. The Hungarian institutions carry on themselves the exchange of their own publications, yet there are certain functions which belong to the sphere of competence of the exchange centre acting within the national library: keeping records, supply of information, bringing together partners, distribution of the contents of collective consignments, exchange of official publications, distribution of a great quantity of books and periodicals arriving here mainly from the socialist countries in accordance with cultural agreements and the dispatch to foreign countries of the most outstanding and comprehensive pieces of Hungarian literature.

We assist the libraries also by rendering it possible to get a survey of the foreign literature arriving in the country. We publish the Monthly List of Foreign Acquisitions containing the material of several hundred libraries. This publication issued monthly in two branches (humanities and social sciences; natural and applied sciences) offers a complete survey in the UDC system of the foreign literature arriving in the country. The same is the case with the foreign periodicals, this list is published every second year.

In Hungary, the exchange of duplicate copies is carried on partly in the network system, partly centrally in the National Library. By this service approximately 200 Hungarian libraries have acquired the literature of interest for nearly twenty years.

2. *Processing. Catalogues* Our circumstances did not allow us to organize a central supply of catalogue cards, although its necessity has several times been discussed. At present the central organs of the book trade prepare catalogue cards of Hungarian publications which are received by the network of Hungarian public libraries together with the books, or they may be ordered subsequently The catalogue cards of the Széchényi Library are delievered only to 1 or 2 scientific libraries (e.g. the University Library in Debrecen). Our union catalogues have an important role. The organization of the union catalogue of books was begun in 1923, nowadays three hundred Hungarian libraries submit regularly the bibliographical descriptions of the new acquisitions. Based on this tool we supply several thousand pieces of information yearly. Our union catalogue of periodicals comprises the *total* holdings of the foreign periodicals to be found in Hungary i. e. not only the current titles. (This material is planned to be published in catalogue volumes in the next years.)

3. *The Interlibrary Loan Service* closely cooperates with the union catalogues, and functions according to the well-known international rules. The loan within the country is carried on, as far as possible, among the libraries directly, whereas the majority of the foreign loans is effected by the central

service functioning in the national library – from this the Library of the Academy and its institutions are exceptions. This service handles yearly about twenty thausand requests, mostly the requests of Hungarian research institutions and enterprises. There is an ever growing number of articles acquired on microfilm or on xerox-copies and the telex is also at our disposal. The service has the deficiency that there is no central Lending Library which causes difficulties in the case of frequently demanded works.

In the following please allow me to mention a few fields of activity which could not be brought into being so far, yet they have a great importance stressed also by the third National Librarians' Conference held in 1970.

a) *Storage*. Preservation of the holdings. The quick growth of holdings resulted also in Hungary in lack of storage space in a great number of libraries. The only solution to this problem is that the non-current material should be placed in centrally organized deposit libraries.

At the same time the damaged condition of old holdings makes the central organization of restoration (National Restoring Laboratory) also urgently necessary. We may not even think of installing separate workshops in each library possessing holdings to be restored.

b) Information. The troubles experienced in the field of information necessitate the establishment of a centre which directs the person interested to the competent place or source ("information on the information"). (In the United States, within the Library of Congress the National Referral Centre was established offering a good example of how the tasks of a national library are becoming more and more wide-spread. By the way, Dr. Humphreys also mentions the establishment of the national bibliographical information centre among the basic functions of the national library).

c) Mechanization. The internal demands of the national library also render necessary the mechanization of work in connection with the national bibliography, the catalogues and other tasks. Yet, in a small country it seems appropriate both from the professional and from the economic point of view to establish this service on a national level.

Centre for Library Science and Methodology

The Centre for Library Science and Methodology belongs to the National Library, yet it enjoys autonomy. Its task it to deal with questions of theory, library documentation, advising librarians on problems of library work, education and postgraduate education of librarians. In its activity an important share falls on the assistance afforded to the public libraries. The centre helps in drawing up plans, in improving working methods, and it deals with questions of modern library building.

Special attention is paid to the problems of readers; i. e. to the investigation and development of their demands.

Summary

In conclusion the question arises of how unity can be established between the two functions and spheres of activity in the national library. Some may think perhaps that it is a question of the symbiosis of two institutions, others tend to consider the services mentioned in part 2 as mere accessories.

Social and scientific development determines (and modifies from time to time) the tasks of the national library. The encyclopaedic national library, born according to demand for universal services and being able for a time to fulfil these requirements, got into a crisis as a consequence of the modern development of science; today up-to-date answers are given to the up-to-date questions and demands of researchers by the special libraries. Who could stop the development which more and more divides the formerly homogenous work among the ever growing number of libraries?

The literature of today cannot be housed in a single library. We can make a choice either to give up the idea of universal services or to formulate it in a modern way. The specialization necessarily entails modern co-operation and integration. The essence of this is that the library cannot renounce the potentiality of having an overview of the "totality". But this cannot be assured in a way that it was in the old encyclopaedic libraries. Co-operation between different library networks, union catalogue, interlibrary loan service, etc. are considered as appropriate means and methods to assure the necessary unity in the best form.

However important it may be, the holdings of the national library are only one of them. We hope that by the development of our collections and by the national services in our charge we can create continuity with the past and participate in the development of the library work of the country complying with the demands of modern life.

The National Library of Nigeria and Library Development in Nigeria

by NAT. M. ADEYEMI

Introduction:

The library is to a developing nation what it is for a developed country, namely a tool for intellectual freedom and economic development; a gateway to political, economic and social happiness and survival. Freedom in its various dimensions means the absence of ignorance of situations. The acquisition of knowledge needed to dispel ignorance derives from studying. Edward Newton realised this when he said in chapter eight of his work entitled "The magnificent farce" that:

> From contemplation one may become wise, but knowledge comes only from study.

The library continues to bring man in contact with the word in the fulfilment of its function as a repository for knowledge in all forms and shapes. It has also become over the years a dynamic centre for research for development. Of the various categories of libraries which exist (Public, Academic, Special, School and College, National) the rôle of the National Library in developing countries in particular calls for an examination, and the object of this paper is to examine the role of the National Library of Nigeria in the context of a national library development.

The National Library of Nigeria

The questions which come to mind when one thinks of an institution of this nature in a developing country are: –

(a) To what extent should it perform the normal functions of a National Library such as:

       1. Bibliographical function
       2. Co-ordinating function
       3. Professional advisory function

Reprinted from *Libri*, vol. 22, no. 1, 1972, p. 77-84, by permission of the author and publisher.

4. Professional training function
5. Research[1]

(b) should it assume total responsibility for library development in the country?

The National Library Act of 1964 and The National Library Decree, 1970

The 1964 Act establishing the National Library of Nigeria was the result of an idea conceived in 1948 when, on 3rd July 1948, the Chairman of the Standing Committee to Advise the Government on the Provision of Libraries wrote to the Chief Secretary to the Government that the Committee: –

> "Feels that a start should be made to establish the National Central Library ... This library would be a copyright library in which would be deposited copies of all books and papers published in Nigeria, would stock the works of reference which are required by serious students but which are not in sufficient demand to warrant their being placed in Regional or local libraries and would serve as a repository and distributing centre for microfilms of rare or out-of-print books in overseas libraries ..."[2]

This idea, which was strongly recommended by the Ibadan Seminar in 1953, was developed by Mr. Gbole Winkina in a document he submitted to the Government two years later entitled: "Beginning a National Central Reference Library Service for Nigeria".[3] The idea was just about to become a reality when, in 1959, the recommendation made by the WALA to set up a National Library Advisory Committee won aid from the Ford Foundation for the Federal Government at Independence which led to the arrival in Nigeria in 1961 of Dr. Frank Rogers. He was asked, among other things, to "consider the problem of a National Library for Nigeria". His positive recommendation for the establishment of this institution met with the usual fate imposed by limited finances in the face of several priorities. Thus when Dr. Carl White arrived in 1962 as the first Library Adviser, he met a situation where the idea of the National Library was passed over as a luxury. However, national pride and Dr. White's "May Report" led to the Bill[4] which established the National Library in September 1964.

The debate of the Bill showed both the interest of Parliament to promote library service, and the ignorance of individual members of the concept and the functions of a National Library. The resulting Act – a political resolution – was frought with handicaps and limitations which aroused interesting comments and recommendations in professional circles. The Act charged the Board *inter alia* with the duty of:

> "providing in accordance with those provisions such services as in the opinion of the board are *usually provided by national libraries of the highest standing*",[5]

but made no mention of the existing publications laws[6] which would deny the National Library of two of its major functions, viz. (1) that of a deposit library, and (ii) the compilation of current national bibliography. Furthermore, the Act had no national application as showed by its clause 7–(1):

> "This Act may be cited as the National Library Act, 1964, and shall apply to the Federal territory only.[7]

The various shades of opinion expressed in professional circles between 1964 and 1966[8] showed beyond reasonable doubt the inadequacies of the 1964 Act and the need to rectify the anomalies therein in order to make the Library truly national. Professional opinion also revealed that for such an institution to be really effective it should not be saddled with more functions than it has capacity to deal with. Accordingly the Council of the Nigerian Library Association (N. L. A.) drafted a memorandum[9] containing a policy proposal to ensure greater effectiveness of the institution and submitted it to the Federal Ministry of Information for consideration and possible adoption. However, the revised National Library Act, the National Library Decree, 1970, took care of only a fragment of the content of this memorandum; but it improved considerably on the Act of 1964 in so far as deposit obligations and bibliographical functions are concerned. Section 2–(2) of the Decree empowers the Board: –

(a)   To assemble, maintain and extend a collection of books periodicals, pamphlets, newspapers, maps, musical scores, films and recordings and and such other matter as the Board considers appropriate for a library of the highest standing.

(b)   To establish and maintain a branch of the National Library in each State,

(c)   To make the facilities of the National Library available to members of the public and others on proper terms, which may include provision for –

      (i)   the imposition of a scale of fees, subject to the approval of the Commissioner, for services rendered to the public,

      (ii)   safe-guarding the property of the Board, and

      (iii)   specifying the categories of persons who may be admitted to premises under the control of the Board,

(d)   To make such arrangements as the Board considers appropriate with respect to –

      (i)   the exchange of matter included in the collection aforesaid,

      (ii)   the preparation and publication of catalogues, indexes and similar aids,

      (iii)   the provision of assistance to other persons in the organisation of libraries and with respect to the manner of using facilities under the control of libraries.

(e)   To make recommendations and give advice on library development or organisation to any department or agency of government of the Federation or a State or to any local government authority.

(f)   To be responsible for the development of the National Bibliography of Nigeria and national bibliographical services, either in a national bibliographical centre or elsewhere.

Section 4 (1)–(4) deals with deposit obligation in the following terms:

4.   (1) The publisher of every book published in Nigeria shall within one month after the publication deliver at his own expense to the National Library three copies of the book, two of which shall be kept in the National Library for permanent preservation and one of which shall be sent by the Director to the Ibadan University Library.

(2) The copies of the book delivered to the National Library under sub-section (1) above –

    (a)   shall be perfect copies of the whole book with all maps and illustrations belonging thereto, finished and coloured in the same manner as the best copies of the book are published, and

    (b)   shall be bound, sewed or stitched together and on the best paper on which the book is printed.

(3) Where any printed matter (other than matter of such descriptions as the Director may specify from time to time) is published by or on behalf of any department of government of the Federation or a State, it shall be the duty of the official in charge of the department to deliver forth-with to the Director for the purposes of the National Library –

    (a)   twenty-five copies of the publication, if it is published by or on behalf of a department of government of the Federation, or

    (b)   ten copies of the publication, if it is published by or on behalf

of a department of government of a State, or such smaller numbers of copies as the Director may determine in any particular
case.

(4) If a publisher fails to comply with any provision of subsection (1)
or (2) above, he shall be guilty of an offence and on conviction shall be
liable to a fine not exceeding £50; and the court before which he is
convicted may in addition order him to deliver to the Director three
copies of the book in question or to pay to the Director the value of
those copies.

The provision made in 2–(2) (b) of the 1970 Decree: "to establish and
maintain a branch of the National Library in each State", gives one the
impression that the institution is now truly *national*. Nevertheless the national
application which this decree has cannot replace the establishment of a
national policy for library development. Such an action demands of the
Federal Government the formulation of a national objective for uniform
development of library resources throughout the country. Furthermore, this
objective should be translated into appropriate legislation with provision for
its adoption by all the twelve states as the basis for the development of a
system of libraries in each state. The result of such a measure would be a
highly developed network of the various categories of libraries aimed at
supplying the needs of the public.

A ready inference from an examination of the decree is that the National
Library is saddled with responsibility for the national library development
in Nigeria. This implication poses some problems because: –

(i)   The National Library is just an institution as any of the other
        categories of libraries in the country, and operating within certain
        physical, financial, and human contexts it can only perform cer-
        tain well-defined duties if an effective and efficient system is
        the goal.

(ii)   Its effectivness as a link between libraries in the country as centre
        for inter-library loan, or even as a clearing house for information,
        presupposes two basic factors: –

(a)   an efficient system of libraries in the country, and

(b)   a good communications network, both of which are virtually
        absent.

Effective communication cannot be possible if the two elements of the com-
municator, medium and audience, are not present in the right framework.
A brief look at the library situation in Nigeria reveals some of the many
problems which need definite solutions.

The library scene in Nigeria and situation role of state branches

Of the other four broad categories of libraries – Public, University and College, Special, and School libraries – University Libraries have been given the attention and support needed to keep them in the forefront of the academic programmes of the various institutions they serve.

Special libraries are well-established in some Government Departments and Public Corporations. The other two categories – public and school-libraries – are still struggling for survival. The greatest progress in public library work was made in the former Eastern Nigeria, where library programme was based on law.[10]

The state branches of the National Library would only fit well into a good network of libraries, for irrespective of whatever political undertone they may have, their social and functional implications are of unique importance. They cannot operate in isolation. The rationale behind their establishment should be seen from the point of view of the creation of national resource centres capable of acquiring in depth the socio-economic-educational, political and cultural materials of the states of their location, and putting these materials at the disposal of the whole nation by means of an efficient communications network.

This exposition has so far placed the National Library where it belongs in the total library scene in Nigeria. It has also pointed out that for the Library to efficiently perform the functions characteristics of institutions of its type, attempts should not be made to give it other functions which can be more effectively performed by another body. The National Library belongs to a system of libraries in the country, and like any of them its activities have to be co-ordinated in certain respects. Its activities will also be enhanced if legislation exits for the development of library systems in the various states of the Federation.

But the fact that its activities spread throughout the country does not give the National Library a right to establish policies governing the development of other libraries, neither can it control the services given by these other libraries.

Some suggestions

Libraries are a necessity in a developing economy because education for development presupposes adequate provision of library facilities at all levels and in all sectors of the economic fabric of the nation. The following possible solutions suggest themselves as answers to the present state of library development in the country.

1. *Legislation.* The Federal Military Government should either (i) take urgent steps, in view of its gigantic economic development programmes, at formulating and implementing a national objective for library development for the whole Federation and by so doing put library development and legislation on the priority list of each state government; or (ii) remove the library from the concurrent list and make it an exclusive matter under Federal control with a body created by law, like the National Universities Commission, to push its case and provide the administration for national library affairs.

2. *A National Commission for Libraries:* The alternative proposal in (1) above calls for the establishment by law of a national body different from the National Library Broad which would be responsible among other things for controlling and co-ordinating the efforts and services of all categories of libraries in the country including the National Library. This idea was contained in the memorandum by the Council of the Nigerian Library Association mentioned earlier on in this paper. However, this was not the first time such an idea was expressed.[11]

The presence of such a body responsible for the provision and development of library services in the country would spell an end to the apathy which has harassed library development in an atmosphere where economic development rests largely on the intellectual capacity of national manpower. The functions of this body, as was proposed by the Council of the Nigerian Library Association, should be among others:

(1)   To evolve national library policies for the provision, development and co-ordination of library services in the country.
(2)   To arrange international exchange of personnel.
(3)   To advise library authorities on their development projects.
(4)   To distribute external and national financial aids to library authorities.
(5)   To establish standards and ensure their implementation.
(6)   To serve as a clearing house for matters generally relating to personel, finance and training.

With such a provision, the scene will be adequately set for a healthy national library programme free from any confusion which could occur from over-enthusiasm that might saddle one unit of a total system of libraries with more than it can cope with efficiently and effectively.

NOTES AND REFERENCES

1. A National Library in a developing country can perform these functions where no other well-established body already exists for the purpose but only as a prelude to the institution of an appropriate body.
2. White, Carl M. The National Library of Nigeria: growth of an idea, problems and progress, Lagos, 1964. p. 2.
3. Ibid. p. 3.
4. Nigeria. House of Representatives. Parliamentary debates. 1st Parliamentary, 5th session, 1964–65. v. 16 p. 33 et seq.
5. Nigeria. Federal Government. Annual volume of the Laws of the Federal Republic of Nigeria 1964, no. VI, D77–77. Lagos, 1964.
6. The Publications Ordinance, 1950, gave legal deposit powers to the libraries of the University College, Ibadan, and the Secretariat Library in Lagos. Successive enactments – the Eastern Nigeria Publications Law 1955, the Western Nigeria Publications Law 1956, the Northern Nigeria Publications Law 1964, and the Federal Government Legal Notice no. 112 of 1964 – gave depository powers to certain institutional libraries in the various Regions of the Federation. None of these laws included the National Library as a depository.
7. See (5) above : D 74.
8.(i) Okorie, Kalu. Library resources in Nigeria : present position and future trends. *Nigerian Libraries,* 1, 3 : 101–112, September 1964.
(ii) The National Library : a review. *Nigerian Libraries.* 2, 3 : 101–107, 1966.
9. Memorandum of the Nigerian Library Association on a National Commission for Libraries, 1968.
10. Agidee, Dickson. Legal provisions for library development in Nigeria, 1946–1968. Paper read at the Nigerian Library Association Conference, 1970.
11. Oderinde, N. O. Nigerian libraries in post-war reconstruction. *Lagos Librarian* 3, 4 : 9–20, 1968.

OTHER REFERENCES

Aje, S. B. The National Library of Nigeria, Lagos. *Nigerian Libraries:* 4, 3: 79–83, December 1968.
Aje, S-B. "Social and other forces affecting library development." Paper read at the Annual Conference of the Nigerian Library Association, 1970.
Bankole, E. B. The Public Library in post-war reconstruction and National development. *Nigerian Libraries:* 5, 1 : 7–10, April 1969.
Chandler, George. Libraries in the modern world. Oxford, Pergamon Press, 1965.
Dipeolu, J. O. Library legislation and Public Library development. *Nigerian Libraries:* 5, 1 : 11–15, April 1969.
Fielder, Fred E. Theory of leadership effectiveness. New York, McGraw-Hill, 1967.
Green, L. E. Nigeria, Ministry of Education Library Service . . . Paris Unesco, July 1969.
Kahn, Tillo E. Transport and communication. Ibadan, NISER, 1969.
The National Library of Nigeria : a tool for economic development. Lagos, 1970.
Nigerian Library Association. Western State Division. Public Library Committee.
I. The case for a central library in Ibadan.
II. Draft legislation for establishing the Western State Library Board: report submitted by the Public Library Committee, Ibadan 1969.

A New National Library: The National Diet Library of Japan

CHIN KIM

In Japan as in other civilized countries, libraries existed from her early history in the form of store-houses where books were kept for the exclusive use of the privileged class of people.[1] The inception of Japan's modern library movement was in 1872 with the establishment of Tokyo Shoseki Kan (Tokyo Books Institute);[2] in 1892 the Japan Library Association was founded.[3] Shortly after the Meiji Restoration of 1868, the social climate and spirit had turned toward modernization of Japan through the importation of Western technology under the Emperor Meiji. Patriotism, a strong sense of national identity and loyalty to the Emperor was made a sacred duty. Preoccupied with the urgency of modernization and promoting the spirit of national identity and unity, Japan's leaders considered individual interest and freedom as luxury. The people were gradually deluded into thinking that the prosperity of the nation was synonymous with their own individual affluence in spite of the economic sacrifices and political deprivation demanded of them. A tragic event took place during the 1930's when political power passed from the political parties to the military, who shaped domestic and international policies.[4] Under such an undemocratic and imperialistic social and political climate, any progressive library movement was severely curtailed.

Immediately following Japan's surrender in 1945, the Allied Powers carried out the provisions of the Potsdam Declaration of July 26, 1945, to "remove all obstacles to the revival and strengthening of democratic tendencies among the Japanese people," and to establish "freedom of speech, of religion, and of thought, as well as respect for the fundamental human rights."[5]

A prime feature of the Constitution of 1947 was that it gave recognition to the principle of popular sovereignty. The new Constitution declared that the Japanese people should exercise their rights through elected representatives in the Diet and that the sovereign

Reprinted from *Journal of Library History*, vol. 4, no. 3, July 1969, p. 225-38, by permission of the publisher.

power resided with the people.[6] In order to put the concept of popular sovereignty into practice, need for the individual's awareness of
his rights and responsibility became urgent and the use of libraries
toward this end became highly important. The program of "democratization of education" was launched in order to eliminate ignorance
among the people so that they could exercise their sovereignty. In
order to implement this program, the reorganization and improvement of the existing library system became necessary in postwar Japan.

HISTORICAL ORIGINS OF THE NATIONAL DIET LIBRARY

Established in 1948 through the enactment and implementation
of the National Diet Library Law, the National Diet Library absorbed
three different government-supported libraries and two privately
endowed collections.[7]

First, the Imperial Diet Libraries, whose history goes back to the
opening day of the Imperial Diet (Teikoku Gikai) in 1890,[8] became
a part of the National Diet Library when the Imperial Diet was
abolished in 1945. Second was the Imperial Library (Teikoku
Toshokan), which has functioned as the hub of the Japanese public
library movement since 1872.[9] Although it has become a branch of
the National Diet Library, its traditional function of public library
is still maintained. The libraries in the executive and judicial
branches of the government were also incorporated into the National
Diet Library. These libraries had developed with the rise of modern
Japan after the Meiji Restoration and became an important part of
the National Diet Library through the branch library system. They
are rich sources of printed materials, although some were badly
damaged during World War II.

The origins of the two privately endowed collections known as
Toyo Bunko and Seikado Bunko are relatively recent. The former,
an extensive collection of writings on Asiatic countries in all languages,[10] was established in 1924, and the latter, which specializes
in Chinese classics, was established at about the same period.[11] These
two collections occupy the status of branches within the National Diet
Library organization.

Imperial Diet Libraries. The bicameral Imperial Diet convened for
the first time in 1890 and continued to exist until the end of World
War II. It consisted of an elected House of Representatives and a
House of Peers which was comprised of hereditary and life peers and

scholars appointed by the Emperor.[12] Patterned after the Prussian
legislature, the Imperial Diet was subordinate to the executive branch
of the government and had done little more than discuss and then
approve the bills submitted by the cabinet.

Each house of the Imperial Diet had a library during its existence.
However, they remained quiet reading rooms for the members of the
legislature despite attempts by legislators to develop well-organized
research libraries.[13] By 1947 there were 36,000 volumes in the library
of the upper House and 60,000 in that of the lower House.[14] This
situation is well summarized in the following statement:[15]

> Both Houses of the National Diet of Japan have had their
> separate libraries since 1890. But because the Diet, prior to
> 1946, had no final responsibilities, its requirements for exact
> and extensive information were correspondingly small. Even
> the wording of the legislation upon which it deliberated was
> prepared by a bill-drafting bureau within the Cabinet. Conse-
> quently, the Diet libraries never developed either the collec-
> tions or the services which might have made them vital
> adjuncts of genuinely responsible legislative activity.

The Imperial Library. The Imperial Library of Japan was absorbed
into the National Diet Library in April, 1949, and named as the
Ueno Branch Library. Currently it is serving the citizens of Tokyo.
This library will be transferred in due course to the Tokyo Metropolitan Government in view of an urgent need for an expanded
municipal library service in the city.[16]

As described earlier, the Imperial Library originated in 1872
when the Tokyo Shoseki Kan was founded. It was the first modern
library established in Japan under the jurisdiction of the Ministry
of Education. In 1880 it was renamed as Tokyo Toshokan (Tokyo
Library) which literally means "institute for illustrated matter and
books." Tokyo Toshokan was designated as the Imperial Library of
Japan in April, 1897, and existed until 1947.[17]

Although the Imperial Library functioned as the first public
library in Japan until recent years, its rule against outside use of
the library materials has been a unique feature. After its establishment, its holdings were steadily increased to reach approximately one
million volumes by 1946.[18] Another important function of this
library until 1947 was its role as the copyright depository, obtaining
one copy of each book officially registered with the Copyright Office
of the Ministry of Education.[19]

The Governmental Libraries. The origins of the governmental libraries can be traced back to the Meiji Restoration in 1868, when the modern form of governmental institutions was introduced in Japan. With the establishment of the modern structure of government agencies, each agency began to set up its own Bunko, which means "container for preserving books." At the beginning they served as archives. However, as the administrative functions of each agency became clearly defined, they were gradually combined with research facilities, and the term Bunko was replaced by Toshokan (Library). Among these governmental libraries, the Library of the Imperial Cabinet (Naikaku Toshokan), whose origin goes back to 1881, was outstanding in terms of its size. It inherited a substantial part of the collections of the government of Tokugawa Shogun and it had already reached a total of approximately 40,000 volumes by 1889.[20]

ESTABLISHMENT OF THE NATIONAL DIET LIBRARY

The Diet as the highest organ of power in the nation under the new constitution needed research facilities in order to discharge its monumental tasks and its responsibility to enact the law and to inspect the affairs of the state. The need was reflected in the Diet Law of March 19, 1947, Article 130 of which prescribed that: "The Diet shall have, as provided for in a separate law, a National Diet Library, in order to help Diet members conduct investigations and researches." Toward the end of March, 1947, the Diet hastily enacted the Diet Library Law. It had seven articles, each full of vague wordings.[21] No one seemed to have a clear conception of the purpose, scope and content of a research library.

This confusion led the Standing Committee for Library Management of both Houses to convene frequently and discuss future plans for the establishment of the new national library. The discussion which began on June 3, 1947, led to a special request to the Supreme Commander for the Allied Powers to provide the assistance of American librarians in the initial stages of planning.[22] Pursuant to this request, the United States Library Mission, composed of Verner W. Clapp of the Library of Congress and Charles H. Brown of the American Library Association, arrived in Tokyo on December 14, 1947. During their two months' stay, they conducted an extensive survey of the local libraries and gradually projected the future of the National Diet Library in close collaboration with officials of both the Japanese government and the occupation forces. Clapp and

Brown envisaged the creation of an institution which would assume commanding leadership in advancing the nation's library system, patterned after the United States' Library of Congress. With a comprehensive collection of Japanese and foreign materials, this research library was to provide extensive services not only for the Diet, but also for the executive and judicial branches of the Government and the general public as well.[23] Their ideas were fully reflected in the National Diet Library Law, which contained thirty-one articles. The law became effective on February 9, 1948.

The dates and principles embodied in the National Diet Library Law needed implementation. Again, there was a need for expert advice. This was provided by Robert B. Downs, Director of the University of Illinois Libraries. As suggested by the Clapp-Brown team, his mission was primarily concerned with the internal organization of the National Diet Library. He was in Japan from June to September, 1948, and his recommendations on the technical aspect of library operation had a profound influence on the subsequent development of the Library.[24] His advice was instrumental in the National Diet Library's developing such devices as a Japanese national bibliography, a national union catalog, a printed catalog card service and periodical indexes.[25]

SPECIAL FEATURES OF THE NATIONAL DIET LIBRARY

In discussing the characteristics of the National Diet Library the legal status of the Chief Librarian, the branch library system, and the legal deposit are essential.

The Chief Librarian and Supervising Organs. The Chief Librarian is appointed by the Speakers of both Houses after they have consulted with the Diet Operation Committees of both Houses and have received the approval of the Diet. The office is non-political and carries the status of Minister of State. The incumbent may be dismissed by joint action of the Speakers.

The Chief Librarian is under the direct supervision of the Diet Operation Committees of both Houses. These two committees hold at least one meeting every six months to consider reports from the Chief Librarian on the program of the library, the rules and regulations made by the Chief Librarian for the government of the library, the budget of the library, and other related matters.

The Chief Librarian is also indirectly supervised by the Coordinating Committee of the National Diet Library. For the improvement of the services of the National Diet Library, this committee makes recommendations to the Diet Operation Committees of both Houses and to the executive and judicial branches of the Government. The committee consists of four members who are: the Chairman of the Diet Operation Committees of the two Houses, a Justice of the Supreme Court appointed by the Chief Justice, and a Minister of State appointed by the Prime Minister. The Chief Librarian may attend meetings of the committee, but he has no vote in its proceedings. The committee was designed to indirectly supervise the Chief Librarian, but it ordinarily provides support for the Chief Librarian in coordinating the services of governmental libraries.[26]

Branch Libraries. Currently the National Diet Library consists of the central library, three branch libraries and thirty libraries of the executive and judicial government agencies in the Toyko metropolitan area. The system of branches in government libraries is a unique one and permits very close cooperation with the network. The Chief Librarian of the National Diet Library appoints the librarians of the branch libraries upon the recommendation of the members of the Coordinating Committee on the National Diet Library, who respectively represent these branches.

As an advisory organ for the Chief Librarian, the Council on the Branch Library System has been functioning since August, 1962. The Council clarifies the official status of branch libraries and reinforces their contents.[27]

How did this unique system of branch libraries come into being? Mr. Goro Hani, Chairman of the Standing Committee for Library Management, House of Councillors, made a revealing statement when the National Diet Library bill was debated in the Diet. Mr. Hani advocated that by unifying all these governmental libraries into the arm of the Diet, the concept of popular sovereignty would be enhanced and the long prevailing fear of executive bureaucracy would be overcome. This system, according to Mr. Hani, enables constituent libraries to make mutual use of printed materials.[28] This idea of an influential solon coincided with the recommendations of the Clapp-Brown team, which elaborated on a program of developing a central union catalog of all books in government libraries to promote maximum sharing of materials by users.[29]

Legal Deposit. From the beginning, there was a consensus as to the depository function of the National Diet Library with regard to gov-

ernment publications. However, publications other than tax-
supported printing presented a problem. During and prior to the
Pacific War, the legal depository system was used as an instrument
of strict censorship of all published materials. At the time of the
deliberation on the National Diet Library bill in 1948, there was
still a lingering fear among legislators that the compulsory deposit
system might lead to censorship.[30] This fear prevailed in the final
version of the legislation. Deposit with the Diet Library became a
voluntary matter for the publishers. The fear of censorship by way
of limitation of legal deposit gradually subsided with the passage of
time. The subsequent amendment of the law prescribes that failure
to make such deposits will be subject to a fine equivalent to no less
than five times the retail price of the publication. In case of deposit
with the National Diet Library, the Chief Librarian provides a
compensation equivalent to the expenses usually required for the
printing and deposit of the publication.[31]

SERVICES OF THE NATIONAL DIET LIBRARY

The services of the National Diet Library extend to the Diet,
the executive and judicial branches of the government, all other
libraries, and the public. Services that transcend the national boundaries are increasing.

Services to the Diet. Services to the Diet are an integral part of the
National Diet Library and are the special responsibility of the Research and Legislative Reference Department, which is similar to
the Legislative Reference Service of the United States Library of Congress in its functions. This department performs four functions: first,
upon request it advises and assists any committee of the Diet in the
analysis, appraisal or evaluation of legislation pending before it, or
of proposals submitted to the Diet by the Cabinet, and otherwise it
assists in furnishing a basis for the proper determination of measures
before the committee; second, upon request, or upon its own initiative, it conducts research work and organizes politically unbiased
materials; third, it provides assistance to committees and members
of the Diet in their bill-drafting; fourth, it makes the information
which it gathers available to other branches of the Government or
to the public.

Within the Diet, inquiries usually come from individual members
of the Diet, committees, and Secretariats of the two Houses. Inquiries
related to legislative drafting numbered 5,518 in 1960 alone as com-

pared with 209 in 1948. There has been a proportional growth in the size of the staff of the Department, from the original 20 in 1948 to 149 in 1961.[32]

Services to the Executive and Judicial Branches of the Government. The branch libraries are established in almost all the ministries, important administrative agencies and the Supreme Court. The central library and all thirty branch libraries cooperate with one another in handling reference questions, using an interlibrary loan system of materials and utilizing the specializations of individual branch libraries. Under this unified system, an aggregate of about five million volumes of the central and branch libraries are open and accessible to the network.[33] Thus, 6,810 volumes of books were placed on interlibrary loan between the central library and the branch libraries and among the latter themselves for the period from April 1, 1966 to March 31, 1967.[34] Copies of catalog cards for the collections of each of the branch libraries are sent to the central library, eventually to be compiled into the national union catalog. It was reported that the reference questions handled within this network numbered 82.715 in 1961, as compared to 3,367 in 1948.[35]

Services to Other Libraries and to the Public. The services and collections of the National Diet Library are available to the public in two ways: first, directly through reading-room service, interlibrary loan, reference service and photoduplication service, and secondly, through prefectural and municipal libraries to the extent that such services do not interfere with the Library's primary responsibilities of service to the Diet, its committees and members and of the other executive and judicial branches of the national government.

There are 850 seats altogether for the public in the main reading-room of the central library and in small reading-rooms in specific subject fields. The open-access system is employed in the latter. Anyone beyond twenty years of age can use the holdings of the library; however, no loans are made to private individuals. Only the interlibrary loan arrangement, which enables him to borrow through other libraries is permitted. Reference service is rendered through correspondence, by telephone, and personally. The number of reference inquiries had increased to 12,094 in 1961 from 1,234 in 1948, and the figure was doubled in 1962.[36] Cases of reference service to the public numbered 55,519 for the period from April 1, 1966 to March 31, 1967.[37] The Library has excellent photoduplication facilities, which were donated by the Rockefeller Foundation, and this service is open to the public.[38]

Indirect services are rendered through bibliographical activities. One of the primary tasks of the National Diet Library is the compilation of bibliographies. The library issues the Japanese National Bibliography, with an exhaustive list of all publications that appear in Japan in each calendar year.[39] The first issue appeared in 1948. In the latter part of each issue of the Japanese National Bibliography there is a complete list of titles of periodical publications the library has received during the year, showing the issues by their respective years. Also for government publications, the Japanese National Bibliography is the most reliable list with the widest coverage. The Union Catalog of Foreign Books, acquired by forty-nine libraries in Japan, has been edited and published by the National Diet Library annually since 1949. There is no such union list of the current domestic publications in existence. A printed catalog card service was organized by the National Diet Library and has been extended to outside organizations.[40]

International Services. Participation of the National Diet Library in the sphere of international service is active and diverse.[41] The National Diet Library manifests vigor and interest in building collections of foreign materials, especially in the fields of science and technology. Scientific and technological materials under the category of official publications are extensively collected, mainly through the international exchange that the library maintains with many countries. Exchange materials are drawn from the legal depository system. The library receives a number of copies of every publication issued by the government and local public bodies in order to use them for international exchanges.[42] It acts as a center for exchanges of materials at home and abroad.[43] According to its records, 79,870 government publications and 3,193 non-government publications were mailed on an international exchange basis during the first period from April, 1962, to March, 1963, while during this period 17,979 government publications and 8,566 non-government publications were received from abroad.[44] This was an advance from the 55,532 government publications and 2,309 non-government publications exchanged during the previous year.[45]

In 1961, the National Diet Library joined the cooperative program of international interlibrary loan initiated by the International Federation of Library Associations (IFLA). There have been increasingly frequent contacts with the major national libraries throughout the world.[46] Reference inquiries and requests for photoduplication coming from other nations are accepted in the same way as those from clients within the country. The transmittal of microfilms abroad is interesting; the figure of 474 was recorded in 1962, more than double that of 219 in 1961.[47] International cooperation with regard to the exchange of bibliographical information is noteworthy.

To promote these activities, *International Exchange of News* has been published on a monthly basis. This publication is designed for domestic enlightenment. A quarterly, *The Indo-Pacific Exchange Newsletter*, came out in November, 1958, to promote the international exchange of publications, particularly in the Indo-Pacific area. This publication is an outcome of the Seminar on the International Exchange of Publications in the Indo-Pacific Area, which was held in Tokyo in November, 1957, under the sponsorship of the National Diet Library of Japan in cooperation with UNESCO and the Japanese National Commission for UNESCO.[48] In January, 1963, the title of this quarterly was changed to *National Diet Library Newsletter*.[49]

The National Diet Library is active in assisting international publication projects such as *Index Translationum*, *Bibliographical Services Throughout the World*, and *Handbook of the International Exchange of Publications*.

Conclusion. The year 1961 marked a turning point in Japanese intellectual history, with the realization of the long dream of opening the new Diet Library building envisioned by the original Japanese founder and American advisors thirteen years earlier.[50] The magnificent eight-story building stands to the north of the Diet building, earthquake- and typhoon-proof and with facilities for preventing mildew. It has storing capacity for 4,500,000 volumes and a seating capacity of 1,500.[51] This event was a material realization of the preamble of the National Diet Library Law, which enunciates:

> The National Diet Library is hereby established as a result of the firm conviction that truth makes us free and with the object of contributing to the international peace and the democratization of Japan as promised in our Constitution.

Housed in its new modern building, the National Diet Library has initiated a reappraisal of its role and service through a series of studies designed to project its future course: improvement of services,[52] closer cooperation of branch libraries[53] and mechanization of information-retrieval systems.[54] An active leadership as a national library was exercised when the National Diet Library initiated annual conferences with university librarians starting in 1965.[55]

Since its establishment in 1948, the National Diet Library has gone through two major organizational reforms, in June, 1961, and in April, 1963.[56] As of March 31, 1967, the National Diet Library consisted of seven divisions: Administrative, Research and Legislative Reference, Acquisitions, Processing, Circulation, Reference and Bibliography, and Interlibrary Service. Currently the National Diet Library is composed of the central library, one detached library in the Diet building, and three branch libraries: Ueno Library, Seikado Bunko and Toyo Bunko. Thirty branches are functioning throughout the executive and judicial branches of the government. The size of the staff, as of March 31, 1967, was 808 persons, including the Chief Librarian.[57]

Incorporation and coordination of tax-supported libraries through the branch library system in Japan present complex problems that do not yield to easy solutions. As discussed earlier, in Japan a great deal of emphasis is placed on the creation and effective use of a branch library system as the best means of promoting democratization. This is one of the basic differences between the National Diet Library and the Library of Congress. Another is that the Chief Librarian of the National Diet Library is under the direct supervision of the legislature and the indirect supervision of the executive and the judiciary. As for the legal deposit, Japan used this institution as an instrument of censoring printed materials prior to 1945. Present Japanese requirement of the donation of a single copy of each non-governmental publication, the measure designed to overcome the unpleasant memories of censorship, needs reappraisal as an important resource for the collections of the National Diet Library.

Through the foregoing discussion, it becomes clear that the functions of the National Diet Library fall within the purview of IFLA's broader definition of national libraries. The term "national," according to this definition, "covers a wide range of institutions, all of which, however, have responsibilities and tasks of national and international significance."[58] Furthermore, the multidimensional functions of the National Diet Library sufficiently meet the most recent inventories on the role of national libraries.[59]

The questions and challenges facing the National Diet Library are three-fold. First, whether such a highly centralized library can effectively cope with the enormous proliferation of knowledge and the resulting vast increase in publication is a question which needs further observation. In this connection, the experience of the United States is worth studying in that she developed separate national libraries for different subject fields, i.e., the National Library of Agriculture, the National Library of Medicine and the National Referral Center for Science and Technology.

Second, the question is to what extent and how rapidly the National Diet Library can cultivate the social needs of libraries among its citizens. Where the society has been indifferent to the raison d'être of libraries, the development of libraries is slow and their contribution to the intellectual growth of society is limited. Creation of an organization such as "Friends of the National Diet Library" may stimulate growth, as this type of organization has proven to be most helpful in promoting the social needs of libraries in France.[60]

Third, the question and challenge are, how to assume the leadership in helping countries of the Asia-Pacific area in their efforts to create and develop national libraries. Because of the stature and maturity the National Diet Library has attained among the international community of libraries, it should undertake an active role in creating an atmosphere in which mutual cooperation, exchange of ideas and knowledge can be stimulated and maintained through regular contacts and communication.

FOOTNOTES

[1]Louise Watanabe Tung, "Library Development in Japan," *Library Quarterly*, XXVI, No. 2 (April, 1956), 79-104.

[2]Noriaki Ono, *Nippon Toshokansi* [The History of Japanese Libraries]. (Kyoto: Ranshobo, 1952), p. 242.

[3]Japan Library Association, *Libraries in Japan*, 2nd ed. (Tokyo: Japan Library Asscociation, 1958), pp. 4-9.

[4]Chitoshi Yanaga, *Japanese People and Politics* (New York: John Wiley & Sons, 1956), pp. 1-8.

[5]*Ibid.*, p. 7.

[6]Verinder Grover, *The Constitution of Japan* (Delhi: Atma & Sons, 1964), p. 32.

[7]"Fourteen Years of the National Diet Library: A Retrospective Outline," *National Diet Library Newsletter* [English], No 16 (January, 1963), pp. 1-3.

[8]Theodore McNelly, *Contemporary Government of Japan* (Boston: Houghton Mifflin Co., 1963), pp. 16-17.

[9]Ono, pp. 242-244; Louise Watanabe Tung, "Library Development in Japan, II," *Library Quarterly*, XXVI, No. 3 (July, 1956), 198-203.

[10]Tung, "Library Development in Japan, II," pp. 203-204.

[11]*NDL* [National Diet Library] *Annual Report 1964* (Tokyo: National Diet Library, 1965), p. 21.

¹²Warren M. Tsuneishi, *Japanese Political Style*: *An Introduction to the Government and Politics of Modern Japan* (New York: Harper & Row, [1966]), p. 86.

¹³*NDL Annual Report 1961*, p. 1.

¹⁴Verner W. Clapp, "The National Diet Library of Japan," *Science*, CVII (May 14, 1948), 500.

¹⁵U. S. Department of State, *Report of the United States Library Mission to Advise on the Establishment of the National Diet Library of Japan*, Submitted to the Supreme Commander for the Allied Powers, February 8, 1948, p. 1.

¹⁶Article 22 of the National Diet Library Law reads: "Effective not later than April 1, 1949, the National Library at Ueno Park shall be operated as a branch of the National Diet Library, especially for the benefit of the citizens of Tokyo. As soon as practicable thereafter, this library shall be transferred to Tokyo Metropolis to be operated under such laws and regulations as may be enacted prior to the date of transfer."

¹⁷Ono, pp. 242-244.

¹⁸Clapp, p. 498.

¹⁹Tung, "Library Development in Japan, II," p. 198.

²⁰Ono, pp. 264-269.

²¹"Fourteen Years of the National Diet Library . . .," p. 2.

²²*NDL Annual Report 1948*, pp. 1-2.

²³Clapp, pp. 497-501; "Japan's Library of Congress," *Library of Congress Information Bulletin*, July 27-August 2, 1948, pp. 11-13.

²⁴Robert B. Downs, "Japan's New National Library," *College and Research Libraries*, X (1949), 381-387, 416; Verner W. Clapp, "R. B. Downs Reports on the National Diet Library of Japan," *Library of Congress Information Bulletin*, September 21-27, 1948, p. 17; T. Ichikawa, "The National Diet Library in Japan," *Journal of Documentation*, VII (1951), 113-118.

²⁵"Fourteen Years of the National Diet Library . . .," p. 3.

²⁶U. S. Department of State, *Report of the United States Library Mission. . .,"* pp. 8-9.

²⁷*NDL Annual Report 1966*, p. 12.

²⁸Goro Hani, "Kokuritsu Kokkai Toshokan no Soritu" [Creation of the National Diet Library], *Toshokan Zassi* [Library Journal], LIX (1965), 304-305.

²⁹U. S. Department of State, *"Report of the United States Library Mission. . .,"* p. 7; Clapp, p. 501.

³⁰Hani, p. 306.

³¹National Diet Library Law, Article 25, Paragraph 3.

³²*NDL Annual Report 1961*, pp. 2-3.

³³Senmon Toshokan Kyokai [Special Libraries Association], *Chosa Kikan Toshokan Soran* [Directory of Research Libraries] (Tokyo, 1956), pp. 14-16.

³⁴*NDL Annual Report 1966*, p. 12.

³⁵*Ibid.*, 1961, pp. 2-3.

³⁶*Ibid.*; *Ibid.*, 1962, p. 2.

³⁷*Ibid.*, 1966, p. 16.

³⁸*National Diet Library: How It Functions* (Tokyo: National Diet Library, 1956), p. 5.

³⁹Article 7 of the National Diet Library Law assigns this task.

⁴⁰"Bibliographical Services in Japan," *National Diet Library Newsletter* [English], No. 22 (October, 1965), 1-5; Robert L. Collison, *Bibliographical Services*

Throughout the World 1950-59 (Paris: UNESCO, 1961), pp. 93-96.

41Tokujiro Kanamori, "Foreign Literature in the National Diet Library, Japan: Acquisition and Availability," *UNESCO Bulletin for Libraries,* XI (1957), 115-117.

42National Diet Library Law, Article 24.

43"The International Exchange Activities of the National Diet Library," *Indo-Pacific Exchange Newsletter* [English], No. 9 (December, 1960), p. 12.

44*NDL Annual Report 1962*, p. 28.

45*Ibid.*, 1961, p. 28.

46*Ibid.*, p. 32.

47*Ibid.; Ibid.*, 1962, p. 32.

48Apparently this Seminar coincided with the meeting of the FALA (Federation of Asian Library Associations) Interim Committee for the Organizational Conference. This is a mimeographed and unpaged booklet which gives the following information: "A Compilation by the FALA Interim Committee for the Delegates to the Organizational Conference in Tokyo, Japan, Nov. 1957. Published in Manila, Oct. 10, 1957."

49"Letter to Our Exchange Colleagues," *Indo-Pacific Exchange Newsletter*, No. 15 (October, 1962), p. 20.

50U. S. Department of State, *Report of the United States Library Mission. . .,*" pp. 22-26.

51"Removal of the National Diet Library into Its Newly Completed Building," NDL Library Science Series, No. 6 (Tokyo: National Diet Library, 1962).

52*NDL Annual Report 1961*, p. 4.

53*Ibid.*, 1962, p. 12.

54"Mechanization of Service in the National Diet Library," *National Diet Library Newsletter*, No. 23 (October, 1966), pp. 2-4.

55*Ibid.*, pp. 4-5.

56Shigeru Kanamori, "History of Libraries: National Diet Library," *Toshokan-Kai* [The Library World] XIX (1967), 157.

57*NDL Annual Report 1966*, p. 56. The report announces that to provide additional shelving space, construction of an annex to the central library was planned and appropriated for in 1966. This building was formally opened on November 21, 1968. See *Library Journal*, XCIV, No. 2 (January 15, 1969), p. 132.

58IFLA, *Libraries in the World; A Long-Term Programme for IFLA* The Hague: Nijhoff, 1963), p. 51.

59K. W. Humphreys, "The Rôle of the National Library: A Preliminary Statement," *Libri*, XIV (1964), 362-368.

60Julien Cain, *La Bibliothèque Nationale pendant les Années 1952 à 1955* (Paris: Bibliothèque Nationale, 1958), pp. 283-284.

THE CHALLENGE OF TWO CENTURIES: CREATION OF IRAN'S PAHLAVI NATIONAL LIBRARY

Nasser Sharify

Dean, Graduate School of Library and Information Science, Pratt Institute, and Chairman, Board of Consultants, Pahlavi National Library

In March 1975, during a conference in Paris, the Deputy Minister for Cultural Affairs of the Imperial Court of Iran asked the present writer to provide him with a comprehensive plan for the country's new national library in one year. The creation of the Pahlavi National Library to serve all people of Iran was the subject of a decree issued by His Imperial Majesty, the Shahanshah of Iran in late 1973.

To plan for a national library reflecting the reality of this century, including the NATIS (National Information Systems) concept as promoted by UNESCO, and capturing the imagination of the next century, obviously required a wide variety of high expertise not possessed by any single individual. I therefore turned to all those whose specialized knowledge was needed for various facets of library, resources, services, programs, and facilities. With the assistance of many, and practically a worldwide search, in a three-month period over 100 experts were recruited, representing many nations and thus bringing with them a colorful diversity in concepts, principles, and practices. Harmony was

Reprinted from the *Bowker annual of library and book trade information* 1977, p. 417-23, with permission of the R.R. Bowker Company, 1180 Avenue of the Americas, New York, New York 10036. Copyright ©1977 by Xerox Corporation.

achieved during a major briefing conference held for all consultants in Long Island, New York, in July 1975, before they departed for a month-long mission in Iran in August 1975.

On March 12, 1976, a 17-volume report composed of approximately 5,000 pages was officially submitted to Iran. These included 11 volumes of position papers by consultants and a 6-volume final report of the chairman of the board of consultants, the last of which was devoted to a detailed building program. Two copies of the entire report are now available at the Library of Congress.

The planning report is now being used as the basis for an open international competition for the selection of an architect for the building. The deadline for the participation in this competition is set for January 20, 1978. Further details about this competition appeared in the January 1977 issue of the *Journal of the American Institute of Architecture.*

It is estimated that the library will be open and ready for service within ten years. Based on the recommendations of the final report, the library's collections will then include 1 million volumes, 25,000 serials and periodicals, and automated data bases with several million items available for on-line retrieval. The library will provide electronic networking among libraries and information centers in Iran and around the world. New communications and information technology will be utilized throughout the service activities of the library.

THE PUBLIC LIBRARY

From the outset of planning, one of the unique features of the PNL concept was that this was to also serve as a public library for the capital city of Iran. The existing national libraries of the developed countries began by serving an official, social, or scholarly elite. Indeed, many of them retain various limitations and constraints on use even today. The Pahlavi National Library will be different. Here will be a dynamic institution, reaching out to touch the minds and lives of all Iranians, however high or humble their station.

In outlining the public library mission, the plan recognizes that Iran is a unique country, standing at a strategic stage of its development. Its national library will reflect its particular needs and opportunities. Iran is now moving rapidly to build a modern, diversified industrial economy and its society is rapidly urbanizing. However, it is also true that Iran has a rich cultural heritage that has been developing for more than 2,500 years. Thus, the library must support both the information demands of today and tomorrow and, at the same time preserve, disseminate, and enrich the cultural expressions of its people.

The library's collections and data bases, its range of staff skills, and its programs of service will all be designed to achieve these two broad objectives. A basic assumption behind the public library concept is that all people should have the opportunity for life-long self-development and self-fulfillment. The time when education ended with several years of only youthful classroom exposure is behind us. Education is now recognized as a continuing experience that occurs in a wide variety of formal, informal, and highly individual ways.

The public library function of the Pahlavi National Library will take place in an open and inviting physical environment. Books and multimedia materials will be on open shelves and available for loan. The staff will create a welcoming and friendly atmosphere and work informally with users, getting to know them personally whenever possible. The activities of the public library will include the following:

To catch the interest of the casual or merely curious visitors and stimulate their use of the library resources

To meet the practical information needs of people facing difficult decisions or complex problems

To provide material for students

To answer ready-reference questions, both in person and by telephone

To advise and guide people in the use of printed and audiovisual materials and to instruct new users, both individually and in groups, in how to take full advantage of the library

To support Iran's literacy campaign by providing appropriate materials and by offering individual assistance to those who have problems in reading

To mount changing exhibits and displays of library materials related to the culture and contemporary activity of Iran

To serve as a model public library that can be studied and experienced by librarians in other parts of Iran and elsewhere around the world

THE IRAN AND ISLAMIC ROOMS

Two notable features of the library will be the Iran and Islamic Rooms. These two related and physically adjacent areas will be located in convenient proximity to the public library areas. These will be the showplace of the library, where both Iranians and visitors from around the world will see, hear, and touch the life of the nation, past and present. This print and multimedia experience will capture the serenity of Islam and dramatize the dynamism of modern Iran in ways that will be vivid and memorable.

The visitor to the Islamic Room will see large-scale, colorful, illuminated maps showing the geography of Islam during different historical periods. Selected objects of Islamic art, including ceramics and tiles and manuscripts, and other examples of early calligraphy, will be on exhibit in well-lighted, atmosphericaly controlled and secure display facilities. Cassette recordings in a wide choice of languages will be used to explain and interpret the exhibits to each visitor. The Islamic Room will emphasize the thoughts, religion, history, and beautiful objects of the past.

The Iran Room will present the dynamic growth and change taking place in Iran today. The exhibits will present and interpret such information as population estimates and characteristics, literacy levels, school and university enrollments, oil production, agricultural output, industrial activity, etc. Multimedia presentations will depict industrial progress and the cultural life of the people. The exhibits and the materials in the Iran Room will concentrate on the post-World War II period, with emphasis on the current decade. Information about the government of Iran—its plans, policies, organization, ministries, services, and regulations—will be readily available. Where possible, this information will take the form of brief summaries and fact sheets that visitors may take with them.

CENTER FOR RESEARCH IN IRANIAN STUDIES

Another unique component of the Pahlavi National Library is this advanced research center, which will be an integral part of the institution, interconnected with its resources, service, and programs. As a center for both instruction and original research in Iranic studies, it will draw together the varied aspects of the field into a unified and integrated research and information program.

The center has been conceived on the assumption that the scholarship of the future will be radically different from what it is today. On the one hand, there will be new disciplinary theories and new combinations of traditional disciplines, such as those now developing in sociolinguistics. On the other hand, the rapidly developing techniques of electronic data processing, storage, and retrieval will permit new forms of analyzing, tabulating, and correlating knowledge.

The goal of the Center for Research in Iranian Studies will be to seek a broadly based integration of scholarship in the area that will create an intellectual environment in which change and innovation can develop and thrive. For example, when dealing with linguistics, the center's task will not be limited to the study of Indo-European Iranic languages; rather, it will extend to embrace all of those languages that have touched historically on what is now the Iranian cultural world, as well as those spoken by peoples with whom Iran has been in cultural or economic contact.

This broadened definition of Iranian studies will maximize opportunities for breaking down the traditionally narrow boundaries of existing disciplines. The center requires a large and capable research and academic staff. These highly trained specialists will bring their diverse talents to bear throughout the library complex. The Iranologists will, for example, teach and conduct research in the center itself, assist in the translation and transliteration of exotic languages for machine-readable bibliographic control, advise on exhibits and displays on Iranian life and Islamic culture, carry out field recordings of oral history of the peoples of Iran, and provide information services on Iranian studies both through a publications program and to individual users of the library.

Finally, it is expected that the Center for Research in Iranian Studies will become an exemplary model for the establishment and operation of other area studies facilities around the world, whether or not they may be part of a national library operation. Such a model will prove particularly valuable for the developing countries of Asia, Africa, and South America.

LIBRARY COLLECTIONS

The resources of the Pahlavi National Library will have great scope and depth and they will be developed expressly to meet the present and future needs of Iran. High selection of standards will be established and maintained, sensitivity to the history and current life of Iran will be demonstrated, and careful selectivity will be exercised. The bulk of the library's resources will be contained in a central and unified collection. In addition to books, the print and near-print holdings will include, for example, serials and periodicals, monographs, theses, microforms, manuscripts and rare books, documents and archival materials, maps, scientific and technical reports, patents, and sheet music and musical scores. Collection development will also extend to include all media that communicate information: films, filmstrips, slides, tapes and other sound recordings, videotapes, film loops, prints, charts, graphs, photographs, globes, models, etc.

In addition to these familiar hard copy holdings, the library will also have central data bases in a wide range of fields. The data bases will contain both bibliographic data for the identification and location of materials and content data, such as abstracts or numerical and directory files.

To ensure maximum use of the library's collections, the concept of intershelving of all types of materials in a unified physical arrangement will be implemented whenever possible. This technique will help the user find all types of materials in all formats and it will encourage the idea of "media browsing," which, in turn, will significantly expand the user's range of learning experiences.

The collection capacity of the Pahlavi National Library is estimated to be approximately 6 million volumes of books and other materials, plus an even larger number of items in other forms, notably archives and microforms. Even with a vigorous program of acquisition, it is not realistic to expect that this capacity will be reached in less than 25 years. During this period, library officials will have the opportunity to develop policies and programs for controlling and balancing the growth of items in the collection. The goal of these measures is to make ever-increasing size unnecessary.

One such method is to develop cooperative regional agreements with other large libraries of the Middle East. Through consultation and coordination, undue duplication of rare research materials can be avoided. As certain categories of material become old and little used, they can be retained by one designated library of deposit that would provide access to the other libraries of the region. Lesser used materials that are identified as important to have represented in the Pahlavi library collections can be systematically converted to microform. A careful policy of materials retention and discard is also essential to controlled growth. Research now underway shows promise of achieving ultra reduction through laser beam technology, which may well become effective and economical over the next decade.

The depth of collections in the various subject areas will also reflect the needs and interests of Iran. In some fields and for some purposes, almost everything will be acquired. In other areas, great scope and depth are desirable without necessarily being exhaustive. In still others, resources at specified levels will be designed to meet the needs of particular groups, such as students. These levels of desirable acquisition have been defined in descending order of depth as comprehensive, research, educational or reference, and token or minimal.

INTERNATIONAL STUDIES

The library will give a special priority in its collection development and staffing to international studies. Never in Iran's history has it been so necessary to understand the motivations, goals, and lifestyles of the other nations and cultures that comprise the contemporary world. On an ever-shrinking planet, faced with declining resources, burgeoning population, and intensified competition by blocks of nations for a larger share of the world's goods, all countries must increase their present levels of mutual understanding.

The international studies program of the library will be shaped to meet the needs of both scholars and specialists, as well as those of the general reader at every level. The holdings in international studies will serve purposes that cut across much of Iranian society and will involve a variety of audiences. The collections will, for example, serve:

As a source of liberal education for young people and students

As a lifelong means for learning about other cultures in order to understand better one's own country

As an aid to officials determining the foreign policies of Iran as it maintains its place as a world power

As a practical source for persons preparing for or engaged in professional and business activities which involve other countries

As a research resource for advanced scholars

The composition of areas was based on some common denominator, such as ethnic, religious, geographic, historic, linguistic, or cultural. These areas consist of the Near and Middle East, Western Europe, East-Central Europe, the Soviet Union, East Asia, Southeast Asia, South Asia, Africa, North America, and Latin America. For each of these areas, the established subject disciplines to be included in the collections are expected to be political science, sociology, social anthropology, economics, education, and social psychology. The size of the collections devoted to international studies is estimated to be approximately 430,000 volumes by the end of this century.

BIBLIOGRAPHIC SERVICES

The technical services department of the library will be equipped to provide cataloging and bibliographic services to the library itself, to other libraries in Iran, and to the international library community. A complete, accurate, and up-to-date national bibliography will make available the intellectual and cultural output of Iran in an organized, computer-based manner. The two principal objectives of a national bibliography for Iran are to provide a current-awareness listing of new material published within Iran and to provide an authoritative and complete historic record of Iranian book production. Bibliographies of nonbook materials, such as maps, printed music, and audiovisual items, will also be included.

The library will also maintain a national union catalog for locating materials held in Iran and provide cataloging and indexing services for other libraries and information centers throughout the country. Through the technical services department, the library will participate fully in the various international bibliographic agreements and protocols now being created or developed around the world. Examples include the International Standard Book Number, International Standard Bibliographic Description, and International Serials Data System.

ARCHITECTURAL CONSIDERATIONS

The Pahlavi National Library concept has been variously described by Iranian officials and others as a "library for the future," a "mother library," and as an "Iranian model for the developing nations of the world." These concepts have been defined and developed by one of the most comprehensive and detailed library planning projects ever undertaken. When the library is completed, it will take its place among the great national libraries of the world.

Although the library is presented as a single, integrated administrative entity, the physical structure will not necessarily be a single building. Such components of the library as the Center for Research in Iranian Studies, possibly including the Iran and Islamic Rooms, lend themselves to distinctive, architecturally separate structures. In addition, some supporting operations, such as technical processing, conservation and preservation services, and the computer center, might well occupy a structure or structures separate from the central collections. Within the limits imposed by the functional requirements of the component involved, the architects will be encouraged to produce a creative and imaginative configuration of structures.

.   Because of the size of the proposed library, it is essential that the architects preserve a human scale for the library, one that is in harmony with its surroundings and convenient for the user. In addition to the functional considerations, it is necessary that the library complex reflect Iranian architecture and be visually exciting, esthetically pleasing and inviting in all of its exterior and interior aspects.

The plan also strongly suggests that architects resist the temptations for monumental design. Rather, the library should be beautiful without being ostentatious and be impressive without being grandiose. Such embellishments as the grand staircase, the magnificent entrance, or the marble colonnades serve no useful purpose and, in fact, tend to intimidate and overwhelm the user, rather than invite him warmly to taste the treasures that the library offers.

DREAM OR REALITY

The consultants with responsibility for submitting position papers on various components of the library proceeded under no constraints of space, staff, or funds. Their mission was to describe a complete national library that would be ideal but achievable. To accomplish this goal, each step in the planning process was firmly rooted in the realities of Iran today. Twenty-nine research papers for the orientation of the international consultants were commissioned from distinguished Iranian specialists. These research and state of the art papers ranged from the status of existing libraries and special collections to book production and distribution, the state of computer technology, and multimedia production and use. Each author was also asked to provide the best possible projections of future trends in each area to the year 2000.

During the month-long mission in Iran during August 1975, the assembled consultants made a total of 204 individual field visits to 73 libraries, government offices, educational institutions, and related agencies. Included in these activities were the officials of the several types of libraries, academic administrators and faculty members, representatives of government ministries, publishers, printers, broadcasters, and others.

The efforts to reach reality through research papers and field visits were enhanced by the continuous, effective interchange between the international consultants and the 37 Iranian librarians and other specialists who worked closely and continuously together. The Iranian consultants reviewed the work of the international consultants as it was being produced in order to relate the emerging recommendations to the existing situations in Iran today. Thus the final design for the Pahlavi National Library, while comprehensive, ambitious, and richly detailed in scope and depth, is nevertheless a realistic and achievable goal for the nation and its people. If the required resources are committed to implementing the plan for the library, the result will be a quantum leap ahead in the provision of library and information services to the entire nation. The Pahlavi National Library of the future will be a large enterprise, an enterprise of excellence, but at the same time it will be efficient, cost effective, and accountable.

The Planning of National Libraries in Southeast Asia

Hedwig Anuar

The term Southeast Asia includes the countries of Brunei, Burma, Indonesia, the Khmer Republic, Laos, Malaysia, the Philippines, Portuguese Timor, Singapore, Thailand, North Vietnam, and South Vietnam – an area of some 1.2 million square miles with a population of over 220 million, characterized by great diversity of people, language, religion, and culture. These countries – apart from Thailand which never came under Western colonial rule, Brunei which is a British-protected sultanate, and Portuguese Timor – achieved political independence only after World War II.

Major factors with which these countries have to contend in their struggle for economic and social betterment include uneven distribution of population, (1) a high rate of population growth with a very high proportion of persons in the younger age groups, predominantly agricultural and dependent economies, low per capita incomes, high unemployment and underemployment, wars, insurrections, and revolutions. Economic development, education, housing, health, and transportation are the priorities in the national development plans of these countries.

The earliest libraries in the region, like early libraries in India, China, and other parts of Asia, served royalty, the nobility, or the priesthood in royal, temple, or monastery libraries. The ordinary folk depended on oral tradition and music and dance for the transfer of knowledge, information, and literature, while the written word or inscription on stone, bone, gold leaf, palm leaf, tree bark, bamboo, silk, and paper was an object of veneration and awe rather than of everyday familiarity and use.

Despite the spread of education, there is still high illiteracy in the region today, which, combined with the multiplicity of languages and scripts and low purchasing power, limits the development of authorship, printing, publishing, bookselling (of locally produced as well as of imported books), a reading public, and libraries. Librarianship itself is a new and barely recognized profession. In most of the countries of the region, there were no professionally trained local librarians until the early 1950s. Some of them are still highly dependent on training abroad that may be prestigious but is often irrelevant to the actual problems they face on

The author is director of the National Library, Singapore. The views in this paper are the writer's and do not necessarily reflect the views of the Singapore government.

1) See Appendix I at the end of this chapter.

Reprinted from VOSPER, Robert *and* NEWKIRK, Leone I., *eds.* National and international library planning: key papers presented at the 40th Session of the IFLA General Council, Washington, D.C., 1974. Munich: Verlag Dokumentation, 1976 (IFLA Publications 4), p. 80-98, by permission of the publisher and IFLA.

their return. Library associations (2) are generally young and have limited resources. Despite the many handicaps they face, they are notably active in the promotion of library and bibliographical services.

The pattern of library development is generally characterized by generous provision for university and special libraries that cater to an educated minority, including university students, researchers, civil servants, economic planners, scientists, technologists, and members of the older professions such as law and medicine. Public libraries, when they do exist, are generally at a rudimentary level of development, while school libraries are usually the poorest and most neglected of all.

It is against this backdrop that national libraries in Southeast Asia have been or are being established. While some trace their origins to the nineteenth century or earlier, most libraries have been formally established only within the last twenty to fifty years. The National Library of Thailand is probably the oldest, having been founded in 1905, while the National Library of Malaysia is the youngest, having been founded in 1971. It should also be noted that the Philippines, Thailand, South Vietnam, and Singapore have new national library buildings, provided within the last fifteen years.

Developing Concepts of the National Library

No Southeast Asian national libraries were mentioned in the July 1955 issue of *Library Trends,* devoted to current trends in national libraries, a further indication of the very recent development of these libraries in the region compared with long established national libraries in Western countries. This particular issue and the report on the Unesco Symposium on National Libraries in Europe, held in Vienna in September 1958, highlight the fact that the concerns of established national libraries such as those in the developed countries were vastly different from those being established in the developing countries. These well-established libraries were concerned with matters arising out of the growing complexity in the organization of large research collections, conservation, microfilming, mechanization, union catalogs, international interlibrary loans and exchanges, and the provision for training of specialist staff.

The functions of a national library and its place in a national library service with reference to Asia were first discussed at the Unesco Seminar on the Development of Public Libraries in Asia held in Delhi in October 1955. The only Southeast Asian countries represented at that seminar were Burma, Indonesia, the Philippines, Thailand, and the "Malayan-Singapore-British-Borneo group" represented by an expatriate British librarian).

The seminar noted that the terms "national library" and "national library services" are often loosely used, and it defined the functions of a national library as follows:

2)   See Appendix II at the end of this chapter.

It should collect all literary and related materials concerned with the nation, both current publications under copyright deposit and historical materials; be a conservatory of materials concerned with world culture and the natural main source in the country of such materials for scholars and research workers; act as the authority for the compilation of the national bibliography, this stemming naturally from its functions as a copyright deposit library; serve as the focal point and organizing agency for national and international interloan of books; and it should be the organizing centre for national and international book exchange.

Though the above are the major functions, the following were also considered desirable for proper co-ordination: it should be the agency to compile and maintain the national union catalogue, again arising from its function as the copyright deposit library. It should provide bibliographical service to parliament and to government departments. In addition, it should assume general responsibility for initiating and promoting co-operation and forward planning in all matters between itself and other libraries in the performance of the above functions, especially in relation to university and special libraries.(3)

In considering what should constitute a viable unit of service for public libraries, the seminar noted that in certain circumstances that concern size of the country and the lack of or limited local government, the country as a whole could be considered as a single unit. In such instances, both the public library and the national library would be serving the entire nation and could therefore be logically combined into one institution. It was thus agreed at the seminar that "in some countries, particularly smaller countries, the functions of the national library and the central library board should be integrated for better and more economical development." (4)

In February 1964, when the Unesco Regional Seminar on the Development of National Libraries in Asia and the Pacific was held in Manila, only five of the twelve countries of Southeast Asia were represented — Indonesia, Laos, the Philippines, Thailand, and South Vietnam. Only six of the twelve — Burma, Khmer Republic, Thailand, North Vietnam, South Vietnam, and Singapore — already had formally established national libraries, while in the remaining countries, other libraries not designated as national libraries were however carrying out some of the functions of national libraries. If national libraries are by definition those that serve nations or independent states, it is a moot point whether Singapore's National Library, established as both a public and a national library in 1958, could strictly be termed a national library a that date or even in 1964 when the country had reached the stage of internal self-government but was not yet a sovereign state.

The basic functions of national libraries, as summarized at the Manila Seminar in 1964, are:

3) Public Libraries for Asia: The Delhi Seminar (Paris: Unesco, 1960), pp. 27–28.
4) Ibid., p. 28.

(1)   to provide leadership among a nation's libraries,
(2)   to serve as a permanent depository for all publications issued in the country,
(3)   to acquire other types of materials,
(4)   to provide bibliographical services,
(5)   to serve as a coordinating centre for cooperative activities.
(6)   to provide services to government.(5)

The seminar also considered it preferable that "national archives should be administered independently of but in close co-operation with the national library."(6) It also agreed "that legislative reference services are an essential adjunct to enlightened government and the pre-requisite finance and facilities must be made available whether the service is offered primarily by the national library or by an independent unit answerable directly to the legislature."(7) On the role of the national library in the fields of science and technology the seminar recommended that "where circumstances permit, the national library should assume its proper responsibilities in the fields of science and technology, since these differ in degree rather than in kind from its responsibilities in other fields. These responsibilities in no way diminish the importance and duties of specialised libraries."(8)

The Meeting of Experts on the National Planning of Library Services in Latin America held in Quito in February 1966 amplified the functions of national libraries still further as follows:

To collect and ensure the conservation of the national book production for which, in addition to other resources, it will receive copies of publications deposited under the copyright laws; it should furthermore ensure that copyright laws are enforced.

To provide national and foreign readers and research workers with an adequate and efficient information service, for which it will assemble the necessary general collections and collections of reference works, prepare a union catalogue of all the country's libraries and compile the national bibliography and any other bibliographies necessary for the performance of its functions.

To organize the national or international exchange of publications.

To centralize inter-library loans with libraries abroad.

To rationalize the acquisition of publications, including periodicals, among the libraries covered by the plan for the development of library services.

To centralize the cataloguing and classification of publications and ensure the distribution of catalogue cards or catalogues published by certain categories of libraries.

5)   Regional Seminar on the Development of National Libraries in Asia and Pacific Area, Manila, 1964. Draft final report. (Paris: Unesco, 1964), p. 2.
6)   Ibid., p. 3.
7)   Ibid., p. 5.
8)   Ibid., p. 6.

To co-operate, whenever its own organization and the development of planning render it advisable, in the extension and improvement of school and public library services.(9)

The Unesco Meeting of Experts on the National Planning of Library Services in Asia held in Colombo in December 1967 laid special stress on the role of the national library as

. . . an active organisation with dynamic leadership geared to a triple purpose:
a) preserving the national culture
b) developing by all appropriate means, systems and procedures which will make available the total library resources of the nation for the benefit of the whole national community
c) establishing relations with libraries of other countries.(10)

Although this seminar stressed the role of the national library in planning for library development, it is noted that only three Southeast Asian Countries — Indonesia, Malaysia, and the Philippines — were represented at the meeting, and these by institutions other than national libraries, although most of the Southeast Asian sovereign states had established national libraries by that time.

Functions of National Libraries

Now, some ten years since the Manila seminar, national libraries have been established in all sovereign Southeast Asian states except Indonesia, where plans for a national library are at an advanced stage. Given the variety of concepts or models of national libraries available, it is enlightening to determine which of these concepts have been accepted as valid in the setting up of national libraries within the Southeast Asian context.

In the first place, it appears that most national libraries have had the advantage of being supported, and sometimes deliberately created, as necessary adjuncts to nationhood, along, perhaps, with other institutions or symbols such as national anthems, national museums, national art galleries, or, in a different context, national steel mills, national shipping, and national airlines. For example, the first proposal for a national library for Laos was made in 1958 by Tay Keolouangkhot and Thao Kene and states that "The establishment of a National Library for Laos will be a sign of its nationhood and a witness to its independence; and it will proclaim the respect of Laos for moral and intellectual values."(11)

However, under prevalent conditions, where the infrastructure of library development is wholly or partly absent, the creation of a national library could well mean

9) "Meeting of Experts on National Planning of Library Services in Latin America Report, Quito, 7–14 Feb., 1966," *Unesco Bulletin for Libraries* 20 (6) Nov.– Dec. 1966, p. 287–88.
10) *Final Report: Meeting of Experts on the National Planning of Library Services in Asia,* Colombo, 1967 (Paris: Unesco, 1968), p. 7.
11) Russell Marcus. "Laos and Library Development," *College and Research Libraries.* 28 (6) November 1967, p. 398.

the creation of an isolated and artificial institution, an apex without a base. This danger has generally been avoided, for an examination of the functions (12) of the national libraries reveals that most of them have some responsibility for library service for the nation as a whole as well as provision for cooperation with other libraries at national and international levels.

The functions of some of the earlier national libraries, such as the Singapore National Library, are clearly derived from the Delhi seminar of 1955 while those of more recent ones such as in Malaysia (and additional functions for the Singapore National Library provided in revised legislation enacted in 1968) emphasize the leadership role of the national library.While there is unanimous recognition of the vital function of collecting the literature of the nation, legal deposit legislation is only partially effective, particularly because of poor communications facilities, the multiplicity of languages, and the underdeveloped and disorganized state of the book industry. Where copyright exists, it may not always be linked with legal deposit. Some national libraries still have archival functions while, more commonly, national libraries and national archives come under the same ministry.

Many have assumed some responsibility for public library service, particularly for the capital city. The Singapore National Library is the only one, in keeping with the concepts emphasized at the Delhi Seminar, that operates as both a national and a public library with a system of full-time and part-time branch libraries and a bookmobile service. The National Library of the Philippines has an Extension Division serving some 446 provincial, municipal, barrio, and deposit station libraries all over the country in cooperation with local government authorities.

There are also great divergencies with regard to bibliographical functions, including union catalogs, current and retrospective national bibliography, indexing of periodicals and newspapers, and centralized cataloging services. Some national libraries serve as exchange centers in the larger countries but are usually not centers for interlibrary loans with libraries abroad, possibly because most libraries that operate interlibrary loans prefer to do so directly.

Preservation of collections through microfilming is gradually becoming more common. The second edition of the *Directory of Microfilm Facilities in Southeast Asia* (13) lists microfilming facilities at the national libraries of the Philippines, Singapore, and Thailand; in Indonesia such facilities are available at the Central Museum Library and the Indonesian National Scientific Documentation Center, which are expected to serve as national centers for the humanities and for science and technology respectively.

In building up their collections of national literature, some national libraries have had the advantage of absorbing or inheriting the private collections of

12) See Appendix III at the end of this chapter for the functions of the national libraries of Malaysia, the Philippines, Singapore, South Vietnam, and Thailand.
13) Patricia Pui Hen Lim (Singapore: Institute of Southeast Asian Studies, 1973).

learned societies or individual collectors. However, because they may be younger
than the university libraries of their countries, their collections may be smaller
and more limited. This in turn limits the bibliographical and research functions
they would normally undertake, which may already be carried out by university or other libraries. Thus the national library, though established to carry out
national library functions such as these, may in reality lack the capability, the
prestige, and the leadership potential required of such an institution.

For example, a Unesco expert's 1968 report on the development of Burmese
university and research libraries noted that the National Library of Burma did
not play an important role in the library system of the country and recommended the adoption of the Scandinavian pattern, "where the functions of the National Library and University Library are combined in a single institution."(14)
In discussing a proposed advisory council on libraries, the report also recommended that "as the National Library has not until now got the central position in
Burma as planned . . . it might be reasonable to affiliate the Council to the Universities Central Library, Rangoon, and to make the head of this library the ex-
officio chairman."(15) It is also interesting to note an earlier instance in 1925
when the Philippine Library Association successfully lobbied in the House of
Representatives against a bill that provided for transfer of the Philippines Library and Museum, predecessor of the National Library, to the University of the Philippines. The archives were not to be included in the proposed transfer.

Something of a vicious circle can thus arise where insufficient support for the
national library leads to bypassing of the institution in favor of other, sometimes
already established, sometimes newer, agencies. This applies particularly to newer
fields such as economic planning or scientific and technical development where
the lack of direct involvement by the national library leads to further weakening
of the institution and the retarding of its potential growth. This danger can only
be avoided if national libraries, as instruments of national policy, are closely identified with and responsive to the nation's development activities and goals.

Library Planners and Plans

How far has planning of national libraries succeeded in the realization of these
concepts and functions? National planning of economic development has generally been accepted as an essential tool of modern government, but national planning of social and cultural development has been evident only to a limited extent,
mainly in the fields of education, housing, health, and transporation; but increasing
attention is now being given to family planning. Most of the countries in the
Southeast Asian region have depended on outside resources for assistance in planning for their national libraries as well as for the planning of library service for
the nation as a whole. The main sources of aid for such planning have been
Unesco, the Ford Foundation, the Asia Foundation, the United States Agency

14)   Palle Birkelund, *Report on the Development of Burmese University and Research
       Libraries.* (Paris: Unesco, 1969), p. 20.
15)   Ibid., p. 4

for International Development, the Colombo Plan, and similar aid agencies.

Among the earliest plans were those for Indonesia, which has had the services of a large number of Unesco and other experts over the past two decades. Recommendations were made in 1953 for the establishment of a national library service (rather than a national library), including a system of provincial public libraries. One of the earliest proposals for a National Library of Indonesia was made in 1960 by J.N. Tairas, at the time a student at the New Zealand Library School. Currently, a Unesco team is advising the Indonesian government on the setting up of a national library that is expected to be established within the next plan period, from 1971 to 1979, as part of an overall plan for library development.

Another early plan was that for Burma, undertaken by Dr. Morris Gelfand on behalf of Unesco in 1958. This plan included a very comprehensive program for a National Library of Burma, covering its aims, organization, and building.

In 1962, Dr. Gelfand, as a Unesco consultant, also drew up a comprehensive plan for the development of the National Library of Thailand and for library service as a whole, in which he estimated that it would require 50 new staff members for the National Library and 25,000 school librarians. In March 1965, an ad hoc committee was appointed to draw up a national plan for library development as part of the government's five-year plan. Subcommittees were given responsibility for details of standards and plans for school, public, college, university, and special libraries and for the national library and library education. In 1968 this national plan for library development was completed and forwarded to the authorities concerned, but it was not accepted.

The first proposal for a national library in Laos was prepared in 1958 by Tay Keoloungkhot and Thao Kene, already referred to. The second proposal, prepared by Unesco expert Georges Chartrand in 1967, on library development in Laos, included the establishment of a bureau of libraries for Laos. The third proposal, by a member of the International Voluntary Service, called for Laos government approval and sponsorship of a Library Development Team that would "help organize libraries requesting assistance, create the materials necessary to run these libraries and set standards for good library practice."(16) The most recent Unesco report of libraries in Laos, Vietnam, and Khmer was made in May 1973 on behalf of the Unesco Regional Office for Education in Asia.

Two Colombo plan experts from New Zealand were appointed in 1962 to make recommendations on the development of a national library, one for a period of four months, while the second expert stayed for a two-year term in order to implement the recommendations made in the report. These called for tremendous expansion of public library service and an accompanying growth in book collections and of staff as well as the setting up of a library school attached to the National Library.

16)   Marcus. *op.cit.*, p. 399.

As a follow-up to the Manila seminar in 1964, the National Library of the Philippines prepared its own detailed survey and development plan in 1967. Subcommittees examined such matters as the administrative organization; resources, including the general reference collection, Filipiniana collection, public documents collection and copyrighted materials; technical services, buildings and equipment, and personnel; financial administration; extension services; publications; and intellectual and cultural activities.

In Malaysia, the first plans for a national system of public libraries rather than a national library were made in 1956 by the Malayan Library Group, predecessor of the library associations of both Malaysia and Singapore. Subsequently, planning for a national library began with the setting up in February 1966 of a National Library Unit attached to the Malaysian National Archives and of a National Library Committee headed by the chief secretary, who heads the Administrative Service. Beginning in November 1970, an Australian expert served as consultant to the government under the Colombo Plan for a three-month period in order to prepare the draft legislation for the establishment of the national library. The National Library Act passed in May 1972 includes the recommendations regarding the role of the National Library given in *Blueprint for Public Library Development in Malaysia* (17) presented to the Malaysian government in 1968 and subsequently adopted with respect to Penisular Malaysia.

The nature and extent of these official plans for the development of national libraries varies from country to country. Some are more detailed and comprehensive, but it may be said that all or most of them have attempted to survey the existing library situation and to make specific proposals on such matters as library legislation, buildings, functions, finance, collections, staffing, and library education, sometimes relating not only to the national library but also to library development for the nation as a whole.

Mention must also be made of the series of surveys on developmental book activities and needs in Laos, Thailand, the Philippines, Indonesia, and Vietnam that were made 1966–67 by Wolf Management Services on behalf of the United States Agency for International Development.

Planning at the nongovernment level has been undertaken by library associations, such as those of Thailand and Malaysia, chiefly for public and school library services. However, some planning for bibliographical projects has also been undertaken. In Malaysia/Singapore, for example, the Joint Standing Committee on Library Cooperation and Bibliographical Services of the two library associations was the first to draw up detailed recommendations for national bibliography, union catalogs, periodicals indexing, interlibrary loans, and other such matters. More recently, however, the trend has been for the national libraries in both these countries to take over these bibliographical and other functions. While there is considerable activity in the bibliographical field by national libraries, university libraries, documentation centers, and library associations of the region, there is

17)   Hedwig Anuar (Kuala Lumpur: Persatuan Perpustakoiah, 1968).

on the whole an insufficiency of planning in this field with the result that efforts
are uncoordinated and duplicated to some extent and bibliographical coverage
is far from complete.

National book development councils, fostered by Unesco since the first Experts
Meeting on Book Development in Asia held in Tokyo in May 1966, have now
been formed in most countries of the region. They were conceived as agencies
that would plan for integrated book development through the coordinated and
cooperative efforts of all sectors, both public and private, of the book industry.
National libraries are generally represented on these councils and will thus share
in the planning.

Planning Implementation

While there has been no lack of official planning for national libraries, the melancholy fact must be recorded that practically none of these plans have been accepted by the authorities concerned or they have been accepted with considerable
modifications.

The planning agencies and the planning processes vary considerably, according
to the legislative, administrative, and financial systems of each country. Some national libraries come under the Ministry of Culture, as in South Vietnam and Singapore; others are under the Ministry or Department of Education, as in Thailand
and the Philippines; the National Library of Malaysia is under the Ministry of
Housing and Local Government. Since most national libraries are government
agencies, the programming, execution, and evaluation of their plans are carried
out in accordance with prescribed practices and procedures and are subject to
bureaucratic and other constraints. A hopeful sign in recent years is the inclusion,
with Unesco assistance, of national libraries and library and book development
as a whole in national development plans, such as those for Indonesia and Laos.

Penna has pointed out that national libraries, public libraries, and school libraries
derive their financial support mainly, if not entirely, from government funds,
whether these be local, provincial, state or national.(18) In the developing countries of the region, universities and university libraries, and even special libraries,
also derive most of their finances from government, although these may be freer
to seek additional funds from individual donors as well as from local and foreign
foundations, business, and industrial firms. The integrated planning of library development as a whole therefore becomes all the more necessary if functions and
services of different types of libraries are to avoid wasteful duplication of efforts
and ensure the most efficient use of scarce manpower and financial resources.

While library plans for the nation are necessary, their very wide ranging and comprehensive character may serve as a deterrent to economic and other planners who
are apt to regard them as overambitious and unrealistic unless they are tempered by
detailed phasing into short-term, medium-term, and long-term periods, with definite

18)   C.V. Penna. *The Planning of Library and Documentation Services,* 2nd ed. rev. P.H.
        Sewell and Herman Liebaers (Paris: Unesco, 1970).

objectives for each stage. A careful and accurate assessment and identification of priorities, including the key one of professional education that has been identified as a major concern of libraries in the region, must be made and regularly reviewed.

In conclusion, the relevance or irrelevance of libraries, including and especially national libraries, in situations where the first imperative is economic development, can only be established when there is a favorable climate of opinion shared by economists, politicians, administrators, educators, scientists, and others involved in national development. National libraries must continually strive to serve such key groups as a priority in order to demonstrate their functional value and to flourish as libraries that are sensitive to the pressures and demands of national goals, eventually providing either directly or indirectly as the libraries' library, service to the nation as a whole.

Appendix I

Populations of Southeast Asia

	Area		Population
Brunei	5,765.3	sq km	141,500 (1972 estimate)
Burma	677,955.7	sq km	28,874,000 (1972 estimate)
Indonesia	2,027,087	sq km	118,400,000 (1971 census)
Khmer Republic	181,035	sq km	5,728,771 (1962 census)
			6,705,000 (1971 estimate)
Laos	236,800	sq km	3,106,000 (estimate for 1 July 1972)
Malaysia	332,631.38	sq km	10,452,000 (1970 census)
Philippines	299,402.79	sq km	37,959,000 (as of July 1, 1971)
Portuguese Timor	19,423	sq km	610,500 (1970 estimate)
Singapore	584.3	sq km	2,110,400 (1972 estimate)
Thailand	514,000	sq km	36,820,000 (1971 estimate)
North Vietnam	158,750	sq km	22,038,000 (mid-1972 estimate)
South Vietnam	173,809	sq km	18,809,000 (estimate for July 1, 1971)

Source: *The Far East and Australasia,* London: Europa Publications, 1973.

Appendix II

Library Associations in Southeast Asia

	Date Founded	Affiliations
Burma Library Association	1958	–
Indonesian Association of Librarians, Archivists and Documentalists (Asosiasi Perpustakaan Arsip dan Dokumentasi Indonesia, APADI)	1953	IFLA, 1973
Indonesian Association of Special Librarians (Himpunan Pustakawan Chusus Indonesia)	1969	–
Indonesian Library Association (Ikatan Pustakawan Indonesia)	1973	–
Khmer	–	–
Lao Library Association (predecessor was Association des Bibliothécaires Lao)	1972	–
Library Association of Malaysia (Persatuan Perpustakaan Malaysia)	1955*	IFLA, 1973
Philippine Library Association	1923	–
Association of Special Libraries of the Philippines**	1954	–
Thai Library Association	1954	IFLA, 1961
North Vietnam	not known	–
Vietnamese Library Association (South Vietnam)	1958	IFLA, 1971 ALA***
Library Association of Singapore	1955*	IFLA, 1974

* founded as Malayan Library Group
** reconstituted as chapter of the Philippine Library Association 1974
*** American Library Association

Appendix III

Functions of Selected National Libraries

National Library of Malaysia (1)

Section 3   Purpose and objectives:

(a)   to provide leadership and promote co-operation in library affairs in Malaysia

(b)   to assist the Government in the promotion of the learning, use, and advancement of the National Language

(c)   to support research and inquiry on a national scale

(d)   to provide facilities for the enlightenment, enjoyment and community life of the people

(e)   to contribute to the development of cultural relations with the people of other countries

(f)   to provide or promote such other services or activities in relation to library matters as the Minister may direct.

Section 4   The functions of the Director General of the National Library are:

(a)   to advise the Minister on all matters relating to libraries and library service

(b)   to promote a nationwide system of free public libraries and library services in Malaysia

(c)   to promote and coordinate the development and use of the library resources of the nation

(d)   to develop and maintain by purchase or otherwise a national collection of library material, including a comprehensive collection of library material relating to Malaysia and its people

(e)   to provide bibliographical service, including national bibliographical services and a union catalogue of library collections

(f)   to provide modern facilities for the storage, retrieval and communication and information

(g)   to promote the advancement of library science and the professional training of librarians

(h)   to act as the agency for the national and international lending and exchange of library material

(i)   to lend, sell or otherwise dispose of library material forming part of the library

(j)   to do such other things as he may deem necessary, in order to give effect to the purposes and objectives referred to in section 3.

National Library of the Philippines (2)

The organization and administration of the national and public library systems in the Philippines is entrusted by law to the National Library. It has the following objectives, powers, duties and functions:

(1)   the preservation of all books, libraries, and library material or equipment belonging to the institution or confided to its custody;

(2)   acquisition of additional books, libraries or other materials;

(3)   supervision over the use of the facilities of the institution by the public at large;

(4)   organization, preservation, equipment and maintenance of a reference library;

(5)   preparation and publication of prints, pamphlets, bibliographic catalogues, manuscripts, or any literary scientific work deserving to be published;

(6)   procurement and collection of books, papers, documents and periodicals relating to the history of the Philippines or to the Philipino people;

(7)   installation and maintenance of a union catalogue for the purpose of cataloguing of National Government books;

(8)   management of the copyright office for registration of claims to copyright; and

(9)   organization of a system of filing, distributing and exchanging official publications with foreign countries.

In addition, the National Library is authorized by law to establish, operate and maintain one thousand municipal libraries for a period of five years under the provisions of Republic Act No. 411, with an annual outlay of ₱ 300,000. The Director is to apportion the libraries among provinces in proportion to their population and divided among the municipalities thereof also on the same basis.

National Library of Singapore (3)

Section 5   The functions of the National Library are —

(a)   to promote and encourage the use of library material and information therefrom by the establishment of lending and reference libraries and mobile library services;

2) Rufo Q. Buenviaje. "Government Policies Affecting the Development and Growth of Libraries in the Philippines." Paper presented at Second Conference of Southeast Asian Librarians, Diliman, Philippines, Dec. 1973.

3) National Library Act, Chapter 311. (In Singapore. *Laws, Statutes, etc.* The Statutes of the Republic of Singapore. Revised Edition. (Singapore: Law Revision Committee, 1970–71.)

(b)   to acquire library material generally, and, in particular, to acquire a comprehensive collection of library material, both current and retrospective, relating to Singapore;

(c)   to collect and receive all books required to be deposited in the National Library under the provisions of the Printers and Publishers Act and to preserve such books;

(d)   to make library material available for reference and for loan subject to proper safeguards against loss or damage;

(e)   to provide reference, bibliographic and interlibrary loan services to Government departments and to Parliament;

(f)   to advise and to co-ordinate the resources and services of Government department libraries and other libraries with those of the National Library;

(g)   to obtain and provide central information on the resources and services of libraries in Singapore;

(h)   to participate in national planning for all types of library service in Singapore, and to conduct research to determine library needs and possibilities;

(i)   to compile a current national bibliography and retrospective national bibliographies;

(j)   to compile and maintain a union catalogue of libraries of all kinds;

(k)   to act as the organizing agency for the national and international lending of library material;

(l)   to act as the organizing agency for the national and international exchange of library material; and

(m)   to initiate and promote co-operation between the National Library and other libraries in the discharge of the above functions.

National Library of South Vietnam (4)

The Directorate of National Archives and Libraries has the following functions:

1   Organizing, directing and supervising the National Library and public libraries.
2   Implementing copyright regulations.
3   Preparing bibliographic aids.
4   Conducting research pertinent to library and archival development.
5   Training specialized personnel to manage records and libraries.

4) Nguyen-Ung-Long. "Library Activities in Vietnam." *Conference of Southeast Asian Librarians, 1st, Singapore, August 1970. Proceedings.* (Singapore: Chopmen Enterprises, 1972.)

Amongst the services envisaged are:

1 The National Library intends to serve as a centre for centralized cataloguing.

2 The National Library intends to serve as an effective centre for the preparation of national bibliography and copyright enforcement.

    (a)   Reference services to the three branches of government

    (b)   Bibliographical services and professional leadership to local public-type libraries.

    (c)   Photographic reproduction services to all other types of libraries.

    (d)   Professional library science leadership in preparation of manuals, classification controls, subject headings, documentation, etc.

    (e)   Inter-library loan services to all other libraries.

    (f)   Union catalogue control of books, periodicals, documents, newspapers and specialized materials.

3. The National Library also intends to serve as a centre for stationary and mobile library branches serving the metropolitan Saigon area.

National Library of Thailand (5)

The chief functions of the National Library are:

1 To render library service to the public through the National Library in Bangkok and through branch units in some provinces.

2 To carry out literary exchanges with foreign countries.

3 To acquire and preserve all kinds of books needed by the public.

4 To translate, edit and publish books and inscriptions from the ancient times.

5 To help other libraries by providing photocopy service and distributing additional books which are needed.

5) Stanley A. Barnett and others. *Developmental Book Activities and Needs in Thailand* (New York: Wolf Management Services, 1967). (AID Contract No. AID/cad-1162).

The National Library
in Latin America

ARTHUR E. GROPP

Former Librarian
Columbus Memorial Library,
Pan American Union

The national library in Latin America has played the usual role in the preservation of publications, documents, and other materials. To the extent of its activity in this role, the national library constitutes a substantial element in the cultural and intellectual heritage of the nation it serves. In a lesser degree the national library has participated in the development of libraries and library services, and in a number of cases has been a leader in the dissemination of national bibliographical and historical information.

The national library has been of particular value in the preservation of publications of national origin. Its collections of nationally published resources, in general, are unsurpassed in volume by any other library, at home or abroad, although the congressional library and the university library occasionally are close seconds. It has made a generous contribution in the issuance of published bibliographies that reflect national periodical and book publishing, general and specialized holdings, and information about persons, places, and subject matter of prevailing importance.

The national library, additionally, has undertaken to generate popular interest and pride in its national culture by organizing lecture series, radio programs, and exhibitions. These programs of popular interest emphasize publications pertaining to national history and significant commemorative dates, life and customs of the country, and prominent contributions by nationals in their specific fields of endeavor.

Reprinted from JACKSON, Miles M., *ed.* Comparative and international librarianship: essays on themes and problems. Westport, Conn.: Greenwood; London: Bingley, 1970, p. 199-226, by permission of the author and the publisher.

The national library, frequently, has gone beyond the physical library to promote cultural and intellectual endeavor. It has aided in the establishment of local libraries, and in lesser measure, to extending reading services to outlying communities. In several instances the national library has taken the lead in the training of librarians, who in turn have made, and are making, significant contributions to their respective communities.

In the countries of Spanish America, the national library emerged with the gaining of independence from Spain. The early desire to establish public libraries forms a part of the record of some nations in their movement for independent statehood. The possibility of libraries available for public use came as a natural consequence of earlier action, when the Spanish government in 1767 ordered the expulsion of the Jesuit Order from its dominions. The newly independent nations in America inherited the libraries of the Jesuits and transformed them into public libraries. Indeed, some had been opened to public use even before independence. These public libraries, subsequently, became the national library as the colonies gained their independence. Two countries, Guatemala and Mexico, used the collections of monasteries and convents for the foundation of their national libraries when they suppressed monasticism in the life of the nation.

Brazil, whose history is linked with Portugal, developed separately from the Spanish colonies. In brief, it became the seat of Portuguese royalty in 1807 during the Napoleonic rule in Portugal when the royal family fled to Brazil, and from exile João VI ruled the Portuguese kingdom until 1821 when he returned to the homeland, leaving his son, Dom Pedro, in charge of Brazil. Dom Pedro proclaimed the independence of Brazil from Portugal in 1822, with himself as emperor. Brazil became a republic in 1889. The Royal Library, established in 1810, is the National Library of today.

Among Spanish American countries, the oldest national library was founded in Bogotá, Colombia, in 1777, followed by Ecuador in 1792, both beginning as public libraries. The national libraries of Argentina, Chile, and Uruguay came into existence as public libraries during the period of struggle for independence, whereas that of Peru was founded within a month after the independence proclamation. Those of Bolivia and Venezuela were created before the middle of the nineteenth century, and those of the Central American countries, Mexico and Paraguay, date from before the end of the nineteenth century. The two remaining national libraries, of Cuba and Panama, were founded in the twentieth century.

Haiti declared itself independent from France in 1804. It remained without a national library until 1939. On September 10 of that year the cornerstone of the building was laid.

Today the only country in Latin America without a national library is the Dominican Republic. Here, functions usually ascribed the national library, such as the depository for nationally produced publications and the government agency in charge of international exchange of publications, are the responsibility of the Universidad de Santo Domingo.

The development of the national library to the present time, in Latin America, has taken place not without hardships. In general, the governments have been confronted with political and social unrest and turmoil throughout their history, thus interfering with continuous and consistent progress and growth of the national library. These conditions of turmoil and unrest likewise have impeded the creation and support of a national system of libraries. Furthermore, an adequate funding of the national library has seldom been forthcoming, particularly in those countries that have had to meet acute economic problems. It is, therefore, evident that fruitful fulfillment of its objectives has been irregular and that the national library, indeed, has been denied accomplishments possible under more normal circumstances.

Most of the materials received by the national library come without cost through the legal deposit of national publications, negotiated exchange, and solicited and unsolicited gifts. A lesser number of publications are purchased. However, on occasion. special provisions are made for the acquisition of private collections. But usually funds are insufficient to enable the national library to obtain materials, generally not available except by purchase, offered in local and foreign markets. It is, therefore, not surprising that important reference materials and periodical collections needed for consultation are lacking in most national libraries.

Among private libraries of outstanding research value acquired by national libraries are the José Toribio Medina library in Chile; the Gilberto Valenzuela library in Guatemala; the library of Pedro de Angelis, an Argentine collector, acquired by the National Library of Brazil; the library of Agustín P. Justo, also an Argentine collector, purchased by the National Library of Peru; the Gabriel René-Moreno library in Bolivia; the library of Cardinal Lambruschini, former librarian of the Vatican, purchased by the government of El Salvador; and more recently the Fernando Ortiz library acquired by the National Library of Cuba.

The national library, additionally, has invited the participation of foreign institutions and governments in important special events as a means for increasing the holdings. These events are in connection with such happenings as the dedication of a new building, the commemoration of the 100th anniversary of foundation, and in one instance, the rebuilding of a collection lost by fire. Responses have been generous. For example, the National Library of Colombia, on the occasion of the dedication of its new building in 1938, received over 6,000 volumes from twenty countries, and the National Library of Peru, after the disastrous fire in 1943, had received a total of 22,894 volumes by the time of reopening in 1945.

In some instances the national library has benefitted from a foreign cultural relations program in the course of which participant countries deposit select national collections in that national library.

The quarters of almost any given national library at the time of foundation were, at best, modest, usually a room in a government or university building. Sometimes an old convent, monastery, or church was conditioned for use. As the library outgrew these early quarters, various of them eventually constructed more suitable buildings for occupation. Most of the buildings were erected at the turn of the century, or soon thereafter. These have long since proved inadequate, and even the buildings constructed more recently, although adequate in size, have not always incorporated features best suited for administration and organization. There remain some Latin American countries that still do not have a building especially constructed for national library use. The National Library of Mexico is still quartered in the St. Augustine church. Plans are being developed for the construction of a new building for the national libraries of Panama and Costa Rica. Bolivia, Ecuador, Nicaragua, and Paraguay have not yet erected buildings especially designed for library purposes. Argentina, whose present building was inaugurated in 1901, has chosen a new site for the relocation of the National Library, and was developing plans for a modern building. Terms for the acceptance of bids for construction were published in the official government gazette.[1] No further action seems to have been taken.

The national library, in some cases, has suffered heavy physical losses. For example, the National Library of Uruguay, during the struggle for independence, and the National Library of Peru, during the conflict with Chile, were used for quartering invasion troops. Although in Uruguay the collection was stored in a basement, an apparently safe place, many valuable items nevertheless disappeared. In Peru most of the collection disappeared at the time of the conflict. Subsequently, only about fourteen thousand volumes of the fifty-five thousand volume collection were recovered. Then, tragically, in 1943 disaster struck this National Library again, when a fire completely destroyed the building and nearly all its contents.

It would be difficult to estimate damage to library materials credited to dampness and insects, losses particularly heavy in libraries and archives in tropical zones. The writer, in his survey of libraries and archives in Central America and the West Indies, 1937-1938, found evidence of dampness. In relation to Nicaragua he stated, "On the patio gallery the cases are placed along the wall and along the outer edge, facing each other . . . . The books in the outer row of cases are subject to dampness during the rainy season."[2] However, the current trend of concern for library materials is evident in the construction of modern buildings which assure control of dampness and insects, and security against losses by fire.

The national library disseminates information of its resources and activities through the media of publications. Most libraries, in greater or lesser degree, have published bulletins, journals, and catalogs of the collections and of exhibitions, current national and special bibliographies, reports of activities, commemorative leaflets, brochures, and historical documents.[3] They are important contributions to cultural and intellectual activities of the nation. Among the most valuable publications, particularly for those concerned with Latin American studies, is current national bibliography for which some national libraries have made themselves responsible. Greater effort and support should be given to this activity. The compilation of current national bibliographies has been carried on by the national libraries of Brazil, Chile, Costa Rica, El Salvador, Guatemala, Honduras, Panama, Peru, Uruguay, and Venezuela.[4] The National Library of Haiti is represented by a comprehensive bibliography, 1804-1950, compiled by the director of the National Library, but published commercially in the United States. Current national bibliography, however, is not up-to-date, and its continuing publication on a regular schedule is doubtful.

The publication record of any given national library is usually in direct ratio to the funds allocated for this purpose, the output ranging from creditable to disheartening.

The national library differs substantially from other libraries in emphasis on use of library materials. For instance, municipal and popular libraries emphasize liberal use of library materials and are administered in a manner that will produce maximum use in areas such as reading and consultation within the library, circulation of books to the home, provision of reading rooms and special services for children, in some cases bookmobile units, and in others a central library with branches. The national library on the other hand, in keeping with its primary objective—that of preservation of materials—generally restricts the use of its collections to consultation on the premises. Users of the national library, for the most part, are students, professors, and researchers.

Education for librarianship in Latin America is a recent development. In 1929, modern universally recognized techniques were introduced in a teaching program in São Paulo, Brazil.[5] In 1943 a similar program was initiated in Buenos Aires.[6] Earlier librarians in charge of administration and organization, more often than not, were highly individual, leading to the use of widely divergent practices from one library to another and from one country to another. Because library schools and courses for the training of librarians now are functioning in most of the Latin American countries, the younger generation of professional and resourceful librarians is able to operate from more standardized and interchangeable methods—from one library to another and from one country to another.

Two national libraries, Brazil (1946) with a reorganized course of study, and Peru (1944) with a newly established school, aimed for the training of their own personnel, but the courses were opened to personnel from other libraries. A library school, reported in 1957, for the training of librarians was being established in the National Library of Argentina.

The training of librarians has led to significant changes in patterns of library service, and in some instances the government has recognized librarianship as a profession. For example, in Uruguay the law creating the library school requires that all vacancies of technical positions in state and municipal libraries be filled by graduates of the school; more recently, the government added the category of librarian to the professions accorded minimum wages.

A consequence of training for librarianship is the formation of national, local, and special library associations. These associations have contributed considerably to the formulation of standards for the organization of libraries and for personnel qualifications, and they are setting the course of professional activity.

In 1948 the writer found eighteen associations on record in the Latin American countries. Only a small number of these had progressed beyond the organizational stage. However, by 1966 a total of fifty-six library and archival associations was listed.

Argentina

In 1796, at the time of his death, Bishop Manuel Azamor y Ramírez left his collection of books for the establishment of a public library. The provisions of the will were not carried out until the Junta Revolucionaria on September 7, 1810, authorized its establishment. The library of Bishop Rodrigo Antonio de Orellana and the books of other supporters of the opposition were added to the collection left by Bishop Azamor y Ramírez. Quarters were designated in the Colegio de San Carlos. Mariano Moreno was named protector of the library and Saturnino Segurola and Fray Cayetano Rodríguez became the librarians. On March 16, 1812, it was opened for use as the Biblioteca Pública de Buenos Aires.

The Library continued to function as a public library until September 9, 1884, when the government proclaimed it the National Library. The first director of the new administration was José Antonio Wilde, who was succeeded in 1885 by Paul Groussac, an eminent scholar, for the next forty years. During this period the library grew from 32,000 volumes to nearly 230,000 volumes, aided by the law, adopted in 1870, requiring the deposit of nationally published materials. The publications which had accumulated during the period 1870-1884, in the Library of the Oficina de Depósito y Reparto de Publicaciones, were incorporated in the National Library.

The present building of the National Library was dedicated on December 12, 1901. These quarters have become crowded, and a new building is projected. Land was acquired for this purpose, adjacent to the Facultad de Derecho y Ciencias Sociales, and the terms for bidding on the construction were opened in 1961. However, no further action seems to have been taken.

The National Library has a good record of publishing: reports of activities, regulations, explanation of the classification system; reproduction of documents; catalogs of its book collection and of manuscripts; catalogs of gift collections; lists of acquisitions; history of the library; several editions of the most used books; catalogs of documents related to the Río de La Plata region in the Archivo General de Indias in Spain; and a journal, published as *Revista* (1879-1882) of the Biblioteca Pública de Buenos Aires; *La Biblioteca* (1896-1898); *Revista* (1937-1951); and again as *La Biblioteca* (1951-).

Bolivia

On 30 June 1838 the president of Bolivia decreed the establishment of a free public library in the capital of each province, to be supervised by the national government and the director of the Instituto Nacional through a local literary society. At that time two such libraries were established, one in La Paz and the other in Sucre. The latter became the National Library, now administered under the Ministerio de Instrucción Pública. In 1936 the Archivo Nacional was merged with the Biblioteca Nacional.[7]

At the Third Pan American Scientific Congress, Lima, 1924, the Bolivian delegate reported that his government was establishing a second National Library at La Paz, but the plan was not carried out.

The initial collection of the National Library was formed from the library of Antonio José Sucre, first president of Bolivia. In 1907 it added the extensive collection of Gabriel René-Moreno, historian and bibliographer.

Editors, authors, and government offices are required to deposit two copies in the National Library of every publication printed in the country.

The Library published the *Revista* (1920, no. 1-2; 1932; 1936-1943).

Brazil

In 1808 Dom João VI, fleeing from the Napoleonic invasion of his country, brought with him his library containing many rarities, Portuguese history, pamphlets, pictures, and maps. This collection became the foundation, in 1810, of the Real Bibliotheca do Palacio da Ajuda. It was housed in the Hospital of the Ordem Terceiro do Carmo. In 1811 it was opened to the public. When D. João returned to Portugal in 1822 he took a part of the collection with him.

From 1853 to 1870 the Library was housed in the Casa do Largo de Lalå, where for the first time reading room space was provided. In 1910, on the 100th anniversary of its founding, the National Library was transferred to the present building, a granite and marble structure rising four stories above the basement.

In 1853 the government purchased the library of the Argentine bibliophile, Pedro de Angelis, which contained some 2,700 volumes and 1,300 manuscripts rich in the history of the Río de La Plata region. In 1886 the government established its office for international exchange, and in 1890 transferred the operation to the National Library. Additional acquisitions come from the requirement of deposit of any work registered in the copyright office, which is located in the Library.

In addition to the book collection, the Library has many pamphlets, periodical publications, newspapers, maps, and manuscripts. One of the largest single acquisitions by the library was the special collection of Dom Pedro II in 1889, numbering some 48,236 volumes. It possesses a Gutenberg Bible and other incunabula.

A library science course was made a part of the National Library in 1914, offering studies in bibliography, paleography, iconography, and numismatics. In later years cartography replaced numismatics. However, in 1946, with the reorganization of the Library under the direction of Rubens Borba de Moraes, the course was completely revised and modernized.

The National Library continually, throughout the years, particularly since occupying the present building, frequently has featured special exhibits of library materials.

It has a long list of publications, many of them catalogs of exhibits. However, in the series *Documentos históricos* (1928-), already totaling 110 numbers, the Library has published numerous historical documents. Another series of outstanding note is *Anais*

(1876-) formerly *Annaes*, in which it has published historical documents, catalogs, bibliographies, inventories of manuscripts, a history of the Library, and so forth. Many numbers of *Anais* have been reprinted as separates. The most recent issue contains a 208 page catalog of newspapers and journals published in Rio de Janeiro, 1808-1889, in the collection of the National Library. In 1951 the Library began publication of manuscripts from the Pedro de Angelis collection, of which six volumes have appeared. Among other publications are the regulations governing the Library, reports of the director, and courses of study of the Library School. It publishes *Boletim bibliográfico* (1918-1921; n.s., 1951- , semiannual). Issues of the *Boletim* appeared for the years 1931, 1938, and 1946, in which only Brazilian imprints were listed.

Brief accounts of the national libraries and bibliographic activities in the following countries occupy pp. 209-225 of this article: Chile, Colombia, Costa Rica, Cuba, Ecuador, El Salvador, Guatemala, Haiti, Honduras, Mexico, Nicaragua, Panama, Paraguay, Peru, Uruguay and Venezuela.

NOTES

1. *Boletín oficial*, Buenos Aires 69, no. 19,534 (mayo 18, 1961):1.
2. Arthur E. Gropp, *Guide to Libraries and Archives in Central America and the West Indies*, p. 522.
3. For a listing of the publications of national libraries, the following publication may be consulted: *Bibliografía sobre las bibliotecas nacionales de los países latino-americanas y sus publicaciones,* compiled by Arthur E. Gropp, 1960.
4. The *Bibliografía brasileira* is compiled by the Instituto Nacional do Livro, an independent body, located in the National Library.
5. Adelpha Silva Rodrigues, *Desenvolvimento da biblioteconomia em S. Paulo* (Rio de Janeiro: Impr. Nacional, 1945), pp. 9-10.
6. Arthur E. Gropp, "Education for Librarianship in Latin America," *Library Quarterly* 18, no. 2 (April 1948): 110.
7. Arthur E. Gropp, *Bibliography of Latin American Bibliographies* (Metuchen, N. J.: Scarecrow Press, 1968), p. 338, item 5723.
8. *La Nación,* San José, mar. 1, 1969.
9. C. K. Jones, *Bibliography of Latin American Bibliographies.* 2d ed. (Washington, D.C.: Government Printing Office, 1942), item 2641.

Cliff Lashley

West Indian National Libraries and the Challenge of Change

It is impossible to say exactly what a national library is because each nation is unique and each national library attempts to serve its nation's peculiar needs. There is however widespread agreement on the basic functions of any national library. In the words of Sir Frank Francis, Director and Principal Librarian of the British Museum, 'Speaking broadly the national library in any country is the library which has the duty of collecting and preserving for posterity the written production of that country.' If you ask why collect and preserve for posterity the written production of a nation, the unanimous reply would be that the national library is 'the mind of society,' 'the only effective repository of the racial memory,' 'a live depository of the cultural past' or something like it. There is also agreement on some of the basic formulas, such as legal deposit, and some of the basic activities, such as producing bibliographies, which a national library uses to fulfil its duties. It seems likely that if and when national libraries are established in the West Indies they would have the same basic duties for the same reasons and would fulfil them in the same manner as elsewhere. So what is interesting to speculate about is the cultural uniqueness of the various West Indian nations--Barbados, Trinidad, Guyana and Jamaica--and the consequent peculiar needs their national libraries would have to satisfy. It is in satisfying these needs that national libraries in the West Indies might meet the challenge of change.

There is no literature describing the unique cultural characteristics of the various West Indian nations though we natives sense and are jealous of our insular differences. There is a substantial and growing literature, largely written by West Indian historians and social scientists, which attempts to characterize West Indian society as a whole, developing models which could serve as bases for social planning and action. The two models which have been fully elaborated-- the plantation society model and the plural society model--do clarify our vision of West Indian reality, showing up our history of economic exploitation, the deep structural nature of our race and class divisions and the neo-colonialism of our post-independence policies. But these models are not only too static; they do not focus the cultural aspects of West Indian society narrowly conceived. They do not allow us to see, for example, the role of written production and its preservation in West Indian society. So, ironically as you shall see, we must adopt a 'foreign' model.

West Indian culture, and the role of written production in it, are clarified by the great tradition/little tradition model elaborated by the American anthropologist Robert Redfield in *Peasant Society and*

Reprinted from INGRAM, K.E. *and* JEFFERSON, Albertina, A., *eds.* Libraries and the challenge of change: papers of the International Library Conference held in Kingston, Jamaica, 24-29 April 1972. London: Mansell, for the Jamaica Library Association and the Jamaica Library Service, 1975, p. 47-50, by permission of the author and the publisher.

Culture, (1956). A great tradition is an autonomous cultural system
with its own mutually adjusted and interdependent parts which do not
require another system for its functioning. Of course it interacts
with other systems, but it is not dependent. It is a literate tradition with specialists--priests, teachers, philosophers--and insti-
tutions--temples, maybe with embryonic libraries and schools--to
consciously preserve and transmit the tradition. A little tradition,
by contrast, is not autonomous. To maintain itself, it requires
continual communication with a great tradition. It is oral, not
literate and according to Redfield 'is for the most part taken for
granted and not submitted to much scrutiny or considered refinement
and improvement.' Great traditions and little traditions are interdependent, feeding, and feeding on, one another. 'The teachings of
Galen about the four humors may have been suggested by ideas current
in little communities of simple people becoming but not yet civilized;
after development by reflective minds they may have been received by
peasantry and reinterpreted in local terms. Great epics have arisen
out of elements of traditional tale-telling by many people, and epics
have returned again to the peasantry for modification and incorporation into local cultures.'
    Writing and what it makes possible is the crucial difference be-
tween the great and the little tradition, in spite of Redfield's
implication that it is scrutiny, reflectiveness and the resultant
refinement and improvement which is the source of the fundamental
difference. McLuhan has galvanized us into the awareness that writing
and print determine our modes of perception--our scrutiny and re-
flectiveness--and consequently what we perceive and the models we use
to represent our perceptions. We are now aware that oral, tribal man
perceives, conceptualizes and organizes his social life differently
from visual typographic man and that television and Telstar might be
remaking the world into a global village and presumably establishing
a universal little tradition. What is important is the realization
that writing and its analogues profoundly affect the structure of
society. Large-scale enterprises like sugar production are impossible
without the technology of writing which not only gives speech a
material correlative but permits its preservation and transmission
over time and space. Thus writing permitted the absentee landlord to
give instructions, receive reports, keep records and compute profit
and loss, with disastrous consequences--because of his absence--for
the development of West Indian society. The technology of writing also
made possible the British Empire, the late failure of the sun to set
on the Union Jack and the near hegemony of British culture.
    If we look at Jamaica by the light of Redfield's model we see that
Jamaica has no great tradition. I cite Jamaica because of the obvious-
ness of the distinctions there, its possession of the only nearly
national library, the West India Reference Library. Give and take a
little, the pattern in Jamaica fits the other West Indian nations as
I can show. Jamaican culture is obviously dependent on autonomous
systems and their specialists and institutions elsewhere. As Redfield
might have put it, Jamaican culture cannot be fully understood (in
its historical or contemporary dimension) from what goes on in the
minds of Jamaicans alone. We need to know something of what goes on
in the minds of remote teachers, priests or philosophers, not to
mention industrial designers, advertising agents and millionaires,
achieved or in process, whose thinking affects Jamaicans. Redfield says
the specialists of the great tradition are affected by the little
tradition but it is doubtful if any of Jamaica's little traditions
affect even a significant number of Jamaicans living abroad.

There are three little traditions in Jamaica. There is a little
colonial tradition which is the literate, fully institutionalized
and officially transmitted tradition. Because it is literate, institutionalized and official the other two little Jamaican traditions
sometimes relate to it as if it were a great tradition. The other
two traditions are the African folk tradition and the Rastafari
counter-tradition. They are both essentially oral. Although the
African folk tradition is in some degree a tradition of all Jamaicans
(everybody speaks and/or understands Jamaica creole) most Jamaicans
regard it as a lesser tradition than the colonial. It is viewed as
the dark tradition of dark people from the dark continent. Because of
this, its oral nature, its lack of institutionalization and the
refusal of the specialists to give it recognition, the African folk-
tradition has remained a little tradition although it has been independent of its African great tradition since just after the last
infusion of people from Africa.

The counter-tradition of the Rastafari is partially an amalgam of
the other two traditions although Rastafari are brutally critical of
both traditions. The Rastafari's great book is the Authorized Version
of the Bible most fundamentally reinterpreted and their explicitly
claimed great tradition is African, geographically Ethiopia. The
Rastafari counter-tradition is the local manifestation of an international rejection of Western culture and the concurrent attempt,
inevitably using some of the West's legacy, to replace it. There is
also in Jamaica, as throughout the world, a small group of literate
specialists who belong to and are trying to advance the counter-
culture. While this group is not Rastafari they have essentially the
same analysis of the little colonial and little African folk traditions, use some inevitable Western legacy, claim an African heritage
etc. Of course all Jamaica's little traditions interrelate and they
all interrelate, at least negatively, with the foreign blond, blue-
eyed great tradition.

In Jamaica the unique cultural situation is that there is no great
national tradition and only that little tradition which is most para-
sitic on a foreign great tradition is literate, institutionalized and
officially presented and transmitted. So the peculiar need a Jamaican
national library would have to satisfy would be the enfranchisement
of the African and other folk and Rastafari and other counter-
traditions. This is the challenge of change for all West Indian
librarians.

To meet this challenge we must first have an adequate concept of
change. We must intend change in the infrastructure of the society.
And since positive change in the West Indies means development we
must not tacitly assume we know what development is and then let it
mean the present state of supposedly developed Western society. We
must spell out the goals of development, the good life, in terms of
the folk and counter-traditions. Next we must recreate the profession
of librarianship. It has been customary to say that a librarian
should have no politics, no religion, no morals, that he/she must be
objective to be impartial. That notion of objectivity was partial,
as the history of colonialism and our destitution makes plain.
Librarians in 'developing' societies must have as their passionate
concern to work for the health of the whole body politic; they must
be political.

Consequent on this conception of our profession comes new tasks.
We might have to find a new formula for obtaining the nation's printed
production free of cost because, maybe, copyright should be abandoned
in developing countries so that all knowledge would be free.

Certainly we will not primarily collect and preserve written materials. We will use electronic technology to collect, preserve and disseminate the spoken word. Our collecting must be active. We can train as oral historians and folklorists, decide what to collect and go out and get it. We must beware when we organize materials that we do not automatically use classifications which only reflect the little colonial written tradition. A classification scheme is ultimately a cosmology. In helping readers of whatever level we must help them to all the various kinds of sources. We may even have to persuade them that their real task is the collection of the very sources they came in search of.

These conceptions are not only the concern of a national library and its staff though it is the essential responsibility of the national library to lead in their realization. All West Indian librarians must help identify, collect, preserve and transmit in all its variety of origin, form and content the total racial memory and build ultimately a great West Indian tradition.

Twelve years' work at the National Library of Cuba

by Sidroc Ramos,
Director of the Biblioteca
Nacional 'José Martí'

Immediately before the 1959 Revolution, the collections of the Biblioteca Nacional 'José Martí', which had previously found refuge in a succession of forts and ancient buildings, were moved to imposing modern quarters. It was however only after this turning-point in history that the library, founded in 1901 and the most important in Cuba, became properly organized on a scientific basis, with an appropriate budget, adequate staff, and expanding collections—thus entering on a new phase of its existence.

Reorganization and a fresh start

The first task of the director appointed by the Revolutionary Government to be in charge of the National Library and the centralized network of public libraries in Cuba was to review the purpose and functions of these libraries.[1]

In addition to providing services for researchers and educated readers with a great variety of interests, the National Library was thrown open as a public library for use by a large number of inexperienced readers who had previously had no regular access to books.[2] To that end it was necessary to carry out a vast cultural information programme, and to institute new services to attract a wide public, going beyond the normal work of lending books and periodicals to include the provision of facilities such as equipment for listening to music and the loan of pictures and other works.

This meant that, in addition to its normal role as a national library, namely, that of conserving and studying library collections throughout the country, the library had conferred upon it an important public mission helping to make its action more dynamic and effective.

As the headquarters of the National Library Administration, coming under the Consejo Nacional de Cultura, the library has also taken over laboratory work, methodological guidance and the active leadership of the national network of public libraries in Cuba. It advises these libraries on standards and structures, preserving them from the temptation of slavishly imitating its example by devising special ways in which they may more effectively promote a more dynamic service to the public.

1. In 1959 the first incumbent of this post was Dr María Teresa Freyre de Andrade, the most eminent authority on librarianship in Cuba today.
2. Apart from other reasons, it is only since 1961 that illiteracy has been stamped out in Cuba; and before the Revolution, books were very expensive.

Reprinted from *Unesco Bulletin for Libraries,* vol. 26, no. 4, July–August 1972, p. 210-13.
©Unesco 1972. Reproduced by permission of Unesco.

The reorganization of the library resulted in the setting up or activation of departments and services such as cataloguing, reference, selection and acquisition, exchange, etc.—basic facilities which had not existed or had previously operated intermittently—and in the judicious maintenance of services such as stack-rooms, a periodicals library and reading-rooms (to include, in due course, a technical room) (see illustration).

New departments and services

The Cuban Bibliography Department was set up in order to bring together, preserve and classify valuable national publications and documents and to take over responsibility for bibliographical research on books, manuscripts and periodicals, especially of an historical nature, as well as research on Cuban history and literature. The recent opening of the Martí Room, in commemoration of the great writer and national hero, has given a new impetus to research into his life and work.

This department produces the *Bibliografía Cubana*, both past and present, and classifies collections of manuscripts by famous Cubans, whose personal archives are preserved by the library. It contains collections of old Cuban engravings, catalogued according to a special system, and photographs and cuttings from periodicals.

Special mention should be made of the map collection, which already comprises more than 20,000 maps and plans of Cuba and the rest of the world, appropriately catalogued, as also a large number of ancient and modern atlases, which are made available to scholars and research workers. A comprehensive guide to Cuban place-names in their current form has recently been completed, and work is proceeding on lists of maps by continents and countries.

Other departments have been created for the visual arts and for music. The former provides the reading-matter and other information required by those concerned with the plastic arts (painters, architects, film-makers, the theatrical profession, designers, teachers, students, researchers), lending books and journals on the premises and lending out to individual readers or institutions reproductions of famous works, prints and slides. It encourages a taste for the plastic arts by holding discussions and small exhibitions. It preserves and studies valuable documentation concerning Cuban art, such as posters, exhibition catalogues, etc.

The Music Department (see illustration) performs similar functions for music, providing facilities for listening to recordings and lending out books and scores; it also houses and studies valuable Cuban collections of both learned and popular music. Its activities include concerts and conferences at which well-known composers and musicians, both from Cuba and abroad, give performances and discuss their creative work.

Both departments have played an important part in fostering aesthetic appreciation of the arts and in circulating a substantial quantity of material.

Departments such as the Library Extension and the Juvenile Department have demonstrably increased the services which the library is able to offer. When first opened, the extension stimulated the creation of a number of small libraries in factories and other working premises, while at the same time providing basic technical training to their staff and the staff of libraries in other institutions by holding courses at regular intervals, assisting them in organizing their collections and developing action to spread the reading habit (a function which was for some time performed by a separate department).

The Juvenile Department has been planned, and operates specially, for children and adolescents. Its services include the loan of books, prints and pictures, an information register, the holding of exhibitions, competitions for its users on a great variety of subjects, film shows and concerts, and the provision of courses or clubs for those interested in painting, stamp collection, art appreciation, literary criticism, the theatre, etc.

One of the most interesting initiatives, welcomed by people from many countries, has been the opening of an annex to study the great wealth of native legends and folklore of Cuba and other countries, as well as children's stories well-known the world over, with a view to selecting and adapting stories to be told to children.[1]

Thanks to this activity, at present the responsibility of the Juvenile Department, the library has spread the custom of story-recitals throughout Cuba, with a view to stimulating children's imagination and sensitivity, helping them to develop their ability to express themselves and encouraging the reading habit.

To this end it has been necessary to develop the technique of story-telling, by providing courses at frequent intervals and recording their content in a series of texts published by the library.

The 'short story hour' has become an institution which is now an integral part of our library life. Story-recitals have spread to schools, hospitals and infant groups, arousing active interest also in other institutions.

The Juvenile Department further promotes studies on and provides information about collections of children's books in libraries throughout Cuba and organizes seminars on children's books for the benefit of teachers, writers and research workers.

Information on science, technology and the humanities

The library has instituted a highly important service with the creation of a Department for Scientific and Technical Information, which has assumed responsibility for establishing the union catalogue of scientific and technical journals in Cuba. Today this catalogue lists more than 18,500 such journals, which are circulated to more than 120 libraries throughout the country, thus providing information on how to obtain issues of any journal in existing collections and making a saving to the national budget by minimizing the duplication of subscriptions.

In addition, the department compiles and brings up to date, either on request or in accordance with its own national-development forecasts, bibliographical information on specific economic and technical subjects. A study of the material circulated keeps readers informed about the latest publications in each field of science or technology and free photocopies are provided as necessary. The department is responsible for the national inter-library loan service for each special subject.

In 1971 the department provided 18,000 services of this kind to a large number of bodies and institutions; its experience is also useful in advising and training the staff of a great number of specialized information centres which have been, or are about to be, set up by other institutions. Lastly, this department is also working on the *Guía Nacional de Bibliotecas*.

In the field of the humanities and the social sciences, a similar function is fulfilled by the staff of the Department of Information on the Humanities. This operated formerly as a separate unit, but is now part of the Periodicals Department and provides indexes of periodicals and a variety of bibliographical and other information. It is also preparing a catalogue of periodicals concerned with the humanities.

It is worth pointing out that, primarily due to the work of the Periodicals Department and the Department of Information on the Humanities and the Cuban Collection, the National Library has in ten years indexed eighty Cuban journals of the nineteenth and twentieth centuries, whereas throughout the whole

1. This initiative was due to the eminent Cuban poet, Eliseo Diego.

of the preceding period, since the constitution of the republic, only sixteen journals had been indexed, usually by individuals without any official standing.[1]

For the first time, work has been undertaken and successfully completed on a general index of Cuban periodicals.

Other activities

The library publishes the *Revista de la Biblioteca Nacional José Martí*, which is primarily devoted to historical and literary research carried out on the basis of national bibliographical and documentary collections. It also produces the *Boletín Bibliotecas*, dealing with questions and experiments of interest to librarians.

As part of its advisory function, the library provides headquarters facilities and administrative support for the Encuentros Nacionales de Información y Actualización Bibliotecarias, attended by head librarians and professional staff members from public libraries throughout Cuba. Several of its departments provide specialist training for the staff of other libraries.

A final aspect of the work of the library consists of activities directly related to its main task, for example, bibliographical exhibitions about well-known figures, historical events, countries or periods and many other activities of a general cultural nature, such as lectures and discussion groups for those interested, in which writers, composers, artists and other representatives of Cuban or foreign culture take part; also concerts, art exhibitions, outstanding films, etc. All these activities secure a better use of the everyday facilities of the library, which in 1971 provided more than 350,000 services to members of the public.

International Book Year

When 1972 was proclaimed International Book Year by Unesco, the Revolutionary Government of Cuba appointed a national committee, under the chairmanship of the Minister of Education, to set in motion an extensive series of activities relating to books, reading and libraries.

To mention only a few of these: both the National Library Administration and the National Library will take part in the organization of a large-scale exhibition on the history of books in Cuba; a panoramic display will be mounted of world book production and its origins; exhibitions will be held in the provincial libraries of Oriente, Camagüey, Las Villas and Matanzas, showing books published or written in each province; and the library will draw up a list of Cuban bibliographies and a catalogue of scientific and technical works published in Cuba.

Above all, International Book Year will be marked by the exceptional growth planned for the national network of public libraries, which is at present a small one. A library service will be opened for the first time in many small towns. Mini-libraries will be set up (service points, with no professional staff) in a number of rural areas. In the aggregate, plans have been made for a 25 to 30 per cent increase in the number of established libraries and an even greater increase in services through the provision of a large number of mini-libraries. Progress on this scale is without precedent in Cuba.

1. Tomás F. Robaina, 'Los índices de publicaciones periódicas en Cuba', *Bibliotecas 70* (Habana), año VIII, no. 5, septiembre-octubre 1970.

4. CONCLUDING NOTES

Among the various ways in which national libraries can be categorised, one is by type of country. There are fairly clear differences between large developed countries (which can generally afford dedicated national libraries, even if they sometimes find other solutions), small developed countries (in which national library collections and functions are usually dispersed), and developing countries (where national libraries commonly perform other — academic or public— library functions, and where they have a major role in national library planning, not to mention library training and leadership generally). A fourth category might be added: socialist countries, developed or developing, with strong centralised national libraries which have as important a national role as in non-socialist developing countries, though perhaps for different reasons. This categorisation is complicated by federal countries where separate states may have their own national libraries, and where there may or may not be a national library for the whole country.

National libraries are or may be 'national' in several different senses. They may be national in the sense that they contain the literary production of the nation; or in the sense that they are the nation's main book museum, containing a high concentration of the nation's treasures; or in the sense that they are leaders, perhaps co-ordinators, of the nation's libraries; or in the sense that they offer a national service (to the nation's libraries or population). In developed capitalist countries, the emphasis tends to be on the first and last of these senses; in other countries, on national leadership and co-ordination. In the latter, the ostensible power of the national library is greater, but the power of a comprehensive central service must not be underestimated.

Several key issues emerge, and their resolution will differ according to the type of country in question:

1   How far should the National Library collection duplicate other collections in the country? How do the costs of duplication compare with the benefits?

2   How can collection and conservation of the nation's literary production and treasures be combined with positive information, lending and bibliographic services? These functions require different qualities and motivations in staff, and different organisations and procedures. Is the division of the National Library into two main sections a possible answer?

3   Should reference and lending functions be combined, or separate provision be made? Separate provision may be appropriate for large developed countries, combined provision for developing and smaller developed countries.

4   How far should the National Library be responsible for planning and managing the nation's library resources? Should its leadership be confined to pre-eminence and example, or should it devise policies and supervise their carrying out? If this is not the role of the National Library, by what sort of body should it be carried out, and should such a body have some control also over the National Library?

5   Should the National Library be a library training centre for the nation, and if so should it confine its activities to practical training or serve also

317

as a library school? This may depend largely on whether the National Library is seen as an ordinary library on a large scale or as a different sort of library from others.

6.   Should the National Library aim to make a fully comprehensive collection of the nation's imprints, or should it be selective? How far in any case can it go with ephemeral publications? Should it, and can it, also serve as a national archive of non-print documents such as sound recordings, films, etc?

7.   Can a National Library successfully combine a full national role with more general services to other clienteles or to the public? If such a combination is necessary initially for economic reasons, should there be a long-term aim to have a dedicated, or at least a less diversified, national library?

8.   Should National Libraries confine their national information role to that of switching centre and resource supplier to other agents, or aim to supply information direct to users? There is a large difference between acting as a referral centre and supplying computer tapes, and setting up as a direct supplier of information to individuals, bypassing other libraries.

9.   How far can a true and comprehensive national library service be achieved without a National Library as such? Does the future lie in more co-operation and networking, or in greater centralisation? What is the optimum combination of co-operation and centralisation?

Two potentially important aspects receive little attention in most writings on national libraries. The first is the national library as a national repository — an important role in the socialist countries and in the UK, but not even mentioned in Humphreys' analysis. The second is the national library's international role, as the natural focus for communication with other countries. Many national libraries do in fact serve as such a focus, but the role has rarely been made explicit or emphasised, although it is of growing importance as the need to obtain access to the bibliographic records and book resources of other countries grows greater. Certainly, IFLA'S programmes of Universal Bibliographic Control and Universal Availability of Publications depend to a considerable extent on the adequate performance of this role.

GENERAL

1. ESDAILE, Arundell. *National libraries of the world: their history, administration and public services.* 2nd ed., by F.J. Hill. London: Library Association, 1957.

    A descriptive account of the historical beginnings and development of libraries that had emerged as the most comprehensive collections in their respective countries.

2. FRANCIS, F.C. The contribution of the national library to the modern outlook in library services. *Aslib Proceedings,* 10 (11), November 1958, 267-75.

    The author gives his own view (just prior to the Vienna symposium) of the role of the national library in the present world and of developments he would like to foresee, with emphasis on the need for decentralisation in large comprehensive libraries and co-ordination by the national libraries of bibliographical and information work in the country as a whole.

3. FRANCIS, F.C. Problems of large national and learned libraries. *In* IFLA, FID *and* IAML. *International Congress of Libraries and Documentation Centres, Brussels, September 1955.* The Hague: Nijhoff, 1955, vol.1,p.106-12; Discussion: vol.2A, p.185-95.

    Size (of collections and catalogues), space in which to expand, acquisitions and cataloguing are some of the common problems discussed. Suggested solutions involve co-ordination, co-operation, decentralisation, subject specialisation and standardisation.

4. INTERNATIONAL FEDERATION OF LIBRARY ASSOCIATIONS. *Libraries in the world: a long-term programme for the International Federation of Library Associations.* The Hague: Nijhoff, 1963, p.50-3.

    The special chapter on national libraries, built around the deliberations of the Vienna symposium of 1958, discusses the development and responsibility of the national library, "questions of a general nature and of extreme urgency which accordingly require to be studied at the international level".

5. LIEBAERS, Herman. Asian and Pacific librarianship from a European angle: comments on Unesco's Regional Seminar on the Development of National Libraries in Asia and the Pacific Area, Manila, Philippines, February, 1964. *Libri,* 14 (2), 1964, 168-75.

    Comments on the special problems of national libraries in countries with tremendous differences in social, economic and cultural levels of development, and discusses recommendations made by the Seminar. The potential value of IFLA for helping Asian libraries is considered.

6. MEYRIAT, Jean. Responsibilities of national libraries for international co-operation in bibliographical activities. *In: National libraries: their problems and prospects. Symposium on National Libraries in Europe, Vienna, 8-27 September, 1958.* Paris: Unesco, 1960, (Unesco Manuals for Libraries -11), p.56-62.

    The national library will, in most cases, have the responsibility of supplying the international centre directly or indirectly with all the data concerning national publications; and in this paper the author considers what this responsibility will involve according to the types of publications concerned and the possible difficulties that may arise.

7.   RUPEL, Mirko. Bibliographical activities of national libraries. *In: National libraries: their problems and prospects. Symposium on National Libraries in Europe, Vienna, 8-27 September, 1958.* Paris: Unesco, 1960, (Unesco Manuals for Libraries -11), p.49-55.

> Discusses the tasks which devolve upon the national library (including compiling and publishing bibliographies and co-ordinating bibliographical work in general), also cataloguing and classification problems, and new methods for the storage and retrieval of information.

8.   WORMANN, Curt D. Co-operation of national libraries with other libraries in the same country and in other countries. *Unesco Bulletin for Libraries,* 18 (4), July-August 1964, 165-71, 183.

> The main types of co-operation are discussed (national, regional and international) with reference to the problems and situations in Asia.

9.   WORMANN, Curt D. National libraries in our time: the Unesco Symposium on National Libraries in Europe. *Libri,* 9 (4), 1959, 273-307.

> The various stages (conferences, important publications, etc.) are described by which the national libraries began to regain their central position in the 1950's, leading to the Unesco Symposium in Vienna in 1958. The article attempts to evaluate the conference, to analyse national libraries as a type, and also to give some impression of the discussions which took place after the conclusion of the Symposium itself.

BY COUNTRY

Useful articles on the national libraries of many countries can be found under the appropriate country in KENT, Allen *and* LANCOUR, Harold, eds. *Encyclopedia of library and information science.* New York and London: Marcel Dekker, 1969.

10.   AJE, S. B. National libraries in developing countries. *Advances in Librarianship,* 7, 1977, 105-43.

> Some background is provided on the concepts and evolution of developing countries and of the national library as known today. The review itself provides facts and data from 26 countries, in Africa (13), Asia including the Pacific area (5), Central and South America including the Caribbean (6) and the Middle East (3) on the state of their national libraries.

11.   CHANDLER, George. *Libraries in the East: an international and comparative study.* London and New York: Seminar Press, 1971.

> Includes brief accounts of developments in national libraries in 8 countries (the Lebanon, Egypt, Iran, Pakistan, India, Thailand, Hong Kong and Japan), which are related by the author to the various recommendations made at Unesco seminars.

AFRICA

12.   Meeting of the directors of national libraries in countries of the Maghreb. *Unesco Bulletin for Libraries,* 27 (3), May-June 1973, 188-9.

> Lists recommendations agreed at a meeting held in Tunis in August 1977 for co-ordination and co-operation by the national libraries of Morocco, Tunisia and Algeria, and for more participation in the international scene.

13.   PANOFSKY, Hans E. National libraries and bibliographies in Africa. *In* JACKSON, Miles M, *ed. Comparative and international librarianship: essays on themes and problems.* Westport, Conn: Greenwood Publ. Corp.; London: Bingley, 1970, p.229-55.

> Attempts to indicate briefly the state of national libraries and national bibliographies in Africa, as well as bibliographical work pertinent to Africa performed elsewhere.

Nigeria

14.   AJE, S.B. The place of the national library in a multi-state federation with special reference to Nigeria. *Nigerian Libraries,* 6 (3), Dec. 1970, 170-7.

> Other countries (USA, USSR, United Kingdom and Egypt) are examined, analysed and compared. Ways are suggested for direct involvement and assistance by the National Library of Nigeria in the largely underdeveloped public library area, in line with the important role of national libraries in developing countries in the area of the development of national library services and networks.

South Africa

15.   TAYLOR, Loree Elizabeth. *South African Libraries.* London: Clive Bingley, 1967, p.21-6.

> Contains short historical accounts, and notes on the collections, bibliographical work and publications, of the two national libraries in South Africa (the South African Library in Cape Town which concentrates on reference functions, and the State Library in Pretoria which acts as the centre of the national interlibrary loan system).

AMERICA

Canada

16.   DONNELLY, F. Dolores. *The National Library of Canada: a historical analysis of the forces which contributed to its establishment and to the identification of its role and responsibilities.* Ottawa: Canadian Library Association, 1973.

> Detailed account of the many years of recommendations and studies which culminated in the emergence of Canada's National Library in 1953, and of developments from then until the passing of the new National Library Act in 1969 which allocated to the National Librarian a statutory responsibility for the co-ordination of all aspects of library resources and services at the federal government level. Implications of these enlarged powers are discussed.

17.   LAMB, William Kaye. Canada — National Library. *In* KENT, Allen *and* LANCOUR, Harold, *eds. Encyclopedia of library and information sciences.* New York and London: Marcel Dekker, 1970, vol. 4, p.165-9.

> A short account of events leading to the formation of the National Library in 1953, and of its development from then until the separation from the Public Archives and the passing of the revised National Library Act of 1969.

18.   SYLVESTRE, Guy. The role of the National Library, Ottawa, in an integrated Canada-wide information system. *Infomation Science in Canada,* 1 (2), Spring 1970, 42-4.

> Describes the role of the National Library as co-ordinator at the govenment and the national levels, by providing guidance in planning systems and help in their implementation. A Research and Planning Branch has been created to this end.
>
> *See also 20.*

United States of America

19.   CHARTRAND, Robert L. Three national libraries. *Bulletin of the American Society for Information Science,* 2 (8), March 1976, 41.

> Re-examines the roles and resources of the three national libraries (Library of Congress, National Library of Medicine and National Agricultural Library). Mention is made of recent attempts to tie more closely together the services offered by them.

20.   COLE, John Y. The national libraries of the United States and Canada. *In*
        JACKSON, S.L. *and others, eds. A century of service: librarianship in the
        United States and Canada.* Chicago: American Library Association, 1976,
        p.243-59.

        A brief historical account of the development of the Library of Congress (the
        de facto national library of the USA) during the past 100 years, and of the
        creation and development of the National Library of Canada.

21.   LEACH, Richard H. A broad look at the Federal Government and libraries.
        In KNIGHT, D.M. *and* NOURSE. E.S., *eds. Libraries at large.* New York
        and London: Bowker, 1969, p.346-86.

        The central position of the Library of Congress is demonstrated by a few statistics,
        then reasons are suggested as to why it has held back from offering the nation the
        kind of leadership envisaged by Humphreys (see p. 7). The activities, holdings and
        services of the other two national libraries (National Library of Medicine and
        National Agricultural Library) and the relationships between all three national
        libraries are described.

22.   LORENZ, John. The national libraries, *In* COSATI. Task Group on
        Library Programs. *Federal information resources: identification, availability
        and use.* Proceedings of a conference, Washington, D.C., March 26-27,
        1970. Beltsville, Md.: The Group, 1970, p.8-11.

        Outlines some of the services and some newer developments provided by the
        three national libraries (Library of Congress, National Library of Medicine and
        National Agricultural Library), and suggests ways of improving their performance.

23.   SCHMIERER, Helen F. *and* PASTERNACK, Howard. The National
        Advisory Commission on Libraries. *Library Quarterly,* 40 (4), October
        1970, 436-47.

        Describes background and reasons for setting up the Commission, its terms of
        reference, composition and activities. This is followed by a review of *Libraries at
        large . . . the resource book based on the materials of the National Advisory
        Commission on Libraries,* ed. D.M. Knight and E. Shapley Nourse. New York:
        Bowker, 1969.

24.   The Library of Congress as the national library: potentialities for service.
        In KNIGHT, D.M. and NOURSE, E.S., *eds. Libraries at large.* New York
        and London: Bowker, 1969, p.435-65.

        A statement of the Library's view of itself as the National Library of the United
        States, summarising some of the points made to the National Advisory Commis-
        sion on Libraries in 1967, and looking into the furture. Possibilities for the
        future national library and information service network are considered.

ASIA AND THE PACIFIC ISLANDS

25.   ANUAR, Hedwig. Patterns of library service in Asia and the Pacific Islands.
        Library Trends, 8 (2), October 1959, 130-4.

        Indicates how the functions of a national library in this area are being extended
        beyond those usually regarded as essential in Western countries.

26.   HATCH, Lucille. The National Diet Library, the National Library of the
        Philippines, and the Singapore National Library. *Journal of Library
        History,* 7 (4), October 1972, 329-59.

        The 3 national libraries described exemplify the differences that may occur in
        libraries attempting to provide the services identified as appropriate to a national
        library by the Unesco Regional Seminar on the Development of National Libraries
        in Asia and the Pacific area in Manila in 1964 - mainly through adaptation to a
        particular region and to the needs of the nation the library is designed to serve.

27.   JAAFAR, S.B. Reference and extension services in national libraries.*In* LIM Huck Tee *and* RASHIDAH Begum, *eds. Proceedings of a PPM and LAS Conference . . . Penang, March 1974.* Penang: Persatuan Perpustakaan Malaysia and Library Association of Singapore, 1975, p.114-9.

> Discusses the reference services provided in a national library, with reference to those of the national libraries of Singapore, Philippines and Malaysia.

28.   KASER, D., STONE, C. Walter *and* BYRD, Cecil K. *Library development in eight Asian countries.* Metuchen, N.J.: Scarecrow Press, 1969.

> The current state of library activities in eight selected nations of East and South East Asia is described (Vietnam, Laos, Thailand, Korea, Philippines, Taiwan, Malaysia and Singapore). A summary of problems and also recommendations are given in most cases.

Bangladesh.

29.   HUQ, A.M. Abdul. National library for Bangladesh. *International Library Review,* 9 (1), January 1977, 95-112.

> Suggests the duties that the national library must perform, the responsibilities it must undertake, the status it should have, and how the library itself may be brought about.

India

30.   KAULA, P.N. *The National Library of India: a critical study.* Bombay: Somaiya Publications, 1970.

> A brief historical account of abortive attempts to establish a national central library in Delhi is followed by an analysis of the activities of the National Library at Calcutta, with suggestions for its improvement. The author emphasises, however, that the main issue is the location of the National Library.

Indonesia

31.   POON, Paul W.T. A proposed national library system in Indonesia. *Australian Academic and Research Libraries,* 6 (1), March 1975, 20-30.

> Describes how different institutions in the country have been carrying out the functions of a national library to a limited extent, suggests that these could be considered as the nuclei of the future national library, and discusses its functions and administrative framework.

Iran

32.   SHAFA, Shojaeddin. *The Pahlavi National Library of Iran, its planning, aims and future: summary report.* [1976]

> A very brief history of libraries in Iran is follwed by an account of the planning process for the new National Library and a detailed description of its objectives and proposed organisation.

Japan

33.   DOWNS, Robert B. Japan's new National Library. *College and Research Libraries,* 10 (5), October 1949, 381-7, 416.

> The writer's mission to Japan in 1948 was concerned principally with the internal organisation of the National Diet Library. Various problems are discussed and recommendations made in line with procedures already known to Japanese libraries.

Malaysia

34.   WIJASURIYA, D.E.K. The National Library of Malaysia: problems and
       prospects. *In* LIM Huck Tee *and* RASHIDAH Begum, *eds. Proceedings of a
       PPM and LAS Conference . . . Penang, March 1974.* Penang: Persatuan
       Perpustakaan Malaysia and Library Association of Singapore, 1975, p.1-11.

       Gives brief historical background, followed by description of organisation and
       administration, services and staffing.

Singapore

35.   ANUAR, Hedwig. The National Library of Singapore. *In* LIM Huck Tee *and*
       RASHIDAH Begum, *eds. Proceedings of a PPM and LAS Conference. . .
       Penang, March 1974.* Penang; Persatuan Perpustakaan Malaysia and Library
       Association of Singapore, 1975, p.22-47.

       Describes the legislation affecting the library (which is also the public library for
       the Republic of Singapore) and examines the developmental processes (planning,
       implementation and evaluation) with reference mainly to its national library
       functions.

AUSTRALASIA

Australia

36.   BALNAVES, John *and* BISKUP, Peter. *Australian libraries.* 2nd ed. rev.
       London: Clive Bingley, 1975, p.42-55.

       Contains a description of the Australian national library, its collections and the
       comprehensive bibliographical services it provides.

EUROPE

Bulgaria

37.   KALAIDZIEVA, K. On the post-war development of libraries in Bulgaria
       and the reorganisation of the National Library "Vassil Kolarov". *Libri,*
       12 (1), 1962, 13-24.

       Describes the re-organisation of the National Library "Vassil Kolarov" (which is
       the centre of the system of all Bulgarian public and scientific libraries), in parti-
       cular the special efforts made to acquire scientific literature and provide access
       to it.

France

38.   DENNERY, Etienne. Bibliothèque Nationale de France. *In* KENT, Allen
       and LANCOUR, Harold, *eds. Encyclopedia of library and information
       science.* New York and London: Marcel Dekker, 1969, vol.2, p. 435-48.

       Summary of the history, followed by an account of the various Departments of
       the Bibliothèque Nationale and the services it provides.

39.   FERGUSON, John. *Libraries in France.* London: Clive Bingley, 1971,
       p. 15-18.

       Contains a brief account of the Bibliothèque Nationale, indicating the main lines
       of its work and touching on current problems.

Ireland

40.   HUMPHREYS, K.W. The National Library of Ireland: the library today
       and tomorrow. *An Leabharlann,* n.s. 1 (4), December 1972, 19-23, 26.

       Attempts to answer two questions in the context of the Irish situation: why a
       national library? and what is a proper one?

Poland

41.   HORODYSKI, Bogdan. La bibliothèque nationale: son rôle et ses devoirs. *Libri*, 13 (1), 1959, 89-97.

>   Attempts to bring together and throw light on tendencies in the library world which have served as a basis on which to build the programme for the establishment of a new national library in Warsaw. Topics discussed are subject specialilisation in the large universal library, the microfilm solution to space problems, and the desirability of bibliographical, information and research functions for the national library.

42.   PREIBISH, A. Polish libraries: their structure, organization and aims. *International Library Review*, 9 (2), April 1977, 161-74.

>   Historical background is followed by description of the collections, structure and activities of the National Library, which is the focal point and the link of all the elements of the national network of libraries and information centres.

Scandinavia

43.   GRONBERG, Lennart. University libraries − national libraries: aspects of the problems in Scandinavia, especially in Sweden. *Libri*, 17 (1), 1967, 59-62.

>   Indicates the distribution of functions in Scandinavia, supplementing Rojnić's article on 'University libraries in a double function' (on p. 112 of this volume).

44.   HARRISON, K.C. *Libraries in Scandinavia.* 2nd ed. rev. London: André Deutsch, 1969.

>   Includes historical background and description of the services provided by the national and university libraries in the Scandinavian countries, including Finland and Iceland.

United Kingdom

45.   THE BRITISH LIBRARY. *In* SAUNDERS, W. L., *ed. British Librarianship today.* London: Library Association, 1976.

The British Library: introduction.	Harry Hookway	p. 37-44
The British Library Reference Division		
The Division as a whole.	Donovan Richnell	p. 45-57
The Department of Printed Books.	R. J. Fulford	p. 56-66
The Department of Manuscripts.	D. P. Waley	p. 66-69
The Department of Oriental Manuscripts and Printed Books.	G. E. Marrison	p. 69-73
The Science Reference Library	M. W. Hill	p. 73-83
References		p. 83-85
The British Library Lending Division	Maurice B. Line	p.86-108
The British Library bibliographical Services Division	Richard E. Coward	p.109-35
The British Library Research and Development Department	John C. Gray	p.136-48

>   The achievements of the British Library are surveyed in five chapters: an introduction by the Chief Executive of the British Library, tracing the events that led up to its formation, is followed by chapters on the Bibliographic Services Division, the Lending Division, the Reference Division (containing sections on each of its four departments), and the Research and Development Department. Each chapter or section is written by its head.

46.   GREAT BRITAIN. DEPARTMENT OF EDUCATION AND SCIENCE.
        The scope for automatic data processing in the British Library: report of a
        study into the feasibility of applying ADP to the operations and services of
        the British Library. London: HMSO, 1973.

> Analysis of the activities of the various organisations that came to make up the
> British Library, with recommendations for their development and extension (by
> no means all of these involving automation). Chapter 1 includes an outline of exis-
> ting and proposed functions of the national library.

47.   GREAT BRITAIN. DEPARTMENT OF EDUCATION AND SCIENCE.
        National Libraries Committee (F.S. Dainton, Chairman). *Report.* London:
        HMSO, 1969. (Cmnd. 4028).

> In this report — which endorsed the practicability, and also virtually the necessity,
> of a single authority, centrally financed and managed — an examination is made
> of the functions and organisation of the national library institutions in the United
> Kingdom, and of their activities and services, to see how far they, together with
> other types of library and information services, could provide an adequate national
> library service for the future.

48.   HUMPHREYS, K.W. The British Library. *Journal of Librarianship,* 4 (1),
        January 1972, 1-13.

> Describes attempts made in recent years to determine the essential functions of
> a national library and considers these in relation to the recommendations of the
> Dainton Committee and the proposals in the White Paper on the British Library.

49.   HUMPHREYS, K.W. The need for a national library service: what organi-
        sation do we require for total library service in Britain? *Journal of Li-*
        brarianship, 5 (4), October 1973, 259-69.

> Discusses the present system of library organisation in Britain, compares it with
> those of other European countries, and suggests a new administration based on
> regional systems.

50.   LINE, Maurice B. National libraries. *In* WHATLEY, H. A., *ed. British*
        librarianship and information science, 1971-1975. London: Library Asso-
        ciation, 1977, pp 132-45.

> A brief historical account, in the form of a review article, of the five years covering
> the planning, creation and early years of the British Library.

51.   RICHNELL, D.T. The national library problem. *Library Association*
        Record, 70 (6), June 1968, 148-53.

> A survey of the historical development of national library provision in the United
> Kingdom from the conferment of the privilege of legal deposit on the libraries
> of Oxford and Cambridge Universities to the setting up of the Dainton Committee
> in 1967 is followed by a consideration of the Committee's terms of reference and
> the possible lines of future development that they suggested.

52.   ROBERTS, E.F.D. National library services: a Scottish view, *In: Papers*
        from the 43rd Conference of the New Zealand Library Association, 1976.
        New Zealand Library Association, p.16-22.

> Describes the development of national library services in the United Kingdom
> over the previous five years, and the way in which Scotland has been affected by
> or contributed to that development. A sketch of the historical background of the
> National Library of Scotland is followed by a discussion of the extent to which
> it has been able to carry out the functions of a national library considered to be
> essential or desirable.

U.S.S.R.

53.   KALDOR, Ivan. National libraries and bibliographies in the U.S.S.R. *In*
        JACKSON, Miles M., *ed. Comparative and international librarianship:*
        Essays on themes and problems. Westport, Conn.: Greenwood Publ. Corp.;
        London: Bingley, 1970, p. 167-97.

> Historical background to the creation of the modern Soviet library system is
> followed by a description of the system of national libraries and their functions,
> and of two of these libraries in particular — the Lenin State Library and the Nat-
> ional Library of Uzbek S.S.R. There follows a brief review of the Soviet national
> bibliographical apparatus and activities.

AUTHOR INDEX

Page numbers in bold type refer to papers reprinted in this volume. All others refer to entries in the *Further Reading* Section.